THE AUTHORISED BIOGRAPHY OF

JOE MERCER OBE

FOOTBALL
with a

By Gary James

ACL & POLAR PUBLISHING

DEDICATION ONE

To Heidi for all her support.

DEDICATION TWO

To Norah Mercer - special thanks for allowing me to tell the story.
G.J.

First published in Great Britain by
ACL Colour Print & Polar Publishing (UK) Ltd
2, Uxbridge Road, Leicester LE4 7ST
England

Text copyright Gary James
Design Copyright ACL & Polar 1993

ISBN 0 9514862 9 2

Edited by
Julian Baskcomb and Andy Ward

Designed and Printed by
ACL Colour Print & Polar Publishing (UK) Ltd
2, Uxbridge Road, Leicester LE4 7ST
Telephone: (0533) 610800

Cover photographs:
Front: *Joe as England Manager during a training session in May 1974. (Photo: Colorsport)*
Back: *(Top) Joe shows off the League Championship trophy at Manchester City in 1968.*
Joe as Arsenal skipper with the 1950 F.A. Cup (bottom) and Joe as a pre-war star player with Everton.

I have no complaints, no chip on my shoulder.
Football has been good to me. I have enjoyed some
success, felt the warmth of the fans, known
tremendous challenges. I never wanted to do
anything but become a footballer and I have been
able to spend all my life so far in the game. I could
have asked no more. Football is my life.

JOE MERCER, circa 1964

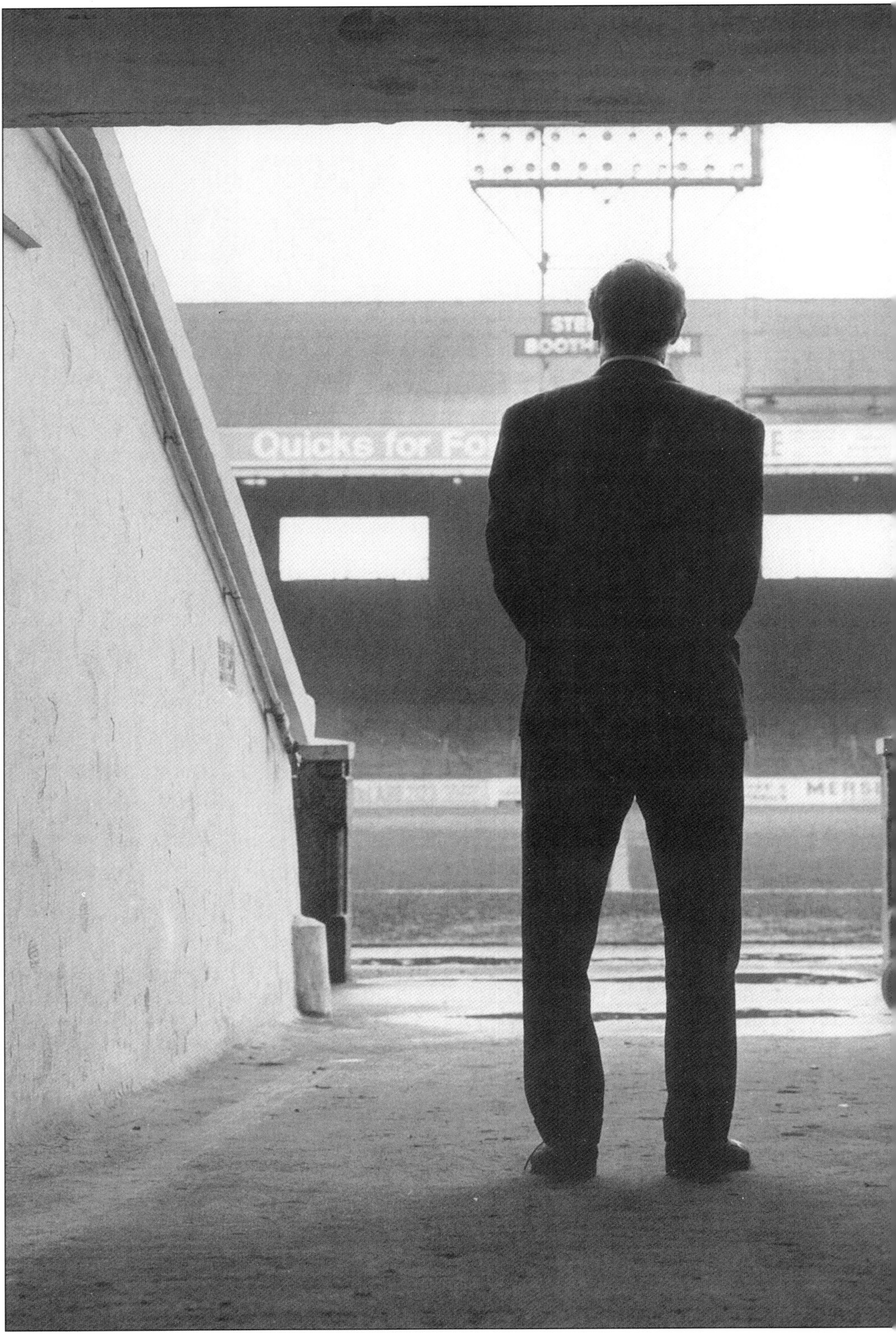
Quicks for Fo

CONTENTS

	Introduction	7
1	Born into Football	9
2	Happy Days at Everton	19
3	Man of the Match	33
4	England's Wartime Captain	41
5	Everton's Loss, Arsenal's Gain	57
6	Superstitious Gunners	71
7	Footballer of the Year	79
8	Honour in Defeat	93
9	Time to Retire?	107
10	End of an Era	117
11	'We're Going to Sheffield'	127
12	The Move to Villa	139
13	The Push for Pomotion	147
14	League Cup Villans	157
15	Joe Without Football	165
16	Restoring Faith	173
17	City of Hope	187
18	The Blue Ballet	197
19	'Mars Next Stop'	203
20	The Glory Continues	219
21	European Success	231
22	Ruining The Dream	247
23	End of The Road	257
24	The Fun Returns	267
25	Retirement	281
26	Tributes	293
	Bibliography	303

INTRODUCTION

ONE OF the first people I interviewed whilst researching this book, Colin Bell, warned me that I would have tremendous difficulty writing a biography of Joe Mercer because he said 'everyone would say the same things'. He believed everyone would mention Joe's tremendous personality, his friendly nature, his humour... and so on. I have found Colin's comment to be true, although I must admit it has been a real pleasure listening and meeting so many different people, each with such a high regard for Joe. Although it has proved difficult at times, the thought that I could write a biography on such a great man spurred me on throughout the difficult periods.

The name Joe Mercer immediately conjures up two images. The first is of his huge grin, a welcoming smile that instantly made you feel you were with a truly nice man. The second is of his bandy legs. They may not have looked much like an athlete's but, after over twenty years of playing professional football, they proved they were more than good enough.

Joe's record as a player and a manager is incredible. It is difficult to think of any other man who has achieved as much. As a player Joe won three League Championships, the F.A. Cup, and a Cup finalist's medal. He was also voted Footballer Of The Year, and he captained his country with great power and strength through an extremely difficult period when Joe and his colleagues provided vital morale building entertainment. He also appeared for the Football League.

Excluding wartime games, he played 184 League and Cup games for Everton the local giant, then after playing for Aldershot during the war, he found further fame with Arsenal - the nation's greatest club at the time - where he featured in 247 League and 26 Cup games.

His managerial career commenced at Sheffield United, then after several other clubs had shown an interest in him, he moved on to Aston Villa, where he won promotion and the League Cup. After a short absence from the game Joe arrived at Manchester City where he guided the Blues to promotion in his first season, and then even greater success with the League Championship, the F.A. Cup, the League Cup and the European Cup Winners' Cup all arriving within his first five years at Maine Road.

In 1970 he was the first person to guide an English side to a European and domestic cup double, and the year before that he became the first man to win both the F.A. Cup and the League as a player and as a manager. The only man to go one better than Joe and win all three domestic trophies in his playing and managerial career is George Graham who was brought to England by Joe in the first place! Had the League Cup, or any of the European trophies, been in existence during Joe's days at Everton or Arsenal then I am convinced Joe's record would, even today, be the best. As it is, Joe must surely be one of, if not THE most successful player of his era.

After Joe left Manchester City he became general manager at Coventry City, before he was asked to be caretaker manager of England following Alf Ramsey's dismissal. During that period Joe managed to put the fun back into international football - a feat that only he was capable of.

I have always believed Joe to be the best player and manager of his period because, in addition to all that success, Joe was a truly genuine man. He never allowed himself to get carried away with his glory and, as I hope this book proves, he always remembered his family, friends, and the struggles he had encountered growing up in difficult circumstances in Ellesmere Port.

Whilst researching for my first publication in the late 1980s, I was persuaded to contact Joe to discuss my book. I did not believe he would really be interested, after all he did not know me, and to be honest he had nothing to gain from meeting me. As it turned out Joe and his wife Norah welcomed me into their home and treated me, and my father (a typically obsessive Mancunian blue), like friends. It all went so well that Joe agreed to write the foreword to that book and I continued to visit the Mercers over the years that followed.

Because of the kindness and assistance Joe and Norah gave, I was determined to write a book based on Joe's life, or at least his time at Maine Road, whilst he was alive. Unfortunately, due to other commitments I was unable to do that. Joe passed away on 9th August 1990 - his seventy-sixth birthday. He would probably have been amused that his contract of life had expired exactly 76 years after it had began, and then it had to be during the close season! Once he passed away, I realised that his story had to be told immediately. Since that date I have spent considerable time researching his life and interviewing the people who knew him best.

Anyone who met Joe knows what he was like, and I hope this book portrays Joe in the way we all remember him. I must admit though, it has been extremely difficult describing a man who was such a popular figure. He was such a remarkable person who always remained the same despite achieving an exceptional amount of success. This book is merely one impression of Joe, and I make no claim to have covered every moment of Joe's long life. I see this book as being a taste of Joe - not the man himself. Wherever possible I have used Joe's own views to add flavour but, I must be honest, there were so many questions I wished I was able to ask him, or stories I wanted him to tell. Nevertheless, I hope this publication provides enough of Joe, in the way he deserves to be portrayed to satisfy any follower of football. Joe loved the game and I hope this book demonstrates that love.

This is the story of a man who achieved tremendous success, yet he will probably always be remembered more for playing 'football with a smile' I think he would prefer that.

Gary James
Ripponden, North Yorkshire
August 1993

ACKNOWLEDGEMENTS

As with any project of this size a great number of people have helped along the way. Firstly, I must thank the Mercer family, especially Joe's kind wife Norah and son David. Norah has given me access to so much information and has helped in so many ways that a simple thank you is not enough. I hope this book goes some way towards repaying Norah for all the assistance and support she has given. Norah must also be thanked for the way she made both myself and my wife, Heidi, welcome on so many occasions to her home. It is obvious that Norah gave Joe tremendous support throughout their life together.

In addition to Joe's family, a number of other people have greatly assisted with details concerning Joe's non-football related life. Falling into this category is Alan Percival, a lifelong friend of Joe's. He was able to reveal what the 'young Joe' was really like, he also supplied information from many other periods of Joe's life and I am extremely grateful.

As far as Joe's footballing life is concerned there are so many people, from all different areas of the game, who I must thank. Special thanks must go to the following: Malcolm Allison, Colin Bell, Peter Bishop, Tony Book, Ian Cook, Stan Cullis, Willie Donachie, Tom Finney, George Graham, George Highham, Jimmy Hill, Tommy G Jones, Francis Lee, John Motson, Glyn Pardoe, Norman Penny, Peter Shilton, Mike Summerbee, Bob Wilson, and Ron Wylie. Others who have helped include Noel Bayley, Bill Borrows, Mike Cairns, Ian Devon, Phil Fletcher, Charlie Hawkins, Bryan Horsnell, Max Kester, Eddie Large, Ron McKenna, Bill Peel, Darren Rackham, Tom Smith, G.A. Upton, Dave Wallace and Dave Woodall.

The present-day staff of the following clubs, listed in order of assistance, all helped: Arsenal, Tranmere Rovers, Aldershot, Coventry City, Aston Villa, Manchester City, Everton, and Sheffield United.

Thanks are due to library staff throughout Britain, especially Gillian Brown at Ellesmere Port Library and the staff at Manchester Central Library. Also, thanks to Nicky Shaw of the Alzheimer's Disease Society (158-160 Balham High Road, London, SW12 9YY) for supplying much needed information on a topic that is hard to understand and, for all those either suffering with the disease or caring for sufferers, is extremely difficult to cope with.

Julian Baskcomb and Julia Byrne at ACL & Polar need thanking for supporting this project from the start. They, together with their colleagues, have put considerable effort into this book as they do with any project they take on and deserve more than a simple thank you. They have spent time ensuring that this book is a quality publication.

Over the final six months Andy Ward was brought onto the project to assist with the editing of the book. He offered his skills and knowledge at a time when a fresh pair of eyes were urgently required to ensure the book achieved its goal. I am grateful to Andy for all his assistance during those final months.

Finally, the greatest thank you of all goes to Joe Mercer, OBE. No one will ever forget what Joe achieved throughout his life.

There could never be another like Joe.

PICTURE ACKNOWLEDGEMENTS & ARCHIVE SOURCES

Most of the photographs and newspaper cuttings in this publication have come from either the Mercer family, or from the author's personal collection. Other articles, interviews and photographs have been taken from or supplied by the following:

Manchester Evening News & Guardian, Colorsport, Empics, The Hulton Deutsch Collection, The Daily Mail, The Daily Express, The Daily Mirror, The Ellesmere Port Pioneer, The Liverpool Echo, The London Evening Standard, The Birmingham Sports Argus, The Sheffield Green 'Un, The Observer, The News Of The World, Picture Post, the BBC, Granada T.V., Thames T.V., Radio City, Piccadilly Radio, and GMR.

There are a number of other photographs included in this book, the source of which we have been unable to trace. The owners are cordially invited to contact the publishers in writing providing proof of copyright.

Chapter One

BORN INTO FOOTBALL

I was born into football - although in the close season! My grandfather had played for Primrose Rovers, a well-known side once, almost before professionalism began. My father was centre-half for Nottingham Forest when I was born. When my parents went out, Noel Watson, the referee, was my baby-sitter. Now he is an elder statesman of the FA.

Joe Mercer, *The Great Ones*

Joe Mercer's earliest memory was that of his father, Joe Mercer, senior, returning home from World War One in 1918. His Dad walked through the door, took a football out of his kit-bag and threw it for the four-year-old boy to kick. From that day on, it was football, football, football.

Joe Mercer was born into football, in August 1914, the month that war was declared on Germany. Thousands crowded the streets of London, cheering in anticipation of a swift victory, perhaps by Christmas. They sang the National Anthem outside Buckingham Palace and along Downing Street, and expressed their loyalty to King and Country.

In the Mercer household, in the Cheshire town of Ellesmere Port, the declaration of war was somewhat overshadowed by the birth of their son. Joseph, the first child of Joe and Ethel Mercer, was born into a divided world with Germany attempting to change the face of Europe. On the actual day of his birth, 9 August 1914, Germany and Austria-Hungary threatened to attack Italy if it refused to renounce its neutrality. It was one of many threats made during a long war that eventually contributed to the death of Joe Mercer, senior.

Ellesmere Port is situated at the base of the Wirral peninsular, at the junction of two canals, the Shropshire Union and the Manchester Ship Canal. The town expanded quickly in the first decade of the century. The opening of the Manchester Ship Canal, in 1894, heralded a succession of new industries - ship builders, flour mills, cement works, iron and steel, and, of course, the Mersey docks. With the industries came immigrant workers from different parts of the country and with varied backgrounds.

Despite this expansion, Ellesmere Port was still a relatively poor town. Most people struggled to survive. Few could realistically hope to achieve much success, other than a steady job in the town. Joe Mercer, senior, however, found an escape.

In industrial areas, sport is a common form of release. For Joe Mercer, senior, sport meant only one thing - association football. Reports show that he was an outstandingly clever centre-half who, in October 1910, was spotted by a Nottingham Forest scout when playing for Burnell's Ironworks, a local club. He signed for Forest at the age of 21 and soon became a first-team regular. But Forest were not the first club to show interest in him. He had previously been spot-

Joe was born in Queen Street, Ellesmere Port.

The Ellesmere Port Flour Mills.

ted by Everton, the giants from across the River Mersey. Apparently, Everton had heard of his local reputation and decided to see if he really was as good as their sources had implied.

Will Cuff was the Everton representative who went to watch Joe Mercer, senior. Cuff, later Chairman of the Football League, saw Joe on a bad day. Joe was not on his best behaviour. He made full use of his 6ft 2in height and 13st weight to intimidate the opposition. Cuff was impressed with Joe's general play but was a little concerned, to say the least, about his physical style. Said Cuff: "He's a good player all right, but he'd get us thrown out of the League!"

Instead, Joe Mercer, senior, signed for Nottingham Forest, then a lowly First Division club (and soon to become a lowly Second Division one!). He developed into a superb footballer, said by many to be on the verge of an England cap when war was declared. The *Birkenhead Advertiser* summarised the signing on 17 October 1910: "We hear that Joe Mercer, the clever centre-half of Bur-nell's Ironworks, has been signed by Notts Forest for

Cartoon from the *Birkenhead News* in 1921 depicting Joe Mercer Senior playing for Tranmere.

whose reserve side he appears today. Mercer was originally with Bebington Vics, from whence he went to Bolton and he has since played for Chester Castle, Tranmere Rovers and Burnell's Ironworks. He is 21 years of age, 13st in weight and he stands 6ft 2ins in height. We wish him luck."

In spite of government promises, the Great War, as it was to become known, was not over by Christmas 1914. Instead, there was deadlock in the despicable, muddy trenches that stretched from the North Sea to Switzerland. There was one alleged incident that both surprised and pleased the British soldiers stuck on the bloody Western Front, when on Christmas morning the German soldiers gradually came out of their trenches offering cigarettes. At first, the British believed it was a trick but then when a football appeared all thoughts of deception

Joe Senior (centre) pictured at Forest in 1913/14.

disappeared as both sets of troops engaged, not in battle, but in a game of football. Sadly, the realities of war were never far away, and soon the men were re-armed and fighting not for goals but for lives.

The news that the Germans were holding almost 600,000 Allied prisoners shocked the British public. As the colonies of Britain and Germany, and other European powers were brought into the conflict the government asked for more volunteers and mounted the famous and highly successful Lord Kitchener 'Britain Needs You' campaign.

Thousands joined up immediately. In 1915, Joe Mercer, senior, along with fellow Forest players Tom Gibson and Harold Iremonger, went to the Kingsway Recruiting Office in London to join the 17th Service Battalion of the Middlesex Regiment, known as "the Footballers' Battalion". It had been set up by the War Office and allowed the footballers, while still in Britain, to be absent on Saturdays to enable them to play for their club. By the end of 1915 there were two Footballers' Battalions. The first left for the front in November 1915 and went into battle in France the following month. The second followed soon after, and was in France by early 1916.

In the Mercer household, Joe Mercer, junior, was far too young to understand what was happening and why. All he sensed was that his father was missing. He knew little about his father's whereabouts, or indeed about the sacrifices that both his parents were making.

On the battlefields, Joe Mercer, senior, became a victim of Germany's lethal new weapon, the deadly chlorine gas, capable of both choking and blinding its victims. He was also badly wounded in the shoulder before being captured. He was a prisoner of war for 18 months at Meschede in Germany. Like most POWs held by the Germans during this period, he suffered considerably and endured terrible deprivations. It must have been clear to him that he would never again play top-level football. However, that was a small price to pay, as he knew that many of

Above: Joe Senior (centre) joining the army with fellow Nottingham Forest players Tom Gibson and Harold Iremonger in 1915.

Below: The Forest trio (back row, Joe Senior in the centre) as members of 'The Footballers' Battalion' of the Middlesex Regiment.

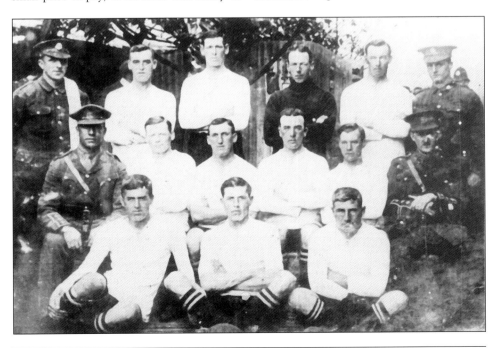

his friends and comrades had lost their lives and would not have the chance to return home, let alone play sport.

When the war ended, Joe Mercer, senior, returned to his native Ellesmere Port and sought a normal life with his wife and the son he hardly knew. His first objective was to make up for lost time with his family. The baby he had left behind was now a young boy. Joe, senior, was far from a fit man - he was severely affected by POW camp deprivations and the gas attack - but he still managed to find some energy to play sport and pass on a few of his old footballing tricks to his eager young son. His chances of returning to full-time professional football appeared slim. It seemed essential to find regular employment away from football in order to support his family, so he took a job as a bricklayer. Then, at the start of the 1919-20 season, he returned on a part-time basis to the Wirral's major non-League side, Tranmere Rovers. At the age of five or six, young Joe's interest in football developed as he went to Prenton Park to watch his father captain Tranmere Rovers.

During the course of the following years, the health of Joe Mercer, senior, declined, and his appearances for Tranmere became less frequent. In the latter stages of his career he did, however, achieve something he had previously thought was beyond him, when he returned to Football League soccer. In 1921-2, he played 21 games during Tranmere's inaugural Third Division (North) season. Sadly, this was to be his last season in the Football League as his condition deteriorated further, culminating in his premature death five years later.

Following his father's death, 12-year-old Joe had to take on more responsibility. Three more children had been born to the Mercers in the years following the war, and Joe now had a six-year-old sister, Betty, a three-year-old brother, Stan, and a baby brother, Arthur. Once Joe Mercer, senior, passed away, life was always going to be difficult for Ethel and her children.

By the 1920s, Ellesmere Port's economy had been boosted by the construction of a large Shell oil refinery, and an ironworks from Wolverhampton had moved to the town. The ironworks brought many workers from Wolverhampton to Ellesmere Port. They lived in the area to the north of the railway station, retaining their Black Country accents, of course, while the

Joe's father returned to football after the War. He is pictured here (back row, third from the right) with Tranmere Rovers in 1919/20.

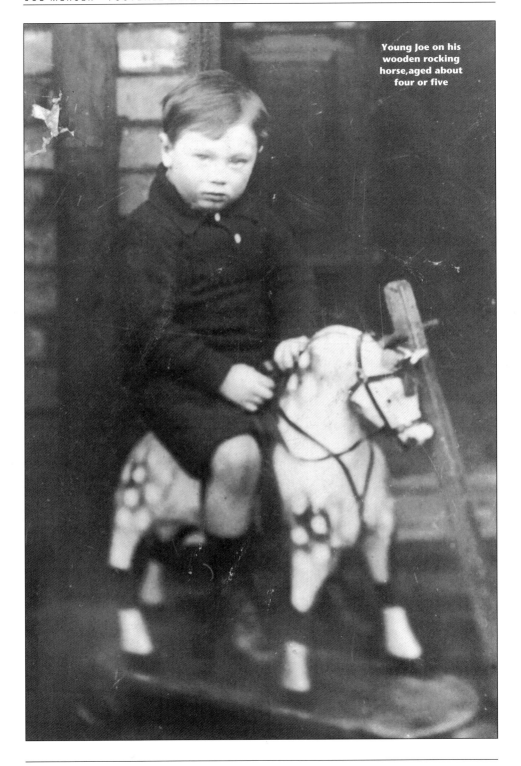

Young Joe on his wooden rocking horse, aged about four or five

southern half of Ellesmere Port was mainly made up of locally born 'Portites' who spoke in typical Cheshire twang. Naturally, there was a certain amount of rivalry between the two factions, although it must be said that this was generally only 'friendly rivalry'. There was never any major trouble between the groups.

Joe Mercer, junior, was, of course, a Portite. Among the Wolverhampton set was Stan Cullis, another boy with a huge interest in football. Says Cullis: "There existed a division amongst the population, a mild cold shoulder was quite evident with the unwelcome attitude arising on the part of the Portites towards the migrant Midlanders."

Joe believed the Midlanders, nicknamed 'Wufflers', were to blame. Despite being rivals within the town, however, Joe and Stan would eventually find fame together in the same England international team, and later as rival managers.

Although young Joe faced more responsibility, he found time to enjoy himself. He had always been a mischievous boy. If there was ever anything going on Joe would always be at the centre of it. Life may have been difficult but Joe was determined to get as much fun out of it as was possible. With his friends he would often go 'scrumping' (stealing apples), or would participate in any boyhood prank that would bring him a sense of joy. He was known as a "bit of a devil" because of his antics and tricks, but his intentions were not malicious, and one can imagine that they were carried out with a mischievous grin that warmed people's hearts. However, like most boys in the area, Joe frequently found himself taking part in fights, but only when picked on or when he saw one of his 'mates' in danger. He got involved in a few scuffles with the 'Wufflers'.

At school, Joe was certainly not an academic. He found it hard to concentrate. His mind was on what he could do when it was time to go home - football, cricket or swimming. Joe and his friends would go to the Manchester Ship Canal and dive in from any of the high bridges that crossed the industrial waterway. Most of the boys learnt to swim in the polluted canal, as it was the closest they could get to a lake or swimming-pool. They obviously did not care what chemicals or pollutants were in the water. All they cared about was enjoyment.

Ellesmere Port Schoolboys, circa 1924. Joe (with the ball) has Stan Cullis sitting to his left.

On cold or cool days they would often swim near the steelworks as the water expelled from the works was hot, making the area warm. The boys could swim there and daydream about being in a hot bath or pool somewhere else. Occasionally, they would venture further afield, cycling, two to a bicycle, the seven miles to Chester. There they would find the nearest real swimming-pool, and make a day of it if they had enough money.

Although Joe would participate in many sports, football was the one he loved and the one he excelled at. It had been his first love, and he had played the game for as long as he could remember. His father had not only given him a ball, but had issued a challenge: "See if you can do more in the game than I have."

Before his death, Joe Mercer, senior, managed to pass on some important tips to his son. He repeatedly fooled the young Joe, who was naturally right-footed, into thinking he was totally useless with his left foot, and by doing so forced him to work hard on his left. This made young Joe a much better all-round footballer and, years later, would help him become a world-class player.

Joe was always grateful for the time his poorly father spent teaching him a few tricks and giving him advice. At a presentation in the 1950s he spent a few minutes outlining how much he thought of his father: "If anybody ever inspired me it was he. I was only 12 when he died, but his personality has always had a big influence on me, and it is amazing how much it has helped me in my career. He had a lot of confidence in me making the grade in the football world, and, after all, I was Joe Mercer's son. I basked in his glory in my younger days, and it did help me enormously to reach the top. It is difficult to explain, without getting too sentimental, how much he did mean to me."

Joe's father encouraged him and advised him: "The only way you will learn to play football is to play it - and the better class of football you play the quicker you'll learn. Keep playing in better-class football all the time."

This was the kind of advice Joe followed. He continually played with boys older and more developed than himself, and they recognised his skill. According to Alan Percival, one of Joe's lifelong friends, even then Joe was a fantastic dribbler who could play in any position. More often than not he played as a centre-forward but he could play equally as well in defence. To Joe it was the prospect of playing that appealed, not the position.

Joe's love of football at this time perhaps can be best illustrated by a story he told when recollecting his childhood. It concerns a time when he was given a place at a holiday camp for underprivileged children at Dyserth, North Wales. For many children in the Merseyside and Manchester area, this was their only opportunity of a holiday, and the prospect of staying in a different country, away from home, was seen as an enormous treat. Joe, like the others, was excited. However, when he got there his excitement turned into despair as he discovered that there were plenty of activities arranged but no football. Typically, Joe decided to return to his beloved sport. That night he decided to 'escape'. He sneaked out of camp and made a bid for freedom. He stole, or, rather, 'borrowed', as Joe would have put it, a bicycle, and started cycling back to Ellesmere Port, where he knew he could find football. Unfortunately for Joe it was not too long before the Dyserth officials discovered he was missing. They quickly set about searching for him, and early the following morning he was captured some distance away on the main road back to England. There was no chance of football now as he was taken back to 'enjoy' the rest of his holiday.

Football really did mean everything to Joe. To help with the family's finances, he took on a paper round. This could have severely reduced his 'footballing time', but he made sure it did not. On Saturday nights he rushed to the railway station to collect the *Liverpool Echo*, or the *Liverpool Express*. Then he ran through the town and called at all the pubs, knowing that he could sell papers to men waiting for the football results. Other boys helped Joe sell his papers; they were keen on Joe finishing his round quickly, so that they could all play football. Joe was one of the 'star' players. A game without him always lacked something.

There were other occasions when Joe was almost prevented from playing football, such as when he was told to look after his youngest brother, Arthur. This was probably the last thing Joe wanted to do. After all, a boy of around ten years his junior would "just get in the way, wouldn't he?" To avoid incurring the wrath of his mother Joe obliged and took young Arthur with him. Little did Mrs Mercer realise that Joe actually found his young brother quite useful. He decided that Arthur was just about perfect to play the part of a goalpost. At least Joe could honestly say to his mother that he could see Arthur all the time, especially when he was shooting for goal.

Often these games of football were played between ever-increasing numbers. Boys would come along midway through and join one of the teams, always trying to balance the sides. Often there would be between ten and twenty a side, with the game continuing until the last few boys were called in by their parents. Joe often commented that these games started at nine in the morning, had half-time at midday, and a second half from two until five. If there was any light left they played extra-time!

Games took place whenever and wherever possible. The boys often played in the street with newspaper wrapped in string. These were the days when footballs were not readily available; few in Ellesmere Port possessed them. Occasionally, tennis balls would be used. Joe preferred this because he could kick the ball against kerbstones or the gutter to get around his opponents. In the unlikely event that there was nobody to play with, Joe would practice alone, again kicking the ball against the gutter or the wall, judging the angles, learning all about ball control. Sometimes a couple of old men would watch him and the others play, and Joe loved this. Years later he admitted that playing before an audience, any kind of audience, inspired him.

Despite all Joe's footballing activity outside of school, there was not much chance of him progressing into serious competition through the school. Before being taken seriously as a footballer you really needed to be recognised as a player at school, but the schools in Ellesmere Port did not pay much attention to sporting activity. It was only when a new teacher arrived that the situation began to change. Alan Percival, who grew up with Joe, tells the story: "In those days schoolteachers were on the other side as far as we were concerned. It was an 'us and them' situation. Then Bill Roberts came as a young teacher from Llanberis, North Wales, and he used to join in! He'd come on to the fields with us and play on the weaker side and very often he'd also play on the streets. Now he took us all in hand and he organised teams in Ellesmere Port. This was all new to the boys. Then both Joe and I were in the school team, and Bill Roberts started organising practice matches on the Ellesmere Port ground, or other local works grounds. Players recommended from the school would go along. Joe and I and one or two others from our school used to go to the various venues and have trials for the county. Until Mr Roberts came we had no chance of getting into the county side because we were not represented. Anyhow, both Joe and I got into the county side. I think there had only ever been one before us. Mr Roberts started it all!"

Schoolteacher Bill Roberts.

After only one year of competitive school football, Joe was in the Cheshire county side. At that time he played at centre-forward. Bill Roberts often joked that he played him in that position because of his 'crooked legs' - he wanted to give him plenty of room!

At 14, Joe was approached to play for one of the local village sides, Elton Green. Remembering his father's advice about stepping up a class whenever you can, he joined them. While playing for Elton, Joe was paid sixpence for his bus fare and was given a bag of vegetables. Although this unusual method of payment caused a great deal of amusement during Joe's professional career, it actually proved quite popular in the Mercer household at the time.

Since the death of Joe's father, life had been difficult for the Mercers. Joe's mother, Ethel, supplemented her widow's pension of 21 shillings a week the best she could. She took in washing, and Joe helped her by collecting the baskets. Even with the extra money from that, it was a struggle keeping the four children clothed and fed. Somehow though she managed it. Years later Joe often paid tribute to his mother: "I am very proud of my mother - and we have had an 'up and down' career. There have been wonderful times, bad times, but always a wonderful home. It has been poor at times, but always clean and honest, and a mother in the true sense of the word."

It was not long, however, before Joe himself started bringing more home than his famous 'bag of vegetables'. When he left school, he joined the Shell oil company at the local refinery. He was paid seventeen shillings and sixpence a week. To save money Joe used to walk the three miles to work every morning before clocking in at 7.30. Sometimes he was so hungry that he ate the sandwiches he'd brought for dinner on his way to work. At Shell, Joe delivered petrol, worked in the wagon repair office, and acted as a fitter's mate. He did not really enjoy any of it. How could he? After all, it was not what he wanted to do.

Working at Shell, however, did give him the opportunity of joining their football team, and as you would expect, Joe readily moved up another grade. He became a regular in the side. His thoughts were still on playing football, even though he was the family's breadwinner. He knew he was a good player. By this time he had played in a number of decent sides - the village side Elton Green, his home-town side of Ellesmere Port, and the Shell side. What Joe really wanted though, was to emulate his father by playing for a League club.

The local Shell Oil refinery where Joe started work for 17s 6d.

Chapter Two

HAPPY DAYS AT EVERTON

We understand that Joe Mercer has signed a Central League form as an amateur for Everton, and will take his place in the Reserves to meet Manchester City tomorrow (Saturday). As this will be in the nature of a trial for Joe, we join with all football 'fans' in wishing him the best of luck and a good match. At the present rate of progress we can visualise the Everton team round about 1936 containing quite a good sprinkling of ex-Town FC players!

Ellesmere Port Pioneer, 1932

IF ANY ONE FOOTBALL CLUB held a special place in Joe Mercer's life, it was Everton. This is how he put it in the 1980s: "I was an Evertonian because Sam Chedgzoy, who played for England, came from Ellesmere Port, and my Dad and Sam Chedgzoy played for Ellesmere Port Ironworks together in 1909. Sam Chedgzoy came to Everton, and my Dad went to Nottingham Forest, so I've always been an Evertonian ... I've been an Evertonian all my life, but I had an uncle who used to take me to see Liverpool play. Hold your hat on, this was 1921-2, when Liverpool won the Championship, and the side then was Scott, Longworth, McKinlay, McNab, Wadsworth, Bromilow, Lacey, Forshaw, Johnson, Chambers and Hopkin."

Liverpool did indeed win the Championship in 1921-2, and again the following season, but Everton soon took over as top club on Merseyside, and one of the most important and popular sides in Britain. They were helped by the emergence of William Ralph 'Dixie' Dean, who joined the club from Tranmere Rovers for £3,000 in March 1925. In 1927-8, Everton won the Championship, and Dean scored 60 League goals (100 in all matches). "There's only one man who will break that record," Dean once said. "That's that man who walks on water."

Dean was a magnificent centre-forward and a popular personality. His spirit helped Everton to further success - the Second Division Championship in 1930-31, the Léague Championship in 1931-2 and the FA Cup in 1933. In the middle of this success, Joe Mercer, junior, signed professional forms for the club. He had been an amateur with Everton for two years after being approached at the age of 15 while at Ellesmere Port. Numerous other clubs had shown interest in the young player; Bolton wanted him, Chester made an offer, and Blackburn had given him a trial in which he scored three goals. Despite the interest of these clubs, Joe wanted to sign for Everton. At 17, he was reluctant to sign amateur forms again, but Everton were not too keen on the idea of paying him wages just yet. And so the spindly-legged youngster continued to play games for Ellesmere Port and Runcorn while Everton gave him further trials.

Joe's employer, Shell, must have become a little impatient with him around this period. More and more of his time was devoted to football. He had managed to get away with it while at school but now he was supposed to be working for a living. Joe later recalled the period before he signed professional: "The old manager at Shell grabbed me one day and said, 'You'll have to make up your mind - work or football' and I said football, which was my only quality, my only asset. And then Everton signed me - after two 'final' trials - the last one my last game as an amateur, for Everton's third team against Manchester City at Maine Road."

Sam Chedgzoy

Joe's agreed salary owed something to his mother's insistence on a fair deal. She had discovered a great deal about the uncertainties of professional football while her husband was with Forest and Tranmere, and she knew how quickly and cruelly a career could be cut short. Ethel Mercer insisted on being party to all discussions between Everton and her son, and she saw no reason why she could not discuss her son's future with Tom McIntosh, the Everton secretary. The outcome was that the youngster was offered a salary of £5 a week. Joe was overjoyed: "I went to Everton as a pro and got a fiver. I used to count it about four times before I got home. I said, 'Over my dead body am I going back to Shell.' It was twice what the average working man got and I was only a lad. But my mother recalled a maxim of my father's: 'It's no use turning pro unless you get the money.'"

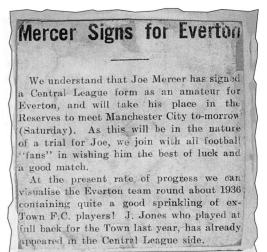

Mercer Signs for Everton

We understand that Joe Mercer has signed a Central League form as an amateur for Everton, and will take his place in the Reserves to meet Manchester City to-morrow (Saturday). As this will be in the nature of a trial for Joe, we join with all football "fans" in wishing him the best of luck and a good match.

At the present rate of progress we can visualise the Everton team round about 1936 containing quite a good sprinkling of ex-Town F.C. players! J. Jones who played at full back for the Town last year, has already appeared in the Central League side.

Alan Percival remembers Joe's elation with his regular wage. At the end of the week, when Alan left his job at the flour mill, Joe was waiting at the gates with a grin from ear to ear. Joe was so happy that he had to meet his friend Alan to tell everything about his week and about this vast wage he had received. He was not there to gloat - that was not his way - but to share his happiness. In those days a salary of £5 was an absolute fortune and not many young men had even seen a £5 note. Typically, Joe himself could not believe his luck at being able to earn money by doing something he enjoyed.

One action showed just what type of man Joe was becoming. One of his friends asked him what he was going to do with the money. The friends probably expected some form of extravagant celebration, but Joe dashed all hopes of that when he simply informed them that he was giving his full wage to his mother. Joe felt it was far better to help others, and in this case his family, than to take it for himself.

At Everton, Joe had to train alongside some of the most famous players in the land. As Joe often said, "Everton at this time were the leading team in England and therefore the leading team in the world."

One of the biggest characters at Everton was, of course, Billy Dean, who disliked the name 'Dixie'. Dean was the first player Joe encountered on his initial day at Everton. Joe, the

9st youngster from Ellesmere Port, began undressing while Dean, the strapping 6ft international centre-forward, was performing exercises on a mat. Joe knew his body did not look much at that time. He was so skinny and his legs were bandy and peculiar, and it was obvious that Dean began to notice as Joe undressed. He stopped his exercises, and shouted across to the other players: "Hey, lads, look at those legs. They wouldn't last a postman a morning."

Right from his first moment in professional football, Joe Mercer was known for two distinctive characteristics. The first was an infectious grin which encouraged warmth and humour. The second was his pair of spindly, bandy legs. The legs might not last a postman a morning, but they saw Joe Mercer through a 22-year career as a footballer!

Nobody laughed more about the legs than Joe himself: "My father was 6ft 2in. I would have been, too, had my legs been straight." In fact Joe was 5ft 9in. Stories about Joe's legs continued throughout his life in football. His family remember an incident when Joe stepped out of a taxi and, as he stood up straight next to the car, a dog ran straight between his legs. But the most outrageous comment is recalled by Joe's son, David: "He played a charity golf match at Coventry. I went caddying and he played with Douglas Bader. Some fellow in the crowd said, 'Christ, Joe Mercer's legs are worst than Douglas Bader's!'"

Bill Dean's ribbings drew Joe close to the tough 25-year-old Everton star. During their first conversation, Dean asked if

Dixie Dean

Joe's father was the same Joe Mercer who had played for Tranmere in the early 1920s. The answer was yes. "I was in with a bit of a chance to start off with," Joe said later. From that moment, young Joe became a sort of batman for Dean, collecting his mail and running errands for him. In return, Dean gave Joe advice and treated him like a younger brother.

Everton Boys Who Will Make Their Mark

Here is a trio of Everton youngsters at present being kept "in pickle." Frank King, the young goalkeeper, is on the ground staff, and Norman Higham is a likely centre forward—how necessary this is you all know; and, finally, Mercer, the Ellesmere Port young man, who is growing better and better in a football and physical manner.

As the friendship between Billy Dean and Joe developed, Billy let Joe borrow his golf clubs. Joe treasured them as if they belonged to a golf champion. One day, however, Joe fell out of Dean's good books when he borrowed them without permission: "Off I went to the old Fazakerley course on a day ticket supplied by Everton. They used matting tees and with one mighty lunge I hit the deck and the head of Dean's brassie flew further than the ball. His club was shattered.

Liverpool Sunday Express, 1933

My hero was angry. He administered the accepted punishment - a dressing-room thumping."

In retaliation, Joe and Charlie Leyfield, who moved on to Sheffield United in 1936, decided to whitewash Dean's car. Unfortunately for Joe the prank backfired. It was a blistering hot day and the paintwork of Dean's precious car was ruined. Naturally an even bigger hiding than the earlier one followed as Joe discovered that it was perhaps best not to retaliate.

At first Joe may have found it a little difficult to adjust to the professional way of life. He would still play in the streets with his friends, but every time his club found out they reprimanded him. Joe could not understand why, because, after all, he was playing football, which is what he was paid for. Obviously they wanted to prevent him being injured.

Joe now waited for his call-up to the first team, but with so many outstanding players at Everton he realised it could be a long wait: "I joined Everton after they'd had that marvellous run. I don't know the years but they won the First Division, got relegated, won the Second Division, won the First Division, won the FA Cup. Just imagine the atmosphere when I walked into that Everton dressing-room, in those days, 1932. Ted Sagar in goal, Ben Williams, Warney Cresswell. They had four international centre-halves - Tommy Griffiths, Hunter Hart, Tommy White and Charlie Gee. Then TG Jones came after. Then there was Jimmy Dunn of the Wembley Wizards and Dixie."

His first-team chance came sooner than expected, at the end of the 1932-3 season. Everton had reached the FA Cup Final and were due to face Manchester City at Wembley Stadium on 29 April. Before then came a fixture pile-up - four games in a fortnight. Naturally the club were reluctant to field their first team throughout this period, but Football League regulations forbade the club from fielding a weakened side. Joe was given the news that he was to replace right-half Cliff Britton in the team to play Leeds United on 18 April 1933. The two teams had also met the previous day at Goodison Park when Leeds won 1-0. Cliff Britton played in that game but was rested for the return, so Joe stepped on to the field at Elland Road before a crowd of almost 20,000. His hero, Billy Dean, was also rested but must have been watching as his young protégé took his first step in the big time. Joe, like all professional footballers, never forgot his first-team début: "My first game for Everton was against Leeds. Everton were playing Manchester City in the Cup Final so they rested a few players. I played against Potts, Milburn, Willis, Edwards, Hart, Copping, and they kicked the stocking tops off everybody."

Albert Geldard, with ball, and Dixie Dean, holding the Cup, offered Joe some Wembley turf.

Joe knew all along that he was merely a stand-in, but that did not deter him from playing to keep his place. The game ended as the previous one - 1-0 to Leeds - and Cliff Britton returned to the side for the Cup Final. But Joe had now experienced the pleasure of first-team football: "After my first game for Everton I thought, 'Well, I've played. No matter what happens now, no one can take that away from me.' I was brought up to believe that Everton was the best team in the world and nobody was going to beat us. The players knew what they were supposed to do and got on with it. We always had fun. I probably learned more about the game at Arsenal, but I learned how to laugh at Everton."

On the day of the Cup Final, while Everton were overpowering Manchester City 3-0 with goals by Jimmy Stein, Billy Dean and Jimmy Dunn, Joe was playing for Everton Reserves at Preston. The following day, he could not resist going to Goodison to see the victors. At the ground he found two England internationals, Billy Dean and Albert Geldard, cleaning their boots. Albert, who Joe often described as the team's worrier, pulled off a piece of mud and grass from his boots and kindly offered Joe a piece of Wembley turf. Joe replied: "No thanks, I'll get some myself eventually!" As the years went by, and Joe's chance of a Wembley Cup Final seemed to recede, he perhaps wondered whether he had been unwise to reject Albert Geldard's offer.

Cliff Britton

After another season in the Reserves, Joe began to compete for Cliff Britton's right-half spot. The two players trained together and both concentrated on improving their soccer skills. Joe appreciated Britton's skills and commitment: "Cliff was the exact opposite to me. While I roved and ran and relied on my undaunting energy, Cliff was cool and poised. He had the most educated right foot I ever saw. We used to work for hours together hitting a ball to and fro. We must have gone through the coaching manual and back again - just two youngsters trying to improve themselves."

Joe made eight first-team appearances in the 1934-5 season, always as cover for the injured Cliff Britton. At one point, towards the end of the season, Joe thought there was some doubt about his future. Players were on one-year contracts, and those put on the transfer-list near the end of the season were soon without pay. This worried Joe, especially when he overheard the great prankster Billy Dean talking in the bath: "You'd have thought they would have signed up young Joe again. He hasn't had much of a chance." Joe moped for days until he discovered that he was in fact retained. It was just a typical Dean joke.

Everton's Lancashire FA Senior Cup winning team of 1934-35
Back row (left to right): T. Kavanagh, Joe Mercer, A. Clark, J. Deighton, B.D. Williams, J.E. Jones, J.W. Archer, A. Tucker. *Front:* A. Geldard, S.J. Bentham, A. Dickinson, C.R. Webster, J. Stein.

The next season, 1935-6, Joe found himself part of an Everton team that had to move with the times. It was a story about football history that Joe never tired of telling: "Dixie never had a negative thought in his head. Tactics? He never worried about tactics. He used to say, 'Get it up the middle to me and I'll knock them in.' Everton were winning all these things, and all of sudden the Arsenal came. From 1930 to 1938 Arsenal won five Championships and two Cup Finals with this third-back game. We'd play them, we'd have a lot of the play, and they'd break away. Big Herbie Roberts would nod one down, Alex James would knock one about 60 yards for Joe Hulme, who goes down the wing and crosses for Ted Drake to knock one in. We'd say, 'Lucky so-and-so. With all that luck they'd win the Grand National.' But it was more than luck, it was well-planned. In 1935 Arsenal beat us the first match of the season. They beat us four-nothing, so we had this tactical talk and decided to play the third-back game. All us kids had come into the side, and Everton had their first tactical talk of all time. Dixie Dean put his feet on the board-room table, leaned back, pulled his hat over his eyes, and said, 'It's you buggers, you can't play.' And that was the end of the team talk as far as William Ralph was concerned.

"We went to Middlesbrough playing the 'third back' game. Middlesbrough

WATCH THIS PLAYER

*E*VERTON have always been famous for their half-backs, and their present line, Britton, Gee, and Mercer, is one of the best ever to wear Everton's blue shirt.

The last-named, Joe Mercer, the baby of the middle line, is one of the most promising half-backs in the game. Mercer joined up from Ellesmere Port three seasons ago.

Equally at home on the right wing, he is as fast as most wingers he is opposed to. This may be due to the fact that he first earned a reputation as a wing forward.

Last season, when Britton was injured, Mercer was introduced to the side, and so well did he play that Britton, when fit, could not get back into the side.

Jock Thomson, who has helped Mercer a lot, has now lost his place to this smart lad whom Bolton turned down after a couple of trials. A cap on form, must surely soon be his.

Everton 1935-36
Back row (left to right): C. Britton, Joe Mercer, E. Sagar, J. Jones, T. White.
Front: A. Geldard, S. Bentham, W. Dean (capt.), J. Cunliffe, C. Leyfield, W. Cook.

had Ralph Birkett, ex-England and Arsenal, on one wing, and Jackie Milne, ex-Scotland and Arsenal, on the other. They had Yorston, Camsell and Fenton as an inside trio. Camsell had scored 59 goals in one season. They beat us six-nothing. Coming back on the train, Dixie Dean said, 'Bloody good job we weren't playing the attacking game.'

"We persisted in playing the new way, and we were still getting beat, but not by many, then all of a sudden the directors found out. We went in one day and were told, 'In the billiard room, Mr Cuff wants to see you.' Cuff was a Football Association man, a right autocrat. 'I understand you've been playing the third-back game,' he said. 'Everton plays the attacking game. I don't care if you get beat six-five.' The next day we got beat six-five."

Joe's details are a goal or two in error, but his account was full of wisdom and always drew smiles to match his own.

In September 1935, Joe established himself at left-half in Jock Thomson's place. At last Joe was thankful that his father had fooled him into thinking his left foot was totally useless. The work he had put in all those years earlier was now paying off. Joe remained in the side for the rest of the season and even played in his first FA Cup tie. But his Cup début must have been jinxed as Preston North End defeated the Blues 3-1 at Goodison.

When Jock Thomson returned to the side, in the latter part of the season, Joe switched to take Britton's place at right-half. In fact during this particular season, while playing at right-half, he scored the first of his two League goals for Everton. It came on 14 March 1936 at Goodison when Blackburn Rovers were well and truly beaten 4-0. 'The most spectacular goal of the day was scored by Mercer, the most improved half-back of the season' reported the *Liverpool Echo*. 'He gathered the ball near the half-way line, got into his long stride instantly and wended his way beyond four or five opponents before he shot beyond Binns and into the net'. Billy Dean scored two, and Jimmy 'Nat' Cunliffe the other. Although this is on record as Joe's first League goal, he did actually score one prior to this. The earlier one was in fact an own goal and, as so often in these cases, was scored in a way that must have made the spectators either laugh or cry depending on which team they supported. Joe often recounted the story: "I remember the game at Stamford Bridge. The mud was up to our eyes. I decided that the best way to deal with one situation was to pass the ball back to Ted Sagar, our goalkeeper, which I did, not realising he had already raced out of goal to take the ball himself. I was horrified when I saw the ball go past Ted. I was sure it was going to be an own goal, and I ran forward in a desperate, hopeless effort to catch it. In the meantime Ted, a superb athlete, made an amazing acrobatic dive and managed to push the ball onto a post. That would have saved the situation but unfortunately I had to rush back to help, and I tried to kick the ball clear and pushed it into the net. What Ted said to me does not bear repeating! It was my most embarrassing moment in football."

The following season, 1936-7, Joe replaced Thomson more permanently. He always believed that he benefited from the changes to the game: "The stopper centre-half game came in. Before that wing-halves played wide, then after that the idea of putting wing-halves on inside-forwards was adopted. This was a change from wingers being the man the wing-halves watched. The change to the third-back game made me. Before that full-backs were largely clog-and-bang, although the great full-backs like Cresswell were quick as well as having a beautiful kick. The wing-halves were expected to hit these long balls. 'Over to the outside-left,' I was told, and I was thinking it would take me three kicks to get it out there. But after the change, I could tackle a bit, run a bit, beat a player, play short passes. Willie Cook, the full-back at Everton, used to volley clearances over his shoulder. He never shoved anything to me. He was more likely to hit me with it.

"The game was more black and white in those days. If their inside-right scored four goals it was a question of 'Where were you? You're the left-half, you're supposed to be marking him.' The game was not quite as simple as some try to make out though. We always pushed wedges in. When we attacked and the right winger had the ball, the inside-right would go with him.

Arsenal 3 Everton 2, Highbury August 1936. Everton goalkeeper Ted Sagar punches clear, Joe Mercer (far left player) lends his support.

The centre-forward would spearhead the attack and the outside-left converged on the far post. The right-half and the right-back would then push in as wedges to support."

Joe's team-mates at Everton remember him as a wing-half with great skill. Inside-forward Stan Bentham: "Joe used to get the ball, and he was a good dribbler, as good as any inside-forward, and he used to come on these weaves coming up to us, and I thought, 'Well, I'm not going to get the ball off him, he won't want to give it me or anybody else,' so I used to go back in his position, and then if he was robbed we still had cover."

Joe was often compared with Matt Busby, who was playing for Liverpool in the late 1930s. Both had the poise and energy to bring the ball forward "as if it were tied to their boot-laces". They could mesmerise defenders before clipping the ball out to the wing or through the centre.

Joe seemed capable of doing anything with his long, bow-shaped legs. Some players likened him to a spiral staircase, his legs full of bends and angles, the direction of the ball uncertain. He could stretch a leg deceptively to gain an extra half a yard and nick the ball. He was also a studious player. He never forgot an opponent's strengths and weaknesses, and adapted his style accordingly. He never missed anything that happened during a game. He could recall it afterwards.

Liverpool Echo
1937-38

Like all 1930s wing-halves, Joe was an all-round player who could attack and defend. He was up and down the field with enthusiasm. According to one full-back who played behind him, Joe "could get stuck in". On first sight, opponents sometimes mistook him for a light-weight defender. "He's got legs like sparrows' kneecaps," someone once said. And a journalist once wrote that Joe's legs were so bowed that he couldn't stop a pig in a tight corridor except with a sliding tackle. All through his career, opponents would stare at the shape of his legs, and his rolling gait, and think it would be easy to push the ball between his legs. But it wasn't.

During the 1936-7 season, his first as a regular, Joe took part in the game that he always classed as one of the greatest he ever played in. It was a Cup-tie replay against Second Division Tottenham Hotspur. The first game, on Saturday 20 February at Goodison, ended 1-1. The fifth round replay was two days later. Joe told the story at length in the 1950s: "It was a Monday night and the ground was saturated with a week-end's rain. This was right up our street, because in those days on the right wing for Everton was Albert Geldard who, on a heavy ground with the brilliant Cliff Britton behind him, was almost unplayable. We had a few changes in the side, Torry Gillick coming in as outside left to partner a boy playing only his second game for the 'Toffees'. The boy? - Tommy Lawton. Our side read: Sagar; Cook, JE Jones; Britton, Gee, Mercer; Geldard, Cunliffe, Dean, Lawton, and Gillick.

Right from the start the Everton side got on top, and in the mud the plan of playing to Albert Geldard soon paid dividends. Albert created havoc in the Tottenham defence, and very soon we were two goals up - Jimmy Cunliffe getting the first and Tommy Lawton with a brilliant left-foot goal which rattled into the back of the net from 30 yards. Morrison reduced the lead, but we went in at half-time with the score three-one, thanks to some brilliant work and a goal by the one and only Dixie Dean.

"The second half was a repetition of the first. In fact, kicking down the slope towards the end where the teams come out, I think we were playing more easily than ever. Then, with four

Action from a game Joe classed as one of the greatest he ever played in, the 1937 FA Cup Fifth Round replay between Spurs and Everton at White Hart Lane. Ted Sagar is seen clearing his lines.

minutes to go, the score 3-1 in Everton's favour, it happened. I played a ball on the left wing, which I agree was over the line, but no whistle went, so I crossed it into the penalty area. Dixie fastened on to it and was in the act of shooting when Arthur Rowe, later to become the Spurs manager, was adjudged to have fouled Dean. The referee pointed to the spot and there we were 3-1 up, the ball on the spot for a penalty and four minutes to go; and if that game didn't appear to be won then I have never heard of one that was.

"But in the meantime the linesman was flagging, and after some arguing the referee was persuaded to consult him. The outcome was not a penalty for Everton but a throw-in for Tottenham, and no one knew better than me how fair that decision was. Unfortunately the remainder of the side took a poor view of this and were still arguing when the throw-in was taken. Before we could bat our eyes the ball was whisked across the field to the left wing, back into the centre and Morrison had headed a goal.

"Right from the restart away went Tottenham again, and in next to no time they had got the equaliser through a similar movement, Morrison again being the scorer. Then with the game reaching the last few seconds their inside-forward Meek fastened on to a ball in midfield and wormed his way towards the penalty area. All of a sudden he hit a terrific shot which must have been from well outside the box, and to my terrible anguish it finished up in the back of the net.

"I was immediately behind him when he shot and I saw the ball so very clearly every inch of the way. It had goal written all over it from the moment it left his foot. As the ball hit the back of the net the referee blew the whistle for full-time, and for a fleeting second the majority of the players didn't know whether the goal had counted or not. I remember Billy Cook, our full-back, saying 'Was that a goal, ref?' and the referee replying 'It certainly was.' Then the Tottenham lads realised the game was won and, of course, their joy was quickly transferred to the spectators."

Joe always said that the atmosphere after the final whistle was incredible; hats were thrown up in the air, as were programmes, and the Tottenham supporters in a crowd of over 40,000 roared with delight. Incredibly many spectators had left before the end and so missed the final exciting moments. Even a famous reporter from a leading newspaper had departed early, causing some to wonder what sort of a match report he was going to submit.

The 1936-7 season, like all the seasons since Everton's 1933 Cup victory, was a let-down for a side that had achieved so much at the turn of the decade. Also, it saw the emergence of a man who would eventually end Joe's Everton career, and almost his footballing life.

The change was brought about by the death of Tom McIntosh early in 1936. McIntosh's role as club secretary was not just one of administration it was also, more or less, the role of a manager. He was replaced by Theo Kelly, an outstanding administrator who had difficulty liaising with the players. One man who quickly took a dislike to Kelly was Billy Dean. Dean, at 30, still felt he had a lot to offer the club. Indeed he was club captain and was still scoring plenty of goals. In September 1936, Dean passed Steve Bloomer's goalscoring record of 352 League goals. That day Joe, using his one-time 'useless' left foot, got the ball across to Dean at about chest height. Dean had his back to the goal at first, but went to head it into the right-hand corner of the goal. Suddenly he changed his mind and sent it the other way into the far top-left corner.

Dean's goalscoring prowess didn't really seem to change the way Theo Kelly felt about him. The two men, along with various directors, had to meet frequently to discuss team selection and club affairs. There were often niggling disagreements and arguments and it became obvious that Kelly and Dean had little time for each other. It all came to a head when Dean was dropped for a home game against reigning League Champions Manchester City. Tommy Lawton was his replacement and although Dean fully appreciated Lawton's skills, many of them improved upon by coaching from Dean, it was still a bitter time. Joe liked both centre-forwards and recognised their strengths: "Tommy was technically a better all-round player than Dixie but not in the air. Dixie was so confident - I've seen him toe-end the ball into the net - and had such a good temperament. Dixie's greatest secret was that he would never retaliate. They would push him and he would stand there. If he'd had pockets in his shorts he would have put his hands in them. But when he moved a goal was on the way.

"He was always so kind with praise to Tommy and all the young lads. I remember Tommy coming into the side for a Cup replay at Tottenham. He scored a goal in the first half, turning on the ball beautifully, and Dixie said, 'Well, that's it. That's the swan song. That's the end of it.' They were two great players."

Dean's last match in the Everton first team was at home to Birmingham on 11 December 1937. He moved to Notts County at the end of the season.

Seniority changes quickly in football, and Joe Mercer was now one of the longer-serving Everton players. In 1937 he received a benefit of £650 as reward for his first five years as a professional. He used £600 of the money to buy his mother a house in Eastham.

EVERTON BENEFIT CHEQUES

Cheques to the value of £2,600 were presented to five Everton Football Club players by the chairman, Mr. Ernest Green, at Goodison Park today.

They constituted benefit cheques to Billy Cook, Jimmy Cunliffe, Jack Jones, Joe Mercer and George Jackson.

Mr. Green was supported by directors, Messrs. A. Gates and W. R. Williams and Mr. Theo Kelly, secretary, and all the players were present (writes Pilot).

Mr. Green expressed the hope that all the beneficiaries would remain with the club long enough to receive second benefit cheques.

" I hope the younger players will do their best to qualify for similar cheques," he said.

Mr. Green emphasised the fact that four of those receiving cheques—Cunliffe, Jones, Jackson and Mercer—graduated through the Everton " A " team.

Mr. Green also presented medals to the following players in last season's Central League championship side: Gee (captain), Thomson, Jackson, Lyndley, Jones (T. G.), Davies, Watson, Bentham, Bell, Gillick, Trentham, and Andy Tucker (trainer).

Liverpool Senior Cup winners' medals were presented to Cook (captain), Morton, Jackson, Mercer, Edwards, Lindley, Merritt, Stevenson, Bentham, Bell, and Trentham, and special medals were handed to Mr. Harold Pickering, who is in charge of the " A " team, and Mr. Frank Blundell, a member of the ground staff.

In May 1936 Everton played five games on a three-week tour of Germany. The tour party is seen at Sans Souci near Potsdam, shortly before touring the Olympic village in Berlin.

The Everton party outside the Cosmopolite Hotel, Copenhagen, in May 1937.
From the left: Albert Geldard, Tom Lawton, Joe Mercer, Charles Gee, George Jackson, Jack Jones, Stan Bentham, Jim Cunliffe, Alec Stevenson and Harry Morton.

Without Dean and Albert Geldard, who had also left the club during the close season of 1938, many people expected the 1938-9 season would be another where success would elude the 'Toffees', but they couldn't have been more wrong. Even though Jock Thomson, in his last season with the club, returned to the side as left-half there was a place for the now vitally important Joe Mercer at right-half. Cliff Britton was playing mainly in the Reserves, where he also acted as a coach and advisor. The season commenced with six straight wins including a fine 2-1 victory over Arsenal, the reigning League Champions. Tommy Lawton was proving a good replacement for Dean as he scored eight goals in those opening games.

Everton, the League leaders, lost their seventh match when the previous season's FA Cup Finalists, Huddersfield Town, won 3-0 at Leeds Road on 24 September. The next game was to be the all-important derby match with third-placed Liverpool, but that was preceded by news of world events that preyed on the mind of the population.

Germany, led by Adolf Hitler, was building up her armed forces and was bidding for control of much of Europe. It was becoming obvious to many, especially the Everton players who had visited Germany on close-season tours, that Hitler was preparing for war. Back in 1936, prior to the Berlin Olympics, the Germans were keen to test their players against the other top European sides. Everton were invited on a tour and, as Joe put it, "Everton were going out as trial horses."

That tour had been interesting as the Everton players witnessed the Nazi propaganda machine in full working order. The Germans went to great lengths to demonstrate their alleged superiority. Aside from the experiences in the country, the journey to Germany was, in itself, a bit unusual to say the

EVERTON F.C. PLAYERS IN LINER CRASH

NIGHT THRILL IN FOG

FOURTEEN Everton Football Club players, en route for their tour in Germany, had a thrill when the Hamburg-America liner New York, on which they were travelling, came into collision with the Dutch steamer Alphard north of Ostend, last night. All the players are reported safe.

The collision occurred during fog.

The Alphard was sunk, but the crew of 27 were taken off by the New York, which is proceeding to Hamburg—her scheduled destination.

The Everton party includes Messrs. E. Green, Jack Sharp, G. Evans and Dr Cecil Baxter, directors; Mr. Theo. Kelly, secretary; Mr. Harry Cooke, trainer; and the following players: King, Jackson, Jones, Britton, White, Gee, Thomson, Archer, Mercer, Leyfield, Geldard, Stevenson, Bell and Gillick.

Mr. Hunter Hart, assistant secretary of Everton, states that he has received a message stating that the New York sustained only slight damage, and will arrive at Hamburg late today.

Mr. George Evans, who recently retired from the position of Public Assistance Officer in Liverpool, was concerned in a sea accident on his last voyage.

He was a passenger on board the Cunard-White Star liner Laurentic, which came into collision off the Isle of Man last summer.

The New York is a vessel of 23,337 tons gross, and the Alphard was 3,551 tons gross.

least. Joe often told the story of the trip: "We set off for Germany on a liner travelling from New York to Hamburg. We joined it on tender out of Southampton. The ship was filled with Germans, either coming home from holiday or visiting relatives, and everyone was having a good time - until we were hit by a Dutch steamer ... smack, right in the middle. The steamer went down like a stone, but fortunately everybody was saved and we continued the journey. As usual, we made a joke. Charlie Gee was always having his leg pulled about being slow, and Jimmy Cunliffe, the quickest thing on two feet, said, 'What do you think? When I got in the top boat Charlie was already there!'"

From the summer of 1938, there was no chance of Everton touring Germany again in the immediate future. Hitler's first claim was on the Sudeten region of Czechoslovakia. A proportion of this region's population were of German origin, hence Hitler's claim the area was part of the German state. The British and other western Europeans were deeply concerned and Prime Minister Neville Chamberlain met Hitler to obtain guarantees that war would be prevented. On 30 September 1938, the day before the Liverpool derby, Chamberlain returned home waving the Anglo-German agreement which he believed guaranteed "peace in our time".

At Goodison the following day the crowd of over 65,000 celebrated by singing the national anthem while the German forces marched into the Sudetenland. By half-time the score in the derby match was 2-1 to Everton. Stan Bentham and Wally Boyes had scored for the Blues while Liverpool's Willie Fagan replied in the 43rd minute. There was no further scoring, and the blue half of the city celebrated further.

Despite the continuing threat of war, the 1938-9 season was completed and Everton won the Championship in style. "We won it by Easter," the players would later recall. It was a skilful side, known as 'the School of Science', and its great strength lay in the half-back-line of Joe Mercer, TG Jones and either Jock Thomson or Gordon Watson. It was also a young side. The average age was only 25. Centre-half TG Jones was only 22, centre-forward Tommy Lawton only 19, while Joe Mercer was by now 24 years old.

Confidence was high and for Joe Mercer life was just perfect. He was at a club he loved with people he could relate to. Joe loved the big-match atmosphere and was caught up in it from the moment he left home on match-days. During his journey from Ellesmere Port he was surrounded by Evertonians going to the match. The supporters knew Joe was one of them, a man who loved football and would do anything to play. He loved hearing the comments of his followers, and those for whom Joe was the enemy. When running out before a packed Goodison Park Joe always felt tremendous excitement, and often commented about the pleasure he felt when he heard the crowd roaring. Or of the times when he was forced to take throw-ins from amongst the crowd, as they always seemed to be packed tight to the touchline.

1939 started out as Joe's year. As well as his constantly superb performances for Everton and a League Championship medal, he also received his first international honour. He was one of the country's finest wing-halves. What more was there to life?

Everton 1938-39: 'The School of Science' championship-winning side. *Back row (left to right)* - Lawton, TG Jones, Sagar, Cook (trainer), Mercer, Greenhalgh. *Front* - W Cook, Gillick, Bentham, Thomson, Stevenson, Boyes.

Chapter Three

MAN OF THE MATCH

If the flags are not out in Ellesmere Port, a little town in west Cheshire, they ought to be. The honour is due to Joe Mercer, the Everton half-back, born there 24 years ago, who at Hampden Park, Glasgow, on Saturday gave for England one of the greatest displays I have ever seen in a representative game.

Henry Rose, *Daily Express*, April 1939

NORAH FANNY DYSON was the only child of a successful Wirral grocer. She was born in Liverpool in March 1920, and her family moved to Ellesmere Port just a few months after her birth. They lived north of the level-crossing in the area where Wolverhampton folk had settled, whereas Joe lived in the south as a true 'Portite'.

Albert Dyson, Norah's father, had been a grocer since the age of 12 and had successfully built up his business. He was a strong Everton supporter and had become friendly with many of the Everton players and staff. It was through these connections that Albert Dyson met Joe Mercer.

Tom Corley, an Everton scout and the man who "spotted" Joe, organised an event at the Wolverhampton Corrugated Iron Company Social Club in Ellesmere Port and, because of the relatively small number of players with cars, he arranged for one or two Ellesmere Port people to collect some of the players from the Woodside ferry. Albert Dyson collected Archie Clark, Cliff Britton and their partners, and went on to develop a particular friendship with Archie Clark, who visited the grocer regularly.

During their discussions about Everton, Archie Clark revealed that there was a young 'Portite' on Everton's books called Joe Mercer. It was decided that Archie would introduce him to Albert by inviting the young player to tea at the Dyson home. Norah tells the story: "My father and Archie Clark contacted a boy called Johnny Meredith who knew Joe and was a bit of a footballer. They asked Johnny if he would go with them in the car to collect Joe and if they both would like to come back for tea. But unfortunately Johnny Meredith was a shy type and he didn't come, but old cheeky face Mercer came! Of course at the time I was 11 and Joe was 17, and he treated me like a sister. Six years is a big difference at that stage of life. Then the gap narrows. I didn't meet him again until I was about 14, when I bumped into him at the Cottage Hospital garden fete. He challenged my friend, Joan Hollingsworth, and I to a swimming-match at the Rivacre baths. So we went there, had a swim and a chat and I then used to see him quite often just walking around the town. And then I was rather poorly at the Christmas of 1936 and my father had a message on the Boxing Day to say Joe Mercer was stuck down the

Port, couldn't get on the bus, and could my father, by any chance, run him to Everton because he was playing in the afternoon against Arsenal. A cousin of Joe's had offered to take him on a motor-bike but that wasn't allowed in case they had an accident. So, of course my father took Joe to the match and told him that I was unwell and Joe came to see me. By this time I was 16 and it naturally developed from there."

As the relationship blossomed, Joe and Norah enjoyed the pictures, swimming and walks. As Joe could not drive, Norah took him for day trips into the countryside, to places like North Wales. In fact, it was Norah who taught Joe to drive, during the war years.

Joe also became close to Norah's father, as Norah recalls: "My father was fond of Joe. I think they struck up a friendship, relationship, call it what you will, because Joe was the son my father never had, whilst my dad was the father Joe had lost when he was twelve. They were very close and they got on very well."

Joe spent much of his free time with Norah and her parents. In fact it was while Joe was at the Dyson home in 1938 that he received the news he had always hoped for. Norah well remembers the day: "Joe was at our house when he heard he had been selected to play for England. It was different to how it is now because in those days the international side was announced first on radio. Few people had telephones. Luckily Joe was at our house when the announcement was made on the radio. He was delighted - a dream come true!"

Joe is on record as saying that the selection was his "biggest individual thrill in football" and it was certainly a major achievement. At this time England was spoiled for choice of wing-halves and Joe came into the side as left-half instead of the more familiar right-half spot. Huddersfield Town's Ken Willingham was the permanent right-half and, as Joe admitted at the time, it would take a miracle to relieve him of that position. Willingham was a very good runner and tenacious footballer, playing for the Yorkshire team at a time when they were still a major footballing power.

Once again Joe's father's insistence on practising with the left foot had paid off. Joe was able to play left-half for England against Ireland at Manchester United's ground, Old Trafford, in November 1938. Joe replaced Wilf Copping of Arsenal, who had a reputation as a hard man. Stanley Matthews said of Copping, "He never shaved before a match to try and frighten the forwards. He was very dark - and he was tough. Great to have on your side. You can't have 11 gentlemen in a team."

NEW ENGLAND CAP v IRELAND

MERCER EVERTON

Joe's style was a bit different to Copping's but was nevertheless very effective against Ireland. England won 7-0, with Tottenham's Willie Hall scoring an incredible five goals. Most of the press reports focused on Hall's goalscoring exploits and an outstanding performance from Stanley Matthews. Years later Joe reflected that this match was Matthews' finest: "In the match against Ireland Stan Matthews was at the top of his form for the whole 90 minutes. We won 7-0, five of the goals being scored by inside-right Willie Hall - an England scoring record - and Stanley had a part in almost every goal."

Joe also summed up his own role in the game: "I had a great view of this terrific game but I hardly kicked the ball! When it came into our half, Ken Willingham had it, and he was playing it to Stan Matthews. When Stan didn't have it, Willie Hall was scoring goals!"

With Everton colleague Tommy Lawton and former Ellesmere Port team-mate Stan Cullis both in the side, the experience of playing for England was made a little easier for Joe. Also,

England's team against Ireland in November 1938
Back row (left to right): Willingham, Cullis, Woodley, Morris, Mercer, Hapgood.
Front: Matthews, Hall, Lawton, Stephenson, Smith.

once the game started all the attention was on the goalscorers, preventing Joe's own role from being closely examined. It is true, though, that the credit for the result didn't lie entirely with Hall and Matthews. Many reporters regarded the result as a team achievement. The *Daily Mail* reporter Frank Carruthers stated: "It is doubtful whether there was ever an era of the game richer in talent than was revealed by the England team at Old Trafford. It may be suggested that a defence which concedes seven goals is woefully weak, but the Irish halves and backs were overwhelmed."

England's next game was against Scotland at Hampden Park. Joe retained his place as England attempted to defeat the Scots at Hampden for the first time since 1927.

The Hampden bogey was well and truly ended. The game, played in appalling conditions, began with "England looking rather shaky", as one reporter put it. Joe was given full credit for his performance at this point, however, as he tried to establish stability in defence.

Scotland were first to score, the goal resulting from an error. Tommy Walker of Hearts sent a pass through the middle. England's Morris pushed the ball back wide of goalkeeper Woodley as the England 'keeper ran out. Before Woodley managed to get the ball Dougal of Preston had slipped past him and tapped the ball into the net.

From that point on, England controlled the game. Even though Joe wasn't captain, he rallied the side in the pouring rain. The conditions deteriorated further and by half-time both sides were drenched. England did not have a spare set of shirts, so they borrowed a set from Queen's Park, the Scottish club who played at Hampden.

In unfamiliar shirts, England now dominated further. They scored 20 minutes into the half. After a mistake by Third Lanark's Carabine, Huddersfield's Beasley slammed home the equaliser. In the final minute West Ham's Goulden passed the ball to Stanley Matthews on the right, who in turn centred the ball to Tommy Lawton's head. The Everton forward snatched the winning goal with a perfect header with only seconds to spare. Lawton's winner was greeted with an eerie silence from the stunned Scottish crowd.

The following day Joe Mercer took the headlines with his sterling performance. Reporter

MERCER WAS THE MAN OF THE MATCH AT HAMPDEN

Inspired Display Against Scotland After Dougal's Early Blow

By CHARLES BUCHAN

Scotland .... 1 England 2

AFTER waiting since 1927 for a win at Hampden Park, England gained only her second victory on this ground in the last minute of a thrilling game when Lawton's head connected properly with a Matthews centre. History was made in dismal, rainy surroundings.

A pronounced second-half superiority brought a just reward to England. During this period the 150,000 crowd tried in vain the "Hampden Roar." It dwindled to an agonised groan as the England half-backs repelled the mild onslaughts of the Scots. Not only was the roar stifled, but the Hampden bogy well and truly laid.

NEW ENGLAND SPIRIT BEAT SCOTS

Matthews and Mercer Brilliant

By ARBITER (Frank M. Carruthers)

WHEN Edris Hapgood, England's captain, flung his arms in the air as the signal of

of his tremendous strength.

By his artistic brilliance Matthews provided most of the highlights, but Mercer was the outstanding figure. I have not seen a man exercise such a compelling influence since Arthur Grimsdell, and it is curious that both have the same unusually shaped legs. I wonder whether their power to go through with the ball in a tackle can be traced to this.

Mercer's display came from the heart, and surely the authorities will now decide that they must take him on the Continental tour. I believe he wa

Mercer was hero of England win

Scotland 1, England 2

IF the flags are not out in Ellesmere Port, a little town in west Cheshire, they ought to be. The honour is due to Joe Mercer, the Everton half-back, born there 23 years ago, who at Hampden Park, Glasgow, on Saturday gave for England one of the greatest displays I have ever seen in a representative game

36

John Macadam declared: "Mercer was magnificent all through, even in the first half, when it looked as if Scotland were going to have a runaway win."

In the *Daily Express*, Henry Rose wrote: "I happened to meet Mercer before the game. As he thanked me for my good wishes, I thought he looked pale and drawn, and had a slight suggestion of being over-trained. I could forgive his apprehension, if he had any, for this was his first Hampden. And that is frightening enough for the English looker-on, let alone player.

"His appearance belied his subsequent performance. Mercer was ever in the thick of this throbbing battle, which, with the driving wind and pitiless, ceaseless rain, provided the severest of all tests of skill, stamina, and heart. Mercer had them all.

"He never lost a tackle, never made one without coming away with the ball and never, unless my eyes deceived me, parted with the ball except to a colleague. He commanded a great part of the field, was at centre-half when Cullis hung back, roamed over to the right when Willingham wanted some help in looking after Venters, and yet was mysteriously in his own position of left-half when he had to be. Bravo, Joe."

The *News Chronicle* headline was clear enough: **Mercer was man of the match at Hampden**. Underneath, Charles Buchan, the former Sunderland and England forward, wrote: "Besides demonstrating the superiority of English football for the time being, the exhibition proved how unwise the FA selectors have been in prematurely choosing the England team to meet Italy in Milan on May 13.

"Man of the match was undoubtedly Mercer, the left-half-back. He rallied the side, and prompted them. Yet Mercer will not play against Italy in a month's time. What a pity for England!

"Mercer was the strong man in a crisis against Scotland. He never faltered at any time. His strong forcing work gave Cullis and Hapgood the breathing space they required in the early stages."

Indeed, Joe had not been selected for the tour to Italy, Yugoslavia, and Romania. After the Scotland game Joe admitted: "I was sitting in the bath after the game, thinking to myself. I didn't know whether to laugh ... or cry with happiness ... or sadness!"

Following the game there was a public outcry. This eventually led to Joe being included at the last moment, although there was still some doubt whether the tour would go ahead. With the prospect of war drawing ever closer, it seemed rather foolish to go on a tour which visited one of Hitler's closest allies. The FA consulted the government, who in turn authorised the summer tour of 1939.

Despite the prospect of war between Italy and Britain, the Italian public showed great hospitality towards the English players. When the players arrived at Stresa railway station, the locals showered them with flowers. After a two-day stay at Stresa, the

Lawton and J. Mercer, [Ev]erton footballers, leaving L[iv]eet Station this week to join [En]glish team who play on Continent.

The England team at Victoria Station ready to depart on the Continental tour.
Left to right: Welsh, Matthews, Stephenson, Willingham, Hall, Smith, Woodley, Goulden, Morris, Cullis, Broome, Mercer, Lawton, Hapgood and Male.

squad moved on to Milan, where the international was to be played. On arrival, the players were greeted by a thronging mass of supporters asking for autographs. The crowd was such that a simple two-minute walk to the Piazza Duca d'Aosta, where the players were to stay, took half an hour. When the English party got inside the hotel, the tremendous crowd demanded that the players come to the window as they chanted *Viva Inglesi!*. Naturally Joe and the other English players obliged.

The game itself was to take place at the impressive San Siro stadium. Not everything about the stadium impressed the English, however, as when they arrived, they were presented with the incredible sight of high wire netting being erected around the pitch. On investigation they discovered that the high fencing was being installed to prevent bottles and other missiles being thrown at the players during the game. After the treatment they had received from the Italian public, they could not understand the reasoning behind the fences.

Although Italy were one of the greatest footballing sides in the world - they had won the World Cup twice while England were obstinately refusing to participate - England were still regarded as the best international side. This match was seen by many as the unofficial Championship of the World. The two sides had not met since 1934, when the English won an ill-tempered game 3-2, an occasion that went down in football history as 'The Battle of Highbury'.

In comparison to the Highbury match, this game started in a sporting manner. The Italians had an air of confidence about their game and perhaps felt that instead of using physical force to defeat the English, they would use their plentiful skills. For the first ten minutes the English were in command. The crowd of approximately 70,000 acknowledged the skills, and England were rewarded when Tommy Lawton headed a goal. Then the Italians gradually began to outplay England, and left-winger Bievat scored a brilliant and deserved equaliser.

The Italians soon scored another, more controversially. Here's Joe Mercer's account: "George Male and the Italian centre-forward, Piola, went up together for the ball in our goalmouth. Male seemed sure to get it, but Piola struck out with his fist - punching the ball into the net. Following through, his fist landed a fierce blow on George's forehead and George fell - knocked out!"

May 1939. England line-up in the San Siro Stadium, Milan.
Left to right: Hapgood, Woodley, Broome, Lawton, Willingham, Matthews, Mercer, Male, Goulden, Hall and Cullis.

The foul seemed so obvious that the English players didn't appeal, but the German referee, Dr Bauwens, awarded a goal. Perhaps the alliance between Germany and Italy extended to the football field!

The English now played with more determination as they themselves piled the pressure on the Italian defence. Joe Mercer and Ken Willingham moved up in support of the forwards as the last moments of the game ticked away and England attacked with eight players. The pressure led to England's equaliser as Willie Hall scored after Len Goulden's shot was blocked.

After the game, the press acknowledged the overall improvement in the Italian method of play, and the Italians impressed their English counterparts by admitting their second goal should have been disallowed. Most of the praise given to the English was in recognition of the fine work of the side's defenders, in particular Joe Mercer. Fellow team-mate Stanley Matthews commented: "We never recovered from the brilliance of Italy's first goal, and if it hadn't been for a sterling performance by Joe Mercer, who held our defence together, we might well have gone under."

From Milan, the English touring party travelled to Belgrade via Venice. On arrival in the Yugoslavian capital they were greeted yet again by another remarkably large crowd. For many of the players, the tour was beginning to take its toll, as the crowds demanded more and more of them wherever they went.

In a difficult game the English were defeated 2-1 by a strong, impressive Yugoslavian side with England's goal coming from Aston Villa's Frank Broome. Two of England's most impor-

POLITICS UPSET JUGO-SLAV CHOICE
BODYGUARD WATCH
REBEL FULL-BACK

BELGRADE, Wednesday.

SERB-CROAT feeling is blowing up over the composition of the Jugo-Slav team to play England here tomorrow, and a lot of hard words are being exchanged each way

tant players, Stan Matthews and Eddie Hapgood, were injured in the Yugoslavia game and were unfit for the final match of the tour, against Romania.

The tired English party now travelled by boat down the Danube on their way to the final game in Bucharest. Once again large crowds greeted the players and made them feel welcome. A number of visits to local places of interest, such as castles and even a circus, were arranged.

In stark contrast to the welcome they had received, it was an ill-tempered game. Twenty-two year old Stan Cullis had the difficult task of following the injured Hapgood as captain. Throughout the match he had to ensure his players stayed calm and avoided retaliation. He even had to calm the normally placid Mercer. Cullis recalls: "One of the Romanians took off the sole of Joe's boot, and I saw Joe threatening him, so I had to tell him 'If you do anything, I'll send you off, never mind the bloody referee! We're going to finish with eleven men, and win!.'"

Joe stayed on the field, of course, and England defeated the Romanians 2-0 with goals from Len Goulden and Don Welsh. The home side had far more of the play and, in the closing moments of the game, piled on so much pressure that the entire England side was needed in defence. The England players were relieved when the match ended. After two weeks of travelling across Europe, being mobbed everywhere they went, and three tough games, it must have been a great feeling of relief when the final whistle was blown.

Most of the England players then returned home, but Joe Mercer and Tommy Lawton travelled to join their Everton team-mates in Holland. Tommy Lawton gives the details of their exhausting journey across Europe: "We said good-bye to the homeward-bound England team at Basle, on the frontiers of France and Switzerland, and, after a brief two hours' rest, travelled direct to Amsterdam, which we reached at five on Saturday evening, only an hour and half before the kick-off time. Our time-table had been: Thursday morning, 11.15, left Bucharest, Romania; Friday, 7.15 am, Budapest, where we had a short stop of one and a half hours in order to be greeted by Hungarian FA officials; on through Hungary and Austria, until Basle was reached at 3 am Saturday morning. And so at last we reached Amsterdam."

After that kind of journey, anyone would expect that Everton would allow Joe to miss the game, but, no, after a brief rest he made his way onto the pitch. Tommy Lawton was impressed: "I was too exhausted to play against the Dutch side and sat in the stand, nodding sleepily most of the time, I must admit. But the indefatigable Mercer turned out ... and gave his usual 90 minutes' display!"

Joe Mercer was not the type of person to let anyone down. However, it seems that Joe was paying the price for being a successful international player. If Joe had failed in the match against Scotland over a month earlier he would have missed England's gruelling tour and could have settled for an easier time in Holland. But Joe admitted that playing for England and Everton were both great honours, and neither was something he wanted to miss, no matter how tired he felt.

Finally, Joe returned home to his family and girl-friend Norah, and his thoughts turned to further success with his club. As his 25th birthday approached, Joe had become a vital player in the Everton team, won a League Championship medal, and established himself as an England player with five successive internationals. Joe, like all Evertonians, was hoping the reigning League Champions would achieve further success during the forthcoming 1939-40 season ... but the prospect of war was ever closer.

Chapter Four

ENGLAND'S WARTIME CAPTAIN

In 1943 I was chosen to replace Stan Cullis as captain of England. It was a great occasion for me when a letter from Sir Stanley Rous gave me the news, for I wanted the job. To do a good job as captain you must want to lead and to take responsibility. You must be the sort who is able comfortably to tell people what to do and what not to do - but this must come in a natural way and not be forced. Captaincy must be spontaneous. Players who want to take this responsibility are not common and I think good captains are born to the job. I'm sure Stan Cullis was.

Joe Mercer, *The Great Ones*

THE 1939-40 season commenced with League Champions Everton drawing 1-1 at home to Brentford. Joe Mercer resumed his club position at right-half. His performances the previous season had earned him the reputation of being one of the best and most consistent players of the period, and the News Chronicle Football Annual recognised Joe as one of their four Players of the Year. The others were Willie Hall (Tottenham Hotspur), Stanley Matthews (Stoke City) and Billy Morris (Wolverhampton Wanderers).

Two days after the draw with Brentford, Everton won 2-1 at Aston Villa. The attendance was under 30,000, somewhat less than might have been expected to see the League Champions. The reason was simple - it was obvious that war was almost upon Britain. Hitler and his followers had relentlessly shown signs that some form of German military action was being planned for Europe. All forms of heavy transport, motor vehicles and civilian aircraft were now being commandeered throughout the German nation.

The continuing concerns disrupted the day-to-day life of all British civilians. Over a million children were evacuated from British cities during the week of 31 August. At the time few parents knew exactly where their children were going, or who they were to stay with. Surprisingly, in the midst of these disruptions and fears of war, the footballing authorities announced on 1 September that the following day's League programme would carry on as normal.

Throughout the summer months, as the prospect of war increased, many players had enlisted in the Territorial Army or other such national service organisations. Everton's great rivals Liverpool went one stage further than most when they became the first side to join the Territorial Army as a club. West Ham United and Bolton Wanderers followed their example and volunteered en masse, while the directors of Manchester United took a less patriotic view: "It is a matter for the individual to decide". On 30 August, most of the West Ham players received their call-up papers for the Essex Regiment searchlight section. There was little chance of a normal League season.

Joe and Norah

On Saturday 2 September Everton travelled across Lancashire to face newly-promoted Blackburn Rovers. A subdued crowd of over 17,000 saw the Lancashire derby. The result, if it mattered, was a 2-2 draw with that man Tommy Lawton scoring twice, his third and fourth goals of the season. During the previous day the Germans commenced their invasion of Poland. On the Saturday an air-raid on Warsaw, the Polish capital, resulted in the death of 21 people. On the Sunday, 3 September, at noon in the House of Commons, Prime Minister Neville Chamberlain announced: "This country is now at war with Germany. We are ready".

A ban was immediately placed on the assembly of crowds. The Football League and Football Association concluded that the League programme should be cancelled and that all players contracts should be suspended. Everton's chance of building on their success had ended. As Joe often put it: "All of a sudden we were a good side again. Then, of course, the war came."

By the end of the month, the FA had relaxed their rules and had given permission for the organisation of mini-leagues or competitions consisting only of teams within the same region or district. One proviso was that games could be played on either Saturdays or Bank Holidays, and that the attendance had to be either less than 8,000 or half the capacity of the ground, whichever was the lower figure. Later, crowds of 15,000 were allowed, provided the match was all-ticket.

During this time of confusion, most of the players who hadn't previously enlisted now joined the forces. Stanley Rous, the FA secretary, sent letters to all players with coaching experience urging them to join the Army Physical Training Corps. As part of the circular, Rous stressed that the players would be able to retain their fitness and that they would be made Sergeant Instructors immediately. After a few days working at Cammell Laird's, Joe Mercer was one of the first men to sign up for the Army PT Corps, in mid-September, and was in the first batch of men sent to Reading for training. As Joe said, "I'd never worked at Cammell Laird's before, and I wasn't going hiding."

In Reading, Joe and the others realised that Rous' promise of promotion wouldn't materialise. He had no right making the promise, and as soon as the players realised the truth they rebelled. Joe recalled: "Only our ignorance let us assume that we should be accepted immediately as Sergeant Instructors on the same terms as gymnasts who had worked for years and undergone specialised courses to win their tapes. But we were ignorant - and when we were told we were not going to become Sergeants right away we mutinied. We refused to obey orders."

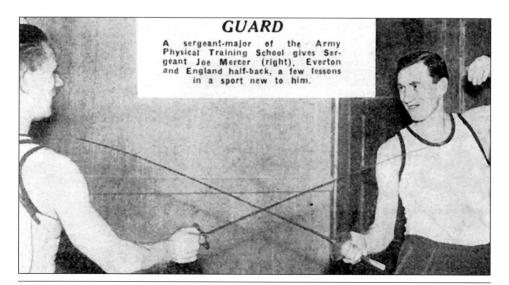

GUARD

A sergeant-major of the Army Physical Training School gives Sergeant Joe Mercer (right), Everton and England half-back, a few lessons in a sport new to him.

Army School of Physical Training, Aldershot, 1941.

An urgent message was sent to Stanley Rous at Lancaster Gate and following lengthy discussions, Joe and his comrades achieved their first victory of the war - they were made temporary Sergeants. Understandably, the other Sergeants, who had spent considerably longer training, gave Joe and the others a rough time.

At the end of his course Joe was presented with his 'real' stripes and the crossed-swords emblem of the PT instructors and then, much to his delight, was sent off to play football as entertainment for the troops. The Army, and the other forces, sent representative sides touring through the areas of Europe occupied by the Allies. Often the representative games took place only a short distance from actual fighting. Matt Busby, a man who was to play with Joe in these games, commented: "Often we played matches only a few miles behind the front lines with the noise of gunfire sometimes tending to drown the sound of the referee's whistle."

In his autobiography, *The Great Ones*, Joe recalled that his first such match was a victory in Paris against the French Army. The only part of the game he could remember was when a barrier behind the goal collapsed causing the packed crowd of soldiers to fall in piles ten deep.

In addition to Army games, Joe continued to represent England at international level during the war. The FA insisted that these games be regarded as 'unofficial' internationals and refused to award caps. There was no doubt at the time that these games were true full-blooded international affairs and that the same amount of commitment was shown in them as was in the pre-war internationals. In fact the boost these games gave to the troops' morale probably meant that the players deserved more for these matches than any other. The stubborn refusal to issue caps was an insult.

Joe's first wartime international was against Wales at the Racecourse Ground, Wrexham. A restricted but still significant crowd of 17,000 saw the English side win 3-2 on 18 November

1939. Stan Cullis and Tommy Lawton were both in the England team, while Joe's Everton colleague, Tommy G Jones, was the Welsh centre-half. Joe's friendship with 'TG' developed at Everton when the Welshman joined the club from Wrexham in 1936 for £3,000. Like Joe, TG had established himself as an international before the war.

This match was followed two weeks later by another England victory, 2-1 against Scotland, at St James's Park, Newcastle, before a 15,000 crowd. What was incredible about this match was that there were actually more Scottish players on the pitch than English. This occurred because two Manchester City players, Sam Barkas and Eric Brook, were involved in a car crash and were unable to play. England recruited two Newcastle players, and one of them, Tommy Pearson, was actually Scottish.

F.A. says Mercer must play: Club answers "No"

By HENRY ROSE

THE Football Association: Mercer must play for England against Wales at Wembley.

Everton: We are expecting Mercer to turn out for us against Liverpool in the Lancashire Senior Cup semi-final at Goodison Park.

Mercer: I am waiting for word from the club.

England's next international was against Wales at Wembley. The FA expected Joe to play in this game. His club, Everton, thought otherwise when they announced he would be playing for the Blues against Liverpool in the semi-final of the Lancashire Senior Cup. The story was later recalled by Joe: "At the time I was under contract to His Majesty's Forces at Chester Camp and requests for my footballing services had to go 'through the proper channels'. The red tape got mixed up somewhere. Anyway, the day Everton wanted me for the semi-final, England wanted me for a match against Wales at Wembley. To read the headlines, you wouldn't have believed we were fighting for freedom in a World War.

"The papers had a field day. 'Everton Must Climb Down.' 'Mercer Will Not Play For Everton.' 'Next Step In The Mercer Sensation.' 'Behind The Scenes Crisis.' 'Army Decision Day.' 'Everton Declare War On The FA.' It sounded as if we were preparing for the El Alamein campaign. But it was all a bit sad. No player likes to be kicked by both sides in public. It all happened because there was some doubt whether England had applied to my CO for my services. In the end I was released from duties at Chester at noon on Saturday. I couldn't have made Wembley and played for Everton. After the game, I was smuggled away by car."

On the day itself neither Everton nor

Named in the Wembley programme to play for England, Joe arrives at Goodison Park to play for Everton against Liverpool in the Lancashire Senior Cup semi-final.

England appeared to know which game Joe would turn up at. Both expected him. When Joe arrived at Goodison Park, the Everton staff were naturally excited, and as he entered the field that excitement was quickly passed on to the supporters. Prior to the game the 13,563 crowd was subdued. They believed that Joe was on his way to Wembley. As the players were led on to the pitch the crowd remained fairly peaceful, until they caught sight of Joe, then the ground erupted and chanted "Good old Sergeant". They made Joe realise that they were delighted that he had turned out for them instead of for his country.

After the game, which Everton won 4-1, an FA investigation cleared Joe of any blame and resulted in two Everton directors being suspended. As far as the FA were concerned, Joe, because he was under contract to Everton, had been put in a difficult position by his club. They were responsible for deciding who he played for, therefore they were the guilty party.

Joe regained his place for the next England game, against Scotland in Glasgow, although it was uncertain whether the game would take place. At the time, a notorious German propagandist known as Lord Haw Haw was intercepting British radio programmes, and now he threatened that the game would be stopped before the second half by a bomb attack on Hampden Park by Hitler's Luftwaffe Airforce.

The Scottish public were determined to see the game and their response was typical: "Let's ring Hampden with anti-aircraft guns to keep the Jerry out, then settle down to whip the English!" The game was played, although 6,000 supporters failed to turn up.

Apart from the worry of military action, the FA had another worry. They were concerned that Joe, Stan Cullis, Bert Sproston and Don Welsh wouldn't be able to play as there seemed doubt over whether the Army had granted them leave. When all four arrived at Glasgow station together on the same train, the FA officials were naturally overjoyed. Such was the uncertainty of wartime football. Each game had to be planned like military manoeuvres with players travelling from all over the British Isles in already difficult circumstances to meet at one location, for a 90-minute game. Joe recognised the importance of these wartime matches. He often commented on the need to keep up morale at home and, of course, abroad. A few of these wartime games were filmed with copies distributed to the troops to convince them that life was continuing as normal.

One of Joe's most farcical wartime football experiences was a game between the Army and the RAF at Leeds. The fog was so bad that any match other than a charity match would probably have been postponed. Radio commentator Raymond Glendenning couldn't see through the fog so he ran up and down the touchline with a microphone shouting to the players, "What's happening? What's happening? Where's the ball?" "I haven't the foggiest," Joe replied. He and Raich Carter, the RAF inside-left, set off to look for the ball and yelled back to Glendenning in relays what was happening.

England's greatest wartime achievement, indeed one of the greatest-ever England achievements, was the 8-0 victory over arch-rivals Scotland in front of 60,000 spectators at Maine Road, Manchester, on 16 October 1943. The English team that day was one of the finest of all time: Swift (Manchester City), Scott (Arsenal), Hardwick (Middlesbrough), Britton (Everton), Cullis (Wolves), Mercer (Everton), Matthews (Stoke), Carter (Sunderland), Lawton (Everton), Hagan (Sheffield United), Compton D (Arsenal).

The eight-goal margin is still the biggest ever recorded in England-Scotland fixtures and Joe often insisted that this game was "the greatest game I can remember". In Brian James' book *England v Scotland*, Bill Shankly recalled: "When I heard the team I said two prayers. One of thanks to the Scots for leaving me out, and one on behalf of Adam Little who had taken my place. I knew then we'd do well to get away with less than five goals against."

The match stood out for Frank Swift, the England goalkeeper: "The finest team I ever played in was the England eleven which beat Scotland 8-0 at Maine Road. Taking into consideration that it was a wartime game, with both sets of players affected by wartime conditions, and lack of training facilities, long hours of travel to get to the match, it was a magnificent, if

England 8 Scotland 0 - 'The greatest game I can remember,' Joe (far right, with hands on hips) often insisted.

one-sided match. I've yet to see such perfection of movement, unselfishness, or team spirit as England showed that afternoon. Or the courage to equal that of the Scots, beaten though they were, but never humbled.

"It was sheer delight to be the goalkeeper on this great side. For long periods I was able to watch the machine swing into action, to note the brilliant half-back play of the three muske-teers, Britton, Cullis, Mercer, the terrific shooting of Lawton, the methodical destruction of the Scottish defensive plan by Carter and Hagan, and the sheer wizardry of Stanley Matthews.

"I was glad that afternoon at Maine Road that it was Joe Crozier in the Scottish goal, and not yours truly. I had no wish to test my skill against this goal-hungry line. Lawton was shoot-ing too accurately for any goalkeeper to stand much chance of saving his shots. Strange that the easiest chance of the match, a penalty by Carter, was missed!"

Tommy Lawton scored four, Hagan two, Matthews and Carter one each. Despite the scoreline and the obvious demolition performed by England, Scotland did have a few chances, with the heroic Swift making an incredible swallow-dive save from one of Campbell's shots during the second half. Nevertheless the day belonged to England.

Joe appeared in three more internationals before he received an official invitation to cap-tain the team. Former schoolmate Stan Cullis had been posted overseas, and Joe was the obvi-ous choice as his successor. It was a job Joe loved. He felt it a great honour and tried to ensure he put in as much effort and commitment as possible. He would lead by example. Joe com-mented in a 1960s interview: "I had been lucky. My apprenticeship had been served under such natural captains as Billy Dean, Charlie Gee, Jock Thomson and Stan Cullis. The time had now come to see how much I had learned. Of one thing I was sure. No youngster who came into the side would suffer what I suffered under Hapgood. On my international début I was left alone and felt like something the cat had brought home. Stan Cullis and Tommy Lawton did

TELEPHONE:
3504 PRESTON

F. HOWARTH
T. CHARNLEY
(SECRETARY)

The Football League Ltd.

30 Winckley Square,

Preston, 8th., October 19~~4~~1.,

Sgt. Major Ins. J. Mercer,
Blacon Camp,
Chester.

Dear Mr. Mercer,

<u>International League Match at Blackpool</u>.

Will you please be good enough to report at the
ground before 2-30 p.m.

The Mayor of Blackpool has invited all
players and officials to have tea with him at the Winter Gardens
after the match at 6 p.m. Any player desiring to stay in
Blackpool on the Saturday night will on request to the undersigned
have reserved for him a bedroom at the Danum Hotel South Shore,
Blackpool.

Yours faithfully,

F. Howarth

THE FOOTBALL ASSOCIATION.

PATRON:
HIS MAJESTY THE KING.

PRESIDENT:
THE RT. HON.
THE EARL OF ATHLONE, K.G.

SECRETARY:
S. F. ROUS.

TELEGRAPHIC ADDRESS
"FOOTBALL ASSOCIATION
PADD. LONDON."

22, LANCASTER GATE,

LONDON, W. 2.

Our reference SFR/DMM/F

17th May, 1943.

C.S.M.I. J. Mercer,
A.P.T.C. Staff Army School of P.T.,
Queen's Avenue,
Aldershot.

Dear Mercer,

I am sorry to hear from Major Sloan that you will not be able to make the journey to Aberdeen.

Would you be so kind as to give me some details of the match in which you took part on Saturday last at Gillingham. I understand that the match was played in aid of the Red Cross Prisoners of War Fund.

I wish to find out who issued the invitation to you to raise a team for this purpose. who sanctioned it from the Red + Committee.

Yours sincerely,

C. S. Rous.

49

THE FOOTBALL ASSOCIATION.

PATRON :
HIS MAJESTY THE KING.

PRESIDENT :
THE RT. HON. THE EARL OF ATHLONE. K.G.

SECRETARY:
S. F. ROUS.

TELEGRAPHIC ADDRESS :
" FOOTBALL ASSOCIATION
PADD. LONDON."

Our reference SD/HH

22, LANCASTER GATE,
LONDON. W. 2.

6th October, 1941.

Dear Mercer,

    I am sorry that I did not see you in the Hotel on Saturday evening to congratulate you upon your splendid contribution to an all round display which resulted in such a successful match.

    I was sorry to hear from your wife that you felt over-tired, and much hope that you were better on Sunday and able to make the return journey in comfort. I was pleased to meet your wife and members of your family, and wish you much happiness in the future.

Yours faithfully,

[signature]

Secretary.

C.S.M.I.J. Mercer,
5th Training Battalion, R.E.,
Blacon,
CHESTER.

the honours and I felt a lot better. I learned later that Hapgood was a 'loner'. He even did his own private training schedule at Highbury.

"To this day Billy Wright calls me his football 'fairy Godmother'. All I did was to welcome him when he arrived. He had a ton of talent but was nervous. On one occasion we were going out of the tunnel at Hampden. The famous 'roar' nearly blew us back again. I saw Billy's face and told him, 'Pretend they are shouting for us instead of at us.' It seemed to work."

Joe's first game as England captain was a 2-2 draw with Wales at Anfield, Liverpool, before a crowd of almost forty thousand. Joe felt especially proud as the venue was so close to his home on the Wirral. Although he was disappointed with his performance, his captaincy was acclaimed for getting the most out of his players by his encouragement and his tremendous personality. Stan Mortensen of Blackpool, who made his début against Wales, later commented on Joe's leadership: "His captaincy is easily the best I have known. He has some trick of personality, perhaps connected with that broad grin of his, which made you pull out every little bit of effort that was packed within you. He has a level head too. Sometimes I have seen a player shaping for a first-class row with a referee, but a couple of quiet words from Joe has soon put an end to that nonsense. He watches over his team-mates like a shepherd, always on hand. Those of us who played alongside him during and just after the war, learned a lot in the shape of on-the-field manners."

Tom Finney, the great Preston North End winger, was another who made his international début when Joe was captain. At Deepdale in 1992 Tom talked about playing under Joe: "It was in wartime, and I was actually in the forces in Italy when the information came through that I'd been selected to play for England in an international against Switzerland - we had two matches against them, one at Berne and one at Zurich. Joe was the captain, Frank Soo and Frank Swift and other well-established internationals were there. Anyhow, we lost the first game and won the second. I'd made my way through from Italy, of course.

"Actually, through Joe I was given a fortnight's leave. I hadn't been home for three years

Joe (left) with Scotland forward Tommy Walker, Frank Swift and Tommy Lawton.

Six of the F.A. team which flew to Belgium in a RAF Dakota in March 1945.
Back (left to right) - Joe Mercer, Frank Soo and Maurice Edelston.
Front - Frank Swift, Stanley Matthews and Matt Busby.

and I was supposed to report back immediately after this match. I talked to Joe and he said he would try to get me some leave. I told him that I was courting and that I hadn't been home for three years. Somehow he managed to get me a fortnight's leave which was really marvellous for me. I'd been away so long, then was given my first international, and then was given a fortnight's leave. It was really fantastic.

"I don't really know what Joe did to get me the leave. All I know is that the chap who was in charge of the England side was connected with the services. Joe somehow persuaded him.

"It was funny. When I had to return to the station, I had to hand my pass in and I was asked where I'd been. So I had to try and explain that I'd played for England, then I was given a fortnight's leave. I was asked who'd given me the leave. All I could say was, 'I don't know,' All I was interested in was the piece of paper to say I'd been granted 14 days leave. I was extremely grateful to Joe for all he'd done."

Joe tried to get involved in every aspect of the team. He also believed in the team as a unit. Talking of his own captaincy he commented: "I believe in the 'collective' idea. Pre-war, England players met before the match and chatted. It wasn't much different from the bath-tub tactical chat at Everton ten years earlier. In the war, we not only played together, we lived together. We saw more of each other in a week than we had in a season pre-war. We came to know each other on and off the field. I was convinced that it was no good 11 individuals turning up, often from nine different clubs and extemporising. Unknown to us, Hungary was bringing collective football to a fine art. We were soon to learn a bitter lesson.

"When I became captain I said to the lads, 'We've all got to sacrifice some individuality for the sake of the team.' I then got the forwards talking and thinking as a unit. The same applied to the defence. It was a long way from the elaborate tactical talks of present-day football, but it was a start. It gave me the chance to have my say and the lads had the same chance.

You can't afford to be haphazard. You can't get to the top in a professional game with an amateur approach.

"In the war, circumstances were right for introducing the 'collective' idea. After the war we missed the boat. We went back to the amateur approach. We had selection committees, and sports writers giving them hints like tipsters at Aintree racecourse."

When the war ended, England played a series of Victory internationals. The first one was against Ireland at Windsor Park, Belfast. Joe was captain, and Stan Mortensen scored the only goal less than 10 minutes from the end. Ireland could easily have won had they taken their chances.

For Joe one incident stood out above all the others. Before the game, he slipped out of the Windsor Park stadium to give a friend a promised ticket. Surprisingly, he was refused re-admission by an over zealous commissionaire. Joe tried to explain that he was England's captain, but the commissionaire treated Joe with scorn until a passing Irish FA official recognised Joe from a photo he had once seen. The two Irishmen apologised, while poor Joe became the butt of a number of jokes in the England dressing room.

Joe knew that he had been fortunate to continue playing the sport he loved at a time when so many had lost everything. Even so, life was not easy for him. In addition to international and Army representative games across Europe, Joe found himself, in his role as PT Instructor, helping soldiers to get fit for forthcoming military action. He also performed the soul-destroying task of helping soldiers rebuild their enthusiasm for life after periods of sustained fighting abroad. Joe's famous spirit and happy nature lifted himself, and many others, during this difficult time.

For a period Joe was stationed at Aldershot. Throughout the war the town had been fortunate to have a vast number of footballers based at the army camp. They included internationals like Frank Swift, Andy Beattie, Matt Busby, Stan Cullis, Jimmy Hagan and Tommy Lawton. Naturally, these players were keen to play football, and so played for the local club under the wartime guest system. In fact, during Aldershot Football Club's sad demise in the 1990s this time was repeatedly being hailed as the club's greatest period. Joe made 24 guest appearances and scored four goals while finding immense pleasure playing alongside many of his friends.

The Aldershot manager was Bill McCracken, a former Newcastle right-back and Irish International. He had a tremendous tactical brain and was responsible for perfecting the offside trap, making it almost impossible to play against him. Joe and

THE
FOOTBALL ASSOCIATION
INTERNATIONAL MATCH

J. MERCER
Everton (England's Captain)

M. BUSBY
Liverpool (Scotland's Captain)

ENGLAND v SCOTLAND
AT
VILLA PARK,
BIRMINGHAM

Saturday, February 3rd, 1945

KICK OFF — 3 p.m.

OFFICIAL PROGRAMME SIXPENCE

Sport & Play (1900) Ltd., Birmingham, 7.

Army School of Physical Training, Aldershot, 1945. Jim Morris is on Joe's right (with the Sergeant's stripes). Joe and Jim were involved in a number of scams.

the other players used to pull McCracken's leg something terrible. Regularly Joe jokingly accused him of being so good with tactics because he was "too lazy to play football properly".

On a few occasions Joe and the others would attempt to claim some highly fictitious expenses, and McCracken responded to Joe's claims by saying "Ah bejebers! You and Hagan, and Lawton, and Swifty, and Britton - Dick Turpin was a gentleman compared to you lot!"

At the start of the 1943-4 season McCracken was fortunate enough to field an Aldershot side that included England's regular half-back line of Mercer, Cullis, and Britton. No wonder they remained unbeaten until their sixth match. The "three musketeers" played together 10 times during that season, and their familiarity with each other's play must have helped England's performances as well as those of Aldershot.

Joe also played for Reading while Joe Edelston was manager, and had a few games for Chester. When he could, he returned home to Everton, where he alternated between wing-half and inside-forward. The record books show him as making 119 wartime appearances for Everton, and he scored 23 goals.

Joe had some enjoyable times at Aldershot, although there was at least one occasion when Joe thought he would try and improve his situation. The story was told by Joe's close friend Jim Morris: "It was a very cold night and we decided that we'd go and pinch some coal. Joe hoisted me over the wall and I was going to throw the coal over, and when Joe had got sufficient coal he was going to shout, 'That's it.' I would come back and away we'd go. "Well, I was throwing this coal over for quite a while and I thought, 'There's something wrong', so I jumped back over the wall and fell into the arms of the Regimental Sergeant-Major. Well the RSM immediately said, 'Who is your accomplice?' I wouldn't tell and he said, 'Right, in the morning you'll be in my office!' I went back to the bunk and found our friend Joe, feet up in front of a nice warm fire from the bits of coal he'd salvaged beforehand.

"Next morning I had to appear before the Regimental Sergeant-Major, who again asked me who it was. I wouldn't tell. He said, 'Alright, you've got a severe reprimand.' I turned away, and as I went for the door he said, 'You'd better tell your bow-legged friend, Mercer, that if he could run as fast on a football field as he did away from the scene of the crime last night, he wouldn't be a bad player!'"

Joe and Jim remained friends throughout their lives, despite Joe's sudden disappearance at the coal bunker! They also became involved in a number of similar events while together in the army, one of which Walley Barnes revealed in his autobiography, *Captain of Wales*. Barnes was told the story by Joe during their time together at Arsenal. The tale, as Barnes remembered it, ran like this: "Apparently, after playing in a wartime league match in London, Joe and Jimmy had been invited to stay the night at the London District PT School. They spent a convivial evening together and were returning through the grounds of Hendon Police College, where the PT School was situated at the time, when Joe lost sight of his companion.

"Joe found Jimmy Morris eventually. He was on his knees beside a large goldfish pond, watching the fish swim placidly round and round. 'Did you ever see such beautiful fish?' asked Jimmy. 'I'd like to have one of those to keep in my bunk at Aldershot.'

"Joe looked at Jimmy, and then at the goldfish. 'If you want a goldfish you shall have one!' he declared, and so saying he rolled up his battledress trousers and waded into the pond up to his knees. After a few minutes he held one bare hand triumphantly aloft, and in it was a plump, slippery goldfish.

"Carrying their prize with great care, the bold fishermen retired to the guest bedroom. 'It'll be alright here,' said Joe. He placed the goldfish lovingly in the wash-bowl, put in the plug and turned on the tap. 'Now you can swim about all night if you like, my beauty,' said Joe, and he and Jimmy hit the hay. Unfortunately, however, Joe forgot to turn off the tap, and the next morning, when he and Jimmy awoke, not only was there no sign of the goldfish, the bedroom was flooded and the water had flowed down the passage and was steadily trickling under the door of the RSM's bunk opposite. "Joe and Jimmy decided not to waken the RSM and put him in the picture. Instead, with great presence of mind, they hastily mopped the water from their own floor, exchanged their sodden doormat for a dry one from a neighbouring bunk, packed their bags, and stole away to the railway station, leaving the RSM with a mystery to solve that would have taxed the best brains ever housed in Hendon's celebrated Police College."

Away from football and the army, Joe's family life developed further when in March 1941 he became engaged to Norah Dyson. Some six months later, on Wednesday 3 September 1941, Joe and Norah married. The wedding was reported in a number of newspapers. The *Ellesmere Port Pioneer's* headline was 'Star Footballer's longest "Match"': "The centuries-old church of St Lawrence, Stoak, was the scene of the wedding on Wednesday of Company-Sergeant-Major Joseph Mercer, Everton and England half-back, and Miss Norah Fanny Dyson, only daughter of Mr and Mrs AE Dyson, of Hoylake and formerly of Ellesmere Port.

"The bridegroom, who is the eldest son of Mrs and the late Mr JP Mercer, of New Chester Road, Eastham, was accompanied by Mr Tommy Jones, Everton's Welsh international centre-half, as best man."

The article and adjoining photograph took up a good proportion of the front page, indicating the town's pride in Joe Mercer. The ceremony, and subsequent reception at the Stanney Village Hall, was followed by a honeymoon at the Old England Hotel, Windermere. However, the honeymoon, much to Joe's delight, was cut short by a day. Norah remembers the story with great affection: "Archie Clark, who had been responsible for the friendship of course, and his wife were staying over for the wedding. They were going home on the

TO WED NOTED FOOTBALLER

Joe Mercer, England and Everton half-back, is to marry Miss Norah F. Dyson, only daughter of Mr. and Mrs. A. E. Dyson, of Hoylake. Miss Dyson's family is well known in is well known in Wirral. Her father is well known in the grocery trade, and has businesses at Hoylake and Ellesmere Port. Mercer is now a Company Sergeant-Major-Instructor.

Miss N. F. Dyson.

Sunday and so I said to Joe, 'Seeing as Arch and Lil have come all this way, perhaps we ought to go home on Saturday instead of Sunday and see them off.' So of course Joe had the bright idea that if we were going home on Saturday, we could leave early and he could play for Everton. So we left early Saturday and he played Saturday afternoon. So that's how our marriage started ... with football! And that's how it went on."

Norah knew that Joe's life was devoted to football. She understood Joe's passion for the game, and loved him because of how he was. And, of course, Norah knew something about football herself, much more than most footballers' wives. Indeed, some of Joe's teammates teased him that Norah knew more about football than he did!

Joe's decision to cut short his honeymoon turned out to be a good one. Not only did Everton beat Stoke 3-1, but Joe scored one of Everton's goals. And all of this took place just seven days after Stoke had humiliated the Evertonians 8-3!

Joe and Norah's wedding day. Everton team-mate T.G. Jones (seen behind the couple) was the Best Man.

Joe training at Everton in September 1946. Just over two months later he left for Arsenal.

Chapter Five

EVERTON'S LOSS, ARSENAL'S GAIN

I was shocked when I saw his leg, the muscles of which had wasted after he had been in collision with Willie Waddell in an England v Scotland game at Hampden Park, Glasgow. Joe had misguidedly tried to carry on with the bad injury. All he succeeded in doing was to make an operation necessary, and play on so badly that he was never again selected for the England team. Things went from bad to worse after Joe had spoken to me, and finally he was dropped from the Everton team. For a while he contemplated giving up the game, but soccer is in Joe's blood, and he determined to carry on.

Tom Whittaker, *Tom Whittaker's Arsenal Story*

"ALL FOOTBALLERS ARE INSECURE," Joe Mercer once said. When the Football League programme resumed in August 1946, Joe faced one of the most insecure times of his career. His home life was now settled, following his wartime marriage to Norah, but his hopes of maintaining a top-level career had suffered a serious setback following an incident in the international against Scotland in April 1946, when Willie Waddell of Rangers innocently landed on his leg.

Joe played through the rest of the match, but some people thought that he was not trying. This hurt him tremendously - he was not a man to idle his way through a game. Joe documented his views some years later when making notes for his autobiography: "I was staggered to learn that some people thought that my poor performance in the international match was because I wasn't trying. I am a competitor. I never played a 'friendly' game of football in my life - not even in the streets of Ellesmere Port! For me, football is about one hundred per cent effort. If I tried as a kid there was no way in which I wasn't going to give a hundred and ten per cent as captain of England. I had a bad game because I was injured."

What concerned Joe even more was the fact that the Everton managerial staff believed he had not tried. They seemed convinced that he was now making excuses for his poor performance, and were uncertain about his injury. Joe was devastated by their attitude and was determined to prove how wrong they were. He consulted an orthopaedic surgeon and even paid for a

Joe in his last international, against Scotland in April, 1946

Theo Kelly

cartilage operation because Everton, the club he had given over a decade's service to, refused to pay.

Joe's relationship with Theo Kelly, the Everton secretary-manager, became more strained than normal. Kelly, more than anyone else, seemed to doubt that Joe was injured, and was convinced the player's career was almost over. For a man as committed and in love with the game as Joe was, it was difficult to accept what Kelly was suggesting. The injury occurred when Joe was 31, and it became a family joke that he stayed 31 for several years.

The situation worsened when Joe failed to find his true form for the Everton side. His knee regularly hurt and he began to struggle rather too often. After one game at Goodison Park against Arsenal, Joe popped in to the visitors' dressing room to see Tom Whittaker. As the trainer of both Arsenal and England, Whittaker knew Joe well. When he inspected Joe's leg he was shocked and shouted to the Arsenal players: "Look at this lads - you've been playing against only ten men."

The muscles above and below the knee were wasted away, and the knee itself was swollen. Whittaker told Joe that he was amazed he had lasted for the full 90 minutes, never mind the many months since the injury took place. The Arsenal trainer insisted that Joe visited Highbury when next in London to allow him to have a serious look at the leg.

Joe continued to play on, although the more he played, the more mistakes he made. He was still attempting to perform as an attacking wing-half, roaming wherever the game took him. It wasn't a style of play that suited a 32-year-old with a damaged knee. Eventually he was dropped.

Nearly 40 years later, on a radio phone-in programme, Joe fielded a blunt question from someone who suggested he was playing badly to get away to another club. Joe replied: "It's quite right that I wasn't playing too well at the beginning of that 1946 season. Don't forget, I'd just had a cartilage out. My last game against Scotland was at Hampden Park and I did my cartilage, and I wasn't fit. I tried to get fit, but I wasn't playing like I used to play. I used to be an attacking wing-half in those days. I used to run all over the place, wherever my feet took me. I wasn't playing well. It wasn't because I wasn't trying. I wasn't fit, and 70 per cent of football is fitness."

Perhaps Theo Kelly should have guided Joe more. Quite simply, though, Kelly probably did not want to help Joe. Their relationship had become openly hostile and Joe, realising he had no future at Goodison, decided it was time to move on. He had only ever been with one professional club, and had never dreamt of leaving Everton until he felt Kelly's hostility. Years later he looked back on the final period at Everton with sadness: "It was a terrible blow for me to go, because I was so crazy about Everton. Mind you, I wasn't easy to handle. I was captain of England at the time, and I had been a sergeant-major, running my own show.

"Theo Kelly was the manager, and I had one or two ups and downs with him. The funny thing was, he wanted me to play centre-half - me a wing-half who used to go diving into the action, when the club had TG Jones, the best centre-half of all, in my opinion. 'Right, I'll give him centre-half,' I thought. 'I'll pull the ball down on the penalty spot, dribble it out of the box, everything.' We played Preston, and I tried all those things - and they came off! I just had one of those games. Things became so bad between Theo and me that one day I went to see the directors at the old Exchange Hotel, where they held board meetings."

Joe met Cecil Baxter, the Everton chairman, and asked for a transfer. Baxter was a persuasive man who Joe respected. If the situation with Kelly had not been so bad, then there is no doubt that Baxter would have been able to persuade Joe to stay. Unfortunately for Everton, Joe knew he could not remain. "I want a transfer," Joe told Baxter. "And if you won't transfer me, them I'm packing up. I'm not going to play again!"

For a man who had dedicated his life to football this was a drastic action. He loved the game and wanted to play on, but his manager had made it extremely difficult. In the end Joe walked out on the club he loved.

Joe believed that this was now the end of his playing career. He threw himself into a new business in the grocery trade. Norah's father, Albert, had been a grocer since he was 12, and knew the trade inside out. He encouraged Joe to get more involved and together they obtained a wholesale business in Wallasey, not far from Joe's home on the Wirral. Said Joe: "I passed out as a qualified grocer, but whereas I had all the education, my father-in-law had all the experience. Norah was a great grocer. She was managing shops at 16. I dressed a window one day and my father-in-law took a look at it and said, 'As a grocer you're a good footballer.'"

Albert Dyson decided Joe needed help, and suggested Charlie Hawkins. Charlie, a man who understood the world of grocery, takes up the story: "I first started with Joe in 1946. I should say first that I was an absolute avid Evertonian, I never missed a match unless I was working. I always saw games played on Wednesdays. I'd come out of the army and was working for a local firm - I'd worked for them before the war. One night at home, the doorbell went and I answered and there was Joe on the doorstep. Of course, although I'd never met the man or spoken to him, it was instant recognition. He was a hero to me.

"On the spur of the moment I just couldn't understand why he was standing on my doorstep. So that was the first question. At that point, he told me he was going into the grocery business. I had the experience where, of course, he didn't, and so he asked me if I would throw my hand in and go along as a sort of guiding hand. At that point I was only 27 but I thought I knew enough to help Joe. Anyway I did. I don't know if it was the offer of a better wage or the fact that I was going to work for Joe Mercer, I just had to accept the offer. We worked together then for almost 17 years."

Although Joe was now fully involved in his new-found occupation, he missed football tremendously. His wife Norah could sense that he wanted to return to the game. He really disliked grocery ... despite comments made in the press to the contrary.

While Joe was away from Everton, the club were in the process of transferring him. Tom Whittaker, the man who had realised the full extent of Joe's injury, was tipped off: "Joe was on the transfer list and I got a letter from a great mutual friend, Ernest Edwards - the sporting journalist who wrote under the pseudonym of 'Bee' - saying that Joe would like to come to Highbury, and what were the chances of Arsenal signing him? The 'chances' were that we went in up to the hilt for Joe, and never regretted one penny of his transfer fee!"

Whittaker immediately contacted Theo Kelly at Goodison, who in turn telephoned Joe's grocery shop at Wallasey. Joe later explained the sequence of events: "The 'phone

Tom Whittaker

at the shop rang one day. The voice at the other end was Theo Kelly. 'Arsenal are interested in you', he said. Since he obviously wasn't, except to get rid of me, I was excited. If Arsenal asked you to play with two good legs, you jumped at the chance. If they were interested in a grocer with a gammy leg, well, I was prepared to go on all fours.

"I didn't have to. My father-in-law, who had set me up in the grocery business, went with me to meet George Allison [the Arsenal manager] at the Adelphi Hotel in Liverpool. We had the shortest transfer talk ever, I didn't even sit down. Allison made it clear that Arsenal wanted my services. I was honest and said that I didn't want to leave my new business. George said that I could live and train in Liverpool, and so we shook hands.

"Theo Kelly brought my boots to the Adelphi - that was the last straw. I was hurt and said, 'You'll regret selling me, Theo.' I don't know if they did, but I went to Arsenal for £7,000, just half the fee they gave for Bryn Jones in the days of the Depression. At least I was not responsible for inflation in football!"

Norah Mercer remembers receiving the news: "Players in those days didn't have agents. Joe went over to the Adelphi. He said, 'I'm going over to have a talk to Tom Whittaker,' and about half past eight the phone rang. 'Mrs Mercer?' I said, 'Yes.' He said, 'It's the hall porter at the Adelphi. Would you pack an overnight case for Mr Mercer. He's just signed for Arsenal.' That was it."

For Norah, the news that Joe was going back to football was not really a surprise. Unlike most football transfers, it didn't involve a move of house. Joe became one of the first commuter-footballers.

Instead of leaving one of England's biggest and best clubs to end his days with a lower-division side, Joe was moving to an even more impressive club, probably the greatest club of the 1930s. Everything about Arsenal was the best. Under Herbert Chapman, then George Allison, the Gunners had been hugely successful. The club had also developed the Highbury ground into one of the best in Britain. They had built two magnificent stands and rebuilt the huge North Bank terracing. Arsenal had even figured in a feature film, 'The Arsenal Stadium Mystery', such was the popularity and interest in the 1930s side.

In the weeks that followed Joe's transfer, he was persuaded by Tom Whittaker to adapt his method of play. The knee injury inhibited his natural style, so Whittaker advised him to play more defensively. Joe's attacking play simply drained him, and left terrible gaps in the defence that his spindly legs could no longer cover. Under Whittaker's guidance, he lay well back and became almost a fourth full-back. He later claimed that Arsenal were the first to introduce "the flat back four".

His new role suited him well and it was not long before his fellow professionals recognised the skill and commitment of the man in the number-six shirt. Yes, Joe was back at left-half. "I was a left-half because everywhere I went the right-half was a good 'un," he said later, thinking of Cliff Britton at Everton, Ken Willingham in the England team and Archie Macauley at Arsenal.

Liverpool centre-forward Albert Stubbins noticed the change in Joe's style: "Joe told me that when he went to Highbury he was told never to cross the halfway-line, which shows the sort of way they would hold a team. They would say, 'Let them come, let them come,' and they would back up and pack the defence further back. It obviously worked. Joe was a very fine passer of the ball. He could give you a beautiful pass over 30 yards, as straight as anything."

At Arsenal, Joe began to conserve his energy sensibly. He was still enthusiastic, still passionate about the game, but he was more watchful, more disciplined. He played more with his head than his legs. Rarely did he pass back to the goalkeeper, rarely did he clear into touch. He got the ball in a defensive position but used it constructively.

Joe's injury still troubled him, however. After a Saturday game he was unable to run a circuit of the football pitch until the following Thursday. He put considerable effort into regaining full fitness. After every game Tom Whittaker treated his leg by putting on cold compresses

Joe at work in his grocer's shop.

and bandaging it up until the following Monday. Twice during every week Joe was visited at home by a physiotherapist, who massaged his leg.

Joe Mercer and Tom Whittaker had a great deal of respect for each other. Whittaker, more than anyone else, was responsible for giving Joe the chance to continue playing the game he loved and needed. Without football Joe was unhappy. He did have the grocery business but that was a poor substitute for the people's game. He always told the press that Arsenal had allowed him to continue living on the Wirral because of his business interests, yet when he was in the shop he was desperately aching to get back down to Arsenal to play football.

Norah, her parents, and his colleague Charlie Hawkins all shared the view that Joe was happiest on a football pitch. During the week he was just looking forward to getting on the

train to London and absolutely detested being 'locked up' in the shop. Norah knew what football meant to her husband: "He was alright, quite happy, whilst he was playing football. When he was injured, he hated the grocery business because he couldn't get away from it. He loved getting away at a Friday lunch time and catching the 5.30 train to London. Of course in those days there wasn't any floodlights, so the game would kick off at two or two-thirty on Saturday. So he would be back on the six o'clock from Euston - he was home for 10 o'clock."

Soon, everybody on those trains knew Joe. Norah Mercer: "He was coming back one weekend and he was thirsty, and as the waiter went through he said, 'Would you bring me a Guinness?' The waiter said, 'No, I won't.' Joe looked at him and said, 'Why?' The waiter said, 'You once put me through it on a PT course. I'm not bringing you any Guinness!'"

TELEPHONES:
270 and 5971

T/A A. B. TODD

JOE MERCER

Wholesale and Retail Grocers

105-107 BRIGHTON STREET, WALLASEY

According to Joe's grocery colleague, Charlie Hawkins, it was obvious that football was all that really mattered. The grocery business was something Joe did, but did not really like. By lunch time every day Joe was bored, and could not wait to go training. Despite the lure of football, though, Joe got involved in the day-to-day running of the business. Charlie realised that Joe's name would bring in the customers: "When he first took over, he took over a business that was in decline. There's no doubt about that. We quickly pulled that sky-high. His signature was the sign on the windows and

FOR POINTS GOODS——
PERIOD No. 8

JOE · MERCER

Late A. B. TODD   Est. 1911

Wholesale and Retail Grocer,
105 - 107 BRIGHTON · STREET,
'Phone: Wallasey 270.

All Family Registrations Will Receive
Prompt and Careful Attention
POINTS LIST:
Canned Meats, Fish, Milk, Vegetables.
Cereals, Breakfast Cereals, Dried Fruit,
DELIVERIES TO ANY PART OF THE BOROUGH

vehicles - it wasn't just J Mercer, it was his signature. Of course, with him being a former Everton player he was so well known, a big attraction. Youngsters used to come in the shop wanting autographs, and you never ever saw Joe turn his back on them, or lose his rag. He was a great man, a nice man. No doubt at all.

"Then once a year I used to get my reward for the hard labour - it was hard, long hours too. Joe and his father-in-law - Pop, as we used to call him - and I would go to Ascot each year for the Royal meeting. After a couple of days, Joe had had enough racing and he would go to London or somewhere for his football training. Then he would rejoin us as if he hadn't been away. They were great days with Joe."

Arsenal 2 Manchester United 1, September 1947. United's Stan Pearson gets between Walley Barnes (left) and Joe.

Football was everything to Joe. He just could not keep away from it. Norah accepted that and supported him through difficult times, like his recovery from his leg injury. Norah believed a wife's role was to provide support and help in whatever way was possible. She knew he loved the sport and she ensured she helped him. She backed him in whatever he wanted. Whenever she could, she watched him play.

When he first signed for Arsenal, Joe trained at Anfield, the home of Everton's great rivals Liverpool. There is little doubt that Theo Kelly would not have wanted Joe to continue training with the Everton team, especially when the press started giving great reviews of Joe's progress in London. As Joe's fitness returned, many Evertonians expressed regret at the club selling him.

As Joe returned to full fitness, so did Arsenal. The club that had been such a pre-war power was now saddled with a debt of nearly £200,000. The manager, George Allison, who was also the second largest shareholder, was worn out after having to keep the side together through the difficult war years. When the war ended, Allison asked Tom Whittaker to assist him.

As Allison's assistant, Whittaker persuaded the players to work together for the good of the club. According to Bernard Joy, the former Arsenal and England amateur centre-half who played between 1935 and 1946, Whittaker alone was responsible for saving Arsenal from relegation in 1946-7. The club finished in a credible 13th position. During the close season Whittaker was installed as manager, replacing the ageing Allison.

With Whittaker in his new role the club had new hope and optimism, and started the 1947-8 season in the best possible mood. The captain, Les Compton, brother of Denis, the England cricketer and Arsenal team-mate, was missing for the start of the season as he was wicket-keeping for Middlesex. Whittaker appointed Joe as temporary captain.

Joe revelled in the confidence shown in him. After six games the club had maximum points with victories over Sunderland (3-1), Charlton (4-2), Sheffield United (2-1), Charlton again (6-0), Manchester United (2-1) and Bolton Wanderers (2-0). In the Bolton game, although the Gunners were winning 2-0 at half-time, they were without two key players, Lewis and Fields, in the second half. Joe reshuffled the side, moved himself to centre-half and inside-forward Logie to left-half. Joe relied heavily on his three forwards, two of whom appeared to be limping. Leading by example, Joe guided his eight accomplices through to victory and won rave reviews from all who witnessed the game.

With Fields injured, and the cricket season over, Les Compton returned to the side for the next game, at Preston. Naturally Joe expected Compton to return as captain, but Compton had other ideas. The story was told by Harry Homer, who witnessed the event for the Arsenal programme: "In our dressing-room before the match at Deepdale - atmosphere of boots and bandages and tucking-in of shirts. Ian McPherson deep-breathing, George Swindin loosening up by throwing the ball against the wall, Laurie Scott skip-jumping and Ronnie Rooke running on the spot. Tom Whittaker looks at his watch. 'Time to go out, boys, remember what I've told you.' He takes the ball from George and tosses it to big Les Compton. Our centre-half takes it over to Joe Mercer. 'If you don't mind, Tom, I think Joe should have this, he's not done too badly with it so far.' Joe looked embarrassed, Tom smiled, and our left-half held the captaincy."

Such events increased Joe's love affair with Arsenal. His previous club, Everton, had ultimately treated him shabbily. At Arsenal the complete opposite was true - the club made him more than welcome. This boosted his confidence and enabled him to perfect his more defensive role with the assistance of so many kind, friendly colleagues.

Under Joe, Arsenal set a new club record of being undefeated in their first 17 games of the season. The run ended on 29 November 1947 at the Baseball Ground, where Derby County's Reg Harrison scored the only goal of the game.

The matches that followed saw Arsenal score fewer goals, but their strong defence ensured they gained more points than they lost. Typically, the British public began to criticise Arsenal for playing so-called 'negative football'. What Arsenal were doing was using their forwards to support their defence when an opposition attack was made. Likewise, when Arsenal attacked, the whole team attacked. To Whittaker, Arsenal were the all-attacking, all-defending side.

In one game, however, this policy brought about their downfall. The result of the FA Cup match against Bradford Park Avenue, a struggling Second Division side, at Highbury was regarded as a foregone conclusion. The League leaders, Arsenal, expected little trouble from Bradford. Joe, together with Archie Macauley, played more of an attacking role than usual. Bradford defended well and by half-time were leading 1-0. Billy Elliott, who later played for Burnley, Sunderland and England, volleyed the goal following a corner-kick. And 1-0 it stayed.

Norah Mercer recalls Joe's depressing trip home: "Bradford knocked Arsenal out - Ron Greenwood was playing for them. Joe had a new trilby hat, and he was a bit annoyed about being knocked out of the Cup. I don't know whether he kicked the hat or tossed it in the air, but one of the porters salvaged it and brought it back, but Joe told him he could keep the so-and-so thing."

The defeat shocked Arsenal. Tom Whittaker and his captain were determined to make sure the upset did not affect their League performance. Although the Gunners were leading the race for the Championship, Burnley and Preston were close behind. Another threat came from the ever-improving Manchester United, where Joe's long-standing friend Matt Busby had taken over as manager.

For most of the pre-war era, City had been the better supported and more successful Manchester team. Indeed, United almost slipped into the Third Division (North) in 1934. Now, however, Busby was building a real footballing side for United supporters, and City had started the post-war era in the Second Division. The Reds were playing at City's Maine Road Stadium as Old Trafford had been badly damaged during the war, and the loyalty of City's supporters became severely strained. This shift in the balance of power in Manchester would provide Joe Mercer with another great career challenge almost two decades later.

Following Arsenal's Cup defeat, the Gunners had to travel to Maine Road to play Manchester United in their next League game. United were expected to test Arsenal like no other League side had managed all season. Whittaker realised the importance of the match. If Arsenal were to lose it would severely dent their chances of winning the League. Confidence had to be regained if the Gunners were to stand any chance of success.

Back on the Wirral, however, Joe's health was poor. He was struggling with influenza and unable to train. Norah Mercer telephoned Whittaker on the Tuesday before the United game and broke the news: "Joe won't be fit for Saturday, I'm afraid. He's ill in bed with a heavy cold."

It was a real setback for Whittaker. It was bad enough playing against United, only a week after the Bradford defeat, but to face them without their inspirational captain was just too much. He begged the Mercers to postpone the decision until later in the week. He would gladly wait until the last possible moment.

In a determined bid to play, Joe had seven penicillin injections and tried to fight the illness. As you might expect, his determination and enthusiasm ensured he was ready for the game, although he was still a long way off full fitness and had managed only one morning's training.

Manchester United 1 Arsenal 1, Maine Road, January 1948. The crowd of 81,962 is to this day the largest ever to watch a League match in this country. Here, United's Jimmy Delaney heads over.

The game attracted a crowd of over 80,000. Supporters just had to be there, despite the fact that it was raining heavily, the vast Kippax terracing was not roofed, and most spectators were set for a drenching. The attendance, though not the highest for Maine Road, is to this day a record for a League match.

The game itself saw Arsenal back to their best with a strong defence and hard-hitting attack, while United played an exciting attacking game. Joe played a fine game against United's speedy Johnny Morris, and the result was a 1-1 draw. Arsenal took the lead through an early goal from Reg Lewis, and Jack Rowley equalised for United.

After the game, a United director went over to Tom Whittaker in the Maine Road board-room and declared: "What a dream team we'd have, if we could field your defence and our forward line." Whittaker smiled and responded: "But our forwards are part of our defence, and our defence is part of our attack!"

Arsenal were leading the League because of their reliance on team work. As captain, Joe ensured the team played for the benefit of one another. From his time as England captain in the war, he had recognised that every player relied on the others, and that a team of individuals was useless. Every team member had the chance to speak his mind and all views were considered and essential - if the players were to work as a team everyone needed to be free to discuss their beliefs.

The Arsenal side continued to play well together and on Good Friday, after beating Middlesbrough 7-0, they were eight points clear with only six games to play. The players started to believe the Championship was theirs. Perhaps they became too confident. On Easter Saturday they lost 3-0 to Blackpool.

Joe, once again, took the leading role and acted swiftly to help his colleagues back to winning ways. The return match with Middlesbrough on Easter Monday ended in a 1-1 draw. This was followed by a victory over Blackburn, and then a 1-1 draw at Huddersfield, despite being without Laurie Scott and Archie Macauley, who were both on international duty.

The train journey back from Huddersfield on 10 April was exciting. If the other results had gone Arsenal's way, then the Gunners would be crowned League Champions with games still to play. Denis Compton sneaked out of the train at Doncaster station. He rushed up the platform to buy a newspaper and came running back with a pile of papers joyfully shouting: "We've won the Championship!"

The team had conceded only 32 goals - a defensive record - and had answered their 'negative football' critics by scoring 81 goals. Only one First Division side had scored more - Wolverhampton Wanderers, now managed by Joe's schoolboy pal Stan Cullis.

Arsenal had won the League by playing fine football in packed grounds. Their average attendance of 54,982 was the season's second best - Newcastle bettered it by 1,300 as they headed for promotion from the Second Division. For Joe the Theo Kelly experience at Everton was now over. He had proved that he was still a great footballer, albeit with a different style. He may have been past his physical peak, but his skill, tactical brain and foresight easily made up for any shortcomings in speed, while his endeavour could not be faulted. Whittaker had given Joe a second chance in football, now Joe had proved worthy of the opportunity and support given to him.

Arsenal's sixth Championship was in many ways Joe's!

Arsenal's championship-winning squad of 1947-48

Chapter Six

SUPERSTITIOUS GUNNERS

Any side that wins the Cup must be lucky; and the fact that it's been lucky is always the first thing those of you who have been watching it point out. But in one way we were lucky. All through the Cup ties we only had to travel thirteen and a half miles from Highbury to Wembley. Not only that. We were able to stick to our ordinary training. We could eat at home. We were never jolted out of our routine. Oh yes, we were lucky there all right.

Joe Mercer, *interviewed by Denzil Batchelor, May 1950*

FTER A SEASON disrupted by injuries, when Arsenal finished fifth in the League and went out of the FA Cup in the fourth round, Grocer Joe's team returned to the limelight during the 1949-50 season.

Joe was 35 years old at the start of that season. "Pick me on how I'm playing, not on my age," he told Tom Whittaker, and the Arsenal manager kept picking him.

Joe's one remaining ambition was to play in the FA Cup Final. He had played at Wembley Stadium for England, but, as his playing career was supposedly nearing its end, the prospect of playing in the country's major sporting event was disappearing. Deep down Joe almost regretted turning down a piece of Wembley turf when Albert Geldard had offered it to him in 1933 after Everton's success over Manchester City.

As the 1949-50 season began, Arsenal's League form was exceptionally poor. Only one of the first five games brought any points, a victory over London rivals Chelsea. The side struggled in the lower half of the table, and were soon out of the Championship race. All that was left was the FA Cup.

The third-round draw saw them pitted against Sheffield Wednesday at Highbury. Long before the draw was made, Arsenal goalkeeper George Swindin told Joe, in the room they shared at the Great Northern Hotel before every game, that the Gunners would be drawn at home four times in the competition and would then go on to win the trophy. Joe adopted a sceptical stance and told Swindin: "I'll believe those home draws when I see them." Swindin was convinced, however, and told everyone his prediction.

Against Second Division Sheffield Wednesday, Reg Lewis scored the only goal of the game two minutes from time. The game was very close. Wednesday could have won, despite being down to ten men after full-back Vic Kenny dislocated his shoulder early on. They deserved more out of the match, but, as Swindin predicted, it was to be Arsenal's lucky year.

The Fourth Round draw brought another Second Division team, Swansea Town (later renamed Swansea City), to Highbury. Len Thompson, a former Arsenal player, was given the task of checking out the opposition, just as he had done for the game against Wednesday. Ever

Arsenal enjoyed enormous popularity at the time. Here fans queue for tickets for the third round North London 'derby' with Spurs in 1948-49.

since the shock defeat by Bradford, Tom Whittaker had asked Thompson for a comprehensive report on the opposition. The report was always passed round the management and players on the Monday before the tie. Whittaker and his captain, Joe, had always known and understood the value of preparation and team discussion. If the team could sit down together and debate tactics then they would work together on the field. This type of discussion took place before every Cup tie.

In addition, the players also found themselves adopting several rituals on the day of every Cup match during the 1949-50 season. Superstition played its part in Arsenal's success. Alex Forbes discovered that the boots of Arsenal's legendary Alex James fitted him nicely, and he saved their 'magic touch' for the Cup games. Les Compton ensured he cleaned the windows of his Hendon home on the morning of every tie. Even Joe became wrapped up in superstition. He and George Swindin would have a shave every Saturday morning from Dick, the hotel barber, and would then go for a walk down Euston Road until they reached a set of traffic lights outside the Hearts of Oak building (and not a step further).

Swansea came to Highbury in determined mood, and, although Arsenal led 2-0 early in the second half, the Welsh side piled on the pressure. Their two wing-halves, Burns and Paul, forsook defence for attack, and Roy Paul was in terrific form. Scrine pulled a goal back and then with only minutes to spare it looked as though Swansea had equalised, Burns netting with a terrific drive. The referee, however, ruled that Burns had handled the ball before shooting and so Arsenal scraped through, once again, into the next round.

The game made a lasting impression on Joe: "Roy Paul was one of the best players I've ever seen. He gave us a hell of a fright when Swansea came to Arsenal in 1950."

After the game Tom Whittaker made an offer to the Swansea directors for Roy Paul. The Arsenal manager had been trying to sign him for approximately a year and his performance against the Gunners heightened Arsenal's determination. The Swansea board refused to sell him to Arsenal - it was bad enough losing! Within six months, though, Paul was on the move to Manchester City, where he found glory as a Cup Final captain in the mid-1950s.

In an interview during the season Joe was asked about the Swansea game. The interviewer was of the opinion that 'lucky' Arsenal would not have won if the game had been a boxing

Joe in action against Birmingham City at Highbury in September 1949. Arsenal won 4-2.

match. He believed that Swansea would have won on 'points'. Joe responded: "I admit Swansea gave us a very rough time in that last quarter of an hour, when they were one goal down. We were a bit 'lucky' to get home with our lead. But don't forget that they weren't in the game for three-quarters of the match. And don't forget that our defence is part of our side. People talk as if we are 'Lucky Arsenal' because we've a good defence. As if it were a sort of fluke we could rely on."

The fifth-round game was once again at Highbury, just as Swindin had predicted it would be. This time the Gunners faced Burnley. For the game Whittaker replaced Ian McPherson with Denis Compton at outside-left. The move caused great sensation and controversy in London, yet when the game was over Compton had given all the justification needed to prove that Whittaker was correct in his decision. Compton set up the first goal for Reg Lewis and then scored the second himself from about 25 yards.

For Joe Mercer, however, only one moment from the game seems worth recalling. Late in the game, played on a slippery, rain-soaked surface, Joe handled the ball in his own penalty area! The referee failed to see it, but Harry Potts, the Burnley manager, did. From that day on, Potts reminded Joe of the incident whenever they met, and claimed it cost Burnley the game. Once again 'Lucky Arsenal', as they had become known, had survived. The whole country started to believe that the Arsenal's name was already on the Cup.

Leeds were the sixth-round visitors to Highbury, and Swindin had correctly predicted four home draws. The game ended 1-0 with a goal from Reg Lewis, and the Gunners were in the semi-finals without leaving Highbury. Joe enjoyed the Leeds game. He was pleased with his team's performance: "Another clear-cut victory. The whole team played safe and strong football. Of course Leeds put on the pressure just before the end. Well, the team that's behind always does in a Cup tie."

Chelsea were Arsenal's semi-final opponents, and the other tie was between Joe's former club, Everton, and the side he trained with, Liverpool. The all-London clash almost took place at Wembley Stadium. The FA were considering the idea, but Everton raised two objections: It would give the London victors too great an advantage in the Final; and Wembley, being pri-

Denis Compton finds the net for the Gunners' second goal against Burnley in the fifth round of the Cup in 1950.

A goal from Joe in Arsenal's annual fixture with Racing Club de Paris.

vate promoters, would take some of the gate receipts, which, in Everton's view, should stay in the game. Wembley responded by agreeing to give the clubs almost all the tickets available. The FA eventually decided to use Tottenham's White Hart Lane ground, as they agreed that Wembley would give an unfair advantage to the winners of that semi-final. Similar arguments arose in 1991, when Arsenal played Tottenham in a semi-final at Wembley. Then the question of ground safety was seen as being more important than ground advantage. The victors in 1991, Tottenham, may have had a ground advantage in the Final against Nottingham Forest, as Everton suggested over 40 years earlier.

On 18 March 1950, at White Hart Lane, Arsenal surprised many by dominating the early play. Chelsea were known for coming out and attacking at breakneck speed, but the Gunners were determined to get the early goal. Their determination worked against them as, after 20 minutes, Chelsea's Roy Bentley reached a ball before Arsenal's goalkeeper Swindin and lobbed it over his head into the net. Five minutes later Bentley scored Chelsea's second.

Joe urged his team-mates to keep calm. As far as Joe was concerned, Arsenal were losing after 25 minutes but they had not lost - there was plenty of time for them to fight back. Joe kept his side together and with only a minute of the first half to go the Gunners won a corner. Joe described what happened next: "Freddie Cox took it with the outside of his boot, it travelled a yard inside the line and suddenly curved in. Whether it was a particularly cunning in-swinger or the blustery wind, I was never sure and nor was anyone else. But Harry Medhurst, the Chelsea 'keeper, was late going for it and the ball was in the net before he punched it."

Freddie Cox modestly claimed "I just hit it" when he was asked to explain how he had scored such an unusual goal direct from a corner-kick.

Half-time came seconds after the goal. Joe and the rest of the team were now confident that they could pull back the deficit. Sure enough, Arsenal took a hold on the game in the second period, but Chelsea hung on for most of the half. With barely 13 minutes to play, it looked as though Arsenal would fail in their bid to equalise. Fate, though, was once more on the Gunners' side as they forced their 15th corner of the game. Denis Compton went to take the kick and signalled to his brother Les who moved up field from his position on the halfway-line. Joe, remembering that in the first half Les had moved up for corners on a couple of occasions and had been caught out each time, ordered him back. Les took no notice. Again Joe ordered him back. This time Les increased his pace as he made his way up field. Realising nothing else could be done to bring Les back Joe moved to the halfway-line where Les should have been and held his hands up in protest.

Denis Compton took the corner to coincide with the arrival of his brother in the Chelsea penalty area, and watched as Les Compton's powerful header rocketed into the Chelsea net. Les had met the flag-kick so hard that he somersaulted over with the momentum and, actually missed the sight of the ball entering the net.

This sequence of pictures shows Les Compton's dramatic late equaliser for Arsenal in the 1950 FA Cup semi-final with Chelsea at White Hart Lane.

Arsenal had equalised with their former captain's first goal for the club since the war, and after disobeying his current captain's instructions. Joe rushed over to Les and helped him to his feet and congratulated him, while at the same time pretending to chastise him for not following his instructions.

The game ended 2-2 with a replay scheduled for the following Wednesday. After the game Joe went up to Les Compton in mock seriousness: "What is the good of my giving orders on the field if you ignore them? One word from me and you do as you like!"

Les entered into the banter by apologising excessively over and over again. He was also on the receiving end of more ribbing from his team mates for costing them their 'Sunday off'. With a replay to prepare for, Whittaker demanded the men in on Sunday.

The replay took place before around 65,000 spectators in light rain on the Wednesday night, and although Arsenal were determined to win the tie it took them until extra-time before they scored. Freddie Cox netted in the 104th minute with a low shot after a great run into the penalty area. Cox's wife had actually seen the goal in a dream the night before, and had spent much of the day telling everyone about it. The goal, both in the dream and in real life, put the Gunners into the Final.

Cox's goal prompted widespread celebrations. Arsenal supporters swarmed on to the pitch to congratulate their heroes. On seeing this, Joe assisted the police and stewards in clearing the pitch and shepherding the supporters back to the terraces. He helped because he feared the referee might abandon the game.

When the tie ended, the Arsenal fanatics raced back on to the field in their hundreds, but Joe rushed over to Johnny Harris, Chelsea's gallant captain, threw an arm round him and headed to the dressing room consoling his opponent. He understood the disappointment that Harris must have felt and, realising that it could have easily been himself on the losing side, made sure he treated Harris in the way he would have wanted to be treated. Joe knew that losing a semi-final was devastating, especially if, like Chelsea, you are within minutes of forcing another replay.

Arsenal's win was another step towards George Swindin's prediction coming true. Fate, luck and prophecy had all played their part in Arsenal's march to Wembley. By this time, the newspapers, like the rest of England, had christened them 'Lucky Arsenal'. They had reached the Cup Final without travelling outside London. In the semi-final replay the Chelsea players had tried to match Arsenal's luck by each having a rabbit's foot in the pocket of their shorts ... without success.

Liverpool had spoiled Joe's chances of a fairy-tale Arsenal-Everton Final by beating their Merseyside rivals 2-0. All Arsenal had to do now was to beat Liverpool in the Final.

Arsenal at Villa Park, January 1949.
Back: Archie Macaulay, Walley Barnes, George Swindin, Billy Milne (trainer), Lionel Smith, Joe Mercer.
Front: Don Roper, Jimmy Logie, Ronnie Rooke, Doug Lishman, Ian McPherson, Leslie Compton.

Arsenal 1949-50
Back row (left to right): Joe Mercer, Walley Barnes, George Swindin, Lionel Smith, Arthur Shaw.
Front row: Ian McPherson, Reg Lewis, Peter Goring, Jimmy Logie, Don Roper, Leslie Compton.

Chapter Seven

FOOTBALLER OF THE YEAR

If there is a happier man in Britain this morning than spindle-legged Joe Mercer, captain of the Arsenal football team and voted 'Footballer of the Year' by football writers, then I'd sure like to meet him. Arsenal won the FA Cup by defeating Liverpool 2-0 in the Final yesterday and joined Bolton Wanderers as the only clubs to record three FA Cup victories at Wembley.

George Casey, *Sunday Pictorial, 30 April 1950*

AFTER THE semi-final victory over Chelsea, everybody connected with Arsenal faced a multitude of requests for Cup Final tickets. For Joe, living on the Wirral, so close to Liverpool, the problem was doubled. Not only did he face Arsenal supporters, but Liverpool fans, too. Joe was unable to supply everyone with tickets but did his best to send supporters away in good mood.

He continued to train at Liverpool's ground, Anfield, although their trainer, Albert Shelley, reluctantly advised the Arsenal captain that he should train away from the Liverpool first team. The directors feared that Joe would find out all about the team's tactics and would pass his knowledge on to Tom Whittaker. To avoid his opponents, Joe trained in the afternoons with the future Liverpool star, Jimmy Melia, who was then on the Anfield groundstaff.

The Arsenal captain teased Jimmy and anyone else connected with Liverpool, claiming that the Merseysiders should easily overcome the Gunners as they had already beaten them twice in the League! Whether this psychology helped convince the Liverpudlians it is difficult to say but, one thing was certain, most of the Arsenal players were confident of victory. Joe was uneasy though. He was worried about the game and simply hoped that all his fears would disappear by Cup Final day.

Joe had other options for his training. He would run through mud and sand to Hilbre Island with the family terrier, Taffy, and then stop for a cup of tea with the Cliftons before running back. Or he could train a couple of nights a week at Tranmere, where he was very popular. However, he had a theory about training for the Cup Final, something he would stick to throughout his career: "The best day's training is the Saturday game. It's so important to play flat out. It's the only way they're going to get fit for Wembley. In the interests of the team, they've got to go and play flat out."

One event that did give Joe the chance to forget any worries about the game was the annual Footballer of the Year presentation on the eve of the Final. The award had been instigated by the Football Writers' Association just two years earlier, and was the first real form of recognition for England's greatest players. The first two recipients were Stanley Matthews, the legendary Blackpool player, and Johnny Carey, Manchester United's influential captain.

In 1950, the journalists' overwhelming choice was Joe Mercer. He was presented with the trophy at the annual banquet at the London Press Club. To Arsenal's 35-year-old captain the award was a triumph. He had been written off by Theo Kelly at Everton, and had virtually retired from the game just before Arsenal showed interest in him. No-one believed that a few years after setting up a grocery business Joe would end up one step from Wembley glory. To come back to the very highest level was a major achievement, and the whole of the country recognised this. There is no doubt that Joe's award was more than justified, and Joe himself was extremely proud that he was chosen. He had always recognised the skills of others, and the commitment shown by his fellow professionals, now he was the one elected above those same men.

Joe receives the 'Footballer of the Year' trophy on the eve of Arsenal's Cup Final with Liverpool.

Joe's qualities of leadership, devotion to the game, motivation, and encouragement had stood out during the Gunners' progress to Wembley. Tom Whittaker's Arsenal relied heavily on their experienced captain. Joe encouraged his colleagues to participate in team discussions, and anyone could speak about any subject. For that reason Arsenal were a real team.

The 'Footballer of the Year' award glowed with Joe until his death in 1990. He was immensely proud of his achievement, and always made sure he attended the Football Writers' Association Award ceremony every year, unlike many of the other recipients. Even when Joe was quite ill he went to the ceremony. In fact there were only a couple of occasions when Joe failed to attend - one of them in the last few months of his life - and Norah admits that if he had known he was going to miss the awards he would have been devastated.

On the presentation night in 1950, Joe was unable to enjoy the ceremony as much as some subsequent recipients as he had to leave at nine-thirty. He would have liked to have stayed longer, although he did meet one person who thought nine-thirty was late: "What are you doing here? You should be in bed! All the Liverpool players are in bed!" Joe responded: "Yes, but I bet they're not sleeping!"

He eventually left the Press Club to rapturous applause, and journeyed to his room at the Great Northern Hotel. Arsenal had taken the unusual step of allowing the players to spend Cup Final eve at home instead of in a top-class hotel "away from it all". Joe, of course, had to travel from Liverpool anyway, and he stayed at the usual place, sharing a room with George Swindin, Arsenal's Yorkshire-born goalkeeper.

MERCER AND LIVERPOOL

LIVERPOOL F.C. directors have decided that Joe Mercer, Arsenal captain, can continue training on their ground, but he will do so in the afternoons, when the Liverpool players have finished their work. A goalkeeper and two or three other players will be provided to help him.

On Cup Final morning Joe woke up at approximately ten-thirty and, together with George Swindin, went through their usual Cup-tie routine. They ate a leisurely breakfast, had their hair cut by Dick, the hotel barber, and then strolled along Euston Road as far as the Hearts of Oak building. As usual they ventured no further and returned to the Great Northern Hotel.

Joe and George met the rest of the Arsenal squad at Highbury for lunch. Everyone was in good spirits,

The Evening News

NO. 21,281   LONDON, SATURDAY, APRIL 29, 1950   ONE PENNY

100,000 CHEER IN THE RAIN

Cup Final Teams 'Mobbed' as They Reach Wembley Stadium

SHUT-OUT CROWD SURGE ROUND ROYAL ENTRANCE

"EVENING NEWS" REPORTER

HEAVY downpours of rain could not keep down the spirits of the thousands packing Wembley Stadium for the F.A. Cup Final this afternoon.

It was the customary scene of laughing, shouting, rattle-waving partisans.

They cheered at every little incident as they waited for the arrival of the King and Queen and the appearance of the teams—Arsenal and Liverpool.

few nerves were showing. Joe was still nervous, but was confident his fears would disappear once the game started. As the team boarded the Wembley bound coach at one o'clock, the cheers and good wishes from the supporters made Joe more determined than ever to bring success to the Arsenal faithful.

As the coach journeyed to the stadium, the heavens opened. A deluge drenched all the waiting supporters, those along the route and those already standing on Wembley's open terraces behind the goals. Tom Whittaker, realising that the team would arrive at the stadium far too early, asked the driver to stop in a convenient spot to allow the players to go for a short walk. The rain was so heavy, however, that the team sat patiently in the coach listening to the radio. They were less than half a mile from the stadium, but supporters rushing past the coach failed to recognise the team. The fans all had their heads down to combat the pouring rain.

After a 15-minute halt, the coach set off again, and the team arrived at Wembley to a fantastic welcome. The rain had eased a little when the players entered the stadium and walked into their Wembley dressing-room. These were the new dressing-rooms, developed for the 1948 Olympics. The old dressing-rooms, the ones Joe and other Arsenal players were used to, were at the opposite end of the ground.

Joe changed into new kit. Arsenal were to play in old-gold shirts with white collars, white shorts, and black-and-gold hooped stockings. As both Arsenal and Liverpool normally played in red shirts the FA ruled that both sides must wear change strip. This was again not possible as both sides' second strip was white shirts. The two sides tossed a coin, with Liverpool winning. They elected to wear white shirts.

Arsenal supporters expected their side to wear blue, but Whittaker opted

The two captains, Joe and Liverpool's Phil Taylor lead the teams out at Wembley.

Joe introduces Peter Goring to the King.

for old gold. He wanted them to be different, he had an idea that gold indicated success. To retain some piece of Arsenal's famous colours George Swindin was to wear a crimson goalkeeper's jersey. Whittaker actually believed that this would distract Liverpool's attackers as the colour was so brilliant.

At 2.48, Arsenal were ready. They stood alongside Liverpool in the tunnel ready to take the field. Joe was immensely proud as he finally achieved his last ambition as a player. He followed his manager on to the famous Wembley turf. As they walked out in the drizzle, Joe held a conversation with the opposing captain, Phil Taylor, who was walking on Joe's left behind Liverpool manager George Kay. Joe and Phil wished each other luck as the atmosphere reached a crescendo.

The players lined up in front of the Royal Box, and Joe introduced his side to King George VI. Then the referee, Henry Pearce, whistled the two captains for the toss. Joe spun the coin which, on the first throw, ended up sticking on its side in the wet Wembley turf. He hoped the rest of his actions would have a little more success. When he spun again, Phil Taylor was given the task of choosing ends.

The Cup Final teams were as follows:

Arsenal: **Swindin; Scott, Barnes, Forbes, Compton (L), Mercer, Cox, Logie, Goring, Lewis, Compton (D).**
Liverpool: **Sidlow; Lambert, Spicer, Taylor, Hughes, Jones, Payne, Barron, Stubbins, Fagan, Liddell.**

The game commenced with Arsenal kicking-off in determined mood. Joe's side set the tempo of the match, and made all the early moves. The most controversial moments were a series of tackles by Alex Forbes on Billy Liddell, who Arsenal had obviously selected as the Liverpool dangerman.

After approximately 17 minutes, Arsenal's Peter Goring harassed the Liverpool goalkeeper, Cyril Sidlow, into misplacing a clearance. Big Les Compton flicked the ball sideways to Walley Barnes, who took the ball some 30 yards forward to Jimmy Logie. Logie slid it through the Liverpool defence to Reg Lewis who had moved forward instinctively. Lewis, about 12 yards out, slipped the ball past the goalkeeper and into the net for the first goal of the Final.

Albert Stubbins, the Liverpool centre-forward, recalls the effect that goal had on Joe: "Arsenal scored the first goal, and Joe was a terrific captain, you know,

not only by example but by word of mouth, and the moment they scored he started shouting at his team, roaring at Walley Barnes, big Leslie Compton who was centre-half, and other defenders, and what he was telling them was to tighten up and all this, and they'd just taken the lead, and Joe was in such an emotive state that there were tears on his cheeks. He was really wound up and determined to keep the lead. I always remember, Walley Barnes shouted over to Joe. He said, 'Joe, control yourself.' And Joe said, I remember this, he said, 'I'm the captain of this team, and as long as I'm captain you'll do what I tell you to do.' Now that was the first time I've ever seen Joe in such a determined mood."

Although Liverpool were a goal down they were certainly not finished. The Merseysiders battled hard, but their two danger men, Albert Stubbins and Billy Liddell, were held back by Compton and Laurie Scott, with Alex

83

Thanks for Plaza Stockings

SUNDAY GRAPHIC

No. 1829. April 30, 1950   (C)   A Kemsley Newspaper 2d.

SHAVING Culmak BRUSHES

The King hands Cup to man who was 'finished' four years ago

INSIDE TO-DAY

Forbes assisting Scott in marking Liddell. The first half belonged to Arsenal.

At half-time there was no need for Whittaker to give a long talk as the players were performing as he had asked them to. They were certainly motivated in the right way. The atmosphere was one of confidence, the players knew they could win. Joe was determined, though, not to let any of the team get carried away. He stressed the importance of not getting overconfident.

The players went out for the second half and within minutes realised that Joe's attitude was correct,

Reg Lewis scores Arsenal's first goal in the Final. Joe (No 6) is at the right of the picture with his arms raised.

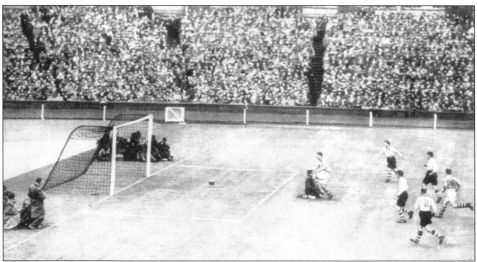

Lewis nets Arsenal's second.

as Liverpool came close to equalising. Billy Liddell crossed a high ball which George Swindin could only get his fingertips to. The ball came down to Jimmy Payne, who headed it towards what appeared to be an open net. Somehow, Swindin reappeared and miraculously smothered the header on the goal-line. Arsenal's lead was safe.

The Gunners immediately came back to dominate the game with Denis Compton, the veteran cricketer-footballer, playing tremendously in what was to be his last game of first-class football with Arsenal. The first half had not seen Denis at his best but now he excelled.

After about 18 minutes of the second half, Arsenal scored again. Goring crossed the ball from the left to Cox, who in turn flicked the ball with his right foot past Liverpool's Spicer, to Reg Lewis. Lewis ran on and rammed the ball into the net from about 12 yards. Sidlow stood no chance of saving the shot.

WOMAN FROM LIVERPOOL WILL SHOUT FOR ARSENAL THIS AFTERNOON

WATCHING the Cup Final at Wembley to-day were 16 wives of the 22 men: eight from Liverpool, eight from Arsenal.

But one of the Liverpool eight was not shouting for the men from Merseyside. She was shouting for Arsenal. She was Mrs. Norah Mercer (pictured here), 30 years old, wife of the Arsenal captain. Joe Mercer is a former Everton player, lives in the north, at Hoylake, and usually practises on the Liverpool ground. Mrs. Mercer has watched each round of the Cup. Now she has come up to see Joe win his first Cup medal. And then she will ask him to retire. He is 35.

She had assistance to-day. With her was her six-year-old son David. He is one of his father's zealous admirers and critical followers.

Cup Final parties

Among the Liverpool eight was Mrs. Molly Taylor, wife of the Liverpool captain. She is medium height, a keen follower of football. The Taylors have two children. But they are too young for football.

To-night Arsenal wives and sweethearts have a party at the Cafe Royal. The Liverpool men take their wives and sweethearts to Grosvenor House.

Before the game Whittaker had contemplated leaving Lewis out of the side as he often appeared lazy, and was occasionally criticised for not "having a go". Joe had defended him, telling Whittaker: "He scores goals, he always scores goals. He's got two good feet, he can play football, he's a clever and brainy player, he can hit a long ball and play them short - and he's good in the air."

Whether Joe's defence had swayed Whittaker or not we do not know, but Lewis thrived on the big occasion with two precious goals.

Two-nil up, Arsenal dominated until a Liverpool rally in the last 10 minutes. Liverpool again came close to scoring. Swindin dived at the feel of Stubbins, causing the ball to run loose. Jimmy Payne fired the ball towards the goal, only for Swindin to save Arsenal again by forcing the ball out for a corner. Everyone packed into the Arsenal penalty area and, following the kick, Payne fired at the goal once more. The ball bounced off another player before Bill Jones headed against the crossbar. A goal seemed a certainty until Joe cleared the danger by pushing the ball into the photographers crowded around the goal.

From then on it was obvious that Arsenal were going to be victorious. Walley Barnes turned to Joe and said, in a confident manner: "How's it feel to lead a Cup-winning team, Skip?" Joe realising that the game was not quite over turned to Barnes and bawled: "Get back to your position, the game's not over yet!"

Joe's mind had flashed back to that 1937 Cup tie, when Everton led Spurs 3-1 with four minutes to play and somehow lost the game. As Joe told Walley Barnes, "The game's not over until the final whistle."

When that whistle came, and Joe had finally achieved all the English professional game had to offer, he could afford to relax. Tom Whittaker, who had shown such faith in Joe four years before, walked on to the pitch and passed several Arsenal players until he reached his captain. Whittaker's recollection of the incident is as follows: "Almost in a dream I walked on to the field, past one, two, three of our players, straight to Joe. I put my arms round him and am not ashamed to say that Joe kissed me. I must confess that the tears were not far away. What a player, and what a man!"

Tears were indeed not far away. As the players lined themselves up ready for the climb up to the Royal Box for the presentation, Laurie Scott noticed tears of joy in Joe's eyes. Scott told him about them, and Joe hurriedly wiped his sleeve across his face. This was without a doubt

Joe's proudest moment. The previous night he had been presented with the Footballer of the Year award, and now his side had won football's most glamorous trophy.

Joe climbed the famous Wembley steps up to the Royal Box, where the Queen (now the Queen Mother) presented him with his medal. As he moved on to the King for the Cup presentation, Stanley Rous, the FA secretary noticed that the Queen had actually given Joe a runners-up medal. He called Joe back. Joe returned the medal and the Queen presented him with the correct winners' medal, before he moved on to the King.

Joe was extremely nervous and when King George VI presented him with the FA Cup the lid nearly fell off. The King suggested that Joe gave the lid to someone else, so he passed it on to Alex Forbes, before climbing down the stairs and on to the pitch to the widespread acclaim of Arsenal supporters. "That was a great feeling," Joe recalled later. "It was all very different from my memory of the Liverpool team at the end of the Cup Final. They were wet and weary. The game had been a bit one-sided but two teams had competed. When the final whistle blew nobody wanted to know men like Albert Stubbins, Billy Liddell, and the others, who had tried their hearts out. All the newsmen and cameras were round Arsenal. Yet Liverpool had also come all the way - their 'crime' was to lose. No team should ever fade away into the lonely tunnel as Liverpool did."

Joe learnt an important lesson that day, one that years later he would pass on to Malcolm Allison, when he told him to "always celebrate your victories." He knew that no-one remembered the failures and that success itself is only short-lived. If a man succeeds then he is right to celebrate. If he fails he never gets the chance! Joe never wanted to be treated in the way his friends from Liverpool were.

Before the players left the pitch George Swindin rushed up to Joe and calmly said, "There you are, 'Cap', I told you from the beginning we'd win it." Swindin, of course, had been proved right. All along he had stated that Arsenal would be drawn at home in every tie, and then would win the trophy at Wembley. The side had never once left London. The furthest distance they had travelled from Highbury was to Wembley - approximately 13 miles.

Once inside the dressing room the celebrations began. The Cup was then filled with champagne. Joe took the first drink and then turned to his manager and said: "Tom, that's the last drink tonight. I'm going to sit back and remember it all."

That night Arsenal celebrated at the Cafe Royal. The place was decked out in red and white, and was full of well-wishers. Naturally, Joe's wife Norah attended. Arsenal also invited all their local dignitaries, most famous supporters, and former players. Amongst the guests were the actress Anna Neagle, Welsh golfer Dai Rees, cricketer Gubby Allen, representatives from all the clubs they defeated on their way to Wembley, and famous players like Cliff Bastin, Charles Buchan, Wilf Copping, Ted Drake, Eddie Hapgood, Joe Hulme, David Jack, Alex James, George Male and Bill Seddon.

Arsenal's celebrations lasted well into the

Mercer, winning captain, with Cup and medal in safe custody, runs the gauntlet of welcoming hands as he leaves the Royal Box.

Joe tastes the sweetness of FA Cup success, another ambition realised.

night, and the reporters gathered their final quotes for the following day's newspapers. Joe got a very good press, with every newspaper stressing his influence on the game.

Don Davies, who went by the name of 'the Old International' in the *Manchester Guardian*, reported: "Arsenal won by superior strategy. They took note of Mercer's ripening years and fading stamina and turned these into positive advantages. Mercer stationed himself well down field, only slightly in front of Barnes and in close touch with Les Compton. This meant that Mercer could move quickly to Compton's aid, if danger threatened down the centre, or to Barnes' aid if Payne showed any signs of becoming troublesome on the wing."

Said Jack Milligan in the *Daily Graphic*: "What a day for Joe Mercer, who once again proved that although he is thinking of retiring, he is still one of England's top-flight wing halves."

Former Arsenal and England centre-half Bernard Joy was full of praise in *The Star*: "Mercer and Forbes were performing great things at wing-half for Arsenal. Spoiling move after move and slipping through accurate passes, Arsenal were well in charge. Although Lewis had taken his goals brilliantly and laid on some passes, the half-back line took the honours. The ineffectiveness of the Liverpool right-wing was due to Mercer's deadly tackling."

Joe thoroughly enjoyed "celebrating his victory". He said later: "I had known that I was nearing the end of my playing days and the Cup Finalist's medal was the one thing I wanted more than anything else. That day I achieved my greatest remaining ambition."

On the Sunday he looked back on his special day for a newspaper interview: "Apart from making a speech, I had a wonderful time. After the dinner and dance, my wife and I set off at about midnight for the Charing Cross Hotel. As soon as we got outside, about a thousand Arsenal supporters grabbed me by the legs, whisked me up on to their shoulders, and marched off with me - like an army that's captured a flag. A squad of police charged to the rescue in Leicester Square. Well, we tottered on, and when at last we reached the hotel my wife said, 'How do you feel?' 'Tired', I said. 'Tired! How can you feel tired? You were carried half way here!' she replied."

Joe shows off the Cup to Arsenal fans before a Civic Reception at Islington Town Hall.

On that same Sunday, Joe spared a thought for the losers. Albert Stubbins: "The next morning, a very nice gesture from Joe and so typical. My wife and I, and our son, Eric, who was about four at the time, were in our hotel room when there was a knock at the door and Joe came into the room. He shook hands with me, and said, 'I know how you must feel,' and he was playing on the floor with Eric, my son, you know, and I thought, 'What a nice gesture. The captain of the winning team still had a thought for the losers,' and that was Joe Mercer."

On his return home to the Wirral after the Cup victory, Joe was given a presentation by the people of Ellesmere Port. Joe had grown up there and had never forgotten his friends and neighbours. Likewise they had not forgotten him. His success was a matter of pride in Ellesmere Port. Joe was one of them and was in turn proud of his roots.

Was it now time to retire?

Joe's footballing career had achieved so much, and this seemed an excellent moment to retire while at the top. After all, he did have his grocery business waiting for him.

At the start of the next season Joe would be 36 years old, although in his own mind he was still only thirty-one. Norah, six years younger than Joe, teased him about his static age: "If you're 31 any longer I'll have caught you up and passed you!"

Astonishingly, there was still a lot more of Joe's playing career to come.

The Victors Smile

Joe is chaired off the Wembley pitch by his happy team-mates.

ARSENAL'S WIN AT WEMBLEY

Liverpool Outplayed Fore and Aft

By an Old International

Arsenal 2, Liverpool 0

LONDON, SATURDAY.

In the presence of the King and Queen, members of his Majesty's Government, the massed bands of the Brigade of Guards, observers from almost every civilised country in the world, hundreds of crushed and harassed representatives of the press, radio commentators, televisionists, ball boys, ticket touts, and close on 100,000 others stolidly enduring the rain, the worst (inasmuch as it was the most one-sided) F.A. Cup-final known to Wembley ended 2-0 in Arsenal's favour here to-day. Even during the preliminary kick-about Liverpool seemed fidgety, on edge, nervous, as though the pomp and ceremony attendant on such events, coupled with the prospect of a gruelling game on heavy going, had upset their balance. Arsenal, on the other hand, trained showmen as they are, performed their loosening exercises with obvious relish, preened themselves before the adoring eyes of their followers, and then strolled to an easy victory at quarter speed.

Arsenal won by superior strategy. They took note of Mercer's ripening years and fading stamina and turned these into positive advantages. Mercer stationed himself well down-field, only slightly in front of Barnes and in close touch with L. Compton. This meant that Mercer could move quickly to Compton's aid, if danger threatened down the centre, or to Barnes's aid if Payne showed any signs of becoming troublesome on the wing. Moreover, this disposition of forces not only puzzled Baron and Fagan, the Liverpool inside forwards, by its unconventionality, but it sealed the middle against frontal attacks and it also left Scott, Arsenal's right back, free to concentrate on his one overriding task—to harass and impede Liddell, the Liverpool sprinter. Naturally Mercer's withdrawal from his normal sphere of influence threw a great deal of extra work on Forbes, the other wing half, who had a correspondingly greater area to cover. But thanks to his own iron strength and whipcord stamina, eked out by the subtle support he received from Lewis and Logie, Forbes's resources proved more than equal to the strain.

Liverpool had only two effective forwards—Stubbins in the early phase, and Liddell at all times. The others, notably Fagan and Baron, were never in the hunt. Never before in the competition have these two appeared so slow in movement and yet so hasty in judgment, and the number of misdirected passes they rolled to their gratified opponents will weigh on their minds for months to come. They lacked either the ability or the confidence to draw a man and beat him by trickery, and their intentions were so transparently obvious that it was easy for the Arsenal players to sense whither the ball was going and to organise a reception committee. Liddell never gave up, and though he could not see his way clear for any prolonged breakaway he nevertheless swept the Arsenal goalmouth with half a dozen centres from any one of which Stubbins, with a slightly longer neck, though at grave risk of dislocating same, might have scored. Stubbins worked hard, and was unlucky. What is more, he was strangely loath to risk a shot with his left foot. Otherwise, on the two occasions when he broke through early on, he might have scored and called forth more snap and bite from his colleagues.

Of the Liverpool defenders—a baffled, toil-worn, and leg-weary set by the end as one may imagine—only Lambert, right back, and Hughes, centre half-back, came through reasonably well. The others at times seemed helpless and bewildered before the beauty and precision of Arsenal's ground passing, a moving sight indeed when, as to-day, the tactical blunders of their opponents gave Logie, Lewis, and friends scope and leisure for a lavish display of their powers. Spicer erred, one thought, in allowing Cox far too much room to work in; Jones, normally a centre half-back, seemed uncertain of his duties on the wing; and even Taylor, the captain, was unusually quiet and submissive until a bang in the face and the prospect of defeat roused him to a magnificent attacking run which almost carried the Arsenal goal by storm. But the ease with which one artful pass by Logie, in the case of the first goal, and a most beautiful concerted move by Compton, Goring, and Cox, in the case of the second goal, twice put Lewis in position to score with ice-cool deliberation proved how far the Liverpool defenders had fallen below their usual wary standards.

Even a badly beaten side at Wembley usually can put in a plea for rank bad luck. Liverpool had theirs in the first half-hour when one swerving, hurling corner-kick from Liddell scraped the bar; when Swindin deflected a centre from Payne against his own crossbar before smothering the ball beneath his body on the line; when a whirlwind centre from Liddell brushed Stubbins's hair and almost bounced through off Payne's shins. A Manchester spectator, who had gone to the match armed with a pair of binoculars and a portable wireless-set, so keen was he on getting his money's worth assured us that when Swindin lay with the ball beneath his body that ball was over the line. Odd that neither the referee nor the other players knew about it but then they had not a pair of binoculars with X-ray powers. But the combined effect of these isolated incidents was as nought as compared with the steady relentless pressure progressively developed by the Arsenal players. Their approach work was notable alike for its skill as for its coolness and unconcern. They might have known they had a trump card up their sleeves. Teams :—

ARSENAL.—Swindin; Scott, Barnes; Forbes, Compton (L.), Mercer (captain); Cox, Logie, Goring, Lewis, Compton (D. C. S.).

LIVERPOOL.—Sidlow; Lambert, Spicer; Taylor (captain), Hughes, Jones; Payne, Baron, Stubbins, Fagan, Liddell.

Referee: H. Pearce (Luton).

Chapter Eight

HONOUR IN DEFEAT

This 1952 Wembley will be memorable for the fiery, unyielding rear-guard action fought by this thin, crippled red line. For me the game will live because of Mercer the magnificent. Joe has reached an age (37) where nature should dictate economy of movement and action. But Joe was ever in the thick of the tense fight rallying his depleted forces. I have watched him with admiration for 20 years, seen his triumphs, but never has he risen to such great heights. Is there such a killer of the ball in soccer, such a pure textbook exponent? Joe never wasted a ball, and when he parted with the ball it never rose more than an inch from the ground. He, Daniel - for most of the game in intense pain - and Lionel Smith were the stars.

Henry Rose, *Daily Express, 5 May 1952*

MOST PLAYERS in their late-30s would have retired, or would be thinking about their next job, especially if like Joe they had just achieved their one remaining playing ambition. He had now won two Championship medals, an FA Cup winners' medal and five England caps, and had played 27 wartime and Victory international matches. In the days before European competition, there were no other medals available. He had done it all.

Joe, of course, played on.

Norah was increasingly concerned about Joe's fitness, especially after the trouble he had experienced in his later days at Everton. By 1950 she insisted that Joe went to see a Harley Street specialist before every season started, to ensure he would be able to cope with the forthcoming demands. Joe dreaded the visit as he did not want to hear anything that might prevent him from playing. He went along to reassure Norah, and to some extent himself.

Joe was passed fit before the 1950-51 season, so he shelved all thoughts of retirement. It was a steady season for Arsenal. Joe played 31 League matches, and Arsenal finished fifth, 13 points behind Champions Tottenham Hotspur. They lost 1-0 to Manchester United in the fifth round of the FA Cup.

Was it now time to retire?

Joe had no worries about a future career. The grocery business was doing well, and he could quit football whenever he felt like it. But that was just the point - he didn't feel like quitting the game he loved. Football, as Norah often said, was his life. Joe loved his family, which now included a young son, David, and they loved him, but everyone knew that without football he would be lost.

In July 1951, Joe settled back into his usual routine: a check-up at Harley Street, regular

Great friends Joe and Matt Busby pictured with the FA Cup. Busby's Manchester United beat Cup holders Arsenal 1-0 in the fifth round at Old Trafford in 1951.

training at Tranmere, runs out to Hilbre Island, a bit of time at his grocery business and the 5.30 Friday night train to London. "Pick me on how I'm playing, not on age," he constantly reminded Tom Whittaker. Joe stayed in the team, and 1951-2 was another famous season.

For most of the season Arsenal not only challenged Matt Busby's Manchester United for the League title, they also headed for the much coveted double of the League and FA Cup. The Cup run began on 12 January with a third-round tie at Norwich City. Third Division Norwich had reached the fifth round the previous season and were determined to match that achievement as they lined up to face the Gunners. However, a bad back pass from the Norwich skipper, Reg Foulkes, allowed Arsenal's Jimmy Logie in to score the opening goal, and Arsenal went on to win 5-0.

The fourth round saw the Gunners drawn against Barnsley at Highbury, and the home side easily defeated their Yorkshire opponents 4-0. Arsenal's inside-forward, Reg Lewis, scored a hat-trick, with one goal off each foot and a third off his head. "That's the way to score a hat-trick," he told everyone afterwards.

In the fifth round, Lewis's luck ran out as he pulled a muscle after half an hour of the away tie at Leyton Orient. Lewis was later forced to leave the field, but by then Arsenal were leading 3-0 through goals by Lewis and Doug Lishman (2). Orient, on their first appearance in the fifth round, had been unable to capitalise on playing against only ten fit men for much of the game.

In the sixth round, Luton gave Arsenal their biggest Cup scare of that year. In the first half,

Typical Arsenal defence for League game with Derby County at Highbury in October 1950. Arsenal won 3-0 before a crowd of 64,750. Next to Les Compton is Derby's Jack Stamps who has just beaten him in the air.

at Kenilworth Road, Bernard Moore headed Luton ahead. It was the first goal Arsenal had conceded in the Cup all season, and they were still 1-0 down at the interval. Tom Whittaker switched his side around during the break. Arthur Milton, in the side because of a chest injury to Jimmy Logie, was moved from inside-right to outside-right, Freddie Cox switched wings, and Peter Goring went to inside-right. This tactical change had the desired effect as Cox charged on to a through pass from Roper and fired a fast rising shot through the narrowest of gaps between Bernard Streten, Luton's England international goalkeeper, and the post. A couple of minutes later, Cox scored another with a similar move. This time his shot was a low one into the bottom far corner. Arthur Milton scored Arsenal's third, before Luton replied with an Albert Mitchell penalty.

The 3-2 win over Luton put Arsenal into the semi-finals for the second time in three seasons, and they were still on course for the League and Cup double. Arsenal trailed leaders Manchester United by only three points, with the gap closing all the time.

On 22 March, Arsenal equalled United's points tally by beating Middlesbrough 3-1, before almost 51,000 spectators at Highbury. On the same day Matt Busby's United suffered a 3-2 defeat at the hands of Huddersfield. United remained in first position on goal average, but with the two sides still to face each other at Old Trafford the title race was far from over.

The week after the Middlesbrough game it was back to FA Cup action for Arsenal, as they faced Chelsea in a repeat of the 1950 semi-final at Tottenham's White Hart Lane. In actual fact, there was no action. A late snowstorm caused the semi-final to be postponed. It was rearranged for 5 April, a decision which also affected two important League games, causing a fixture pile-up for double-chasing Arsenal.

When the semi-final finally got underway, Arsenal took a 35th-minute lead, Cox scoring from Logie's pass. Chelsea soon equalised when goalkeeper Swindin came way out of his goal to cut off a long pass and collided with Chelsea centre-forward Bobby Smith. Arsenal's Lionel Smith probably didn't realise that he had time to clear the ball. Instead he attempted a

Action from the third round of the FA Cup at Norwich in January 1952. Arsenal left-back Lionel Smith makes a tackle, Joe tidies up. Arsenal won 5-0.

dangerous short pass. Jimmy Smith intercepted and centred for Billy Gray to head into the open net.

That equaliser put Chelsea on top. They were the stronger team for the final quarter of the game, but were unable to turn their superiority into more goals.

The replay, a couple of days later, added to Arsenal's fixture back-log. Freddie Cox again opened the scoring for the Gunners with a fierce low drive in the first half. Early in the second half he added a second with a fantastic header into the top right corner from Don Roper's corner-kick. Lishman provided another marvellous header to make the final score 3-0.

For the second time, Joe had captained a team through to the FA Cup Final. This time their opponents would be Newcastle United, the Cup holders.

Because of the number of Cup games and League postponements, Arsenal faced a congested run-up to the Cup Final. At one point, Joe, at the age of 37, featured in no less than six games in ten days. As usual, he put as much effort into his game as the youngest, fittest player. He never once expected to take it easy, and always demanded more of himself than the other players. He certainly led by example, and retained his belief that the best training for a Cup Final was to give everything in the games leading up to it.

Tom Whittaker, however, realised that the fixture pile-up had taken a great deal out of Joe. Knowing how much he needed his captain for the Cup Final and the final League game against Championship rivals Manchester United, he decided to rest him for the penultimate League match at West Bromwich Albion.

As usual Joe telephoned Tom from his Wirral home the day before the game to say he was fit and raring to go. Tom broke the news: "You're not playing tomorrow, Joe, you're being rested". As expected, Joe protested. He felt fine and, typically, wanted to lead his team at West Brom. Tom would not listen to Joe's protestations and ended the conversation in the only way he knew Joe would listen: "Joe, you're being rested tomorrow and that's an order!"

The 1952 FA Cup Semi-Final at White Hart Lane. Joe watches George Swindin punch clear against Chelsea.

Captain Joe hard at work at Arsenal. Often the captain took on some of the managerial duties. All this helped Joe prepare for the day when he too would be a manager.

Joe could not and would not disobey Tom Whittaker's order, no matter how wrong he thought his manager was.

It was not long, however, before Joe realised Tom was right. Later that day he took his son, David, out for a walk. David challenged his father, as he often did, to a race to the "next lamp-post". The two of them started running but within seconds Joe's legs buckled and he finished the race, but only just, by walking. The Arsenal captain went home to rest.

At West Brom, Mercer-less Arsenal were defeated 3-1, while on the same night Manchester United beat Chelsea 3-0. These results meant that Arsenal had to defeat United 7-0 at Old Trafford to win the League Championship. The Gunners conceded that the title belonged to Matt Busby's team. Tom Whittaker sent a telegram to Old Trafford acknowledging the fact, and Joe sent one to his old friend Busby: "Made it at last. I'm very pleased - Joe Mercer."

Manchester United beat Arsenal 6-1, confining Arsenal to third place, behind Tottenham Hotspur on goal average. Only the Cup Final against Newcastle United mattered now. Joe had returned to full fitness, but Arsenal had plenty of injury problems. The most worrying, as the Final approached, concerned centre-half Ray Daniel. Cup Final referee Arthur Ellis, later BBC TV's 'It's a Knock-out' referee, takes up the story: "Ray had broken his wrist in an earlier League game, and the broken bone was still in plaster. It was up to me to decide whether he would play. If I thought the plaster dangerous, Daniel would be out. If I saw nothing wrong with it, Daniel would be allowed to play."

Daniel's heavy plaster was removed on the Tuesday before the Cup Final, and he was told by his specialist that he would be able to play as long as he was fitted with a light plastic shield. One of the Newcastle directors, Stan Seymour, asked Tom Whittaker about Daniel's arm, and then informed him that Newcastle wouldn't object to him playing. However, the decision still rested with referee Ellis: "Although the decision rested with me, and me alone, there had been a lot of publicity in the newspapers about the Daniel case. And some had even gone so far as

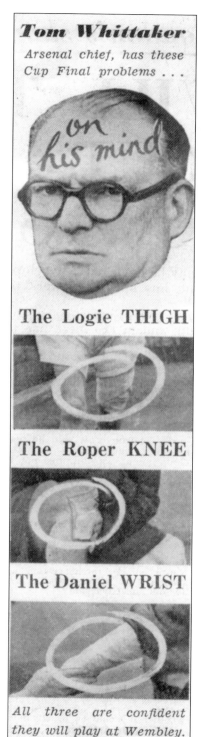

Tom Whittaker

Arsenal chief, has these Cup Final problems ...

on his mind

The Logie THIGH

The Roper KNEE

The Daniel WRIST

All three are confident they will play at Wembley.

Cup Final referee Arthur Ellis arrives at Wembley with his family.

state that Newcastle would protest if Daniel played! I could hardly believe that, remembering the time Jackie Milburn, the Newcastle centre-forward, played in League games wearing the same sort of plaster! I decided I must not pre-judge the case. I went with an open mind and ... well, you know the story - Daniel played."

So did Logie and Lishman, who had both been in hospital. Tom Whittaker had doubts about all three players, but especially Jimmy Logie: "He turned up at Highbury on the Tuesday, and had a walk round in the sunshine, but it was obvious that after five days in hospital, and still with a hole in his thigh big enough to put in a small apple where he had been operated on, it was going to be a desperate gamble to get him fit. But all the players, even those who might stand a chance if Logie couldn't play, wanted him in the side!"

Whittaker added: "I'll make a confession. In my heart I knew that Jimmy wasn't fit to play in any sort of game, let alone a Cup Final, but I felt like the rest of the players. Jimmy just had to play!"

Cup Final day was 3 May 1952, and these were the teams:

Arsenal: **Swindin; Barnes, Smith (L); Forbes, Daniel, Mercer; Cox, Logie, Holton, Lishman, Roper.**
Newcastle United: **Simpson; Cowell, McMichael; Harvey, Brennan, Robledo (E); Walker, Foulkes, Milburn, Robledo (G), Mitchell.**

In the dressing room before kick-off, Tom Whittaker gave his pre-match team talk. Then Joe, who had been nervously bouncing a brand new ball on the dressing-room floor, looked around the room of 'cripples'. There was Daniel with his wrist protected by the infamous plastic shield, Logie with a 15in bandage wrapped round the wound in his thigh, and Lishman recently out of hospital. Joe realised it was going to be an uphill struggle, but reassured his team with a few words of encouragement, ending with "Good luck lads, and don't forget - nobody goes on to the field favourites against Arsenal!"

He hoped those words would be enough to overcome the power of Newcastle.

The players left the dressing room and lined up to be presented to the guest of honour, Winston Churchill, before the toss for the start of the game. Arthur Ellis blew his whistle to start the action, and Newcastle's famous centre-forward, Jackie Milburn, kicked off.

Within two minutes Joe prised the ball from a tangle of legs and then lifted it with ease into the middle of the Newcastle goal area. Doug Lishman got his head to it and then, as the ball dropped, he hooked the ball round his body towards the goal. The Newcastle goalkeeper, Ronnie Simpson, dived but the ball was out of his reach. Fortunately for Newcastle, the ball sailed passed the goal, missing the far post by less than a couple of inches. Shortly afterwards, Jimmy Logie was clean through and poised to score when he mis-hit the ball and fell on to his injured thigh. This time Arsenal were certainly not going to be tagged 'Lucky Arsenal', as they had been two years earlier.

Logie played on in pain, and the Gunners matched their supposedly more powerful opponents move for move in the opening quarter of an hour. But it was not to last. In the 18th minute Walley Barnes tackled Milburn, who attempted a back-heel. Mysteriously, Barnes fell to the ground injured. Either Milburn had made contact with Barnes' leg or the Arsenal full-back

The two Joe's, skippers Harvey and Mercer, lead the teams onto the Wembley turf for the 1952 Cup Final.

had simply twisted his knee as he turned, but it was a serious knee-ligament injury. Trainer Billy Milne rushed on to the field and treated the injured player. Barnes, incidentally, was playing his 58th game of the season.

Barnes played on, but about ten minutes later he went into a tackle with George Robledo and went down again. Billy Milne helped him to the touchline where the courageous Barnes, in immense pain, vowed to return to the pitch. A fully-fit Arsenal side faced a difficult game, but a ten-man side with three 'invalids' and a 37-year-old captain looked to have no chance.

Walley Barnes, sticking to his vow, returned to the field with his leg heavily bandaged, but more injuries followed. The unlucky Ray Daniel aggravated his arm injury in an accidental collision with Milburn. Daniel continued playing even though he was in tremendous pain. It was later discovered that the accident had again broken his partly-knitted wrist.

Soon afterwards, Barnes left the field for the last time. Tom Whittaker felt he could not continue, despite the players' protests to the contrary. Joe Mercer then set about creating a red line of defenders across the field. His team still had the initiative but Newcastle, with the extra man, had the chance to overpower their rivals. Close to the half-time interval, with Newcastle piling on the pressure, Arsenal's goalkeeper George Swindin was beaten, but Lionel Smith somehow managed to head the ball off the line to keep the scores level.

During the interval Joe, knowing that his side would be down to a maximum of ten men for the rest of the game, tried to encourage his colleagues. The team may have been down but it certainly was not out! The game was still goalless, all Arsenal needed to do was score and hold their defence together. Joe would not give up - it was not his way - and he led the players back on to the Wembley turf for the resumption of play. What followed was one of his most heroic performances.

Time and time again Joe showed superb timing as his tackles won the ball. He was magnificent throughout. He encouraged his team, covered well, defended superbly, and passed the ball perfectly to his colleagues every time. Joe, playing the game of his life, was the inspiration Arsenal needed.

As the match wore on Newcastle began to take advantage of the extra man and used sheer weight of numbers in an attempt to outmanoeuvre the Gunners. Joe was not to be beaten and neither were his colleagues, as they all fought with determination.

With 20 minutes to play and the score still 0-0, Joe was convinced his side could sneak a goal. Nine minutes later Joe was almost proved correct. Freddie Cox forced a corner. He took it

Joe introduces the team to Winston Churchill, who is seen shaking hands with Jimmy Logie.

With just minutes to go Newcastle's George Robledo beats George Swindin with a header via the foot of the post for the only goal of the Final.

himself and floated it clear of Newcastle's Frank Brennan and Joe Harvey, straight to the unmarked Lishman who immediately shot at goal. Ronnie Simpson, the Newcastle goalkeeper, described how close Arsenal came to scoring: "The ball, hard hit, whistled over my head. I felt tremendous relief as I saw it strike the top edge of the bar and rocket over. Another two inches lower and it would have been a goal!"

So near and yet so far!

Following that near miss the game continued to be a tense affair, with Mercer's brave side matching Newcastle. With about five minutes remaining it looked as though the Final would go into extra-time. Then disaster came for Mercer's men. Alex Forbes, Arsenal's right-half, lay injured in his own penalty area, while, in the other half of the field, just on the edge of the Newcastle penalty area, Don Roper was also down injured. Arsenal, already down to ten men, now had two down injured and three other invalids who were fortunate to have been included in the side in the first place. The ball spun to Newcastle's outside-left, Bobby Mitchell, who centred it towards George Robledo. Robledo's header sent the ball slowly towards the base of the right-hand post. It hit the upright and glanced into the net. Controversially, Newcastle were ahead.

Joe (No. 6) views the grounded Roper after Newcastle's controversial Wembley winner. Interesting to note that apprentice jockey Joe Mercer was due to ride in the 2.00 at Alexandra Park! Joe often told a story about receiving a cheque from the BBC marked 're: Newmarket'. Joe returned it with a note: "Right name, right legs, wrong bloke!"

MAGNIFICENT MERCER NEVER DID BETTER

By HENRY ROSE

I TIPPED Arsenal. I have no regrets. They won the admiration of their opponents. They won the sympathy of the Soccer world. They won everything except the Cup. And they did me proud. This 1952 Wembley will be memorable for the fiery, unyielding rearguard action fought by this thin, crippled red line.

TO NEWCASTLE THE CUP: TO ARSENAL THE GLORY

Joe's own view was that play should have been stopped the instant Roper was injured: "I was aware that our right-half Alex Forbes was stretched out in one penalty area. In the other, our outside-left, Don Roper, was also out to the wide. As the ball was in midfield, it seemed the classic case for stopping play. Neither side had the advantage. I screamed to referee Arthur Ellis, 'What about stopping the game? The ball is in midfield!' He refused to stop!"

Ellis's own view of the incident is somewhat different: "I saw Don Roper go down after a tackle, but realised he was not badly injured. So I had no right to stop the game. The ball spun away to Mitchell, the Newcastle outside-left, and he centred. Now some people, as well as thinking I should

TO THE NEXT TIME

By Eric Thompson

"THE BAR WAS HIGHER LAST YEAR"

NEWCASTLE FOUND WEMBLEY CHANGED FROM 1951

THEY WERE NOT SURE WHETHER ARSENAL HAD TEN PLAYERS

OR TWELVE

AND JOE MERCER'S LEGS WERE EVERYWHERE

"JUST ONE MORE FOR NEXT YEAR"

BUT NEWCASTLE STILL HOLD THE CUP

have stopped the game when Roper went down, which in my view would have been contrary to all rules, claim Milburn was offside. But I was up with the play and Milburn had Smith and Swindin between him and the goal when he jumped up in an effort to head Mitchell's centre. So he was on-side, and within a split second the ball was in the net via George Robledo's head and one of the goalposts.

"A still picture of the goal does show Milburn in an offside position, but the ball, by this time, is almost at the back of the net. Milburn, from an on-side position, had moved towards Robledo, and then changed direction as soon as he saw the ball going goalwards. When Robledo headed it Milburn was on-side, which is all that matters. The fact that he moved goalwards to take any rebound - as any good centre-forward would have done - proves nothing, because the ball had already been played. And if the ball had rebounded to Milburn from the post he would still have been on-side. And remember, when the ball went into the net I was only three yards from the line."

When the goal was scored, Joe exploded at Ellis. Joe was quick to realise, however, that there was nothing he could do about the decision, and his team was now losing with only five minutes to play. While Roper was being treated the other Arsenal players, who had flopped to the ground when the goal went in, tried to pick themselves up. Joe went over to Alex Forbes, lifted him up, shook him and optimistically declared: "Come on, we are starting to play now!"

When the game restarted, Joe Mercer played with true conviction and, together with Forbes and the others, headed for goal. Arsenal won a free-kick, Forbes placed it right into the Newcastle goal area, and in a mad scramble the ball hit the far post.

Arsenal continued to attack, and Newcastle were relieved when Ellis blew the final whistle. Even though Newcastle had retained the Cup, a feat that had last occurred sixty-one years earlier when Blackburn Rovers defeated Notts County 3-1, it was Arsenal who received the greater ovation. They may not have won the trophy but they had certainly proved worthy of it.

After receiving his runners-up medal, Joe spoke to his colleagues: "We ought to have won. We played our hearts out as a team. We'll go off as a team." And with that remark he led his team towards the tunnel with the crowd cheering wildly. It was as if Arsenal had won the Cup not Newcastle.

Stan Seymour, Newcastle's Vice-Chairman, told Tom Whittaker of his relief when the goal was scored and rightly declared: "Tom, ours is the cup; yours the honour and the glory!"

Inside the dressing room, Joe, completely drained after the game of his life, almost collapsed: "I flopped on the seat in the dressing room just as the 'phone rang. A familiar Midlands accent greeted me. 'Joe, I have been listening to the broadcast. Congratulations. This must have been one of your greatest games.' It was Stan Cullis - the immigrant was congratulating the indigenous. That was a fitting climax to be remembered by your old mate and congratulated - even when you lost."

That evening at the banquet Joe summed up the game and his feelings by saying that it was without doubt "Arsenal's finest hour". He felt immense pride and added a emotive comment that captured everyone's hearts: "I always thought football's greatest honour was to captain England. But I was wrong - it was to captain Arsenal today."

Years later Joe would often refer to the game as his proudest moment, commenting: "We might not have won the Cup but I was thrilled with my lads. We had really battled and at times it had looked as if we were going to pull off the almost unbelievable. The crowd rose to us. That was proof of the heart we showed for 90 frantic minutes. People think I'm pulling their leg when I say that I'm prouder of defeat in the second Final than I was of victory in the first. You sometimes have to earn defeat."

Despite Joe's pride it is true to say that he always felt a little aggrieved by the referee's decision to allow play to go on. He later commented: "My record for fair play was pretty good. But I am no angel. I was so wild at the decision that I gave the referee a piece of my mind. I have a great admiration for Arthur, but I still think that anyone but a tough, hard-headed Yorkshireman might have been a bit more sympathetic and that goal would never have been scored."

The discussions as to the validity of Joe's claims went on for days, even weeks. Most newspaper reporters expressed their own opinions. Some, like Alan Hoby of the *Sunday Express*, dismissed the incident: "But he [Roper] soon recovered. So let there be no stupid talk that the referee should have stopped play before that goal."

Referee Arthur Ellis also played it down: "Actually, the Roper incident meant nothing. Every Cup Final must have an 'incident' that can be discussed in newspapers, on the radio and in the pubs and clubs. The Roper incident was just one of those. In an ordinary League game it would never have been mentioned. I am convinced that not one single soul at Wembley really expected me to stop the game, or thought that the incident was worth remembering."

Forty years on, there are those who remember the controversy. Arsenal failed in the Final not because they were the poorer side, but because their infamous 'luck' had run out. A gruelling season which had promised so much ended with Arsenal runners-up in the Cup and third in the League.

Once again Joe considered retirement, but how could he after such a sterling performance at Wembley, where he was without doubt the hero.

Bernard Joy, the former Arsenal player, praised Joe's legs: "Those legs were the most effective, as well as the oldest, on the field. It was literally the game of his life. Mercer not only did two men's work but was also the driving force as captain. The superb timing of his short lunge into the tackle won the ball time and again; his covering was perfect; and his deliberate passing continued to impose his tempo on Newcastle."

As the close season arrived, Joe knew deep in his heart that he couldn't play for ever, but surely one more season would be possible. He certainly hoped it would. Joe's retirement was fast becoming one of the biggest jokes in football, and Joe was not slow to join in. Years later he would grin and say, "I started to think about retiring when I sprinted flat out down the touchline for a ball at Highbury and the linesman flew past me."

Arsenal 1950-51
Back row (left to right): Les Compton, Arthur Shaw, George Swindin, Lionel Smith, Peter Goring.
Front row: Ian McPherson, Jimmy Logie, Joe Mercer, Laurie Scott, Doug Lishman, Don Roper.

Chapter Nine

TIME TO RETIRE?

And so on Friday 1 May [1953], a 51,586 crowd braved torrential rain, which turned the pitch into a sea of mud, and a freezing wind, to watch us play Burnley. It was a nerve-wracking match. We raced to a 3-1 lead by the 20th minute. That's how the score read 16 minutes from time, and as if conscious of the fact that a draw would give Preston the title, the Burnley players tore into action after Elliott's goal had made it 3-2. Correspondingly, my boys seemed to sag. They were played into the mud, except the defiant, dogged defence who hung on. Finally came the welcome whistle, and we were Champions by the tenth part of a goal with a goal average of 97-64 against 85-60, and both teams on the 54 points mark. There was quite an emotional scene on the main steps outside the East Stand afterwards, as Joe Mercer, after being cheered to the echo, told the crowd that he had decided to hang up his boots for good.

Tom Whittaker, *Tom Whittaker's Arsenal Story*

NORAH MERCER was becoming increasingly worried. She wanted her husband to retire and concentrate on his flourishing grocery business. Joe, though, saw his business as football, not grocery. He did not enjoy the role of shopkeeper. He understood the importance of having a job outside of football but did not really want another career. Football was his life. Nothing else matched it.

After getting the medical all-clear in 1952, Joe decided to play on for another season. He relished the prospect of leading a brave side that had come so close to the League and Cup double. Norah, being Norah, supported him. If he wanted to play, he would play, and his cautious wife would urge him on.

Arsenal's season started perfectly with victories over Aston Villa and Manchester United. Joe, of course, played his part by inspiring his team, and he continued to be revered by the management, supporters and newspaper reporters. Almost every week, however, there was an odd comment suggesting Joe should retire. By April 1953, Jack Peart of the *Sunday Pictorial* was writing, "Joe (Legs) Mercer, pride of England, Arsenal, and Everton, will not thank me for my advice, but, in all sincerity, I say, 'Make this your last season, Joe.' Frankly, there have been signs this season that the strain of 20 glorious years in professional football is beginning to tell."

Joe simply did not want to quit, and whenever the question was raised he would point out that Tom Whittaker still put him in the team. "When Tom stops picking me, I'll stop playing," he argued convincingly.

Joe arriving at London's Euston station from the Wirral - ready for his next game.

Some of Joe's performances certainly belied his age. Take the 5-1 win at Liverpool on 15 November for instance. Eric Thompson's article was displayed under laudatory headlines: "Joe Mercer made it his second best" and "Great Captaincy on his training ground". Wrote Thompson: "Joe Mercer could not have picked better occasions for his best and second best displays of Arsenal leadership. The best was in last year's Cup Final, and a close second came his performance on Saturday at Anfield, where he trains. Mercer was the chief joy of a grand game in which Arsenal beat Liverpool 5-1 - not so much through his own individual play as by his handling of his side."

Joe's leadership, more than anything else, guaranteed him a place in the side, as Arsenal once more bid for the League Championship and the FA Cup. By mid-February they were through to the sixth round of the Cup, and were making a serious challenge for the title. Arsenal's Cup run had started with a 4-0 victory against Peter Doherty's Doncaster Rovers, but Joe's own Cup run began with the 6-2 fourth-round victory over Bury because he missed the Doncaster game with influenza.

In the week leading up to the Doncaster game, Norah and the family doctor had been telling the Arsenal captain that he would not be fit to play. Joe, typically, refused to give in until the very last moment when he admitted he was not fit enough. During the game Joe sat at his home, waiting for the periodic telephone calls from the ground to let him know how the match was progressing. He was probably more anxious at home than he would have been at the game. Knowing Joe, being on the pitch was probably the only place he wanted to be.

In the fifth round, Arsenal visited Burnley, where a comfortable 2-0 victory was attained. In the sixth round they faced another Lancastrian giant of the day - Blackpool.

The week before the Cup match, Arsenal had the opportunity to assess Blackpool's strengths as they played them in a League match at the seaside resort. Arsenal lost 3-2, but the game is worth noting for one reason and one reason only - Joe scored his first League goal for Arsenal. Six years may be a long time to wait for a goal, but within a month Joe had provided the Gunners with his second.

His second goal came in a re-arranged home League match with Preston, who were also bidding for the title, played on the afternoon of Thursday 19 March 1953. It was important for

Arsenal 1952-53
Back row (left to right): Ray Daniel, Alex Forbes, George Swindin, Lionel Smith, Arthur Shaw.
Front row: Peter Goring, Don Oakes, Joe Mercer, Joe Wade, Doug Lishman, Don Roper.

Arsenal to win after only being victorious once in their previous four League games. But Preston came to Highbury with the emphasis on grim, solid defence, and as the game progressed in the second half, this was aided by a well-organised offside trap. The Arsenal supporters became increasingly angry as their forwards were smothered by Preston's tactics. They started booing and then proceeded to slow hand clap the visitors.

Preston quickly silenced their critics as the ball was cleared up to Jimmy Baxter, then Charlie Wayman, and on to Tom Finney who jabbed in a right-footer to make it 1-0. Arsenal, by this time, were struggling with injuries. Lionel Smith had damaged his shoulder, and Joe Mercer had injured his right foot. Joe's leg was heavily

Limping Joe hits target

Joe scores against Preston in March 1953, only his second goal for Arsenal.

Joe gets a shot in against eventual winners Blackpool in a 1-2 FA Cup Sixth round defeat at Highbury in February 1953.

strapped up and he was pushed up to centre-forward "out of the way". This gave him the opportunity to level the score. Desmond Hackett of the *Daily Express* described the momentous occasion: "There is football's grand old man Joe Mercer scoring his first League goal at Highbury. It was gifted to him with extreme courtesy and lack of point appreciation by Preston right-back Willie Cunningham. Instead of allowing the ball to go to goalkeeper Thompson, Cunningham struck the ball into the Mercer chest and good old Joe gleefully plugged the ball into goal with the very strapped up right foot that had so surprisingly made him a centre-forward. Almost as surprising as Arsenal getting away with a point!"

Joe leads his team out at Highbury.

The goal which made Arsenal League champions in 1953 for the seventh time. The Gunners' No. 8 Jimmy Logie stabs the ball home in the crucial final match of the season against Burnley.

Joe's goal against Championship rivals Preston gave Arsenal the impetus to maintain their title challenge, but Blackpool had ended their Cup hopes, winning 2-1 before a 69,158 Highbury crowd. It was Blackpool's first-ever away victory over Arsenal, and most of the action seemed to take place in the last ten minutes. Ernie Taylor scored for Blackpool, Logie quickly equalised, and then there was high drama as Allan Brown scored Blackpool's winner but broke his leg in two places as he collided with Arsenal goalkeeper Jack Kelsey. He was carried off the pitch and, for the second time in his career, missed his chance of appearing in a Cup Final. Blackpool went on to overcome Tottenham in the semi-final and then Bolton in the Final - the famous 4-3 game which saw Stanley Matthews receive his first and only Cup winners' medal.

Arsenal maintained their title challenge with successive April victories against Liverpool (5-3), Chelsea (2-0), Manchester City (4-2), Bolton Wanderers (4-1) and Stoke City (3-1). The press now believed that Joe would announce his retirement if the title went to Highbury. The *Sunday Pictorial's* Jack Peart commented: "Northern fans will scream with rage when I say that I hope Arsenal win the Championship. I do so because I think it will help Joe make up his mind."

After this great run, Arsenal drew with Cardiff, when Joe was absent, and then lost to rivals Preston 2-0 at Deepdale. Joe's great friend, Tom Finney, and Charlie Wayman scored for the home side. Arsenal and Preston were now level on points with only one game to play. Preston completed their fixtures on the

Arsenal title and farewell by Mercer

Arsenal 3, Burnley 2

STANDING on the steps of Highbury Stadium last night, less than half an hour after leading the club to the First Division championship, Joe Mercer, the Arsenal captain and former Everton player, told thousands of cheering fans :—

" Thank you all. This has been the most splendid day of my life; but I am sorry to have to tell you that this has been my last game for Arsenal. I am retiring from football."

Mercer had come out on to the steps in response to repeated calls of " We want Joe " from the crowd (writes **Roy Peskett**).

In gaining their seventh title success—a record—on a sea of mud Arsenal had a brilliant first 20 minutes and piled up a 3—1 lead after being behind.

In the second half they seemed to tire and were quite content to hold on to their lead against a side fighting for every ball, and determined that neighbouring Preston should have every chance to keep the title in Lancashire.

Shephenson opened Burnley's account, and Forbes, scoring his first goal of the season, equalised, the ball being deflected into the net by Brown. Lishman and Logie added to the home score.

The game was going slowly with a monotonous chain of throws-in when Burnley scored a second goal 15 minutes from time through Elliott.

Wednesday, away to struggling Derby County, and won by a solitary goal, a disputed penalty scored by Tom Finney. The result saw Derby County relegated, while Preston were now two points clear of Arsenal.

By the time Arsenal played their last match Preston were on tour. Arsenal played Burnley on the eve of the Cup Final, two days after Preston's last game. A packed stadium greeted the sides as they made their way on to the Highbury pitch. Arsenal had to win to stand any chance.

After three minutes Burnley went ahead, and Joe Mercer was involved. Burnley outside-right Roy Stephenson drove in a hard, low, centre. Joe tried to

Mercer Move

I UNDERSTAND that a special invitation to apply for the post of manager of Liverpool F.C., made vacant by the retirement through ill health of George Kay, will be made to Joe Mercer, the Arsenal captain. The old England international half-back has trained on the Anfield ground ever since he joined Arsenal from Everton. Joe, well known and respected in his native Liverpool, is one of the finest skippers in Soccer today and I have no doubt that he would quickly jump into the forefront of managers.

cut out the danger and, with his first touch of the game, diverted the ball into his own net. What a time to score an own-goal!

Joe quickly set about making amends for his error. He played like a man possessed, as the whole of the Arsenal side gave a tremendous display of forceful attacking play. As the game progressed it was Arsenal who were making all the play, and inevitably their superiority led to goals. Alex Forbes scored his first goal of the season when his shot was deflected into the net for the equaliser. By half-time it was 3-1 to the Gunners as Doug Lishman and Jimmy Logie

Wellington are after Joe Mercer

By BOB PENNINGTON

JOE MERCER, of England and Arsenal, will be on the 10.10 train from Liverpool to London this morning. Object — the Arsenal's championship celebration dinner in Mayfair.

Joe will have company on the trip —his wife, Mrs Mercer, a woman with a mission.

The mission is to keep tags on the retired Joe when he starts getting nostalgic about the old club, the old boys, the old days.

She knows that Joe needs only a whiff of embrocation, a little of manager Tom Whittaker's stately charm to say " I'm good for another season.' "

And that's not the way she wants it. " Not that I'm a nagger," she told me yesterday. " It's up to Joe —always has been. But at 39 his health comes first, and I'm worried stiff lest another season will be too much for him.

" There's our grocery business, too. Why, we're so busy we have to be home by Friday afternoon."

Even if Joe says " no " to Arsenal Mrs Mercer's worries are not over. Wellington Town, the Cheshire League club, have had long talks with Joe about him becoming their player manager.

boosted Arsenal's goals tally. The Gunners needed the goals because the title, if Arsenal won the game, would be decided on goal average.

Burnley's Billy Elliott pulled a goal back in the second half, prompting Arsenal to defend instead of attack. Joe pulled his troops back and they defended superbly. Joe later commented on those final 15 minutes of play: "I never went across the halfway-line and on occasions I had every member of the team back. It was as tense as a Cup Final but we held on and won the match and the Championship."

When the calculations were made, it was discovered that Arsenal had won the title by less than one tenth of a goal. Joe had now won the Championship on three occasions - twice with Arsenal and the 1939 success with Everton.

Was this finally the time to call it a day?

He was still playing well, and was still a great captain. His performance against Burnley received tremendous praise. Someone even sent Joe a cutting, marked the Egyptian Mail, 2 May 1953: "Bow-legged Joe Mercer, Arsenal's skipper, who was probably playing his last League game, was the deciding factor in the Londoners' win over Burnley. In the second-half, Burnley scored again, and piled on the pressure, but Mercer, who returned after a spell on the touchline through a leg injury, managed to rally the Londoners until the final whistle."

After the game the Arsenal supporters gathered outside the main entrance and chanted for the play-

GRAND FINALE

HE used to play for Elton Green, a junior club at Ellesmere Port. He has captained England at Hampden and figured prominently in Arsenal's League Championship and F.A. Cup successes.

He is the head of a provision firm in Wallasey, Cheshire, and a partner in a chain of retail grocery shops.

Yes, it's Joe Mercer, who has now retired from football, after sixteen seasons with Everton and six with Arsenal.

He goes out in a blaze of glory, with Arsenal again League Champions.

Joe, an ideal skipper, continued to live in the north after his transfer from Goodison Park.

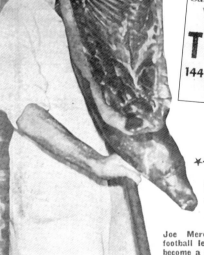

JOE SAVES THE BACON

Joe Mercer, famous England football left half, is training to become a grocer as soon as he's out of uniform. He's so often saved the bacon on the football field that it comes natural to him to save it in his father-in-law's shop at Hoylake.

ers and, of course, for their magnificent 38-year-old captain. Just as the crowd shouted, "We want Mercer", the old 'Portite' appeared on the broad steps of Highbury's impressive main entrance.

The crowd roared as they saw the familiar smiling face. Joe waved to the crowd, and as the noise died down he commenced his speech: "This has been the most wonderful day of my life, and now I am sorry to tell you that you have seen me playing for the last time. I am retiring from football."

Joe had made one of the hardest decisions of his life. He had been promising his wife, Norah, that he would retire for years but had always found it difficult to do. Now, after ending the season with Arsenal as Champions it seemed the right moment to make it official.

Even so, Norah, the person who knew him better than anyone else, was not convinced, and you can guess what happened. Yes, Joe Mercer played for one more season.

SATURDAY, MAY 2, 1953

Mercer And Family Leave

Trio on the Liverpool train at Euston today were Joe Mercer the Arsenal skipper, his wife, and their son David. Joe announced his retirement after Arsenal had won the League championship. ("Star" picture. See Star Man's Diary.)

Chapter Ten

END OF AN ERA

Joe has been promising to retire for years. He has been playing since he was fifteen. I can hardly believe this. In fact I will not believe it has happened until next season has started and Joe is still out of football.

Norah Mercer, *1 May 1953*

AS NORAH SUSPECTED, Joe did not retire at the end of the 1952-3 season. In fact, he spent all the close season training hard. He was 39 shortly before the 1953-4 season started, a remarkable age for a footballer who had pushed himself so hard. Once more he was ready, if selected.

Tom Whittaker and Arsenal supporters were pleased to hear that Joe would play on. He was in the team for the opening match away at West Bromwich Albion, but Arsenal lost 2-0.

All hopes of matching the previous season's Championship success were gone at Christmas, by when Arsenal had won only nine of their 24 games. Joe had played in 13 of the 24, including the 7-1 defeat at Sunderland on 12 September. "Arsenal's worst for 26 years," recorded the headline in the *Sunday Dispatch*. The team's only tangible success in the first half of the season came in the Charity Shield when Blackpool were defeated 3-1 under the Highbury floodlights in October. This was Joe's last trophy as a player, although he did not realise it at the time.

Many now questioned Joe's decision to continue playing first-class football: "Why play on in a side vastly inferior to the previous season's?"

To "put the record straight" and give his own view Joe wrote to the *Sporting Record*. His letter was printed in the 19 September issue: "Sir - The strange and unenviable position in Division One that Arsenal now occupy makes the question, 'Why did you decide to have another year in football?' very difficult and somewhat embarrassing to answer.

"But I want the world of sport to know. I had advice from many friends who said, 'Finish at the top. Don't wait until the game finishes you. The public are fickle. You might injure your health.'

"Despite seeing so many players carrying on just too long, and fully realising the soundness of the advice, after having been given a successful bill of health from a very eminent London specialist, I decided to have just one more season, simply because a man whom I admire, respect and trust thought that the club needed me and I was still wanted to do a job of work. Whether Mr Whittaker will be proved right remains to be seen.

"He thought that I could help the youngsters to feel their feet and assist in establishing them in League football. It just shows how utterly unpredictable this football game is when you think that, except perhaps for the first game against West Bromwich, the boot has been on the other foot. It was the younger members of the team who helped me. I can honestly say that if the younger players had been given the normal support that I am usually able to give, results would have been better."

Joe continued by addressing what had gone wrong so far for Arsenal. He knew the great Arsenal side was at its end and that the team needed new blood and new life. He continued to try hard, and certainly "gave his all". He tried to pass on his experience and knowledge on to his colleagues and the younger reserve-team players, while his manager Tom Whittaker searched for players to strengthen the side.

A LETTER FROM JOE MERCER

To the Editor "Sporting Record"

SIR.—

The strange and unenviable position in Division I that Arsenal now occupy makes the question, " Why did you decide to have another year in football?" very difficult and somewhat embarrassing to answer.

But I want the world of sport to know. I had advice from many friends who said: " Finish at the top. Don't wait until the game finishes with you. The public are fickle. You might injure your health."

Despite seeing so many players carrying on just too long, and fully realising the soundness of the advice, after having been given a successful bill of health from a very eminent London specialist, I decided to have just one more season, simply because a man whom I admire, respect and trust thought that the club needed me and I was still wanted to do a job of work.

Whether Mr. Whittaker will be proved right remains to be seen.

He thought that I could help the youngsters to feel their feet and assist in establishing them in League football. It just shows how utterly unpredictable this football game is when you think that except perhaps for the first game against West Bromwich the boot has been on the other foot. It was the younger members of the team who helped me. I can honestly say that if the younger players had been given the normal support that I am usually able to give, results would have been better.

Everywhere I go these days the question," What's wrong with Arsenal?" is fired at me. The Press is saying, "I told you so. New blood is needed. You must buy."

Jimmy Logie says, " Well, they say that every year. They must be right sometimes!"

Obviously there must be something wrong. I'm not good at excuses. Bad luck can usually be traced to bad play.

The team as a whole are omitting and forgetting those basic principles of play on which Arsenal's method and procedure were based. When we get back to everyone doing his own job and doing the easy thing with the ball more quickly, then we will get more normal results. Arsenal are a side that has been written off many times. We are still here!

Yours faithfully,
JOE MERCER.

EDITOR'S NOTE. Thank you, Joe Mercer, for your very interesting letter. We would welcome the views of readers on the points discussed above, and shall print a selection.

Whittaker signed Tom Lawton, Joe's former Everton colleague, from Brentford to strengthen the attack. Lawton was attracted by the idea of player with Joe again. He made his Arsenal début on 19 September when Manchester City played at Highbury. Joe was out of the side through injury but still travelled all the way from the Wirral to watch. Over 65,000 spectators saw the 2-2 draw.

Arsenal continued to struggle, and were knocked out of the Cup by Norwich in the fourth round. For a short time they were bottom of the First Division, and it developed into Joe's "worst-ever season". Even so, he had a vision of playing on into 1954-5.

At the beginning of April, Joe was in his usual number-six shirt for the visit of Aston Villa. The game, played on 6 April, ended 1-1 with Tommy Lawton scoring the Arsenal goal. Joe was fit, raring to go and had proved himself enough to be selected as captain of Old England against Young England on 30 April. He was excited by the prospect and naturally this prompted further speculation that he would decide to play yet another "one more season".

On Saturday 10 April, the day of Arsenal's match against Joe's friends from Liverpool, *The Star*, under the banner headline "Joe Mercer wants to play on", summarised Joe's position: "Many people seem to have decided that when Joe Mercer leads Old England against Young England at Highbury on 30 April he will be making his final appearance. But the Arsenal captain and left-half has other ideas. Although he will be 40 in August he wants to play again next season. Mercer's idea is to play in Arsenal's reserve side and to use his experience in helping the young players in Combination football. 'I would start right from the beginning of the new season in the Reserves', he tells me, 'and then Tom Whittaker would not be embarrassed by considering me a first-team man.' Mercer is to talk over his suggestion with manager Whittaker, but Arsenal may feel that he should retire now, when his reputation is so high.

Joe knows the answer to that one. 'I can't trust myself not to play. If I finish with Arsenal in May I'm sure I'll be tempted to join another club, and that may be the wrong thing to do'"

Joe seriously intended to play on, and believed he still had plenty to give the game. His experience as a captain couldn't be matched. Like the legendary Billy Meredith 30 years earlier, Joe always believed in playing that extra season. And that was his position on the morning of 10 April 1954, the day of the Liverpool game. Then fate played its part.

The game started with Liverpool, wearing their change strip of white shirts, making the first couple of attacks, before Arsenal started to dominate play. In one Arsenal attack Joe Mercer lobbed the ball out to inside-right Derek Tapscott, whose quick drive was cannoned away off Liverpool's Bill Jones. Tapscott, 18 years Joe's junior, was making his League début, and a few minutes later he had a second chance. Tommy Lawton set him up, and Tapscott hit a powerful shot. Liverpool goalkeeper Underwood got his hands to the ball, but it rolled into the net for the first goal after 20 minutes. Within a couple of minutes Lawton set up Tapscott again, but this time the debutant shot into the side-netting.

What happened next was Joe Mercer's unluckiest moment on a football field. It ended his distinguished top-class playing career.

Joe later told the story many times, always with a smile: "I would have been 40 in the August when I broke my leg playing against Liverpool. It's hilarious, looking back on it. Trainers in our day were sympathetic appointments, as reward for those who'd been with the club for a long time. We had Billy Milne from Buckie, in the north of Scotland, a lovely fellow. He had a wonderful war record - MM, DCM. He was the toughest, hardest and bravest person, but he knew nothing about physiology and anatomy. I was near the halfway-line, about 20 yards from the trainers' box, and I kidded to head this ball, then stepped back and was going to trap it and turn it aside, but Joe Wade came in thinking I wasn't going for it, and we collided. 'It's broken, Bill,' I said to Billy Liddell. All I could think of was Tommy Wright of Sunderland who'd broken his leg on a goal-post, then screamed 'Don't let our trainer on,' and one of our players said, 'Ours is worse than yours.' Fortunately, Albert Shelley, the Liverpool trainer, got there first. Otherwise I might not have had any leg left. There wasn't a lot of pain. In fact, I can still remember, my only thoughts were that I had let the fans and the club down!"

As Joe lay on the pitch, the crowd went silent. Billy Milne signalled for a stretcher and strapped Joe's right leg in splints. The Arsenal captain was lifted on to the stretcher, wrapped up in a blanket and carried towards the dressing room. As the stretcher was lifted up, the

Joe is stretchered off the Highbury pitch after breaking his leg against Liverpool.

Arsenal win 3-0 — Spurs 5-2

MERCER BREAKS HIS LEG RESULTS

ground was as silent as a morgue. Joe Wade held his head in his hands. Joe saw him from the stretcher and shouted, "Don't worry, son," to console his team-mate.

As Joe was being carried off there was still an eerie silence. Joe wanted to let everyone know he was alright: "I tugged at the blankets and just before we reached the tunnel entrance I managed to free an arm. I waved and smiled and it was a genuine smile."

It was a poignant moment and the crowd reacted. How they reacted. The sound of clapping and cheering started in one corner of the vast Highbury ground and then quickly went round the stadium until the noise around Highbury was deafening. Joe was thrilled: "Everyone was cheering. It was a fantastic ovation and I felt none of the pain - only happiness."

Tom Whittaker, Joe Wade and many spectators were in tears. They knew that an era had ended.

At half-time Joe Wade went into the treatment-room, and Joe Mercer again did his best to soothe the Arsenal full-back: "Don't let this put you off your game, Joe. It wasn't your fault."

The Saturday night edition of the *Evening Standard* broke the news to people who had missed the match. Under the headline, "Arsenal win 3-0, Mercer breaks his leg", they printed a photograph of Joe being stretchered off. The other story of the game was Derek Tapscott's two goals on his début. One era was ending, another was dawning.

Joe was taken to the Royal Northern Hospital, where he was given injections. His right leg was broken in two places below the knee, and there was some cause for concern. Tom Whittaker contacted Norah and arranged for her to travel from the Wirral overnight to be at her husband's side. Norah usually watched her husband play, but had missed this particular game as their son, David, had chicken-pox and needed looking after. When she was told the news she said: "I'm glad I wasn't there. I've been on at him for years to give it up." But she knew how important football was to Joe and how difficult life might be for him without it.

Whittaker revealed to reporters that Joe had playfully punched him on the chin as he was lifted into the ambulance and said: "Sorry I made a mess of things, Boss." That was typical Mercer. He also made a joke about being too old to be available for the Old England team.

It was also revealed that Joe had been pestering Whittaker all week about playing against Liverpool. Whittaker told reporters: "I told him to stay at home in Liverpool and forget about football for the rest of the season and just fade out quietly, but he talked me into letting him play today very much against my will. You see, I had a premonition that something would go wrong in this match - but I never thought it would be anything like this. Even today I knew he wanted to see me to plead with me to sign him again next season so he could play for the Reserves and help rebuild the Arsenal!"

Whittaker was quick to point out that Joe's next year was secure: "We will sign Joe up as an Arsenal player for next season in any event, and even if he does not play he will be of great value to us for coaching and other duties."

Newspaper reporters were now convinced Joe's career was over, and they wrote their football obituaries. "Crowd roars for game Joe Mercer" was the headline in *The People*. Wrote Joe

Hulme: "Joe Mercer, who has earned every honour football has to bestow, took his last burst of cheering from the fans yesterday - on a stretcher. He left the Arsenal field in triumph with a wave to the crowd - and a broken leg which has ended one of the most brilliant football careers ever. He was a winner right to the end."

The *Sunday Dispatch* headline was "Farewell to Joe Mercer". The article was by 'Linesman': "Joe Mercer, near his 40th birthday and Britain's greatest and most popular player, waved farewell to football at Highbury yesterday from a stretcher after his leg had been broken. The 33,000 crowd all stood and cheered a tribute as Mercer was carried from the field by ambulance men. They knew he would never play football again, and Mercer, although in great pain waved his good-bye."

Broken Leg Ends Arsenal Captain's Great Football Career
FAREWELL TO JOE MERCER

"Bad luck, Joe!" said the *Sunday Graphic* headline, below which was a half-page photograph of Joe being stretchered off while the Liverpool players watched. The *Graphic's* John Robertson reported: "That grand trooper, 39-year-old Joe Mercer of the spindly legs and untiring energy, has gone from the soccer stage he graced so long. It was sheer love of the game that kept Arsenal's captain in football. Remember that, you detractors of professionalism.

"Mercer had a profitable business on Merseyside. He could have become a manager and sat comfortably in an office chair for £2,000 a year. But Mercer preferred to face the rigours of a young man's game, and give all he knew for Arsenal, who will never have a better servant. Highbury will not forget this great-hearted captain."

In another article, JT Bolton wrote: "For me, this is one of the saddest stories I have ever written for many a day; for the scores of thousands of footballers, it will be an equally sad story to read". He went on to tell the story of the accidental clash between Joe and Joe Wade, but ended with a sad comment: "We may never again see those bow legs in a football match."

On Merseyside, the *Liverpool Echo* recorded: "The whole football world will miss Joe Mercer, a shining light to footballers old and

RETIRE? NOT ME, SAYS MERCER
By JOE MERCER
captain of Arsenal, age 39, who broke his right shin bone in two places at Highbury on Saturday, and is now in a London hospital.

WHAT! Me retire? No fear. When I retire from football it will be on two good legs, not on my back.

It's pretty grim to think that this should have happened at my time of Soccer life. But there's always a bright side. It could have happened at the start of my career.

Season after season for the past few years I've had a lurking suspicion—it's been much stronger than that with my wife Norah—that this was the time to retire.

But as each season has come round I have felt the urge in the old feet and legs to have just another go—you know how it is—and I've a notion that when this job is over and done with I'll feel just the same way again.

My right leg is broken in two places below the knee. It's in splints now, but there's a bit of tidying up to do, and then we'll all have a clearer idea of things.

I know what the medico will say for sure, but I've defied the doctors before now. I shall, of course, be guided by the greatest football boss in the world, Mr Tom Whittaker.

I didn't sleep much last night, and that gave me a deuce of a lot of time to think. I thought a lot of poor old Joe Wade, our back, with whom I came in collision.

I'll wager you never slept. He knows that I am as sorry for him as I am for myself.

I hope Joe heard me shout when I was

MERCER went to trap a bouncing ball, collided with team-mate Joe Wade and collapsed. Here he is being carried off.

being carried off. I noticed he had his head in his hands, poor chap, but I did try to muster up enough strength to shout to him "not to worry, son".

(At half-time Joe Wade went into the massage room to see Mercer and was greeted with: "Don't let this put you off your game, Joe. It wasn't your fault." Said Wade: "I was in tears. I never felt so sick about anything in all my life").

I've played in five full internationals for England, three war-time internationals, won two post-war Cup medals, and two championship medals without the old legs giving way. Now this. What a joke for it to happen in a match where the points were not vital for Arsenal.

(Even when Mercer was being carried off in agony he could still crack. "Just when I got my first cap this should happen!")*

I've been very lucky really. The only serious injury I can remember was in 1946, when I tore some leg ligaments.

In recent years it's been a case of the boss and myself campaigning to conserve the old strength, and playing now and again.

P.S.—Whatever you do, don't write old Joe Mercer off the Arsenal playing list yet awhile. Not on your life!

*Mercer had been chosen to captain an international side against Young England on Cup Final eve.

new. He gained all the honours the game could supply and was acknowledged one of the greatest captains the Arsenal and England ever had."

In hospital, Joe was unaware of the drama that surrounded him. There were problems with his leg - far worse than Joe imagined - and the doctors discussed the possibility of amputation. Joe said later: "At the hospital they gave me an anti-tetanus injection. I was allergic to it. I missed all the chat about amputation because I was delirious and in a high old fever. Poor Norah had to listen. In the end amputation was not necessary!"

Having taken the overnight train from Hoylake to London, Norah arrived at the hospital on Sunday, the day after the accident. She listened to the doctors talking about the seriousness of the injury and then to Joe's hopes and expectations. Joe lay in his bed and told his wife: "I know it looks as if I'm finished in First Division football. But, believe me, if there's the slightest chance of another come back I'll play."

Norah knew that Joe was not a man to quit. He would overcome whatever odds, so long as he returned to football. Norah told reporters on the Sunday: "He'll go back if he gets the chance and play until his leg crumbles under him. Joe's to have an operation tomorrow, which, I believe, is a fairly simple one. But he's in more pain than he'll admit.

"He retired 12 months ago, but he found he could not give up. That is what will happen this time. He's been at football too long. He started playing at four in alleys and streets, with coats as goalposts. He's come a long way since then."

Tom Whittaker also responded to reporters: "Will Joe play again? Of course he says he will play again - he's that type of man. He's brimful of confidence, has a wonderful spirit, and is very happy under the circumstances. But I will try and persuade him not to play again. It is for his own sake."

No matter what was said to Joe, or who tried to persuade him it was time to give up the game he loved,

JOE WILL BE BACK, SAYS MRS MERCER

'He couldn't give up football'

By Daily Mail Reporter

MRS. JOE MERCER, wife of the 39-year-old star footballer who broke his right leg on Saturday, said yesterday: "He'll go back if he gets the chance and play until his leg crumbles under him."

Mercer, captain of Arsenal, former captain of England and "Footballer of the Year" in 1949-50, broke his shin-bone in the match with Liverpool at Highbury.

His wife travelled from their home in Hoylake, Cheshire, to visit him in a London hospital yesterday.

Lying in a private ward with a bouquet from the Arsenal Club he told her: "I know it looks as if I'm finished in First Division football. But, believe me, if there's the slightest chance of another come-back I'll play."

'He's in pain'

Afterwards Mrs. Mercer said: "Joe's to have an operation tomorrow, which, I believe, is a fairly simple one. But he's in more pain than he'll admit.

"He retired 12 months ago, but he found he could not give the game up. That is what will happen this time.

"He's been at football too long. He started playing at four, in alleys and streets, with coats as goalposts. He's come a long way since then."

he was determined. His own view was that he would play again once his broken leg had healed. In a newspaper article, a few days after the injury, Joe gave his views on retiring. He was adamant that he could and would return to football. He pointed out that his retirement would come only when he was back on his two good legs and not while he was lying on his back in a hospital bed.

Sadly for Joe, complications with his leg meant he had to remain in the London hospital longer than he had hoped. His wife Norah, with a young son to look after, had to rush backwards and forwards to comfort him. To help Joe through the long hours of boredom, Joe Wade arranged for a television set to be installed in his private hospital room. This, at least, helped in some small way to take his mind off football.

Despite his situation, Joe always had his friendly smile and appeared cheerful when he

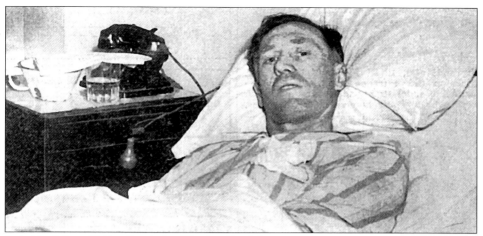

Joe looking fed up with himself at the Royal Northern Hospital.

received visitors. The hospital staff were surprised by his cheerfulness and by the number of telegrams and flowers sent to him. The Sister in charge of his ward spent most of her time answering the telephone to the many well-wishers who invariably asked, quite simply, "How's Joe?" In Hoylake, Norah, her parents and Joe's relatives all faced that same question: "How's Joe?"

Professional footballers of the 1950s, the era of the regional Third Divisions, even shared a joke about the Royal Northern Hospital. The story was that a player with a bottom-of-the-table Lancashire First Division club was taken to the Royal Northern after being concussed during a game in London. "Where am I?" he asked, when he came round. "You're in the Northern?" "What? We've been relegated from the Second Division, too?"

Joe stayed in London for six weeks. A silver plate was inserted in his broken shin, with the help of four screws, and the bone took a long time to begin to knit together. The eventual scar would be the length of his shin.

A smile and a wave as Joe leaves hospital on a stretcher.

Joe has wife Norah by his side as he leaves the Royal Northern on 26th May 1954.

While recovering in London, he thought more about returning to football. He experienced great disappointment at missing the season's end - Arsenal finished twelfth - and couldn't wait to get back. Leaving London was a sign that his leg was getting better, although his journey to the Wirral had to be made in an ambulance, with Joe on his back.

Norah accompanied her husband on that journey. Throughout, Joe talked about returning to football. The conversation was even remembered by the ambulance driver who, in 1970, was re-introduced to Joe by Eamonn Andrews for Joe's 'This Is Your Life'.

Over the course of the following months Joe had spells at a West Kirby nursing home, and the thought of ending his playing career depressed him enormously. Those months after the accident were hugely disappointing for Joe. His family and friends recognised the misery caused by not being able to play football. They tried to walk the fine line between providing Joe with hope for the future but, at the same time, not encouraging him to return to playing.

Typically, as soon as his leg was free from plaster Joe began light exercises. His mission was to play football again. Joe further fuelled rumours that he would indeed play again by training with Arsenal and Tranmere Rovers towards the end of 1954.

Joe's name was often in the papers as speculation about his return increased. However, by mid-1955 Joe appeared on the surface to be more involved in his grocery business. He had now taken on a full-time job with his own company. On the inside, though, Joe was thinking more about football than the grocery trade. Grocery was simply something that prevented him from playing football.

Joe's idea of a comeback at 40 or 41 was only a dream. Certainly it had been an ambition of his to play past 40, and then retire of his own accord. Now his career had been ended by fate rather than choice, and this was something that Joe found hard to accept.

The *Evening Express* recognised Joe's determination in June 1955: "Joe today is a fit man. He has been in training for some weeks, and as recently as a few days ago expressed his belief that he could play again. That to him would be the ultimate triumph. While one admires his desire to attempt to give the game the benefit of his experience and knowledge, I feel that to come back as a player at his age, and after such an accident, would be a mistake. Don't make it, Joe."

What Joe really needed was a way back into football at a level that preserved his dignity and allowed him to prove his abilities once more. League football was not really possible, and non-League football would have been an insult. Joe needed an opportunity to use his experience, and, more than anything, excuses to get away from the grocery business.

Joe latched on to several coaching opportunities. One was with Pegasus, the highly successful amateur side made up of graduates of Oxford and Cambridge Universities. Joe was approached by Harold "Tommy" Thompson, and he went down to meet the Pegasus players at the Royal Military Academy, Sandhurst. In the dressing-room, Ken Shearwood asked Joe how his leg was. Joe smiled, but only showed the scar later, when the other players had gone out. "I didn't want the lads to see it," Joe said. It looked very nasty.

Pegasus weren't the first university side Joe had coached. In the late 1940s he would fly over to Ireland on a Saturday night to coach Bohemians on a Sunday. David Mercer also remembers his father coaching at his school. "Mind you," David adds, "He coached at the opposition schools, too, which was really helpful!"

Another coaching opportunity came with Tranmere Rovers, then a Third Division (North) club. Tranmere had almost gone out of existence in 1955, and were saved by an appeal by the Mayor of Birkenhead. They were without a manager, so Joe went along as a voluntary coach and adviser before the start of the 1955-6 season.

Harold Bell, a long-serving Rovers player, recalls Joe's presence fondly: "Joe Mercer lived for football. It's as simple as that. He came to us, and we were having a bad run at the time, and he took us together, and he was teaching us a new type of football, how to play it, what to do, how to back people up and everything. It was starting to show dividends when he left. Had he stayed there any longer who knows what might have happened. It was rather a pity that we lost him because we were just getting into this routine: Give someone the ball and then run into an open space. It went on, until in the end you seemed to be doing this kind of thing and the other people weren't touching the ball. It seemed a bit of magic to us, instead of just getting it and bang, hoping it gets here, there or somewhere."

Joe's experience at Tranmere taught him one lesson he would never forget. Many years later he said, "Anyone can make a manager at the Liverpools and Evertons and the Cities and Uniteds, but the Tranmeres and the Rochdales, those clubs, that's what fetches the managership out."

The Tranmere directors hoped at one time that they could persuade Joe to stay on as manager, but in the end they approached Noel Kelly, a former Arsenal team-mate of Joe's who was then with Nottingham Forest. Kelly accepted the post of player-manager, and his son, John, later started his career at Tranmere.

But other clubs were now aware that Joe Mercer was getting the appetite for a different kind of football career. In August 1955 he went into management.

Chapter Eleven

'WE'RE GOING TO SHEFFIELD'

Bramall Lane has always been the home of United. It is also one of the big cricket grounds of the country, and the football pitch flanks the cricket square so that spectators are restricted to three sides. The capacity of the ground was tested in 1936, when 68,287 people were admitted to see the game with Leeds United. For the Cup semi-final in 1938 between Preston and the Villa, 55,129 were present.

AH Fabian and G Green, *Association Football, 1960*

FOLLOWING THE DEATH of Sheffield United manager Reg Freeman, Joe Mercer was offered an opportunity to return to football full-time. On 18 August 1955, he was busy in one of his shops when he received a message from a reporter to contact Senior Atkin, the Sheffield United chairman. Joe immediately telephoned Bramall Lane.

Atkin told Joe all about the vacancy and asked him if he was interested. When Joe confirmed his interest, arrangements were made for him to travel to Sheffield that afternoon. Joe then had to tell Norah, who already planned a trip of her own with their son David, who was now 11 years old. Norah Mercer: "What really happened was David was going to Llandudno on the boat and we, the Percivals and I, were going to pick him up and bring him back. Joe rang up and said, 'We're going to Sheffield.' So I said, 'I thought we were going to Llandudno,' he said, 'No, a reporter from *The People* has asked me if I'm interested in Sheffield United, so we're off to Sheffield.' We went to Sheffield straight away, he had an interview with the chairman, Senior Atkin, who owned a big cutlery firm in Sheffield at that time. It was a Thursday and the season started on the Saturday."

The Mercer family, plus Joe's boyhood friend, Alan Percival, and his wife, travelled to Yorkshire with Joe's mind already made up - he wanted to get back into football and this was an opportunity he had waited for. As Norah points out, football was still Joe's life: "Joe hated the grocery business, he just hated and detested the grocery trade. He didn't care what he did so long as he got away from grocery and back into football. That had been the love of his life."

Tom Finney remembers, with a smile, that Joe always claimed to love the grocery business: "When he was in the grocery business and you met him he would tell you he was really enjoying it. But you knew perfectly well that he wasn't enjoying it at all. I knew and I think everybody else knew anyway, that he would have given his right arm to be involved in football again."

During the previous 16 months, while recovering from injury, Joe had taken coaching

From the pain and one worry to one relief... Joe and chairman Senior Atkin, pictured at St. James' Park, Newcastle, during Joe's first game in charge of Sheffield United.

courses and had coached Tranmere Rovers and Pegasus. He had also taken various PT instructor's courses during the war, and had coached local school sides in his free time. He hoped all this experience would work in his favour at Sheffield.

At Bramall Lane, Joe met Senior Atkin and was then introduced to the board of directors. Joe was surprised to find the club had 15 directors. This seemed too large. In the months that followed Joe realised that the United directors could either be his greatest allies or his biggest enemies. He knew there was no way he would be able to keep them all happy, not with so many on the board.

After the meeting, Joe left the board-room to allow the directors time to discuss his credentials. Outside, Joe told Norah and the others that he felt he had the job, and he was right. He was called back into the board-room. Senior Atkin turned to him, held out his hand and said: "Mercer, you've got the job. You're a manager - and I hope you are going to manage, because I know damn all about the game, and ..." turning to the rest of the board, "they know a damn sight less!"

At the time Joe was reassured by this statement. It convinced him that he would be given a free rein. Unfortunately, time would prove that Joe's decisions were rarely accepted without some objection from at least one member of the board. Also, Joe was unaware at the time that there had already been a few internal disagreements. His appointment had not been to the whole board's approval because some directors believed Senior Atkin had more or less given Joe the job before introducing him to the rest of the board.

After the meeting, Joe and the other day-trippers returned home, and stopped for a celebratory meal on their journey. Joe's mind was full of what he needed to do at Bramall Lane. He was keen to develop many of the theories he had gathered during his playing career. He gave several newspaper interviews, telling the press his thoughts on football and football management: "I am what I have always despised - a theorist. But what a wonderful opportunity I now have of putting into operation a lifetime of theories on how football should be run. I believe that the best way to run a successful football club is to put everyone in the picture. Let the players know exactly what is expected of them, exactly what is being planned. My methods may not be revolutionary, but at least they are modern. If football is to maintain its popularity in this age of a hundred and one counter attractions then it must move with the times. If possible we should try to move ahead of the times."

Joe was certainly keen to be seen as a modern manager. With Arsenal, and with England, he had favoured team discussion. To him the game was all about team work and that included the manager. At most clubs during this period the manager was a distant figure. He did not get involved in training - that was left to a trainer. Often, training sessions took place without much thought. Joe wanted to be involved. At the age of 41, he believed a manager's role had to include the role of chief coach. He felt he had to be out on the training pitch with the players showing them what he expected. In typical Mercer style, he would be among the players, promoting team-work, tolerance, and of course humour, while stressing, "I shall do everything to supply our supporters - and the game itself - with entertaining football and a winning side."

The day after accepting the job, Joe travelled with the team to Newcastle for the opening game of the 1955-6 season. He had not had chance to see the side train, let alone play, and did not know what to expect.

By full-time, however, Joe was well aware of the task that lay ahead. His side had lost 4-2 after going three down by half-time. In fact, Newcastle were 4-0 up before goals from Ronnie Waldock and Alf Ringstead in the last ten minutes. The fight-back was some encouragement, but Joe did not like all that he saw. A series of photographs taken during the match show his full range of emotion. One moment he is in despair, the next he shares a smile with the chairman Senior Atkin.

A few days later United drew 0-0 at home to Charlton Athletic, whose legendary goalkeeper Sam Bartram saved a penalty from Alf Ringstead. As Joe left his seat in the director's box after

Bramall Lane moaners are still living in the past

the game, he saw a supporter point him out, and heard him say: "Well, he's made no bloody difference at all!"

Joe had been a manager for less than a week and had already received the kind of criticism that dogs managers. At least he was aware that the supporters needed more than they had been given so far! Joe's third game in charge, a 3-0 defeat at home to Birmingham City, left the club at the bottom of the First Division. Another couple of disasters followed before United's first victory of the season - 2-0 against Tottenham Hotspur, thanks to two goals from Colin Grainger. This was followed by an excellent 1-0 win against Matt Busby's Manchester United, the eventual League Champions.

That form was not sustained. Results proved to be poor, and Joe also had problems off the pitch. Ernest Jackson, the first-team trainer, resigned at the end of August, and Joe searched for a replacement before promoting Harry Latham, the assistant trainer. Illness and injury ruled out key players; and, with little money available, Joe had to be careful who he bought, especially as the directors would question almost every move.

During the season Joe tried for a number of new players. He tried for a long time to sign Aston Villa centre-forward Derek Pace. Villa would not release the player, who ironically scored a hat-trick against United towards the end of the season. Instead, Joe turned his attentions to Arsenal's Jack Wilkinson. The centre-forward was signed in March for around £6,000, but stayed little more than a year. Joe eventually captured his first choice, Pace, towards the end of 1957.

Joe's other signings included Cliff Mason, a £6,500 full-back from Darlington, Des Thompson, a £4,250 goalkeeper from Burnley, and an exciting young Scottish inside-forward called Willie Hamilton.

They weren't enough. United reached the fifth round of the FA Cup, losing 1-0 in a replay to Sunderland, but finished bottom of the table and were relegated to the Second Division for the second time in less than a decade. The supporters were far from happy. They criticised their new manager and, like most supporters, made no allowance for the fact that it had been his first managerial role. But as Joe was later to admit, "Why should they, like everyone else they want the best." What made it even worse was the fact that their city rivals, Wednesday, were promoted from the Second Division at the same time.

"Relegation leaves a scar on the soul," Joe would say years later. It was a tough start in management, and he received criticism from supporters and directors. The large board interfered at every opportunity, although Joe could always count on the support of Senior Atkin, who often pointed out that "Joe is the manager" and that he should be "left to manage".

Said Joe: "I soon learned the value of a good chairman. There were times when Senior Atkin 'mothered' me too much. But it was always encouraging, when directors were shouting the odds at board meetings, to hear Senior's blunt question, 'Have we asked t'manager what he thinks?' He continued to believe that managers were there to manage. On one occasion, a director told him that two heads were always better than one. 'It all depends on what's in the other head!' said Senior."

Joe respected authority throughout his life, but the problems he encountered at United shaped his views on the relationship between manager and directors: "The manager must have confidence in the board and they in him. Each side must know what the other is doing. More trouble is caused in football by what isn't said than by what is. If a manager wants to buy a player, he must be able to make the board see why that player is important. There is no substitute for confidence and communication. If the board want a player, the manager must be kept in the picture. Whoever is bought, the manager is the man who has to fit the player in. One wrong piece of the jigsaw spoils the whole picture."

During this difficult period at Sheffield United, Joe formed one opinion that would be pertinent at one of his later clubs, Manchester City: "Divided boards are no good to any club. It spells ruin in the long run. That is why respect is another important characteristic in managers and directors."

There was one particular United director who believed he knew considerably more about football than Joe. During one disagreement the director moaned: "The manager thinks he knows everything about this game. I played football myself, you know." Joe retorted: "Who did you play for, Liverpool Corinthians?" The director went on: "No, I played football, and as my milkman says to me ..." Joe exploded: "To hell with what your milkman says! You pay me all this money to advise you and you listen to your milkman!"

The same director once informed Joe that he had been watching football for over 40 years and so he must be something of an expert. This time the young manager retorted: "My mother-in-law has been sitting alongside my father-in-law watching him drive for 45 years, but she still can't drive!"

Throughout his time at Sheffield the size of the board and the attitude of certain directors annoyed Joe, but as this was his first managerial appointment he was uncertain of what to expect. He was fortunate, however, in having people he could turn to for advice. He had studied Matt Busby's techniques at Manchester United, while Bill Shankly of Huddersfield Town, and later Liverpool, was always one of the first to phone if things went wrong for Joe. Joe later reflected on his other mentors: "I learned a lot from Billy Walker, who could get the best out of a player, Tom Whittaker, George Kay, Stan Cullis, but Harry Storer influenced me a lot. He didn't like directors and he swore awful."

Harry Storer was a tough, blunt, literate manager, who built promotion-winning teams on shoestring budgets at Coventry City, Birmingham and Derby County. Above all, Storer valued players with guts and speed. Joe was always fond of telling people about the time Storer came into the dressing-room on a Monday morning and asked an inside-forward if he would like to come out on to the pitch to help him find something. After they had been scouring the grass for some time the player said, "What

Harry Storer - a tough, blunt literate manager who built promotion winning teams on shoestring budgets at several different clubs, he had quite an influence on Joe's approach to management.

exactly are we looking for, Boss?" Without halting the search, Harry Storer said, "That bloody hole you were hiding in on Saturday."

Then there was the occasion when Storer took his Derby team to play at Sheffield United, and Joe got a bit incensed at "some of the clog that was being dished out". He phoned Storer and said, "Well, Harry, you gave us a bit of a kicking on Saturday." "Okay," said Harry Storer. "Name the players, Joe. Who was it that was doing the kicking?" Joe quickly reeled off five names and said, "There, what are you going to do about it, are you going to give them a rollicking?" And Harry Storer said, "No, I'm going to give the other six the rollicking."

Storer was once asked what the ideal board of directors should consist of. "The ideal number is three," he replied. "One dead, one dying and one on holiday in South America."

At times, Joe cast his eyes around the 15-man Sheffield United board, thought of Harry Storer and smiled to himself.

The 1955-6 season had one personal highlight for Joe, for he showed the public that his broken leg had healed. He made an appearance for Sheffield United in a friendly, a 2-0 victory over Reading. It was proof, if it was needed, that Joe just could not keep away from playing the sport. Management was a poor substitute for playing, but it was better than the grocery business!

Joe also played for the Starlights XI, a team of managers who played testimonial and charity games. His enthusiasm for playing was to remain for some years yet, as he remembered later in his life: "When we had friendlies or charity games, all the players used to ask, 'Who's he going to drop?'"

Joe's Sheffield United side was not quite good enough to climb out of the Second Division in the next two seasons, finishing seventh and sixth. There were, however, a few bright spots. The most enjoyable one was a fourth-round FA Cup tie at Tottenham Hotspur in 1958.

Tottenham were enjoying great success - FA Cup semi-finalists in 1956, League runners-up

BLADES BATTER SPURS IN CUP TRIUMPH

RESULTS, TABLES

TREBLE CHANCE

TWO GOALS IN 8 MINUTES SHOCK SPURS

Spurs' goalkeeper Ted Ditchburn cannot stop United's first minute opening goal from Derek Pace.

Song thrill for 11 Sheffield heroes

By DAVE PARDON

Tottenham Hotspur ...... 0 Sheffield United 3

SEVEN minutes to go, Tottenham are tottering out of the Cup, throwing a last desperate attack down the left wing in an effort to salvage something from the ruins of shattering defeat.

That attack, like all the earlier ones, is checked From it Brian Richardson emerges to drop a 50-yard swinging pass at Hawksworth's feet. Norman, caught between Hawksworth and Pace, chooses to cover Pace .. and Hawksworth fires a 20-yard shot wide of the diving Ditchburn.

The ends of Tottenham's double-decker stand erupt From one comes a roar that lasts for the rest of the match. from the other, a thousand voices singing " Ilkla Moor Bah' At." The effect is electrifying.

And for long after the match, United players can talk of nothing but that sound. "Spine-chilling," says Alan Hodgkinson. "I've never heard anything like it . . . it made me go wobbly at the knees."

"Wonderful," says Joe Shaw. "In those last eight minutes we could have beaten anyone."

Harry Latham, United trainer who went to Bramall Lane as a player in 1938 . . . never heard

in 1956-7 and near the top in 1957-8. The Spurs stars included veteran goalkeeper Ted Ditchburn and Irish international wing-half Danny Blanchflower, soon to be voted the season's Footballer of the Year.

Joe saw Blanchflower as the major danger to United's chance of success in the Cup tie. He told the players, "Spurs have a key man - cut out Danny Blanchflower and the game's yours."

To deal with Blanchflower, Joe told his left-winger, Bill Hodgson, the former St Johnstone player, to follow Blanchflower wherever he went: "When you get out there, look for the white shirt with number four on the back. When you see it, latch on. That's Danny Blanchflower. Wherever Danny goes, you go. If Danny goes and sits in the stand, you take the next seat. Stop Danny, and the rest of the team will take us through."

Hodgson, a great team man, followed Joe's plan perfectly. Sheffield United's travelling support gave their team the encouragement they needed right from the start of the game, and United scored in the first minute. Young England full-back Graham Shaw lobbed a free-kick into the penalty area. The ball bobbed along the heads of two United players, Brian Richardson and Billy Russell, before Derek Pace brought the ball down and scored from 10 yards with his left foot.

More excitement followed seven minutes later. Johnny Hills, Spurs' right-back, suffering from concussion, picked up the ball with his hands before it had run over the touchline, giving away a free-kick. Graham Shaw again took the kick, and this time floated the ball to the head of Bill Russell who, "with a contortionist's twist of the neck," according to one report, sent the ball spinning past Ditchburn for United's second goal.

Spurs now faced an uphill task on a difficult surface. Harry Carpenter, in the *Daily Mail,* said the pitch was like a skating rink. Bill McGowran in the *London Evening News* said the players "slid like toboggans for yards" when they went down at speed.

Spurs had most of the play yet Mercer's men, especially his hard-working defence, kept the pressure away from Alan Hodgkinson, United's England goalkeeper. In the second half, Spurs made a couple of impressive strikes at goal, but as the game wore on it became more obvious that United would win. Seven minutes from the end, they counter-attacked with a 50-yard pass from Brian Richardson to Derek Hawksworth, who fired a 20-yard shot past Ditchburn for the third United goal.

Sheffield United supporters among the 51,186 crowd erupted with choruses of the Yorkshire anthem, "Ilkla Moor baht'at". The sound was electrifying. Joe could not believe the noise and fervour of his team's supporters. As a player he had experienced this kind of support at Everton, and of course Arsenal, but as a manager it was something new.

After the 3-0 victory, Joe was quick to point out that he was grateful for the way the supporters had got behind the team, especially during the last seven minutes. He told Dave Pardon, the *Sheffield Telegraph* reporter, to "thank them all, from all of us."

The supporters were rewarded with a home tie against West Bromwich Albion in the fifth round. For Joe, the time leading up to the game was extremely busy. As usual, he was participating in all the training. He coached, encouraged, and motivated his players in the mornings, and then, in the afternoons, he set about the administrative tasks that were still relatively new

BLADES FORCE A CUP-TIE REPLAY!

RESULTS, TABLES

TREBLE CHANCE
13 DRAWS

to him. During this period, Joe became more than fully aware of all the other areas of responsibility that fall to a successful manager.

In the build-up to the game, Joe demanded that his players play simple, straightforward, orthodox football, and give one hundred per cent effort. He was convinced that the side would win. Joe was a great believer in letting people play, and for this match he was determined not to let his side get bogged down in tactics: "No gimmicks. Just a hundred per cent fight!"

Something else happened in the build-up - Joe got into trouble for forgetting that his club was Sheffield United *Cricket* and Football Club. Here is his version of the story: "Bramall Lane, the home of Sheffield United, is also a home of Yorkshire cricket, and the cricket ground is, of course, sacred sward, not even to be walked upon by the feet of non-cricketers, let alone footballers in studded boots. We were about to play West Bromwich in the Cup but our practice pitch was impossible to use because of frost, and there was this beautiful cricket pitch. Out of my mind with Cup fever I played across the cricket square. Bells rang, people came running from all sides. They looked uncomfortably like a lynching party. I would not have been surprised to see rope nooses in their hands. No one actually shot at me but that would not have surprised me either. I could hardly have committed a worse blasphemy if I had burst into a bawdy song during a service in York Minster!"

There was already a debate about whether cricket should continue at Bramall Lane, but, meanwhile, the football side of the club had perennial problems. Seeding the football pitch, and pre-season training were affected by the cricket season. For the West Brom Cup tie, the open-air stands near the cricket pavilion were used, but spectators had a poor view because they had to look across the cricket ground to see a football game in the distance. They also got soaked when it rained during the game. Creating a fourth side boosted the attendance to 55,847.

Throughout the game, Joe's side did what he asked. Every player, from confident goalkeeper Alan Hodgkinson, to the non-stop, play-anywhere Billy Hodgson, gave everything to the United cause. West Bromwich Albion, third in the First Division, were an excellent attacking side who had scored 68 goals in 29 matches. United, on the other hand, were a mid-table Second Division side, with only 42 goals to their credit.

West Brom took a 17th-minute lead when Derek Kevan crossed from the left for Ronnie Allen to score easily. The score remained 1-0 in favour of the First Division side until the 77th minute, when Kevin Lewis, a player Joe had discovered in his native Ellesmere Port, scored the equaliser. The game ended 1-1. The replay was the following Wednesday at the Hawthorns.

United's bold bid to reach the sixth round ended at West Brom, where Albion defeated them 4-1 before a crowd of 57,503. If United had beaten Albion they would have faced Manchester United at Bramall Lane less than a month after the Munich Air Disaster. The crash had claimed the lives of eight players, eight journalists and seven others. The Manchester Reds had somehow defeated Sheffield Wednesday, against all the odds, in the fifth round.

The Munich disaster had a profound impact on Joe, as it did with all people in football. He had lost one great footballing colleague and friend, Frank Swift, while another, Matt Busby, hovered close to death in intensive care for a long time before beginning his slow recovery. Joe was also very friendly with the journalists killed in the crash. They included George Follows of the *Daily Herald*, who used to telephone regularly. Years later, when football fans taunted

Joe Shaw stayed put so his side stayed in

Sheffield U. .... 1 West Bromwich A ... 1   By DAVE PARDON

MANAGER Joe Mercer's pre-Cup-tie comments in last Wednesday's "Sheffield Telegraph" were: "No gimmicks ... just orthodox football, straightforward ideas, and 100 per cent. fight."

That is how his team played it, particularly the "100 per cent. fight."

And how they fought!

From a supremely confident Hodgkinson to non-stop, tackle-everybody, play - anywhere Hodgson, they gave all that was asked—and more.

For 45 minutes United's great heart seemed doomed to be broken.

West Brom used every move in the soccer repertoire — wing-to-wing pass, splitting through-ball, close pass, and delicate but deadly chips over challenging defenders. Their game was near-perfection.

To Derek Pace who, against quick - thinking, quick - moving defenders, looked every inch a top-class player. Out-headed by Kennedy, he set about beating the centre-half on the ground. He never gave Kennedy an inch, made him glad to get the ball and get it away—regardless of where.

Master touch

Behind it all was the master-touch of Allen—deep, sinister, fantastically accurate.

To Joe Shaw's everlasting credit is the fact that the centre-half never gave in to what must have been sore temptation to go after Allen ... the move Robson and Kevan hoped Shaw would make so that they would have the middle at their mercy.

Shaw stayed put, blocked the middle, and waited for the inside men to come to him.

Only once, in the 17th minute, did he let Allen through; then, with Kevan swerving to the left wing, United's defence was stretched. The ball was crossed and Allen got an easy goal.

Nagged away

Great saves by Hodgkinson. Coldwell's finest display of the season, and lightning tackles by Graham Shaw, Richardson, and Summers kept Albion to that one goal, and all the time rain increased the glossy appearance of the pitch.

In the second half, United went boldly for the initiative.

The mud told on Allen's accuracy, on the battling penetration of Robson and Kevan, and on the confidence of the defence, but what told even more was the nagging persistence of Pace, Russell, and Hodgson.

Lewis, who had been having a bad time against Williams, was switched to inside-left, Hodgson to outside.

Safety-first move was anything but

Derby Co. .... 2 Notts Co. 1

THIS match looked precisely what it was, a scrappy struggle between two teams at the bottom of Division II.

Neither team displayed skill or even determination in a high cross wind which handicapped ball control. The three goals scored were all helped on their way at some stage by a defender. Brown tried hard as leader but received little help from Parry and Ryan.

GIFT GOAL

Derby were lucky to be presented with a gift goal after two minutes. It came from a back pass from Chatham, which Linton had no hope of collecting. Ryan had merely to tap the ball into the net from a yard out.

Notts dominated much of the play after that, but it was Derby who scored next, Woodhead netting from Brown.

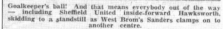

Goalkeeper's ball! And that means everybody out of the way — including Sheffield United inside-forward Hawksworth, skidding to a standstill as West Brom's Sanders clamps on to another centre.

Manchester United about the disaster, Joe was always annoyed, because the whole football world had been damaged that sad day in February 1958.

Although Sheffield United finished the 1957-8 season in sixth place in Division Two, they were only five points behind the Champions, West Ham United. Joe's reputation as a manager was growing, and his name was linked to larger clubs, including Arsenal.

Arsenal had not won a trophy since Joe captained them to their 1952-3 Championship success. They were obviously missing Joe's strong leadership on the field. The 1957-8 season was particularly dire. The Gunners were knocked out of the FA Cup in the third round by Northampton, a Third Division (South) side, and, following a 3-2 League defeat at home to Blackpool, supporters demonstrated outside the Highbury ground.

The club's programme for that match carried an astonishing piece of criticism, which perhaps fuelled the demonstrations. It read: "The present position is the culmination of an insidious trend dating back to 1952 when the team, beginning to wilt in skill, was carried forward to reasonable success by its determination and the superb captaincy of Joe Mercer."

The article was certainly considerably different to the type of club propaganda normally printed in football programmes. It condemned the Arsenal set-up and seemed to promote the idea that Joe Mercer should be the next Arsenal manager. Joe was interviewed by reporters to gauge his feelings. In typical style, Joe spoke of the team spirit he was a part of when he was

Sheffield United directors get their way

MERCER SAYS 'NO'

Turns down the job of Arsenal boss

By ALF BALLARD

JOE MERCER IS NOT JOINING THE ARSENAL.
Last night he turned down the plum £3,000-a-year Highbury job to stay with Sheffield United, the club that gave him his first chance in managership.

He reached this decision after a three-hour meeting with the Sheffield United Board at the end of which he came out beaming. With him, beaming equally broadly, was chairman Leslie Lewis, who issued the following statement:
"The question of the offer

'Mr Sparks' takes over at Leeds

By BOB PENNINGTON

JOE MERCER said "No" to a £3,000-a-year job as boss of his old club Arsenal last night. He stays with Second Division Sheffield United.

Mercer talked over the Arsenal offer in a three-hour meeting with the United board last night.

Then they made this shock statement: "Out of deference to the wishes of his board, MR MERCER HAS DECIDED TO REMAIN WITH SHEFFIELD UNITED."

United chairman Leslie Lewis added: "The fans will be delighted with Mr Mercer's decision."

Mercer's unexpected snub to Highbury is a major defeat for Arsenal's autocratic chairman Sir Bracewell Smith, who

captain, and spoke of the great hope that all at Arsenal would work together to end the current predicament.

As the season ended, Arsenal manager 'Gentleman Jack' Crayston, resigned after 24 years service with the club. Crayston had taken over in October 1956 when Tom Whittaker died of a heart attack. Whittaker, unable to repeat the success of the early 1950s, had become ill as the pressure mounted and, despite being ordered to take a six-month rest when it was discovered that he was suffering from nervous exhaustion, the popular and respected manager passed away. In many ways he had become a victim of his own success, because he had built a hugely successful side, and then, when it broke up, he felt he had to put all his efforts into achieving the same again.

Joe was naturally upset when he heard that Whittaker had died. After all, it was the Arsenal manager who had made Joe believe in himself again following his disagreements with Theo Kelly at Everton. Joe, like so many others, had hoped that Crayston would bring back the club's glory days. Crayston resigned after the board had refused to give him the kind of transfer money he believed was necessary to rebuild the side.

After Crayston's resignation, Joe quickly became the man Arsenal wanted and the newspapers were convinced he would leave Sheffield for a chance to manage his former club. One newspaper even claimed that he had accepted a salary of £3,000 a year on the proviso that he would be left completely in charge of the team. The press pestered Joe, the Sheffield directors, and everyone connected with Arsenal to find out the truth. All was revealed by the end of the first week of June.

On Friday 30 May, four weeks into the close-season, Joe met Arsenal's autocratic chairman, Sir Bracewell Smith, who offered his club's former player a contract for the previously mentioned £3,000 a year. Joe did not accept there and then. He wanted time to think it over and discuss things with his wife Norah and son David.

The Mercers were settled in Dore, Sheffield, and the new post would mean a move to London. As a player Joe could train anywhere and commute to Highbury, but as a manager it was impossible to run the club from a distance.

Apart from family matters and of course his 'much loved' grocery business, Joe had to consider what he had achieved at Sheffield. It was true that he had experienced problems with certain directors, one reason why he was adamant he wanted a free-hand at Arsenal, but over-all he was happy with the support he had received. The people of Sheffield had mixed views of Joe - he had been forced to sell certain favourite players and had taken the club down to the Second Division, thus provoking a certain amount of unrest and criticism. On the other hand the supporters had been magnificent during the 1958 Cup run and their renditions of "Ilkla Moor baht'at" had provided Joe and the team with the backing they needed. The supporters also recognised that Joe had discovered some exciting young players.

The team Joe had built at United was not a great side, but was certainly full of qualities he admired, like team spirit. It had taken him almost three years to get his side to its present level - would it take him the same length of time at Arsenal?

Joe was uncertain, even though he was fully aware of Arsenal's stature in the game. "Arsenal is the greatest club in the world," he had said earlier in the year. "It breaks my heart to see them struggling now. They are too good for this." In fact, Arsenal almost certainly meant more to him than Sheffield United, who he knew did not have the necessary resources to compete at the highest level. The cricket side of United prevented the club from building a great stadium and appeared to hamper football in many other ways.

All of these points crossed Joe's mind that weekend as he pondered his future. On Monday 2 June, Joe met the Sheffield United directors to talk it over. The meeting lasted over three hours and at the end the United board made this announcement: "Out of deference to the wishes of the board, Mr Mercer has decided to remain with Sheffield United." Leslie Lewis, who had taken over as the United chairman, added: "The fans will be delighted with Mr Mercer's decision."

Joe, who left the meeting smiling as usual, commented: "I've made my decision and I feel happy about it. I have been extremely happy with the Sheffield club and greatly appreciate the telegrams and messages I have received today. But beyond that I'm not prepared to say one word. You can understand this is very delicate."

He refused to add any more about what was discussed in the meeting, or about the reasons he turned down the Arsenal job. One thing that was not revealed at the time was that Joe's five-year contract with United, due to run until 1960, was cancelled as part of his agreement to stay. This was at Joe's request, but United felt that the Arsenal job was the one that Joe craved more than any other. If he was prepared to turn that down then surely he would turn down any other club that came after him, or so they believed.

Joe's decision was seen by many as the biggest snub ever given to Arsenal. It astonished most of the footballing public. Joe's act of loyalty certainly boosted his already impressive image and made everyone aware that he still believed he could achieve something at United, even if the cricketers would not let him practice!

Joe covers his ears as son David listens to Elvis Presley records.

Chapter Twelve

THE MOVE TO VILLA

'The Boss' has firm ideas on how players should be treated off the field. "I try to treat my players as I would have expected a manager to treat me," he says. He's a non-smoker and he's hardly a big drinker, but he doesn't frown on players having a smoke or drink.

Peter McParland, *Going for Goal*

JOE'S loyalty to United, after being offered the job as Arsenal manager, proved to the Sheffield faithful that he meant to achieve something at the club, although there were doubts about what actually happened in the meeting. Many believed United had refused to release Joe, a point fuelled by comments made by the Arsenal board. Said Arsenal chairman Sir Bracewell Smith: "Mercer applied for the job. When I saw him he told me he had another two years of his contract with Sheffield United to run. I said he couldn't be considered for the job while still under contract to another club and would first have to get his release from Sheffield. That was the situation."

Those comments created considerable discussion in Sheffield, and many supporters reviewed Joe's period at the club. In the early days the supporters had been unhappy with his dealings in the transfer market. He sold players they loved and appeared to place a lot of emphasis on younger reserve players. What they did not realise was that Joe had to sell players to enable the club to survive. Occasionally his methods were cunning, but his actions were always in the best interest of the club.

United wing-half Jim Iley was wanted by Tottenham Hotspur. When Joe travelled to London to discuss the deal, Spurs offered £20,000, money United urgently needed. Joe did not want to sell but at that figure he could not refuse. When he discussed the matter with Iley, the player was not really interested in a move to London, but Joe had a card up his sleeve. Joe knew that Iley planned to marry Lil Grainger, the sister of United's outside-left, Colin Grainger. Lil and Jim needed a house and Joe knew that Spurs were prepared to provide a club house.

Joe contacted Lil, who lived in a village near Doncaster, by asking the local police station to pass on a message - "Ring Joe Mercer and reverse the charges" - because the house had no telephone. When Lil telephoned, the United manager used all his charm to tell her all about this fantastic house he had seen, and persuaded her to head south and look at it. She travelled to London, viewed the house and immediately fell in love with it. She then returned to Yorkshire to persuade Jim Iley, who was duly sold to Spurs for £20,000.

Then the transfer worked against Joe. United fans hero-worshipped Iley, and could not understand why Joe had "forced him out". "There was almost a public protest meeting to get me sacked!" Joe said later about the strength of feeling at the time.

The same happened in February 1957 when Joe made another sale involving the Grainger family. This time he sold Colin Grainger, an England international, to Sunderland for £17,000 plus Sunderland outside-left Sammy Kemp. The deal almost fell through at the last moment as 22-year-old Grainger had second thoughts during a two-hour meeting on 4 February. The following day the deal was finalised in a York hotel, and Joe returned to Sheffield with Sammy Kemp, his new player. Joe was hurt by the tremendous criticism from the public that awaited him in Sheffield.

Despite Joe's refusal to join Arsenal, he was aware that Sheffield United would never match the truly great League sides. He wanted to further himself and manage a major club. He was ambitious and longed for the feeling he had experienced and enjoyed at Goodison and Highbury. Within only a couple of months of the Arsenal offer, his chance came again. Eric Houghton was sacked as manager of Aston Villa.

Aston Villa was a big club with as much tradition as Arsenal and Everton. Villa had won the League Championship on six occasions and the FA Cup a record seven times, the last time as recently as 1957. To most of the footballing public, Aston Villa was, and still is, a giant, while Sheffield United was a 'nearly' club. Moreover, Villa Park was one of the most famous club grounds in the country. It had been a venue for international matches and many FA Cup semi-finals, and had held as many as 76,588 for a 1946 FA Cup tie with Derby County.

The 1958-9 season had not been going well for Villa. Eric Houghton's team had won only five of the first 21 League games, paving the way for a change of manager. Villa were heading for relegation and the board felt they needed to act quickly.

In Sheffield, Joe was becoming frustrated as his United side ran into injury problems. In the close-season he had signed Ronnie Simpson from Huddersfield Town, with Derek Hawksworth moving in exchange, but Simpson was slow to settle. Joe began to regret not leaving for Arsenal when he had the chance. During December 1958 he took steps towards a change. On Monday 22 December he told the Sheffield United board that he wanted to apply for the Villa job. Afterwards, Leslie Lewis, the United chairman, spoke to reporters: "I was completely astounded when we were faced with Mr Mercer's decision. We discussed the matter in his absence and came to the conclusion we had done everything possible to make him happy and that we had succeeded. But if he wanted to apply for the post we could not stand in his way, so we wished him well."

That night Joe wrote out his application and posted it at approximately nine o'clock. Both Joe and his wife Norah openly discussed the matter with reporters. They did not see a need for secrecy. Norah told them that if Joe's application was accepted then she would be sorry to

MERCER TO APPLY FOR VILLA POST

JOE MERCER, the Sheffield United manager and former Everton and Arsenal player, last night told his board that he intends to apply for the vacant position of manager of Aston Villa.

leave their home in Dore, Sheffield: "Everybody in Sheffield has been wonderful towards us. But where Joe goes I go, and I never attempt to influence him in his decisions. Where he is happy, I am happy."

Norah had been used to her husband's out-of-the-blue statements, such as "I'm off to Arsenal", or "We're going to Sheffield". This time she had been given a little bit more warning, and was well prepared for the new challenges in the Midlands.

On Joe's return from the post-box he told Derek Wallis, a journalist for the *Daily Mirror*, that he had not yet resigned his position at United, but pointed out that he was extremely keen to take the Villa job: "I have not resigned from Sheffield United. I thought it was the best thing to do to inform my board that I intended to apply. I want the Aston Villa job. This time nothing will make me change my mind. It is not a question of money. I must say that. In fact, I have been wonderfully treated at Bramall Lane."

Daily Mirror
TUES DEC 23 1958
THE BIGGEST DAILY SALE IN THE UNIVERSE
2½   No. 17,115

Managers in Soccer shocks

MERCER: I'LL TAKE THE VILLA JOB

FRONT PAGE SPORT

'Protest' umpire chosen

MEL McInnes and Ron Wright were yesterday nominated to umpire in the second Test between Australia and England at Melbourne, starting on December 31.
Peter May, the England

★ JOE MERCER, Sheffield-United boss, said last night: "I want the Aston Villa job.

JOE MERCER, Sheffield United's manager, has finally bowed to the persistent call from First Division Soccer. He wants to be Aston Villa's new boss.

By DEREK WALLIS

night, I phoned Mercer's home after he had surprised the Sheffield board with his decision to apply for the post.
His wife told me: "He'll

He has just gone out to post his application to Aston Villa."
The application, I am told, is a mere formality. The post, carrying a salary of around £3,000 a year, is sure to go to Mercer, who

a question of money. I must say that. In fact I have been wonderfully treated at Bramall-lane.
"It is just that the prospects at Villa Park appeal to me tremendously. I know I have a hard fight ahead but I like the idea of a challenge.
"I want to have the facilities to expand which do not exist at Bramall-lane due to circumstances

He continued to outline his movements and views by saying: "The prospects at Villa Park appeal to me tremendously. I know I have a hard fight ahead but I like the idea of a challenge. I want to have the facilities to expand which do not exist at Bramall Lane due to circumstances beyond United's control. After all, poor gates do not help clubs who want to buy players."

As a final comment Joe revealed that he was more than happy with the way his board had treated him. Relations had improved. In the early days he had a few disagreements with certain directors, but as time pressed on both Joe and the board learnt how to work together: "My relations with the board have been the happiest. No manager could be better treated by a club. It will be a wrench to leave the players who I think are booked for promotion."

Joe's postal application was followed up by a telephone call on 23 December, the day Villa were to hold a board meeting to discuss the position. On that day, every daily newspaper speculated about the salary Joe would be on, and about the reasons why he was trying to leave Bramall Lane. Many blamed the supporters, pointing out that crowds of around 18,000 prevented Joe from receiving the financial backing he longed for.

In addition to the comments about support, the newspapers expressed surprise at the ease of it all. They knew that Joe had been tempted to join Arsenal earlier in the year, and believed that he would not be interested in any other club until his Sheffield contract ended in 1960. What they did not realise, until Joe and the Sheffield board informed them, was that Joe's contract had been ripped up when he turned down Arsenal. Without the contract Joe was free to join whosoever he wished.

As was by now almost a foregone conclusion, Aston Villa offered Joe the post of manager. Joe accepted on the understanding that he was a manager in the true sense of the word. He demanded to be fully in control of team affairs, something that was still rather unusual at the time. Eric Houghton, Villa's previous manager, had made it quite clear and obvious when he left the club that he had not been in full control. Both Newcastle United and Sunderland were similar to Villa, with the team clearly being run from the board-room until the appointments of Charlie Mitten and Alan Brown, respectively.

The major clubs started to realise that success seemed to come from clubs with a strong manager, such as Joe's friends Matt Busby at Manchester United and Stan Cullis at Wolverhampton Wanderers. Aston Villa now wanted that kind of leadership and naturally expected the success that both United and Wolves had experienced.

Before Joe was free to manage Villa, he had one more game to manage at Sheffield United. For the record, the game was away to Grimsby Town on Thursday 25 December - United's last-ever fixture on Christmas Day. Ronnie Simpson and Derek Pace scored United's goals in a 2-1 victory, and Joe left a winning team.

The following day Joe was manager of Aston Villa, when his side were defeated at Old Trafford 2-1 by Manchester United, before a crowd of over sixty-three thousand. On the 27th, Villa met United in the return, but Joe's first home game ended in a 2-0 defeat before a Villa Park crowd of fifty-six thousand. Joe's Christmas may not have been successful, but at least he knew how difficult the task of keeping Villa in the First Division was going to be.

The first game of the New Year saw further misery for Joe, as West Ham United piled on the pressure with a 2-1 win at Villa Park. However, as some respite from the League peril, a 2-1 win against Rotherham United was the start of a good FA Cup run. Villa won away at Chelsea in the fourth round, and a hat trick by the industrious Ron Wylie helped see off Everton, 4-1 at Goodison Park, in the fifth.

Prior to the Everton game few rated Villa's chances. Joe's side were struggling at the foot of the division, while Everton were seven places higher. But Joe really excelled in preparing his players, and stressed the importance of keeping a grip on the key Everton players. He had been really excited about taking a team back to his old club, and was full of pride at how well Villa played, especially as they had performed for much of the time with only ten men. Billy Myerscough had been forced to leave the pitch with a cut eye.

On 28 February, the morning of Villa's sixth-round tie at Burnley, Joe told *Daily Mail* reporter Jack Wood of the boost in morale the club was getting from the FA Cup run. They were still under threat of relegation, but Joe saw the Cup as a way to get away from the hassles of the League: "It's crazy to say we would like to get out of the Cup as soon as possible. Success has taken the boys out of the gloomy mood I found when I went to Villa Park. To be in the semi-final would be a wonderful thing. The public would consider us a good side ... well, at

Scene: Hillsborough. Time: 4.16 Saturday. Down go Nottingham Forest's Quigley (right), and Aston Villa goalkeeper Sims. But only scorer Quigley gets up smiling...

Wembley pass only boast

Nottm Forest ...... 1 Aston Villa 0   By ROSS JENKINSON

At Hillsborough. Att.: 65,107.   Rec.: £16,484.

Cup semi-final, this was a tie to be easily forgotten. It was a run-of-the-l match, with Forest obtaining their passport to Wembley deservedly but unconvincingly.

Villa boss Joe Mercer had no complaints. His players considered referee Ernie Crawford robbed them of an equaliser chance, ruling "hands" against McParland late in the second half, when everybody thought he had dropped an offside-decision clanger.

least a better one than our desperate League position suggests. But I hope for our sake that we win in one game. We cannot afford to go into one of those marathon replay series."

Joe's fears were partly realised. Villa drew no score with Burnley and the tie went to a replay. Then at Turf Moor, Peter McParland scored twice and Villa were through to an FA Cup semi-final for a record-breaking 16th time.

Joe was now only one step away from Wembley in his first season in charge at Villa. He could hardly believe it. At Villa Joe had found a club that seemed quite happy, possessed a never-say-die attitude, with supporters who appeared tremendously loyal. The size of the crowds Villa were attracting were enormous when compared to Sheffield United, and Joe appreciated the support considerably.

In the semi-final, played at Hillsborough, Villa were defeated 1-0 by Joe's father's former club, Nottingham Forest. Joe was convinced that Villa had scored a valid goal: "We thought that Peter McParland had scored a very good goal. I still think that the referee had given him offside and not seen the Forest full-back on the line! The ref's subsequent explanation was that Peter had handled the ball a few moments before. But how that was possible with the ball on the ground all the time, I just don't know."

JOE MERCER. LARGE FINE OLD TEAM SPIRIT

The Cup defeat reduced Villa's determination, and the fight for First Division survival continued right to the last match, against neighbours West Brom at the Hawthorns on 29 April. If Villa won they would be safe and fellow strugglers, Manchester City, would be relegated with already-doomed Portsmouth. Before the kick-off, City and Villa both had 29 points, although Villa had a better goal average.

On the same night, Manchester City beat Leicester City 3-1, before a crowd of over 46,000, so Villa needed a victory. They were winning 1-0 from a 66th-minute Gerry Hitchens goal, and Villa fans thought they were safe. Then, two minutes from the end, Albion's Ronnie Allen fired a shot past the Villa 'keeper Nigel Sims to level the scores. The score remained 1-1 and condemned Joe's side to Division Two.

For Joe it was the second occasion his team had been relegated, but he didn't know the result immediately. He had left the Hawthorns before the late equaliser as he had to attend a banquet in Wolverhampton to celebrate Billy Wright's 100th cap. When he learned the result, Joe was devastated. He had left the Hawthorns believing Manchester City had been relegated and not his Villa side. Joe's anguish was intensified when he received a cruel anonymous telegram from Sheffield: "Congratulations, Joe. You have done it again!"

His managerial career at Villa had started in the same way as that at Sheffield United - with relegation - but Joe still believed he was capable of bringing glory back to Villa Park. Villa were not another Sheffield United. They had great support - an average crowd of 32,837 during the relegation season and approximately 35,000 in their first season back in Division Two. Sheffield United could never match those figures.

In an interview at the start of the 1959-60 season Joe proudly extolled Villa's virtues: "All I am concerned with is Aston Villa. We've got a football empire here, everything. The public is here - we have average gates of thirty-six thousand. The ground is here - the name Aston Villa arouses more enthusiasm wherever we go than even Arsenal did when I was at Highbury. And the directors are right behind me - I am in sole charge. I have a free hand. Aston Villa will rise again. It may take time, but we are coming back. The whole place is begging and praying for a great Aston Villa side again - and I'm going to do my damnedest to give it to them. If I don't, if I fail, then it will be my fault. I shall take the blame."

Joe, like all managers, was aware that the ultimate responsibility was his. He was paid £3,500 a year to manage, a vast amount in 1959, and he would not hide.

By now Joe had developed clear ideas about coaching, and he would not revise his ideas for most his managerial career. This is what he told youngsters: "You learn by playing. Secondly, by playing with and against better players. Third, and a bad third, is coaching. And have some fun out of it. You learn by playing with and against better players, and the only way you'll progress is by playing for better teams. If you get a chance to play for a better team, you must go. You've got to be fit, but it's no use being fit unless you've got a bit of skill. It's no use being fit and skilful unless you play together as a side. It's as simple as that. And you learn by watching."

When Joe first moved to Villa he was told by the chairman, Chris Buckley, that the club had approximately £25,000 available for players. Joe decided that the money would be better invested in a training ground, as this would help him develop younger players. At Sheffield United, Joe had always attempted to develop youngsters and now, at Villa Park, he wanted to provide them with the best possible facilities. The new training ground was excellent. It had two enormous practice pitches, bowling greens, tennis courts, and a clubhouse with all the usual facilities. The ground even had floodlights, a real innovation in the late 1950s.

At that time, no other club could match Villa's training facilities. Other managers would have purchased players with the funds but Joe was looking to the future. Charlie Aitken, the Villa left-back who holds the appearance record for the club, played for Joe during the early 1960s and remembers those first training facilities, and what happened to them after Joe left the club. Says Aitken: "We had the most wonderful training ground, Hercules Sports Ground, about three hundred yards away from the club, just up the road. Beautiful two acres, two football pitches, a beautiful bowling green - which we used for five-a-side, plus accommodation. And they sold that for housing, so we had no training pitch! We used to have to go, beg, steal, and borrow training pitches from all the local factories to train in the mornings. We had nowhere to train. That was from the mid-sixties until 1968 when Mr Ellis came to take over. Before that I was better treated as an amateur!" Joe Mercer made sure training was a priority. He felt it would help him develop the younger players in the way he wanted. Joe worked hard with all the playing staff and Charlie Aitken remembers that Joe used to stress the importance of performing to the best of your ability: "Something Joe told a crowd of us young apprentices at Villa Park has always stuck in my memory. 'Remember, lads, football is a cruel, hard game. Only the best will survive.' he said."

Joe made everyone at Villa aware that he was aiming for the top by the time his five-year contract ended. He did not expect success immediately, but he did expect to be in a position challenging for the game's top honours within those five years: "I came to Villa because I have ambition, and because I wanted to. And remember, you can't work miracles in five months. It may take five years - the length of my contract."

He made sure he considered the strengths and weaknesses of every player. After each game he would write out his views on each player's performance, and would give them all marks. He also made sure every reserve and youth player was considered in the same way. He told reporters that every player in every one of Villa's six sides was graded in the same way. But Joe soon scrapped two of Villa's six teams. "I can't find 11 good players, let alone sixty-six!" he said.

Football through-and-through, that was Joe
... even when ten-pin bowling!

Joe and his Villa squad at a hotel in West Kirby in 1959.

Chapter Thirteen

THE PUSH FOR PROMOTION

Statistics do not tell the true story behind Villa's promotion season. There was much more to it than games won and lost; goals scored and conceded. There was the inspiring leadership and the camaraderie of manager Joe Mercer whose cheery 'Hello, mate' brightened the dreariest winter's day. The famous Mercer grin was an ever-present quantity in victory or defeat.

Peter Morris, *Aston Villa*, 1960

THE FIGHT against relegation had been based on defensive strength. Back in the Second Division Joe Mercer shifted the emphasis to attack. He moved crowd-favourite Gerry Hitchens to centre-forward, and replaced the right-wing partnership of Leslie Smith and Jimmy Sewell with two new signings, winger Jimmy MacEwan from Raith Rovers and Bobby Thomson, a £8,000 buy from Wolves, where he had made only one appearance in five years. The defence relied heavily on goalkeeper Nigel Sims and centre-half Jimmy Dugdale, but John Neal was signed from Swindon to partner Stan Lynn at full-back.

Villa's League season commenced on a hot sunny day in Brighton. Over 30,000 spectators, a large proportion coming from the Midlands, packed into the Goldstone Ground. It was Villa's first Second Division game since 1938.

Jimmy Dugdale was unfit for this match, so Joe selected young Terry Morrall at centre-half. This caused a great deal of surprise in Birmingham as few had even heard the boy's name let alone see him play. Surprisingly, Joe himself had never seen the youngster play in a competitive match but had put his faith in Morrall after hearing rave reviews. Villa were also missing the injured Gerry Hitchens, while Bobby Thomson was suspended after an incident at his previous club.

Villa won that first game 2-1, thanks to a 25-yarder from Jimmy MacEwan and a late winner from Jackie Sewell, and, despite defeat in the next game - 1-0 to Sunderland - they hit a purple patch. They went 14 games without defeat and set their sights firmly on promotion. One of those games was at Bramall Lane, against Joe's old side, Sheffield United. The game ended in a 1-1 draw. However, Villa could claim a moral victory as goalkeeper Nigel Sims was injured and right-back Stan Lynn had to take over as his replacement.

Villa were playing exciting football that delighted their supporters. In one game, against Charlton Athletic in November, the Villa Park faithful witnessed a goal feast as the home side recorded their highest victory at the stadium. Joe's side defeated Charlton 11-1, and Gerry Hitchens scored five. Hitchens had been in danger of losing his place prior to the game

through "lack of goals". Luckily, Joe had kept faith with the great player for "just one more game" and was handsomely rewarded.

In the following match Hitchens continued to show why he was so highly regarded as he scored a hat-trick in Villa's 5-0 victory over Bristol City. Then came two more goals at home to Scunthorpe when again Villa scored five without reply. Vic Crowe, who played for Villa during this period, remembers Gerry Hitchens' strengths: "He was the sort of player you always wanted to have in your team. Perhaps, in terms of skill, he did not have huge natural talent, but he was whole-hearted and very courageous. His main assets were his speed and his strength and the fact that he was very difficult to knock off the ball when he was going for goal. It may seem strange when I say that one of his greatest qualities as a goalscorer was that he was selfish. It is something all the top scorers must have. The great thing was that he was prepared to make mistakes and come back for more and would never hide himself if things were not going too well."

In December the two top teams, Aston Villa and Cardiff City, met at Villa Park. The attendance was almost 55,000, proving that Villa supporters liked the excitement Joe had brought to the club, and were confident that he could guide them to promotion. That attendance was the day's highest. Arsenal attracted only 26,249 for the First Division meeting with third-placed Burnley, and the highest in the First Division was 42,614 (Sheffield Wednesday versus League leaders Preston).

The Cardiff game was a true battle between two well-matched sides. In the first minute Pat Saward scorched the bar with a free-kick. Ten minutes later a shot from Cardiff inside-right Derek Tapscott was pushed out by goalkeeper Nigel Sims and Graham Moore shot narrowly wide of the left-hand post. It was this type of excitement right through the game. (Tapscott, incidentally, was the player who had shared the headlines at Arsenal on the day Joe's playing career came to an end.)

The match against Cardiff progressed towards a goalless draw ... until the last 13 minutes. Then Villa's Jimmy Adam tapped in a goal from six yards and, in the final minute, Hitchens somehow beat a defender and the goalkeeper to a speculative long ball from Jimmy MacEwan to make it 2-0. Joe's side was now top of the table. "One of our greatest displays as well as our most important victory so far." he said afterwards.

Joe was just as elated later that week when Villa's youth side defeated Wolves 5-1 in the FA Youth Cup. Wolves had been second only to Manchester United in youth football throughout the 1950s, so this was a major achievement. "I've never been so thrilled in my life," Joe said afterwards. "They always say there's no substitute for football, and those lads proved it tonight."

The FA Youth Cup also brought Joe another confrontation with Derby County manager Harry Storer. In later life Joe was fond of telling the story: "We had a good youth side at Villa - Tindall, Baker, Sleeuwenhoek, Wright, Aitken, Ashe. We played Derby and they kicked a bit. We fluked a draw. I said something silly afterwards, like 'Next game we'll try and use a ball.' We went to Derby and beat them 4-1. Harry Storer came in afterwards and said, 'Congratulations, Joe, well played.' I said it was a bit embarrassing for me, and asked him how he could take it so well. 'You have to have played cricket, Joe,' he said. 'It's a sunny day and you've won the toss, and the skipper tells you to get your pads on, and you take this long walk out to the middle and take guard and look round the field, and you're just thinking about getting settled in for the day, and then comes the first ball. This big bugger hones in and knocks your castle over and you've got to walk all the way back. And you get to the pavilion and somebody says, 'I could have done as well as that.' And somebody else says, 'You couldn't have done worse.'"

The future looked bright for Villa. The first team was on course for promotion and did not drop a home point until the 1-1 draw against Hull City on 28 December, while the Reserves and youth sides provided strength throughout the club. As the New Year approached, Joe was confident his side would be promoted. Then, in January, Joe's team once again set off on an exciting FA Cup run. The third-round draw put them against First Division Leeds United, a team who had attempted to sign Joe as manager two years earlier. The game, at Villa Park, was played in a blizzard between two committed sides. It could hardly be described as a showpiece but at least it gave Villa the chance to prove themselves against First Division opposition. Although Leeds scored first, through John McCole in the 26th minute, Villa turned the game their way with goals by Peter McParland and Ron Wylie.

The fourth round of the FA Cup took Villa to Chelsea, where a crowd of over 66,000 were

The Villa players take their revenge on the manager after a number of difficult training sessions at West Kirby on The Wirral.

Joe always had time for supporters. Here he signs autographs after taking his Villa side to West Kirby for training. Son David is behind Joe's left shoulder.

thoroughly entertained. There was an abundance of exciting football, most of it coming from Villa. Joe's side played like a true team with his captain, Eire international Pat Saward, leading Villa with conviction. Joe saw Saward as a similar leader to himself, but had been subjected to a great deal of criticism when he appointed Saward captain at the start of the season. The Irishman had always appeared too quiet and serious to be classed as a leader of men, but Joe had recognised his intelligence, fighting spirit, and sense of responsibility.

The Monday after the Chelsea Cup tie, Gerald Williams of the *Daily Mail* was full of praise: "Of Mercer's many astute moves since he took control at Villa Park a year ago, none had had more startling reward than his decision to make Eire wing-half Pat Saward his captain. Three times this season I have seen the bronzed, handsome Saward driving, inspiring, cajoling, and gesticulating Villa to success. He is one of the few outstanding captains in the game today. Yet who, other than Mercer, ever visualised the quiet, serious Saward as a leader? Even Saward shared the general astonishment at his appointment. But the new Villa are powered by a new Saward. How Chelsea could have done with him! How badly they need someone to drive and extemporise, and bolster, and knit!"

Needless to say, Villa won at Chelsea. Peter McParland was carrying an injury after colliding with Chelsea goalkeeper Reg Matthews early in the game, but he opened the scoring after 19 minutes when, from close range, he powered MacEwan's cross into the net. By half-time the score was 2-0 as McParland lobbed the ball for Bobby Thomson, all on his own, to shoot past the advancing Matthews. Chelsea came alive in the second half, but squandered chances and then disintegrated into poor passing and basic errors. Their only reply was a 77th minute penalty from Peter Sillett after Villa's Jimmy Dugdale had brought down Johnny Brooks.

In the fifth round, Villa faced an away tie at Third Division Port Vale. The game, which attracted Vale's record attendance of 48,749, was played in atrocious conditions. The pitch had been turned into a heap of mud and the game was almost called off. Despite the poor playing

'Once more unto the breach'

THE Shakespearean season opened last Saturday, at Middlesbrough. Just as a joke, Aston Villa manager, Joe Mercer startled his team by dispensing with a pep talk and reading a large extract from King Henry V.

" Once more unto the breach, dear friends, once more," read Mr. Mercer to the gaping Villa crew. And they went out to shatter Middlesbrough's unbeaten home record.

I was interested to see if our readers could suggest suitable parts of Shakespeare's works for Mr. Mercer to read to the team before today's big game.

The response was tremendous. All the week postcards have poured in, with dozens of witty, topical quotations. Members of families competed with each other to win one of our guinea prizes.

One lady from Witton sent FIVE cards each containing three quotations. A

member of the Birmingham Repertory Theatre—whose company is this week presenting King Henry IV (Parts 1 and 2)—sent three quotations from the plays applicable to Villa, Blues and Wolves.

☆

Schoolchildren, grandparents, office workers, in fact hundreds of Shakespeare lovers have joined in the fun. Today I give the last of our guinea prize-winners, with my thanks for the response. And my thanks to Joe Mercer for sparking off this Shakespearean soccer festival.

From: Miss D. Latimer, Tame Road, Witton.
Be great in act as you have been in thought;
Be stirring as the time; be fire with fire;

Threaten the threat'ner, and outface the brow
Of bragging horror, so shall inferior eyes
That borrow their behaviours from the great,
Grow great by your example, and put on
The dauntless spirit of resolution.
(King John, Act V, Scene 1).

From: L. Robinson, Lichfield Road, Aston.
Be not tame neither but let your own Discretion be your tutor; suit the action To the word, the word to the action; with This special observance, that you o'erstep Not the modesty of nature.
(Hamlet, Act 3, Scene 2.)

From: Mrs. Cynthia Holder, Welford-on-Avon.
If it were done, when 'tis done, then 'twere well,
It were done quickly.
(Macbeth, Act 1, Scene VII).

'We'll get to London yet . . .'

The local press created their own image of how Joe might dress for his often unorthodox team talks!

surface Joe's Villa seemed to have the edge until Vale scored the opening goal from a penalty. Early in the second half Hitchens equalised from MacEwan's centre before both sides missed chance after chance. The game was heading for a replay when, six minutes from time, Thomson headed the Villa winner from MacEwan's cross.

Next came a sixth-round tie against First Division Preston North End. However, before they could face the Lancastrian giants, they had to play Sheffield United in the League.

In the February return with United, the people of Sheffield finally got their wish of upsetting Joe, as United defeated Villa 3-1 before over 43,000 at Villa Park. Derek Pace, who ironically Joe had signed for United from Villa a couple of years earlier, scored all three Sheffield goals. Pace had also previously scored a hat-trick for Villa against Joe's Sheffield United.

Villa's first home defeat was disappointing, but they soon recaptured form and looked increasingly likely to achieve promotion at the first attempt. They drew with Lincoln and then, the week before the Cup match against Preston, won 1-0 at promotion-chasing Middlesbrough. Prior to the Middlesbrough game, Joe's team-talk was a reading from William Shakespeare's *Henry V*: "Once more unto the breach, dear friends ... "

The Middlesbrough victory reassured Joe that his side were not losing their way in the League: "Winning at Middlesbrough last Saturday rekindled lost fires. No one would dispute that we have been off form in recent weeks, but the tension concerning promotion has indisputably lessened following the win at Middlesbrough. I am not saying we have clinched promotion - there have been too many sides beaten on the post - but this week I have noticed the players going round looking more relaxed and this is a reassuring factor for any manager."

Before the Preston game, Joe talked to his team for almost half an hour. He gave his verdict on Villa's opponents, including their most famous player, Joe's great friend, Tom Finney: "Forget about Tom Finney being a one-man band and if we evolve an intricate plan to stop him we automatically stop Preston. Too many people have been taking this view, and the worst possible disease we could get is the 'Finney-itis'. Cliff Britton, the Preston Boss, is too strong a character to allow any one player to monopolise his side. Mind you he is a crafty chap, full of tricks, and you can't blame him for pulling this red herring over the tie. It's our job to see it doesn't work."

Joe did not bother to watch Preston play in the run-up to the Cup tie. He explained his reasons to Alan Williams of the *Daily Express*: "If the stands fell down Preston would still play the same brand of football - and a very good brand of football by any standards. We must just trust that our overall methods, which have stood us in good stead in a very testing season, will pull us through. But the one thing we must remember is that Preston are a grand all-round team."

The Preston match attracted 69,732 people to Villa Park, and created a ground receipts

record. Villa were determined to prove their capabilities throughout the match and gave everything they had in a tough battle. Typifying Villa's fighting spirit was the giant goalkeeper Nigel Sims who had missed the League game at Middlesbrough the week before through an injury to his shoulder. Kevin Keelan had deputised for him in that game but had himself become injured with a knock to his ankle. Sims, however, had put in a tremendous amount of work in a bid to play in the Cup and Joe, it must be said, gambled with his player's fitness as he selected the goalkeeper to play against Preston. Even an hour before kick off Sims' shoulder was still sore, but he was keen to play. Joe appreciated that kind of determination. As a player Joe proved time after time that he detested missing games and hated quitters.

Villa kicked off and launched an attack down the right. Hitchens centred but Preston cleared the danger easily. Preston quickly replied but Villa's Jimmy Dugdale won his first duel with Tom Finney.

The early part of the game saw plenty of similar duels and attacks by both sides, with the first real scoring chance coming to Villa when Hitchens headed a MacEwan centre wide of the net. A further couple of chances came Villa's way before the tremendous Gerry Hitchens found the net. Hitchens gained possession about 30 yards out, beat a defender, and was preparing to pass to the unmarked McParland. When that option was cut off, Hitchens suddenly turned and went the other way. Then, from about 20 yards out, he unleashed a low drive that entered the net well away from Preston goalkeeper Fred Else. One-nil to Villa after just ten minutes.

As the game wore on, both sides had a number of exciting opportunities but there was no further score until late in the game. In the 78th minute Villa were presented with a gift of an opportunity. MacEwan provided a short centre for McParland to reach. The Villa player collected it, but was closely challenged by Garbutt Richardson. McParland struck the ball, Richardson chested it down but it landed back at the feet of McParland. All McParland now had to do was hit the ball hard and fast into the roof of the net.

Villa dominated the rest of the game, especially McParland who forced corner after corner as the Preston defence tired. The 2-0 win took Joe's team to a second successive semi-final, where their opponents were to be Wolverhampton Wanderers.

Meanwhile, in the League, Villa were close to winning promotion. With nine games to play, they were in second place, 10 points clear of third-placed Huddersfield Town. Leaders Cardiff had a three-point margin, but Villa had a game in hand.

The semi-final was played at West Bromwich Albion's ground, the Hawthorns, on 26 March. The ground was nowhere near big enough. The capacity was around fifty-six thousand.

Villa fans could have filled the ground themselves, but as there was no other large stadium available in the Midlands, West Brom was the only option.

The match certainly captured the public's imagination, and part of the focus was on a small town in the north-west - Ellesmere Port. Not only was it an all-Midlands semi-final, it was also Mercer versus Cullis, the story of how two men from the same schoolboy team had become managers of two of the game's most famous clubs. Ellesmere Port people had just cause to feel proud, although the game also gave the town another opportunity to divide itself between the 'Wufflers' who supported Wolves and the 'Portites' who would follow Joe.

The game was truly hyped in the press, but as sometimes happens, did not live up to expectations. It was, in effect, something of an anti-climax. The players of both sides were affected by the big-match tension, and the two Wolves international wing-halves, Eddie Clamp and Ron Flowers, curbed the menace of Villa's inside-forwards. McParland was not his usual threat, and Hitchens faded once he received a shoulder injury after ten minutes.

Wolves scored in the 31st minute. A right-wing centre was volleyed with tremendous force by Jim Murray. Sims could only parry the ball, and Norman Deeley shot into an empty net. Wolves deserved their 1-0 win, although Thomson caused Wolves goalkeeper Malcolm Finlayson to make a gallant dive to prevent the equaliser. Wolves had looked the more adept and composed throughout. Once more Joe's Villa had failed at the semi-final stage. Two years as manager. Two semi-finals. That night, after the Wolves game, Joe took all the players and their partners back to his house, and they had a party anyway.

The previous season the Cup run had possibly cost Villa their place in the First Division. This season Joe was convinced Villa were on their way back, but he understood that the Cup defeat could have a detrimental effect on his side's promotion drive. The first game after the semi-final was at home to Liverpool, a team in the chasing group. Joe was determined to keep his side on course, but the first 45 minutes of the game tested his resolve to the limit.

Joe shows the way, demonstrating ball skills to young players Jimmy Roach, Alan Baker and Norman Ashe.

Aston Villa 1959-60
Back row (left to right): Peter Aldis, Stan Lynn, Jimmy Dugdale, Wally Beaton, Nigel Sims, Trevor Birch, Peter McParland, Gerry Hitchens. *Middle row:* Ray Shaw (Trainer), Pat Saward, Bobby Thomson, Vic Crowe, Johnny Dixon, Leslie Smith, Joe Mercer (Manager). *Front row:* Jimmy Adam, Jack Sewell, Ron Wylie, John Neal.

At half-time Liverpool led 3-0. Joe went absolutely berserk during the interval. He shouted at the players, kicked the hamper with the remnants of the Villa kit inside, and made everyone aware of just how angry he was. He pointed out that this game was vital to Villa's bid for promotion. He expected more guts and fight from the Villa players during the second-half.

Within 15 minutes of the start of the second half Liverpool added a fourth goal. Joe just could not believe it. Then, as Joe was starting to prepare his post-match diatribe, Villa came back. McParland scored the first in the 66th minute. Six minutes later Jimmy Adam crossed for Bobby Thomson to tuck the ball into the net. Villa continued to fight back and Joe, watching his players power their way forward, was immensely proud of their determination. He still remained angry about the first half, but as he watched his side battle against all the odds he knew that Villa were good enough and determined enough to gain promotion.

With 15 minutes to play, McParland was brought down in the penalty-box giving Stan Lynn the opportunity to score the spot-kick. Villa now trailed only 4-3, and the supporters were going wild. Ten minutes later, Thomson drove Wylie's through-ball past Liverpool's goal-keeper Bob Slater to level the scores.

The final five minutes saw chances at both ends. The best fell to Villa's Jimmy Adam, whose shot was well-saved by Slater. The game ended level at 4-4, and Villa now needed only one more point from six matches to ensure promotion.

Joe hoped, and believed, the one point required would be obtained in the next game, but Charlton Athletic surprised him by beating Villa 2-0 at the Valley. Fittingly, the point was finally earned at Villa Park, when Villa defeated Bristol City 2-1. A crowd of over 33,000 saw Stan Lynn score two penalties.

With promotion achieved, the next objective was the Second Division title. The next game, at Cardiff, would go a long way to deciding the outcome. If Villa could beat their nearest rivals, they would be more or less guaranteed the title. On the day, however, Villa did not really stand much chance of overcoming Cardiff. The game took place in front of a partisan 54,769 crowd at Ninian Park. The noise and fervour generated by the fans was all in Cardiff's favour and, in the end, Joe was grateful that his side were only defeated by a single goal, a goal which guaranteed Cardiff's own promotion.

Joe demanded more from his players, and for the next two games, both at Villa Park, Joe saw his side ease their way to victories against Stoke (2-1) and Rotherham (3-0). The Rotherham victory ensured Villa were Champions and gave Joe his first trophy as manager of a League side.

The Second Division Championship and two successive FA Cup semi-final appearances had done a lot to cancel out the two relegations and prove that Joe Mercer was a good manager who was capable of getting the best out of players. Many people were now tipping him as a future England manager, and his future looked bright. Many felt that if he continued to progress as a manager, he might even match his many achievements as a player. The Villa supporters needed success and it looked as though Joe, and his assistant Dick Taylor, were capable of giving them all the glory they required.

Above all, the 1959-60 season proved that Joe was right to leave Sheffield United for the challenge of restoring Villa to the force they had been earlier in the century. Aston Villa believed in Joe, and he believed that he was capable of bringing real success to Villa. The Second Division Championship was a taste of what he believed would follow.

Let Joe Have A Go For England

THE time has come to scrap the unwieldy England Selection Committee—AND the way in which the teams have been chosen. The flop against Scotland last week, and the hold-up of the players' names to go on tour for England next

J. G. ORANGE

takes you

INSIDE SOCCER

month, lead to one conclusion—the whole system's wrong.

There are nine names on the senior Selection Committee — J. H. W. Mears (chairman), C. N. Banks, A. G. Doggart, H. French, Major H. W. Keys, Lt.-Col. G. J. Mitchell, J. Richards, H. Shentall and D. F. Wiseman.

Of these, I think only Graham Doggart has played serious football. He was in the Corinthian team which met Manchester City, Blackburn and Newcastle, among others, in the FA Cup. The others are mainly administrative heads.

Unwieldy

THE size of the committee is unwieldy and the members on the main see only their own clubs and their opponents in action. They are assisted in their search for international talent by England team manager Walter Winterbottom, who really gets around.

There were lean times for England in the past when we thought that old players and first-class managers like Jimmy Seed and the late Tom Whittaker should have a little say in choosing England's teams. Some even said the job of picking the sides should be given to Matt Busby, disregarding the fact he was a Scot. Later he was manager of Scotland's international teams.

Not for years has England had a selector who played in League and international soccer. The last was Phil Bach, chairman of Middlesbrough and one time Sunderland winger.

But now a real personality, who has proved his worth this season, is available. He's Joe Mercer, former England and Arsenal captain, and now Villa manager.

Let's scrap the present selection committee and give the

job of choosing England's teams to Joe Mercer.

I think his vast experience in all kinds of football would enable him to choose an international team with far more life and skill than that we had at Hampden—and a side with much brighter prospects of winning the World Cup.

Mercer has been through the mill, refused to be "finished" when that was Everton's view. He has unyielding spirit and great judgment.

Mercer has done remarkable things with Villa in a short time. In his first full season he has led them back to the First Division, *and to the F.A. Cup semi-final.*

He has found new players, given new life to others. Left-back John Neal was a discovery who consolidated the Villa defence. He has been mentioned as a possible England full-back though I think he's a bit too old to train for the 1962 World Cup.

Case of Saward

ONE of Joe Mercer's best moves was to restore left-half Pat Saward's confidence and make him captain Saward is an old Millwall player and Eire international.

The man who recommended Saward to the Villa told me at

● *Walter Winterbottom—Let him be Mercer's main assistant and adviser.*

the time he regarded him as one of the best half-backs in the country.

Later he had difficulty in convincing the Villa authorities of that, but Joe, when he took charge, had so much faith in

● *Joe Mercer—give him charge of the England team.*

Saward that he made him captain

Joe has had considerable experience in all branches of soccer. As a schoolboy he represented his country and captained them in internationals. He skippered Arsenal when they last won the League championship and F.A. Cup and was instrumental in saving them from relegation.

Instructor, Too

A BROKEN leg ended Mercer's playing days. Since then he has been through an F.A. coaching course and was an instructor on one occasion. He took his first job as manager with Sheffield United—where John Harris, formerly of Chelsea, has succeeded him—and then moved to Aston Villa.

Through it all and with enough success to turn the head of an average man Mercer has been the same calm gentleman, always telling his men that football intelligence counts for twice as much as muscle effort. He has welded a side that had gone to pieces and lost faith in itself into one that has returned to the First Division in a most confident mood.

Chief Selector

I THINK Mercer could do for England exactly what he did for Arsenal and Villa.

Give him supreme charge of the England team. Make him chief selector and let Walter Winterbottom be his main assistant and adviser.

We would then be able to scrap an unwieldy selection committee, and narrow it down to one man, as do the Continentals. Winterbottom would be free to watch players under consideration.

I am sure we should do better *this* way, revolutionary though it sounds.

For Mercer it would be a thankless job at the start, but he might gain the satisfaction of building up a side worthy of the country

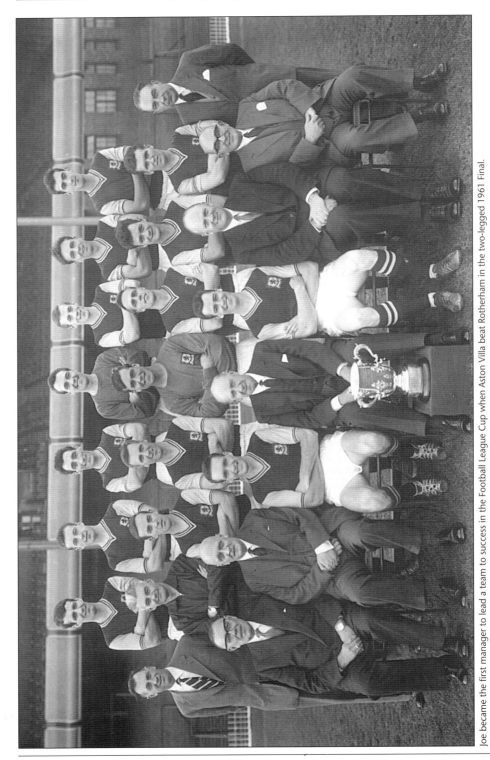

Joe became the first manager to lead a team to success in the Football League Cup when Aston Villa beat Rotherham in the two-legged 1961 Final.

Chapter Fourteen

LEAGUE CUP VILLANS

> Joe Mercer impressed both my mother and my elder brother. They actually tried to judge people to determine which club I should sign for. Joe won hands down with his style, his character, his personality. He was a very likeable man, very honest and my mother was a bit old-fashioned in many ways. She liked people with values and Joe came into this category. He impressed us all.
>
> **George Graham**, Aston Villa player 1961-4

VILLA'S NEXT aim was consolidation in the First Division. Joe was determined that his side would not only survive but reach a mid-table position of respectability. He wanted to restore Villa's prestige and wanted the club to become a dominant force in English football once more. His plans involved bringing in many of his youth and reserve players who had been performing well for the previous couple of seasons. They included Mike Tindall, Alan Deakin, Norman Ashe and Harry Burrows, all of whom had featured in the odd game during Villa's promotion season. These developing players were nicknamed 'Mercer's Minors', in the wake of the Busby Babes at Manchester United, Cullis's Cubs at Wolves and Drake's Ducklings at Chelsea. They attracted a great deal of publicity during the early 1960s. Joe tried to play down the praise as premature. He wanted the players to prove themselves first as he, like most managers, realised that an image of greatness is always difficult to maintain. Joe did not want his young starlets to feel any more pressure than was absolutely necessary.

Joe Mercer's youth policy enabled him to attract top youngsters from all over Britain. George Graham remembers the events that brought him to England from Scotland: "I first met Joe when I was fifteen. He was the manager of Aston Villa, I was still at school. I was in the Scottish schoolboys team. Normally when you get in your international side at schoolboy level, you have a host of clubs wanting to take you on as an apprentice, so you would go down and join a First Division club. I had quite a host of big clubs interested, like Glasgow Rangers, Newcastle, and Manchester United. I was already down at Chelsea looking around. But Joe impressed my mother and my eldest brother. So I tried Aston Villa. Went down there and had a vacation there, enjoyed it, and I finished up joining Aston Villa with Joe as the manager."

As the 1960-61 season started, it was obvious that Joe had to consider team selection carefully. His side for the opening game, a 3-2 win at home to Chelsea, was basically that which had finished the previous campaign. Then, after heavy defeats by West Ham United and Blackpool, Joe began to make changes. He left out crowd favourites like Jimmy Dugdale and goalkeeper Nigel Sims, and even sacrificed his captain Saward for the good of the team. Results slowly improved.

On 15 October, he took his Villa side to Arsenal, and received a good reception from the Arsenal supporters. Villa lost 2-1.

The following week Villa won the Birmingham City derby 6-2, and then beat West Bromwich Albion 2-0. Joe's side quickly found themselves the pride of the Midlands as they went on a run which saw them lose only two games before Christmas. The good results included a 2-1 victory over the eventual League runners-up, Sheffield Wednesday, and a 5-1 thrashing of Manchester City. Villa's good form was not to last, however, as the new year brought a series of defeats and draws.

In fact, the team's first League victory of 1961 did not come until

DIVIDED LOYALTIES

SAT. OCT. 15
ARSENAL
v.
ASTON
VILLA

"Oh, I'll cheer good old Joe with the rest of them! But won't I feel a fool if Villa win —"

22 March when Joe took his young side up to his former club Everton. Everton had not been having a great season, and for this game they resorted to the long ball. Frank Wignall put them ahead after 27 minutes. Joe became angry as the first half progressed because his own side now matched Everton's long-ball tactics. Joe hated this. He enjoyed stylish, exciting football played with a strong defence and a full-blooded attack. At half-time he tore into his players: "For heaven's sake, let's play some First Division football, even if we're going to get beat by ten!"

Villa dominated the second half with much more exciting play. The equaliser came from one of the celebrated 'Mercer Minors', 19-year-old Alan Deakin, who scored after an hour of the game from over 25 yards. Then, with ten minutes to play, Bobby Thomson latched on to a mistimed pass from Brian Labone to score the winner. Joe saw it as a victory for pure football.

As Joe became more experienced in management, so he added to his fund of stories about players. One in particular he would enjoy telling throughout his life. It concerned an Aston Villa player who was known for late nights and enjoying himself. The player was regularly in trouble with his wife over all sorts of things - blondes, redheads, brunettes - and their house was well-known for passionate rows which disturbed the crockery. One Wednesday the Villa trainer came to Joe with the news that the player hadn't been in for training all week. The volatile couple had been rowing and throwing things around since Saturday night, and the neighbours had complained about the noise. Joe took a trip to the house, very concerned, not knowing what he would find when he arrived. He knocked on the door, and was surprised to be greeted by the player himself, dressed immaculately in blazer and tie, looking spruce, beautifully turned out. "Hello, Boss," the player said. "We've just had a slight domestic upheaval."

Joe loved that phrase - "slight domestic upheaval" - and it became a catch-phrase with other football people ... because Joe told the story a lot.

Another time at Aston Villa, Joe confronted a player about a series of late nights. The player defended his behaviour. "I give you everything on a Saturday, Boss," he said. Joe smiled and answered, "You give me everything you've got left."

Like all managers with a sense of humour, Joe was sometimes walking a fine line between wanting to laugh at a player's reaction and trying to ensure discipline. In one game Jimmy Dugdale complained about the referee's eyesight after a penalty appeal was turned down. "What did you say?" the referee asked. "Deaf, too, eh?" came Dugdale's light-hearted reply, and everyone laughed.

Another story of Joe's concerned an occasion when a player went down injured. The trainer came on the field and shouted at the injured player: "Come on, you big softie, get up and get on with it." Then the referee came up and told the trainer to take the player off the field. "I daren't move him, ref," the trainer now replied. "He might have broken his leg."

The 1960-61 season ended with Villa in ninth place. Joe would have settled for that at the season's start. It was particularly impressive because, for the third season in succession, Villa performed well in Cup competitions, especially the newly created League Cup.

In the FA Cup, Joe's side reached the fifth round where double-seeking Tottenham defeated them 2-0. Villa never really functioned during the game and gave Spurs nothing to fear. Villa's supporters were hugely disappointed and so was Joe. After reaching the semi-finals two years running he hoped that his newly promoted side would reach the Final. But the League Cup more than compensated.

Alan Hardaker, secretary of the Football League, had hit upon the idea of having a second cup competition solely for League clubs. The competition had an unhappy birth with five League clubs refusing to enter the tournament. The teams that refused to take part were termed the 'Big Five' by the *Daily Mail* and included Villa's Midlands rivals West Bromwich Albion and Wolverhampton Wanderers. The other three were Arsenal, Sheffield Wednesday and FA Cup holders Tottenham. The following season, other First Division clubs pulled out, and it was not until the 1969-70 season, when Joe again found success, that all the League clubs participated.

Villa were given a bye in the first round of 1960-61 competition. In the following rounds they disposed of Huddersfield, Preston (after a replay), Plymouth (after two replays) and Wrexham. It was quite a season for replays as Villa also had two replays in the FA Cup, and the two-legged League Cup semi-final against Burnley had to go to a third game at Old Trafford.

The League Cup Final was played over two legs, but was held over until the following season because of fixture congestion. Villa's opponents were Rotherham United, the side they had defeated the previous season to win the Second Division Championship. The first leg was played at Millmoor on 22 August before a crowd of 12,226. By that time Villa had played only one League game of the 1961-2 season - a 2-0 defeat at Everton - and they didn't hit anything like form. Villa's Stan Lynn missed a penalty, and Rotherham won 2-0.

Joe was determined his side would overcome the two-goal deficit in the second leg at Villa Park. He put his players on a £90 bonus per man and ensured they followed his methodical plans to overcome Rotherham's tight defence. On a rain-soaked evening, Joe was pleased to see that all the early action took place at the Rotherham goal. Harry Burrows and Peter McParland fired in early shots. In fact McParland had several shots and set up Thomson for an attempt that was so powerful that many reporters said it almost broke the crossbar. By half-time the game was still goalless with Villa having most of the play yet being unable to score.

In the second half, with rain driving into the face of the Rotherham players, Villa finally found the net. Their first goal came when Alan O'Neill latched on to a Alan Deakin pass and shot wide of the diving Roy Ironside in the 67th minute. Four minutes later, with Villa taking full advantage of their dominance, Harry Burrows smashed in the second to level the aggregate score at 2-2. That was how it was after 90 minutes, and the first-ever League Cup Final went to extra-time.

As extra-time began Villa seemed the more determined, and certainly had the backing of a thirty-thousand plus crowd. In the 19th minute of additional play, after almost constant Villa pressure, McParland scored Villa's winner.

Joe had achieved his first Cup success as a manager. Players and supporters celebrated, but

Villa players celebrate the 1961 League Cup triumph.

the success created little interest elsewhere in football. The League Cup competition was yet to make its impact.

One player missing from the League Cup Final team was England international Gerry Hitchens, who had played in the early rounds but had been sold to Italian club Inter Milan at the end of the 1960-61 season. Inter offered Villa a fee in the region of £85,000, and Hitchens himself was to get a signing-on fee of approximately £12,000, a luxury flat, a car, and generous bonuses. Hitchens simply could not refuse the offer, and Joe, the man who had helped make him a better player, could not offer anything comparable. At the time the wealthy Italian clubs could afford to buy virtually any British star. They employed a number of agents who often made offers that infringed FA and Football League rules, but players like Hitchens and Jimmy Greaves of Chelsea could not be faulted for wanting to earn what they felt was a true value for their services. At one stage, not long after the Hitchens move, the League tried to ban transactions with Italian clubs. For Joe and Villa the League's threats came too late, as Joe was helpless to prevent the transfer.

Joe had made a close study of Hitchens, and had even played alongside him on a close-season tour of Sweden and Norway at the end of the 1960-61 season: "The reaction of Gerry Hitchens to my coaching gave me the greatest satisfaction. When he was with me at Villa, Gerry obviously had all the skills at his command but could not co-ordinate them to the best effect. Playing inside-left to him on a tour in Scandinavia, it suddenly dawned on me what he was doing wrong. He could kill the ball perfectly, but then he would freeze on it, giving the defender time to get in his tackle. He also came back square to the ball instead of half-turning to see the opposition coming in."

Joe worked on this problem with the centre-forward: "By putting Gerry into this situation in training, hour after hour, doing the right thing eventually became automatic. Like all good centre-forwards, he often went out on the wing and strangely enough always fancied the left-wing: But, in all respects, his left foot wasn't what it should have been until, again, he put this right by dedication. His fantastic speed and stamina helped him pass players to the bye-line, but then he had a habit of bringing the ball back with his right foot, giving the defence time to recover. By improving his left foot, he was able to cross first time. The other vital point - we were able to improve his shooting. All golfers would appreciate his trouble - he was trying to knock the cover off the ball. We managed to slow his strike down and this did the trick."

On tour, Joe still selected himself for the occasional match, safe that he was far enough away from home to prevent a debate with Norah about whether he should play. During the Scandinavian trip Joe, now 46, looked forward to each game. He even scored a hat-trick in Villa's 7-1 victory over the Swedish side Oestersund. Joe loved it, but Ron Wylie didn't think it was quite so funny. He was the one Joe dropped!

Mercer hat-trick!

OESTERSUND (Sweden), Thursday.—Joe Mercer, Aston Villa manager, scored a hat-trick in his club's 7—1 victory over Oestersund today.—Reuter.

As a replacement for Hitchens Joe signed Derek Dougan, Blackburn's controversial centre-forward, for £15,000. Dougan had caused a tremendous stir by asking for a transfer on the eve of the 1960 FA Cup Final between Blackburn and Wolves. The transfer shocked everyone coming at such a time. Blackburn lost the Final and quickly agreed to his transfer. Dougan scored three times in his first four games for Villa, but was out of action for over two months after breaking an arm and suffering head injuries in a car crash. On the night of the League Cup Final victory, Dougan was in a car driven by fellow Villa player Bobby Thomson when they crashed into a tree. Wolverhampton journalist Malcolm Williams was killed in the crash. Thomson was not seriously hurt but suffered from shock and was out of action until early November. When Dougan returned to the team, he scored only seven more League goals that season, a figure far short of what Joe had hoped for.

Villa were fortunate to have other goalscorers. Burrows, Thomson and McParland all reached double figures. These helped Villa to attain a creditable seventh place in the division. Joe was delighted with his side's performance and was convinced Villa could achieve real success in the years to come. His side had once again progressed in the FA Cup, reaching the sixth round before losing to Spurs. In an interview in 1962 he told a reporter that he was convinced his Villa side would reach their peak in "another two or three years".

Joe takes part in a Villa training session at the Lenin Stadium, Moscow, in 1961.

Joe was happy that his side contained a good balance of experience and youth, and was proud of the way Villa never seemed to give up. In one game at Arsenal the scores were level at 4-4, with only a few minutes to go, when winger Tommy Ewing, a £20,000 signing from Partick Thistle, scored Villa's fifth to secure full points. This gave Joe a great deal of satisfaction, especially as it came at a ground where he had shown the same 'never say die' attitude for almost ten years. It was just a pity there were only 20,000 at Highbury to witness Villa's fighting spirit.

Throughout Joe's time at Villa Park, he tried to work with the players in training sessions. As he was still fit and healthy he tried to lead by example, and show the players the type of game he wanted, but not lay down rigid patterns of play. He wanted his players to think for themselves. He wanted them to know what to do through instinct not through strict rules and training.

One morning, at a training session, Joe got the shock of his life when Derek Dougan arrived with a very short haircut - similar to what was later known as a 'skin head'. Joe looked at the player, laughed and in typical Mercer style came out with a wisecrack: "We shall have to supply him with some billiard chalk for match days - we don't want a miscue when he's heading for goal!"

The 1962-3 season was not as successful in the League as Joe had hoped. It was the year of the big freeze. The bad weather caused so many postponements that Villa played only one game between 19 January and 9 March - and that was a 4-0 defeat at Liverpool.

At Christmas, before the bad weather, Villa had been in fourth place but the disruption affected them badly. A run of 11 League defeats dropped Villa to 18th place. George Graham remembers how the season turned from hope to near disaster: "The atmosphere was very good. There was an outstanding youth policy, I remember that. Some quite famous names - John Sleeuwenhoek, Alan Deakin, Norman Ashe, Alan Baker - and all these youngsters were bursting into the first team. I always remember in 1963 we were going great guns then all of a sudden we hit one of the worst winters in memory. Nobody played. It was iced over for weeks and weeks. Villa had been in the top half dozen, really going well, and after that winter, we came back and really had a bad time, right to the end of that season. I think that really got Joe down. That was one of the reasons he wasn't well at that time."

A late-season recovery lifted Villa to 15th place. The bad run was ended with a 3-1 victory over fellow-strugglers Manchester City at Villa Park, Burrows converting two penalties. Those penalties helped send City into the Second Division. No-one at the game that day could have guessed what the next few years would hold for the two clubs, and the role that Joe Mercer would play in both their histories. At that time City were doomed, while Joe Mercer believed Villa were on the verge of true success. The unpredictable nature of football would soon twist around the fortunes of the two clubs, with Joe Mercer a central character.

First, however, came one of the lowest points of Joe Mercer's life. As George Graham has indicated, the manager was on the verge of a serious illness. The strains of managing a top club were eventually to cause him to leave Villa, but before that happened Joe refused to believe or accept anything was wrong.

At the end of the 1962-3 season Villa's dramatic descent down the division caused him a great deal of worry and this must have affected his health. An added factor was the reaction of the Villa supporters. They were beginning to be intensely critical and could not understand or believe Joe when he predicted a bright future for the club. Joe was hurt as Villa's supporters seemed to forget what he had already achieved at the club, especially as the 1962-3 season had started so promisingly.

Joe's frustration during the season led to him adopting different styles in team-talks. Joe eventually resorted to giving an unusual talk that probably did more for his players and the team than any other: "I tried talking, coaching, pleading, and bullying and none of it helped, so one week I picked the side, pinned the team names on the notice-board and said: 'Right boys, this is the tactical talk - God bless this ship and all who sail in her, may she come safely home to shore! Now go out and enjoy yourselves!'"

Despite the gloom and doom of the League there were a few bright moments for Joe. Villa proved they were still one of the best Cup sides around as they reached the League Cup Final once again. They reached the Final by scoring 22 goals in five ties. Such was the weather, though, that it took over three months to complete the two-legged semi-final. Villa won 3-0 at Sunderland on 12 January and drew 0-0 at Villa Park on 22 April!

By this time Joe's side were hardly the force they had been at the start of the season, and they never really got going in the two-legged Final. Their opponents, Birmingham City, dominated the first leg and deservedly won 3-1. The second leg ended goalless at Villa Park. Ironically, success in the competition would hardly win over any doubters, but defeat just strengthened the opposition that was growing against Joe. Birmingham City had narrowly avoided relegation and for Villa's city rivals to beat them was a major blow. Nevertheless, inside five seasons, Joe had taken his team to two FA Cup semi-finals and two League Cup Finals.

Another bright moment came towards the end of the 1962-3 season. For a game against Liverpool, Joe put his faith in George Graham, one of his impressive youngsters from Scotland. Graham repaid his manager's faith by scoring on his début. Graham remembers the day: "I was fortunate - I think I was just 17 - to make my début against Liverpool, funnily enough. The Liverpool name keeps cropping up in my career! I scored and we were supposedly a very weak team but we beat them 2-0 at Villa Park."

Graham retained his place for the last League game of the season, and for the two League Cup Final games. In later years, when George Graham became Arsenal's manager, Joe and Norah Mercer were immensely proud of his success and they made sure the Arsenal manager was aware of their joy at seeing him guide Joe's former club to glory: "There were actually a couple of times over the last few years when I got nice letters from Joe. I think he was very proud of one of his old boys - one of his young lads who he had first brought to England at fifteen, saw him progress into the Aston Villa first team, then saw him progress as a player here at Arsenal with the double, then into management. Every time I saw him I could feel the pride coming out, as if to say, 'Well, here's one of my youngsters making the grade as a player and a manager.' I could actually feel the warmth and the pride. It was a very nice feeling. It was always a pleasure to meet Joe.

THE MAN FOR BIG JOB

NIGHT S

—says BILL HOLDEN

WITH four days left before applications close, there has been no rush for Soccer's No. 1 job—the England team managership.

Denis Follows, Football Association secretary, told me last night: "We have received a number of applications from foreigners. We have also had some from Englishmen currently coaching abroad.

"I cannot name them, nor can I say whether any League club managers have applied."

Hardly any of these hopefuls stands the slightest chance of being appointed.

I am certain that the man who SHOULD get the job is Joe Mercer, boss of Aston Villa.

Although he told me last night that he is NOT among the applicants, it will not surprise me if Joe is asked to take it on.

He has the background the job demands. He has the ability to succeed—and it is the kind of challenge he would relish.

Villa Lifted Off Floor

He has lifted Aston Villa back off the

Mercer fills the bill as England's team boss—but FA will have to send for him

De

C

By PETER I
Peterborough 3
GOALKEEPE
Carlisle's
signing from a
an impressive d
powerful Peter
London Road I

The eager Po
repeatedly spl
badly - position
wide open, and
faced with a
shots.

But he had
with the goal
Peterborough
lead after 28

Right winger
sent over a nea
although left w

"Joe was a very loveable person, I don't know anybody who has got a bad word to say about him. The thing I liked about Joe was that his whole life was about football, and that included his family. Norah used to come to all the games and she used to know all the players. When I still see her we have a good chat together, and I got to know his son David as well. They are really a nice family."

Joe's son David was on the Aston Villa playing staff but did not quite make the grade for League football. He was released by his father. Joe used to tell the story of how he 'sacked' his son: "He had quite a useful left peg, a fair bit of skill, but lacked pace and I thought the ability to last 90 minutes. So I went across to him one day, put my arm around his shoulder and said, 'I've got a job for you son.' David looked surprised and said, 'But I've got one here dad.' I replied, 'Not any more, son.'"

But David had the last laugh. Some time later someone asked him if he was still a Villa player. When he said he wasn't and was asked why, David grinned from ear to ear and chuckled, "A ruddy awful manager."

Away from Villa Park, Joe was being hotly tipped as the "next England manager". The FA needed a replacement for Walter Winterbottom and, as usual in those circumstances, the press began to speculate as to who should lead England to the 1966 World Cup Finals to be played in England. A growing number of journalists believed Joe was the man needed. Bill Holden of the *Daily Mirror* wrote, at the end of August 1962, under the headline 'The man for the big job': "I am certain that the man who should get the job is Joe Mercer, boss of Aston Villa. Although he told me last night that he is not among the applicants, it will not surprise me if Joe is asked to take it on. He has the background the job demands. He has the ability to succeed - and it is the kind of challenge he would relish. As skipper of England he discovered first-hand just what it's like to play abroad - and just what it takes to win. Joe has firm ideas on that. He believes we have players to equal - and better - the best in the world. He does not believe in sending players out to play to any set plan or pattern. He says they must have a spirit of adventure, they must be encouraged to believe they are great and given freedom to use their brains according to the way the game is going at any particular moment. If the applications arriving at FA Headquarters don't include their 'Mr Right' the next move should be simple - to give Joe the green light."

Alan Hoby, writing in the *Sunday Express*, held the same view as Holden. In an article on 16 September 1962 he went through the favourites for the job, dismissing the claims of Stan Cullis, Bill Nicholson and Alf Ramsey. Who did that leave? Wrote Hoby: "It leaves a sinewy, dark dynamo who, both as a footballer and manager, has always possessed qualities of heart and mind which stand out like the Eiffel Tower. The name ... Joe Mercer - the man I say is tailor made for the England job. Everything he touches he ignites with life and excitement. He is all fire, all faith and, most of all, he is all for England."

Joe was not one of the 59 men who applied for the position, and the FA were not the kind of organisation to approach someone. The man chosen was Alf Ramsey, who eventually guided England to success in the 1966 World Cup Finals.

If Joe had applied for the job, it is purely guess work whether or not he would have been offered the post. If he had been given the task, it's difficult to know whether he would have found success. He would, however, have given it his best shot and, perhaps it would have helped to give him a new lease of life, for at Villa Park he was entering a period of strain and tension. Joe's best days at Aston Villa were now behind him.

Chapter Fifteen

JOE WITHOUT FOOTBALL?

Aston Villa manager Joe Mercer has been ordered by his doctor to withdraw from the England under-23 tour of the Middle East. His place as manager of the party will be taken by Sheffield United chief, John Harris. Mercer, who established himself this season as Alf Ramsey's right-hand man, has been told to take a fortnight's complete rest from work.

Philip Osborn, *Daily Sketch*, May 1964

THE 1963-4 SEASON was Joe's last at Villa Park. The strain and tension of the job was beginning to affect him after seeing his club struggle so much in the latter half of the previous season. And certain sections of the Villa crowd turned against him as they believed Villa should be fighting for the League Championship not fighting to avoid relegation.

Joe now recognised how high the hopes and aims of all the supporters were - they wanted success now! This had been proved by the treatment of Joe's predecessor, Eric Houghton, who managed Villa to FA Cup success in 1957 and was then dismissed 18 months later. True Villa hadn't been performing well in the League, but Houghton was sacked as early as December.

The 1963-4 season was not an enjoyable one for Joe Mercer. The supporters became frustrated and openly criticised their manager. In December, Joe's five-year contract came to an end. At the time there was widespread speculation that Joe's time at Villa was over. Villa had only won eight of their first 25 League games and the supporters were becoming increasingly restless. In mid-October they were even knocked out of the League Cup, the competition which had brought their most recent triumph. Because of the climate at the time, the Villa supporters saw that League Cup defeat, at West Ham, as total failure.

After several disputes Joe and the Villa directors finally agreed on a new contract in January. Unfortunately Joe was not to see it out. Results continued to be poor. The most disappointing one was in the FA Cup. Villa drew 0-0 at home to Fourth Division Aldershot in the third round, and then lost 2-1 at the Recreation Ground, Joe's home ground for a short time during the war.

Joe was seen by supporters as the main reason for Villa's failure. They not only shouted terrible abuse but also threw apple cores and other rubbish at the man who had guided them out of the Second Division and created an enviable youth policy. Joe just couldn't win. In an interview some years later he remembered how low he felt at the time of the Aldershot game: "I recall with shame and humiliation one day at Aston Villa early in 1964. We had been knocked out of the FA Cup by Fourth Division Aldershot. The fans were disgruntled. In a home match soon after this shattering Cup dismissal I went down from the stand to walk to the

DAILY SKETCH, Thursday, April 9, 1964 21

JOE'S COME FAR FROM SELLING PAPERS

SOCCER MASTER

JOE MERCER, of Aston Villa and England, has come a long way since he used to support his widowed mother doing a paper round twice a night, and running all the way to keep fit.

His dad was centre-forward for Nottingham Forest and, though he died when Joe was twelve, Joe still remembers one golden bit of fatherly advice. . . .

"The only way to learn football is to keep playing it and play it against better class, and go on doing so until there is no one better to beat."

Dangerous

That knowledge made me think as I walked round the Robert Diochon Stadium in Rouen last night with Joe Mercer, now manager of the England Under-23s, looking at the scattered glass and sharp stones embedded in the pitch, and wondering how many of his players would be cut to pieces in a few hours.

As I walked at Joe's side, I thought of the April afternoon some ten years ago at High-

Let Mercer be our No. 2

By LAURIE PIGNON

bury when Joe Mercer, captain of Arsenal and England wing-half, crashed with Joe Wade and shattered that famous hairpin left leg.

Mercer was carried off in a shocked silence, never to play again.

But the Mercers are never lost to a game to which they have become dedicated.

Mercer will also take our youth World Cup squad on a tough tour of Hungary, Greece and Israel this summer. He will also sit on the selection committee.

He is Ramsey's right-hand man and this partnership could develop into one of the best things that ever happened to English football.

I should like England to go a step further and officially appoint Mercer as Ramsey's part-time deputy instead of just calling on him when he's needed to fill an Under-23 gap.

Ramsey and Mercer have a first-rate understanding, and think on the same tactical lines.

With the World Cup competition only two seasons away, Under-23 games are as vital as full internationals.

These youngsters are England's insurance policy of the future, and unless half this present side develop into full internationals, the system is failing down.

Together

Ramsey and Mercer agree that there is always something to learn, and when better ideas come along they will accept the challenge, and experiment.

Ramsey proved this in the recent England-Scotland inter-League game.

At present, Ramsey and Mercer are working on a fluid 4-2-4 system, allowing for the stars to use their individual talents.

Ramsey is now preparing for his most difficult match since he took command last May—the clash with Scotland at Hampden on Saturday.

He is sure to find it more difficult to beat inspired individuals like Law, White, Baxter and Henderson. It takes more than a plan to check them.

But a manager must give his men ideas and confidence. Ramsey and Mercer can do both.

Joe Mercer looks to the future

---

trainer's bench, which is on the other side of the ground. Vulgar abuse followed me all the way. I could hear every word as those fans I had slaved night and day for hurled their epithets.

"Apples and orange peel hit me. I had never had the bird in my life before, and it hurt. Should I turn and argue with them? No. I just kept plodding on, praying they would not knock my hat off. That would have been the ultimate in ridicule!

"Perhaps they were still bitter about the previous season, the year of the great freeze-up when football was almost impossible throughout the country for several weeks. Before the ice set in we were high up in the First Division. When play restarted we went for 13 matches without gaining a single point. We roared down the table like an avalanche. I had never known such a disastrous run of results. I started to make changes and I was having battles with the directors."

Much criticised at Villa, Joe was still a hero away from the club. He was given control of the England under-23 team, and, in effect, was Alf Ramsey's right-hand man. The press believed he should have been officially appointed Ramsey's number two. Laurie Pignon, writing in the *Daily Sketch* during April 1964 when Joe was guiding the England under-23s in France, said: "He [Mercer] is Ramsey's right-hand man and this partnership could develop into one of the best things that ever happened to English football. Mercer will take our youth World Cup squad on a tough tour of Hungary, Greece and Israel this summer. He will also sit on the selection committee. I should

MERCER YOUTH PLAN WILL BE A WINNER

By MIKE DEMPSEY: Manchester C. 1, Aston Villa 0 ★★★

THE smile that Joe Mercer beamed round the boardroom was hardly the smile you'd expect from a manager of a side just beaten. But it was understandable.

Unless I'm mistaken genial Joe was thinking: just wait till next season. And no wonder. By then his classy collection of youngsters will have another year of experience, which is all they need to make the Soccer world sit up.

Topping Joe's galaxy is 17-year-old John Sleeuwenhoek. Next is left back Charlie Aitken. Add Harry Burrows, Alan Baker and Alan Deakin. Mix them with old hands Derek Dougan, Vic Crowe and Tommy Ewing and you have a rare Soccer titbit with the emphasis on TEAMwork.

A light ball and tricky wind bothered both sides, but Villa were less frequent victims simply because they kept the ball down.

City improved in the second half, when Bobby Kennedy gave his own classy exhibition of tackling and when Bobby Plenderleith fully justified his recall.

But distribution wasn't City's strong point, nor was it theirs. City, of course, had youngsters to match Villa's.

John Benson, David Wagstaffe, and Neil Young (who hit the winner) each had brilliant moments that no doubt will be repeated many times in the future.

But I must save the last tribute for 15-year-old Glyn Pardoe, who made two astonishing runs, had two headers and a shot that almost scored and even now is remarkably hard to shift off the ball.

Women or no women, Soccer is safe for ever in the hands of our young Pardoes.

Mercer's Minors come up against a Manchester City youth team, some of whom were later to star for Joe at Maine Road.

Joe felt he had to be involved in every aspect of the football club. Here he is at Villa Park checking the nets are up to standard.

Mercer cracks up

By PHILIP OSBORN

ASTON VILLA manager Joe Mercer has been ordered by his doctor to withdraw from the England Under-23 tour of the Middle East.

His place as manager of the party will be taken by Sheffield United chief, John Harris.

Mercer, who established himself this season as Alf Ramsey's right-hand man, has been told to take a fortnight's complete rest from work.

I understand he is suffering from overstrain caused by too much work and too much worry.

The news was passed on to the England boss by Mercer's wife Norah on Tuesday night. This followed an examination by Villa medical adviser Dr. S. Massie.

Last night Villa director Bruce Normansell told me: "We were upset to hear that Joe has had to pull out, and we know it's a great disappointment for him."

"I gather it's merely a question of sheer exhaustion. It's been a very worrying and tough season for him. And I understand his wife hasn't been enjoying the best of health either."

It's clear the strain of yet another unhappy season for Villa has finally caught up with Mercer.

He's been under constant fire from the frustrated Villa fans and there was widespread speculation over his future with the club when his five-year contract expired in December. Eventually, the following month, he signed a new contract but no details were disclosed.

like England to go a step further and officially appoint Mercer as Ramsey's part-time deputy instead of just calling on him when he's needed to fill an under-23 gap. Ramsey and Mercer have a first-rate understanding, and think on the same tactical lines. With the World Cup competition only two seasons away, under-23 games are as vital as full internationals." If the Football Association had followed Pignon's advice, Joe Mercer's England role could have developed and, possibly, by the early 1970s he may have been Ramsey's natural successor. It would have also prevented Joe from further hardship at Villa Park.

Joe's involvement with the under-23 side was to end earlier than he would have hoped. Joe became increasingly tense with the Villa situation. The worry and concern he had previously kept to himself was beginning to show. He became increasingly agitated and, as the season of disappointment ended, it all became too much for him: "I was holding three coaching sessions a day. I was travelling hundreds of miles watching players and opponents. I was fighting all sorts of problems. I was an arrogant one-man band with not enough time to talk to people who wanted to talk to me. I paid for it. One Sunday morning in May 1964 - a beautiful spring day it was - I was happily draining the water from my car radiator when I felt something like pins and needles in my arms and legs. My mind became confused - I went to bed. I knew I was ill, but had never held any real doubts about my fitness until they brought in a specialist."

Norah Mercer remembers that day, too, with slight differences in the details: "I'd come out of hospital after an appendicitis, and I came home this lunch time, and said, 'If I do the lunch will you put the electrolux over the floor for me?' As he's doing it he was dragging. I said, 'What's the matter?' He said, 'I don't feel very well. I haven't got much use of my arm and leg.' He should have got back for a meeting that evening, and I made him go to bed and I rang the doctor. I rang the club and said he couldn't get back for the meeting. When Massie came, he said, 'It's one of two things. It's either polio or a stroke.' He sent for a specialist, who examined Joe. As he was leaving from the room, the specialist turned round and said, 'What about my fee?' And Joe said, 'Well, I must be a bloody bad risk!'"

Joe withdrew from an under-23 tour of the Middle East. *Daily Sketch* reporter Philip Osborn wrote as follows: "Mercer has been told to take a fortnight's complete rest from work. I understand he is suffering from overstrain caused by too much worry. The news was passed on to the England boss by Mercer's wife, Norah, on Tuesday night. This followed an examination by Villa medical advisor Dr S Massie. It's clear the strain of yet another unhappy season for Villa has finally caught up with Mercer. He's been under constant fire from the frustrated Villa fans and there was widespread speculation over his future with the club when his five-year contract expired in December."

While Joe rested at home, Aston Villa director Bruce Normansell told reporters that he hoped Joe would return to Villa Park fully fit after resting. He then went on to tell the press: "I gather it's merely a question of sheer exhaustion. It's been a very worrying and tough season for him. And I understand his wife hasn't been enjoying the best of health either."

Despite Villa's apparently caring public image, the club were beginning to look at Joe's illness in a different way. Joe had been seeing the club doctor, Dr Massie, every week since he first felt ill and each time he had told Joe to "stay in the game". He had always stressed the importance of Joe continuing in football. It was all Joe knew. Without football he would be truly unhappy and ill. Joe remembered the misery he felt the time following the injury that ended his playing career. He needed football, he could not live without it, and the doctor seemed to agree.

Then Joe noticed a sudden change in the doctor's views. During one visit Massie turned to Joe and said: "I've been thinking, Joe. You've got Norah and David to consider. The strain of soccer may be too much for you if you go back to work." He went on to advise him to settle in the country away from the sport. Joe became increasingly suspicious. After all, Massie was Aston Villa's club doctor. He was not just acting in the best interests of Joe, he was also acting on behalf of the club.

It wasn't long before the Mercers discovered why Massie had changed his views. When Joe returned to Villa, within a few weeks, it was not before things came to a head: "I was back at Villa Park, although I was not well by any means. On my first morning back I was sifting

Joe is pictured at his desk surrounded by trophies. The one on his left is Joe's Footballer of the Year trophy, the one on the right belonged to a supporter who just had to show Joe his own trophy.

through the mail. Yet all the time there was an atmosphere about the place that told me some-thing was wrong. The president, Sir Theodore Pritchett, sent for me. He made gentle enquiries about my health - had I considered the future? Halfway through our conversation I realised what it was all leading up to. I had been sacked ... a decision the directors had taken as I lay ill. They paid up my contract and I went home to rest."

It was clear that Aston Villa no longer wanted Joe Mercer. The illness gave Villa a conve-nient excuse, and no one knows what might have happened had Joe rested and returned to Villa.

In football it is virtually impossible for any manager to take a break. In the 1960s, man-agers took most of the tasks on their own shoulders. At Villa, Joe had a trainer, Ray Shaw, an assistant, Dick Taylor, and a scout, Jimmy Easson, but was still out four or five nights a week himself, watching games, training with the part-timers and youngsters, or scouting for players. It was common for him together with Ray Shaw - another workaholic - to drive 40,000 or 50,000 miles a year, in all kinds of weather, and most of the driving was on awkward roads as the modern motorway system was only just beginning to take shape.

The advent of floodlighting somehow made things even more difficult. There were extra midweek games to watch, and kick-offs were later, forcing managers to travel deeper into the night. It was nothing to leave the house at nine in the morning and return at 1am or 2am. And even when he was home, there was little rest. People would be telephoning at all hours.

Football had always been Joe Mercer's life. He had virtually given up all his outside inter-ests as soon as he entered management. Whether he enjoyed the grocery trade or not - publicly he did, privately he did not - his business had been sensibly sold before supermarkets dominat-ed the trade. The lack of outside interests has affected many managers over the years, and the

Joe loved playing. Even after his playing days at Arsenal came to an end Joe could not help himself. He played in any friendly or testimonial he could. Here he lines up in a rather unusual Villa side with his son David, back row - extreme left, who was on Villa's books at the time.

Where do Aston Villa go from here?

By CYRIL CHAPMAN

THE Mercer era at Villa Park, a period first of splendid hopes and then increasing disappointment, came to a shock end yesterday with the announcement that Aston Villa and their manager have parted company "by mutual consent."

breaks are not always long enough for individuals to refresh themselves. Sadly, football does not allow its managers to take a sabbatical. Instead they either resign, like Kenny Dalglish at Liverpool, or are sacked.

Joe, in his tense, nervous state, was forced to leave Villa by "mutual agreement". He did not really resign, for Joe was not a quitter. He wanted to continue: "I felt like a farmer who has ploughed his field, sown his crop, kept it free from weeds, watched it develop and then, when just about to harvest it, is evicted to find another farm."

The parting was announced on 10 July 1964. Many people were genuinely surprised that Aston Villa could treat Joe in the way they did. As expected, the press believed that the "mutual agreement" was a convenient way for Villa to silence their supporters' recent criticisms. Journalist Michael Blair knew the situation at Villa Park well and wrote about the supporters and the board 'living in the past': "The myth is that Aston Villa, forgetting what they once were for that is no longer relevant, are today a major force in the game and that success is theirs by some divine right. Too easily they slip out the references to 'Villa's great traditions' and it is this trite resort to what Villa were in the past that creates the atmosphere that stifles the future. A lot of people have been trying to hoist Mr Mercer on to the tumbrel for some time. Managers are always that vulnerable, but around Aston, Witton, and Erdington there lingers deep resentment that Villa can no longer throw out the bright reflections of more than half a century ago. Joe Mercer looked to the future and was resented because he could not recapture the past."

At Villa, Joe had given them some fine young players and what appeared to be a bright future, but the supporters appeared to demand too much too soon. They had waited since 1910 for a Championship-winning side. They felt that another one was now long overdue, and Joe Mercer had had his five years and failed.

As Joe left Villa, he stressed that it was time for the supporters to back the side. Assistant manager Dick Taylor, who had also worked with Joe at Sheffield United, was left in full control. Villa never did achieve the level Joe believed they could in the 1960s. Unfortunately for Villa, by the time Dick Taylor was sacked, in May 1967, Joe had returned to management and was leading another fallen giant, Manchester City, to glory.

After Joe parted with Villa his thoughts turned to the future. After a short period of relaxation in North Wales, Joe was keen to move back into football in some capacity. Naturally, his wife Norah was concerned about his health and encouraged him to take up other interests. It was difficult. Joe would have taken any job in football.

During the 1964-5 season it appeared that Joe's thoughts were turning away from management. Instead, he became involved in journalism, writing reports on various games and giving his views on football in general. This gave Joe the chance to remain in the sport he loved while keeping him a safe distance from the stress and strain of management. The role would have suited many people, and even Joe claimed it was what he wanted to do for a time. However, he missed the day-to-day involvement with a club. He found it difficult watching two teams instead of urging his own side to victory. He just did not have the depth of involvement he craved.

He also felt he still had something to prove. He was forced out of Villa just when he felt events would justify his management style and the emphasis he placed on youth. He still wanted to manage a truly successful side. Villa's success in the League Cup in its inaugural season can perhaps be equated to Chelsea's 1986 Full Members' Cup victory. Few people apart from the Finalists showed any real interest at all and the League Cup only really became an accepted form of success when the final was switched to Wembley Stadium in 1967.

As he continued to recover, he was persuaded to write his autobiography. The book, *The Great Ones*, was published in 1964. Joe wrote about the most famous incidents of his life, and then talked about the great players he had known. His final chapter, however, looked to the future. It was obvious he wanted to get back into management even though he was far from fully recovered. Management to Joe was a poor substitute for playing. Journalism was a poor substitute for management. In *The Great Ones*, he wrote: "Football has been good to me. I have enjoyed some success, felt the warmth of the fans, known tremendous challenges. I never wanted to do anything but become a footballer and I have been able to spend all my life so far in the game. I could have asked no more. The future for me? Now I am dying to get back as manager of a First Division team. I would like to join a club that is, above all, happy, a club that isn't frightened, a go-ahead club like Coventry or Leeds United. I would not like to join a club that is frightened. Modern soccer has put so much pressure on management and players that there are fewer and fewer happy clubs."

As the 1964-5 season ended, Joe was close to fulfilling his wish. In Manchester there was a club that, like Joe, had previously been hugely successful but, by the mid-1960s, was in its worst-ever state of health. Manchester City desperately needed a pick-me-up, and so did Joe Mercer.

Joe ended his autobiography with these prophetic words: "A lot of people have been discarded and have come back, Winston Churchill among them! Perhaps I can do so too. There is still a great challenge in football. And football is my life."

And so, in July 1965, his life became Manchester City.

Chapter Sixteen

RESTORING FAITH

Joe Mercer came,
We played the game,
We went to Rotherham,
We won one-nil, and we went back
into Division One.

Verse of Manchester City supporters'song
(to the tune of 'Auld Lang Syne')

"**F**OOTBALL could live without Joe Mercer,**" he said years later, **"But I found out that I couldn't live without football. I was out of the game for seven months with a stroke. I kennelled up and then came back to Manchester City. Little Albert Alexander was chairman then, and everything went right, every mortal thing.**"

That year, 1965, began miserably for City fans... those who were left. Their team was struggling in Division Two after being relegated two years earlier. Then, on 13 January, City went to Third Division Shrewsbury for an FA Cup third-round replay and lost 3-1. It was the final straw, especially as near neighbours Manchester United were at their peak. It was one of the lowest points in City's history.

Three days after the Shrewsbury debacle, City were at home to Swindon Town. The attendance was a pitiful 8,015, City's lowest-ever for a League match, and the vast Maine Road stadium had an eerie feel. Thirty thousand absent people were saying, "They didn't come to see me when I was bad."

During that match, City played some good football at times but went behind to a 19th minute goal from Dennis Brown, and further behind to a goal from 22-year-old Mike Summerbee midway through the second half. Today, it seems ironic that Summerbee played a major part in creating City's worst day and yet later would return to Maine Road to play his part in their greatest era.

Although Alan Oakes scored a stunning 30-yard goal, late in the game, City lost 2-1 to Swindon, and supporters expressed their anger. After the game there were demonstrations outside the Main Stand and bricks were hurled at windows. In the days that followed, City fans were embarrassed as United supporters stressed their superiority. In the mid-1960s Manchester City had become the forgotten team of football. City had been a great force between the wars and a successful Cup team of the 1950s, but they were now on a downward spiral, and United had taken over as Manchester's number-one club. More than that, United had become an internationally known team while City struggled to gain the headlines of the local press. City's attendance against Swindon was only 615 more than that of Stockport County, who ended the season bottom of the Fourth Division. United fans joked that Stockport was now the area's second biggest club.

Inevitably, City manager George Poyser left the club, and City finished the season in eleventh place, their second-lowest position of all time. The last game of the season, a 2-1 victory over Charlton Athletic, attracted another meagre crowd, this time only 8,409. Meanwhile Manchester United ended the season as League Champions, FA Cup semi-finalists, and Inter-City Fairs Cup semi-finalists. Something had to be done if City were to achieve the status quo.

That was when Joe Mercer came. July 1965. Norah Mercer wasn't sure it was the right move: "He was very naughty. He was supposed to be resting. One day he said to me, 'Will

Joe's first day at Maine Road, a typical rainy day in Manchester.

you take me to Manchester? They want to talk to me.' We had a hoo-hah about it, because I didn't think he was well enough to go back. David said, 'If you leave him sitting there he'll die of misery. As much as we both love him, if he kills himself playing, at least he's died happy.'"

Norah knew that the stroke had left its mark: "He wasn't quite the same Joe after his stroke. Dr Brown at Manchester said, 'They never are. It's like cutting your finger. It heals, but it leaves a scar. The same with a stroke. It leaves a scar.'"

Joe Mercer was a man with scars. He had a scar the length of his shin as a reminder of the day his playing career ended. He had what he called "scars on the soul" from two relegation seasons as a manager. And now he had a scar on his brain from a stroke. It was no wonder Norah believed that he should stay away from football management. She had seen what Villa had done to him and simply did not think it was worth the risk to his health. Joe kept the news quiet when he was first approached by Manchester City. He knew that Norah would be against the idea. All Norah wanted, though, was for Joe to find some way of returning to the game without it resulting in all the stress and worry she had seen before.

In an interview some five years after his appointment Joe gave his version of how the City job came about: "No hint of returning to football management ever appeared during the year I was out of the game. I had been written off as ill, but deep down the old passions were stirring. I knew I had to be involved with a team. Life was a void without the company of players ... my players. Then one morning in July 1965, completely unheralded, there came a 'phone call from the Manchester City secretary, Walter Griffiths. Would I be interested in joining them as manager? The call of the game, the tang of the dressing-room, the thrill of Saturday afternoons were all alive in my mind again. I was in with a chance of re-entering the great sporting theatre that has always been a part of my life. Yet I had to be a different kind of manager. I could no longer afford to be a loner. I needed to be fit, and I wanted a lieutenant.

"First, I saw a doctor. He told me 'The only way to see if you are fit enough to manage is by managing.' That helped. He knew me, and I could see that he was on my side. Then I 'phoned an extrovert, ebullient, but brilliant coach called Malcolm Allison. Like me he was out of work. Sacked by Plymouth Argyle. It took me two days to find him, but he said he would join me if I took the job. Secretly, I met the Manchester board and accepted the job, telling them of my plans for Malcolm. Then I drove back to Birmingham straight into a row with my wife. Norah argued that I was being plain stupid taking such a job and I knew she was right."

Norah explains more of her feelings at the time: "I did my utmost to stop Joe joining the club. He was still not fully recovered from his illness and I thought the job was too tough. I wanted Joe to wait another six months to get really well and fit, but he wouldn't listen. He's a very determined man. It's his first love. Even when he was laid up I knew he was thinking about getting a job in the game."

When Joe took the job Norah reluctantly accepted that it was what he really wanted and, in many ways, needed: "I married a footballer. I realised he had to go back - it would have killed him not to. I'm one of those old-fashioned folk who believe a man must do what he wants. When you take your marriage vows you make a team job of it."

Joe had met Malcolm Allison at FA coaching courses at Lilleshall. Malcolm Allison remembers their first meeting: "The first time I met Joe Mercer was at Lilleshall. Walter Winterbottom was in charge of the course. There were people like Alan Brown and George Smith who were the coaches, and there were all the old players - it was around 1950 - people like Stanley Matthews, Stan Mortensen, Jimmy Hagan, Joe Mercer. They were all people who were going to Lilleshall to become qualified. All the players there were at the end, or near the end of their careers and all wanted to become managers or coaches. I was about fifteen to twenty years younger than nearly all of them - I'd just come out of the army. I'd been in Austria and I'd played with an Austrian team out there, and I'd become very interested in coaching. So, this was the first time I met Joe. I was practising swerving the ball one day, and he came over and said, 'You want to try kicking it straight first!' Typical Joe. Whenever Joe played any game, like golf, he always hit a straight ball! From then on I used to go to Lilleshall every year, and Joe would always be there. I was like a young whizz kid whilst they were all very famous players."

A player with West Ham in the mid-1950s, Malcolm Allison started in management with Bath City and Plymouth Argyle. His time at Argyle came to an end when the directors overruled his team selection for an Easter Monday game at home to Northampton. They insisted on reserve goalkeeper John Leiper instead of Allison's man, Noel Dwyer. Allison told the board that he was angry that his professional judgement had been questioned, and within hours he was looking for a new job. Malcolm Allison: "Joe rang me up and said 'I've just been appointed Manchester City manager, would you like to come and work with me?' so I said, 'Well it's funny, because yesterday Raich Carter of Middlesbrough rang me and wants me to be his coach.' So Joe said, 'Why don't you call in and see me on your way up and we'll talk about it?' Well, Manchester City had always been my team. When I was a kid I listened to a Cup Final when I was about six or seven. Manchester City were beaten by Everton, 3-0, just before Joe played for them. Anyway, City were my team, so I said 'Okay I'll see you'. When I went to Manchester I saw Joe and agreed to stay there because that was my team."

Joe needed someone fit, strong, and positive to help him correct the faults at Maine Road. Joe knew he was not really ready for the challenge, but he also knew he needed that opportunity to prove to himself that he had not been wrong at Villa, and that he could still be a great manager. Joe's view was that the City job was his chance to prove himself. "I should never have returned to football management so soon after my illness," Joe told a reporter, "My wife, Norah, told me so in no uncertain manner. But she need not have bothered. I knew only too well how ill I had been. I made one stipulation to City before accepting: that Malcolm Allison was to be my assistant. I don't like the word scrap-heap, but quite honestly that is where I found Malcolm. Amazing though it may seem, no one wanted him for he had been out of a job for three months or so."

A Manchester City team in Joe's early days at Maine Road.
Back row (left to right): Dave Bacuzzi, Mike Doyle, Alan Ogley, Johnny Crossan, Vic Gomersall, Neil Young.
Front row: Alan Oakes, Alf Wood, Bobby Kennedy, David Connor, Glyn Pardoe.

In a later interview Joe explained that he and Mal were just right for each other: "Mal and I were a great combination. I had matured by then, I was more tolerant of Mal whereas I might not have been ten years earlier. Everything was right. Earlier in my career I'd wanted to do everything - coach, scout, trainer. I'd gained experience by the time I reached City. Football is a game where you have to look back and say, 'Where are we going wrong?' Inside twelve months you can be born and live, live and die, sins can be forgotten, virtues forgotten, then the next season it's a brand new life and you can be a super optimist again."

When the two men took on the difficult job at Maine Road they had both come through a difficult period in their lives. Joe needed to prove that he could cope with the pressures of management, Malcolm needed to prove that his often controversial ideas could work. Joe believed the City job was a great opportunity for both men to prove their true value: "The chance was irresistible. I knew that people had written me off - and I felt the swell of satisfaction that I had never dismissed myself from anything. There were doubts about my health, but I had no lack of confidence in my ability. Allison was magnificent, as soon as I saw him working with the players I realised I could forget about that department. I knew we had a chance with Manchester City. Although they were in the Second Division, they were a club with a tradition and a ready-made public. We were not concerned with the weakness of the staff. So we got down to the slog. I saw my role of manager as making things easy for Malcolm, smoothing the way for him and helping him along. We got on well together."

Joe saw the concept of "team work" applying to the staff as well as the players: "As far as I'm concerned, managing is a team game. No-one does it on their own. A good manager, a good number-two, and a good chairman. George Kay, Albert Shelley and TV Williams at Liverpool. At City there was Malcolm and I and little Albert Alexander. Matt Busby, Murphy and Harold Hardman at United. It's a combination of things as far as I'm concerned. Nobody does it on their own."

At Manchester City, Joe made sure the chief scout, Harry Godwin, was included in his team. Godwin would later speak of never feeling left out. When Mercer arrived at Maine Road, he put his arm around the chief scout and said, "I've heard you're good at nicking one or two youngsters. Nick a few for me, will you?."

At Maine Road, however, both Joe and Malcolm soon discovered that the situation was worse than they had originally believed. At the time the club had a playing staff of 21 players, but many of these were virtually untried youngsters. There was only one apprentice on the books. Also, Joe surprised many fans when almost immediately he sold the previous season's top scorer, Derek Kevan, to Crystal Palace. Kevan had suffered from a knee injury and had missed the last 15 games of the season, and Joe doubted whether he could regain full fitness and his old goal touch. In fact Joe and Malcolm immediately tried to test if Kevan would fit in with their plans. Malcolm Allison doubts whether Kevan still had the interest he had shown at City before: "I used to do these training sessions whereby I'd create a space for him to make runs through, and I used to say to Joe that he just didn't want to make it. I used to work out training schedules whereby if people really wanted to play or work they would do it, whereas if you just play a normal game it's hard to pick out who isn't really trying. I said to Joe, 'We've got to sell Derek Kevan.'" The transfer was probably a good decision as Kevan was never really the same player again.

The first real chance for Joe to assess the strengths and weaknesses of his new side came in

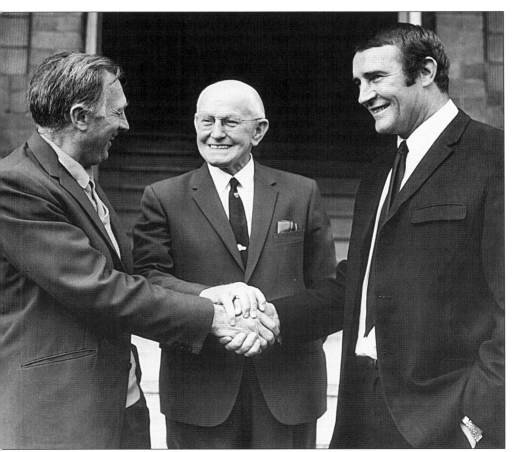

Joe, City chairman Albert Alexander and Malcolm Allison clasp hands to signify the bond that would bind the trio together through the early days.

There's pain on Joe's face as he watches City's appalling performance in a friendly with Dundee.

● At Maine-road, Joe Mercer was another new manager with a big problem.

STUMBLING

This morning he calls in his Manchester City first-teamers for a dressing-room chat . . . to tell them just what he thought of Saturday's stumbling 2—1 defeat against Scottish First Division side Dundee.

Mercer glowered and groaned his way through 90 minutes of City mistakes.

And glumly, he said after the fans had trooped away —most of them early: " I've got a lot to say about this."

The fans were also asking questions . . . and top of the list was this stinger: "Was Mercer right to sell top scorer Derek Kevan without first nailing a replacement?"

That replacement could be Ralph Brand, the Glasgow Rangers and Scotland inside-left. He is expected to join either City or Aston Villa this week.

The Rangers board have agreed to his transfer and a fee around £25,000 has been settled.

a pre-season friendly against Scottish First Division side Dundee at Maine Road on 7 August. Joe did not like what he saw. City were terrible. Mistake followed mistake. Many fans questioned the wisdom of selling Kevan without first finding a replacement. Joe knew that new faces were needed urgently.

Another friendly, a drawn game at Walsall, reinforced Joe's view. The following day Ralph Brand was signed from Rangers. Brand seemed to be just the player City needed. At Rangers he had scored 128 goals in 207 League games, and had scored eight goals in his eight games for Scotland. But Joe's first signing at City was not a success. Brand scored twice in his two seasons at Maine Road.

Following City's third friendly, a 3-2 victory at Tranmere, Joe made his second signing - Mike Summerbee, the player who had twisted the knife on that fateful day seven months earlier. Joe had played with Summerbee's father, George, at Aldershot during the war, and had followed Mike's career closely. During the summer of 1965, Mike Summerbee was supplementing his income from Swindon Town by working as a deck chair attendant at Torquay. He tells the story of the transfer: "I was on £35 a week at Swindon and while on the beach I heard an announcement that Joe Mercer and Malcolm Allison had been signed by Manchester City. John Benson, who much later was to come to Maine Road as manager, was playing for Torquay at the time and was with me on the beach. I knew that Joe Mercer had watched me when he was manager of Aston Villa and had fancied me as a player. I told John that I was going to ring Manchester City immediately and chance my arm. I left John looking after my deck chairs and went out to a telephone and got through to Joe first time."

Summerbee asked Joe if he fancied signing him. Joe asked the player to come to Manchester to discuss terms. "Unknown to me," recalls Summerbee, "Swindon had sent terms of my

A young Mike Summerbee signs autographs outside Maine Road after joining City from Swindon.

contract on ahead of me, but while I was driving up I was telling myself that I was going to one of the top clubs, a club with great traditions and a superb ground. I told myself that I would get a few quid out of them, and as I passed through Birmingham I was telling myself that I would ask for £50 a week. By the time I came through Sale I'd decided that I was worth £75. City had pots of money, were a Super League club, and could afford it. I pulled up outside Maine Road and found Joe in the trainer's room. Joe told me, 'We're in the Second Division, we've had a bad time, we've won nothing for years, and we're skint. You are on £35 a week at Swindon and we'll give you £40.' I accepted like a shot!"

Coincidentally, another man who was to play a great part in City's future, youngster Mike Doyle, was also working in Torquay for the summer when he heard the news that Joe Mercer had been appointed City's manager. Doyle's reaction was not quite so warm: "It was there [Torquay] that I learned of the moves Albert Alexander had been making behind the scenes. The whole thing had been settled, of course, by the time I became aware of developments. I simply learned that Joe Mercer had been appointed manager of Manchester City, and I'll confess my first reaction was, 'Oh, my God, he's a right bastard!' I was jumping to this conclusion on the strength of an encounter the previous year, when several of the City youngsters, myself included, had gone on a course to Lilleshall, and Joe had been there. To my way of thinking, he hadn't appeared to have much time for the Manchester City brigade, and I felt that if he was coming to take charge at Maine Road, some of us - maybe including myself - would get the bullet."

Mike Doyle returned to Maine Road apprehensively, but soon realised that his concerns were unnecessary: "There was never any question of our new manager having it in for the lads who had been on that course at Lilleshall. For all I know, Joe never even remembered or recognised us. Certainly he held nothing against any member of the playing staff, and I found that first impressions are not always the right ones. In many ways, I learned a great deal from Joe, just as I learned a lot from big Mal."

Joe Mercer, of course, was rightly known as a manager who could get angry and autocratic with the players, but he had also strived to be fair. He had mellowed from the days at Villa when he was uptight, constantly under pressure, and perhaps still resenting that he was no longer a player. Now, with the coming of the more volatile, energetic Allison, Joe could step back and slip into his more endearing role - genial Joe, the avuncular figure that brought warmth and wisecracks to the world.

As Joe had told Mike Summerbee, Manchester City were in a desperate state. The new management team needed to restore faith. The club was a laughing stock. At United's Championship celebration dinner the United management and players cracked various jokes at City's expense. Allison and Mercer were present, forced to listen to the glorification of Manchester United. This made them even more determined. Allison, a man who rarely hides his feelings, was soon fed up of hearing the taunts and boasts. He told Matt Busby's son Sandy: "Your father's got a 20-year start, but I'll pass him in three."

Allison's views were laughed at at the time. United's Pat Crerand even bet Allison £10 that City would never again get 30,000 into Maine Road. Three years later it was a different story.

City's pre-season friendlies made Allison and Mercer realise they had a lot to do in 1965-6, but both men publicly expressed the belief that City could achieve great success. The first game of the season was away to Middlesbrough. The 1-1 draw restored some confidence, and the turnaround in the club's fortunes had begun. City were undefeated in their first seven League games. Allison recalls the good start: "It wasn't a good team, it wasn't a very confident team. Going all those games without defeat was important in my mind, it meant we could keep things tight and build the players' confidence. The atmosphere at the place was appalling. The year before they'd finished eleventh in the Second Division and crowds went down to around 8,000, the smallest ever. I remember when we first started off we used to say, 'Hope there's some people coming today.' We used to be so frightened - either Joe or I would walk down the tunnel to make sure there were actually some people there!"

Malcolm and Joe agreed that their main priority was to restore pride and spirit to the once great club. Joe firmly believed he had to build confidence in the team: "We all entered our first season unsure of how we would fare. Our first job was to get team spirit. We did not seek it by pandering, nor by rules. We worked and we talked. We told the players: 'You might think this is a new broom come to sweep clean. It is! And it is going to get harder and tougher!' And it did!"

City's sixth home League fixture, a Wednesday night game against Norwich, saw the attendance reach over thirty-four thousand. Pat Crerand had lost his bet only a couple of months into the season. The previous Saturday, United's attendance at Old Trafford was just 32,716 for the First Division visit of Fulham. City were on their way back and were giving their fans some much-needed pride.

Already, Malcolm Allison had some idea that he might take over as manager himself in a couple of years. According to Allison, there was an important conversation on the coach going to Middlesbrough on the opening day of the season: "We went to Middlesbrough for the first game, and Joe sat next to me and he said, 'After two years you can have this, that will do me, just two more years.'"

At the time Joe probably felt that life at City would be as difficult as it had been at Villa. Two years of that kind of struggle, bearing in mind his illness and Norah's view, would be enough for any man. However, at that time Joe could not possibly have known how successful City would become. Nor could he have realised how much he would recover. Unfortunately for Joe, and ultimately for both men, the naturally ambitious Malcolm Allison would never forget Joe's words.

Together Joe and Malcolm were superb. Their blend of experience and temperament were just what City needed. It enabled Malcolm Allison to develop his potential: "Joe Mercer had shown faith in me, he recognised that I might have something unique inside me, but I remained a nonentity in the game. No one really knew me. But they couldn't put me down once I became Joe Mercer's man. It was very impressive to see the way Joe moved about the game. Everyone knew him and they all liked him. At first his nerves were still shaky ... but as City's health strengthened so did Joe's. Joe taught me many things. He knew how to conserve

Joe, happy to be back in football walks down the steps at Maine Road.

JOE MERCER WON'T BE LED A DANCE

himself and though he had one or two bad days, he usually came into the ground very fresh and very alive. Joe had been a player at Arsenal and Everton and he was a person who was always fit. He kept himself in great condition, he never put a pound of weight on, he wasn't a drinker, and he loved the game. The more he played the more he loved it - he was a brilliant passer, and a great tackler for a small man. His timing was brilliant - he was the first man I ever

THERE may not be much to write home about just now regarding our Sheffield football standards or the positions of our two clubs, yet both manage to preserve some of the dignity that was handed down to them in years gone by. Reason I write this way is because of a remark that Joe Mercer made this week when I questioned him about John Crossan, the Derry City Amateur International, who, by this time, may or may not be a professional.

It was at the beginning of October when the United manager told me that "Billy" Gillespie was over in Ireland and had pretty well arranged for John, who is a younger brother of Eddie, the former Blackburn Rovers and Tranmere Rovers International, to come to Bramall Lane. And, acting on that information, Joe took himself off to Londonderry to sign the player.

By
Fred Walters

Joe had been keen on Johnny Crossan for a long time.

saw tackle in front of the ball. He was brilliant. I admired him so much, and we became very good friends, we had lots of laughs together and we were very fortunate that the team was successful. We won the Second Division the first year, had a good Cup run the second year, we won the First Division the third year. Then we started to go into Europe. That's when I made the famous saying that we'll murder everyone on the planet, then we got knocked out in the first round! Joe just laughed and said, 'Well, that's Malcolm.' It was funny. Well, it wasn't funny for us, but it was funny for everyone else." Malcolm Allison certainly remembers those days at City with great affection, especially his relationship with Joe. Allison had never really been given a major opportunity to use his ideas - few people listened until Joe brought Mal to City. Despite the problems the two men encountered in the early 1970s, Allison admits that his relationship with Joe had been the greatest part of his footballing life. He recognises he owes Joe a great deal: "I had all these new training methods and fancy ideas, and I used to say to him, 'Look, Joe, I fancy doing this,' and he'd say, 'Yeah, okay Malcolm, you do it.' He always gave me great encouragement, he was like a father figure to me. He was wonderful, especially in the board-rooms. Everybody loved him. Everywhere we went people loved Joe."

For both men those early days were good. Malcolm may have needed Joe to give him the chance, but without a doubt Joe also needed Malcolm. Ever since their time together at Maine Road right up until Joe's death in 1990, Joe spoke honestly of his need for Malcolm, and how the younger man helped: "I simply had to adapt myself. The situation reminded me of my days as a player. As a youngster, I used to run wherever my legs would carry me, playing from instinct and energy. But after a knee injury I was forced to play a slower, more calculating game, tucked in behind Les Compton, the big Arsenal centre-half. At Manchester City I was recovering from illness. I could no longer get stripped and charge around the training field. I accepted this. We received tremendous help from one little fellow in the dressing room - Johnny Crossan. In those early days this whimsical Irishman was a wonderful dressing-room influence as we tried to mould players we hardly knew into a fighting unit."

Joe felt fortunate to inherit Crossan at Manchester City. He had tried to sign the player years earlier, a story that Crossan told in the late 1960s: "Mr Mercer was the first manager I ever met from English football. I was a starry-eyed 15 year old at the time playing for Derry City back home. All I knew of Joe Mercer was in photographs and cuttings about him which I used to collect. Anyway, I had apparently been doing quite well as a youngster. I had got into the Derry team when only 14 and Mr Mercer came over to have a look round and weigh up likely prospects. Later, I learned he wanted to sign me for his club, which was then Sheffield United, and a fee of around £5,000 was discussed. I never did find out what went wrong. Perhaps Derry wanted more money, though I could hardly blame Mr Mercer for not wanting to bid any higher. I shall never forget his words when the transfer fell through - 'I'll meet up with you some day!' It took ten years and three or four clubs between - but meet up again we certainly did. I was the first to join Manchester City. Six months later in walked my new boss. He came into the dressing room to meet all the players and as he passed me he said, 'Didn't I tell you?' So for me began one of the most exciting phases of my career - the season City won promotion back to the First Division I was made captain."

Without the help and enthusiasm of people like Johnny Crossan and Malcolm Allison, Joe would have struggled. Mal used all his own fitness and coaching expertise to push the players in a positive, constructive way, while Joe himself was still on the road to recovery. They needed each other, and worked together without the need for self glory. For both men the one aim was to get Manchester City back in the First Division. Their own personal interests did not matter at that point in their relationship.

City's progress in the Second Division continued through the early months of the season, with City's away form being particularly good. During this spell the squad was bolstered by the signing of George Heslop, a strong centre-half from Everton, and Stan Horne, a young player Joe had remembered from his time at Aston Villa.

At the end of October, City were top of the division. This in itself was a triumph. Six months earlier they were a despondent, dying side, now they were full of confidence with terrific team spirit. They maintained a position in the top three for most of the period leading up to Christmas.

On New Year's Day 1966, a crowd of over 47,000 gave the Blues a tremendous ovation as they overcame the division leaders, Huddersfield Town. Interestingly, Manchester United's first home game of the year was watched by just less than forty thousand. City had a long way to go to catch up with United's success, but here was proof that the Manchester public would support a successful City team.

Second Division days - Mike Doyle in action against Carlisle.

In his early days at Maine Road Joe often used to look out hoping fans would turn up... it wasn't long before those terraces were full.

During this period, the outspoken Malcolm Allison boasted about how great City could be, while Joe performed the role of the great diplomat. City fans, who had been deprived of success since the 1956 FA Cup Final, loved it. They loved Malcolm's comments and Joe's elder statesman responsibilities.

The FA Cup brought more publicity, City powering their way into the sixth round. They lost to First Division Everton, but only after two replays. The huge crowds at Maine Road included almost 57,000 to see the Leicester City tie in round five, and over 63,000 for Everton's visit. Had City beaten Everton they would have faced Manchester United in the semi-final. The challenge to United's supremacy was underway. Indeed, the 63,034 to watch Everton was higher than any domestic attendance at Old Trafford that season.

The playing staff still needed strengthening if City were to maintain their challenge for promotion. Joe and Mal showed interest in Wyn Davies of Bolton Wanderers and Colin Bell of Bury. The only problem was a lack of money. Joe was always protective towards the club's funds while Malcolm did not really care about the cash if the player was right. Malcolm was convinced that Bell was just what City needed. Joe doubted whether he was worth what Bury were asking. Malcolm Allison: "I decided on Bell, but Joe wasn't sure. Also doubtful were most of the First Division managers. This gave me a chance, for our directors were clucking about trying to raise money, £42,000, for him. I was telling people in the game that Bell couldn't play, hoping desperately that the board could get the money together in time. They did it with hours to spare. We signed him on the eve of the transfer deadline in March, beating off a late challenge by Blackpool. When Joe first saw him, he was screaming, '£42,000! What have I done, I must be mad!' because Colin Bell was a shy boy, and he was only just twenty. He was an introverted boy in lots of ways. Although he was a great athlete, being shy, he never showed it. He scored a goal at Derby County in his first game, but the ball just hit him - the goalkeeper

Johnny Crossan, Malcolm Allison and Joe with the Second Division championship trophy.

kicked it out and it hit him and went straight back in! I remember Joe was sitting in the stand shouting, 'Oh no, what have I done.'"

Joe soon recognised Bell's great qualities of skill and energy in midfield. He realised that his earlier views on Bell had been false, and freely admitted it. Colin Bell played a major part in the last period of the season, and scored three further goals as City made their way back to the First Division. One of them was the goal at Rotherham that guaranteed promotion. Even now, over 25 years after Bell's goal, City fans still sing their song of celebration. Coincidentally Joe's Aston Villa had defeated Rotherham to win the Second Division Championship and again to win the League Cup.

Colin Bell heads City back into Division One at Rotherham.

Nine days later City won the Second Division Championship by beating Charlton 3-2 at the Valley. City had been leading by three goals before allowing Charlton to come back.

A hallmark of City's history has been the team's inconsistency. There are plenty of examples. Take 1925-6, when City reached the FA Cup Final and beat United 6-1 in the League, but were so inept in most other games that they were relegated to the Second Division. Or 1937-8, when the Championship side followed up their great success by being relegated. Or how about 1957-8, when City both scored and conceded over 100 goals, and some of the results looked like baseball scores.

Joe Mercer and Malcolm Allison had taken City back to Division One, but now they had to overturn history and bring some consistency to the team. As for Joe Mercer, he had proved that he could still be a football manager. He still had a lot to offer.

Manchester City - Second Division champions.

Chapter Seventeen

CITY OF HOPE

> We finished the season comfortably in mid-table and Harry Godwin, the chief scout, came up to me and said, "In the thirteen seasons I've been at Maine Road, we have only been above the bottom six in the First Division four times." I felt we had made good progress.
>
> **Malcolm Allison**, talking about 1966-7

IN JULY 1966 England won the World Cup. For most of the Finals, which were held in England, Joe Mercer worked as a BBC television panellist. He was liked by the "man in the street" for his honest, down-to-earth comments. His was a human face at a time when television was beginning to adopt a more professional image. He caused much hilarity, mainly because of his wisecracks, but also through his pronunciation of the names of foreign players. Also, early on in the tournament, he spotted a player who later became a household name.

Joe thought that Antonio Rattin, the Argentine captain, was a great player. He admired his arrogance on the ball, the skilful way he stroked it around, and, above all, he liked the way he controlled the game, even to the extent of trying to tell the referees what to do! In the quarter-final, against England, Rattin was sent off for arguing with the referee. The Argentinian has always maintained that he was trying to tell the referee he was the captain, nothing more, but the outcome was an unpleasant situation because Rattin refused to leave the field for several minutes.

"What do you think of him now, Joe?"

Joe was as genial as ever in his response. He joked about how he would praise more of England's opponents in the hope that they might get sent off, too!

He was always nervous before going on television. On the set, however, he relaxed, and the familiar Mercer grin transmitted itself to the rest of the nation. He came over as a natural fatherly figure, the type of person you wanted in your front room. He was just himself.

In 1966, the BBC did not always have studio facilities at the ground. Some of the dashes from Goodison Park, Liverpool, to the Manchester studio were particularly breathtaking. One time the driver took them on the central reservation to save being stuck too long in a traffic-jam. Another time, after Portugal had beaten North Korea 5-3, Joe Mercer and David Coleman jumped in a taxi, and Joe was saying what he thought of the game. "I never thought the Koreans would be that fit and strong," Joe said. "They kept coming and coming. They kept on attacking." Then the taxi-driver turned round and said, "They were like that with that bleeding hill in Korea when I was shooting the bastards."

Joe helps Norah into the car outside the Maine Road offices.

The television exposure helped both Joe and Manchester City. Joe was no longer a failed manager. He was a former England captain, a great player in his day and now manager of the exciting First Division newcomers Manchester City.

Joe and Malcolm knew that their side was not yet strong enough to be able to challenge for honours. There was enough talent up front - Mike Summerbee, Johnny Crossan, Neil Young and two promising youngsters, Glyn Pardoe and Mike Doyle - but they needed a stronger defence if they were to stay in the First Division. George Heslop had settled in at centre-half, goalkeeper Harry Dowd had done as much as anyone to get the side up, and Alan Oakes was a dependable wing-half, but Mercer and Allison decided they needed a full-back. Allison knew a player who just might fit the bill - an unknown called Tony Book, who Allison had managed at both Bath City and Plymouth Argyle. Malcolm Allison: "When I wanted to sign Tony Book after we'd won promotion I said to him [Joe Mercer] one afternoon, 'Look, I've been to watch this one, I've been to watch that one, I've been to watch another ... ' I'd been to watch four top full-backs and I said to him, 'There's a player playing at Plymouth, Joe, who is better than all of them.' And so he said to me, 'Who is that?' I said, 'It's a player called Tony Book.' So he just said, 'Oh, right, yes.' Now I knew what he was going to do, he used to go away, he'd go home and he'd ring up all his mates to find out all about whoever, so he came back the following morning and he said, 'That player you want is thirty-one years old, Malcolm!' I said, 'Look, Joe, were you finished when you went from Everton to Arsenal?' So he said, 'What do you mean, was I finished?' So I answered, 'What do I mean? You were *thirty-two* when you went from Everton to Arsenal and you played another seven years!' So he just laughed and then we signed Tony, and he did a great, fabulous job for us. He was the 'Footballer of the Year' when he was about thirty-five. A great player."

Joe did not need much convincing. He had seen Book play for Plymouth against City the previous season, and he knew what 'good old uns' could achieve. He did not think Book could match his own achievements at Arsenal - the game had moved on a pace since Joe's playing days - but he was willing to give Book the chance. It was an inspired signing, and Joe enjoyed watching him play, perhaps thinking of his own twilight years: "I didn't mind him playing well and having plenty of skill, but what made me green with envy was his speed. I mean, it's not right for the over thirties to be skinning the youngsters. It's meant to be a young man's game! We used to hear these First Division coaches shouting from the bench - 'Take the old man on!' No chance! He was a great athlete."

Manchester City paid out £17,000. Book later admitted that he was apprehensive, and believed the fee was too much for a 31-year-old. When Joe met Tony Book in London, he reassured the player: "You look fit enough son. You look like I used to. There's nothing of you. You look really well."

Joe Mercer and Tony Book took the underground to Wembley where they immediately bumped into a northern sportswriter who knew Joe well. Joe did not want to reveal the name of his companion to the reporter as he realised it might jeopardise the transfer, so Joe introduced Tony Book as "Jim Smith, a friend of mine."

The reporter did not recognise Book. After all, he was still relatively unknown in the game. A little later, however, Phil Woosnam, a former City player who had been signed by Joe for Aston Villa, spotted the two men and he did recognise Book. Woosnam seemed a little surprised at seeing them together, but he certainly would never have believed that City were about to sign the Plymouth player. Book soon became an essential part of the City side that aimed to consolidate in Division One. He made his City début on the opening day of the season when the Blues drew 1-1 at Southampton.

City's first home game of the new season let the whole of football know that they were well and truly back. Mercer's men defeated the reigning League Champions, Liverpool, 2-1 before a welcoming crowd of over fifty thousand. Joe and Malcolm no longer needed to fear that the stadium would be empty, as optimism swept through the club.

Old friends, but 'derby' rivals. Joe and Matt Busby at a City-United game.

Don Evans of the *News of the World* wrote a guest column in City's programme for the visit of Liverpool. In his article he wrote that he believed Mercer's City had a great future ahead of them, but first they had to consolidate. He wrote: "Any club entering a higher division must first set its sights on consolidation. Only when this has been achieved can higher targets be aimed for. This, of course, does not mean that City will not be striving to win the League title, the FA Cup, the League Cup and any other trophy available. Anything less than such ambition is foreign to the club. City, always an honoured club in British football, could now be set to embark upon its brightest-ever days. Certainly all at Maine Road have the ambition to match such sentiments. I believe City have a great future, I am impatient for its full development, but I'll still not be upset if this season at least they do not set all the houses on fire. I'll still be around next season - I hope. And I'm certain City will also - around the top of the table!"

Evans had guessed it exactly right. City would first consolidate and then be around the top of the table in their second season back!

City also had an early chance to redress the balance of power in the city. September 17 1966. Manchester United at Old Trafford.

Matt Busby welcomed City to Stretford, and congratulated the Blues on winning the Second Division. He also made a special mention of Joe in his programme notes. The two men had known each other since their early playing days. Busby of course had played for Manchester City and Liverpool when Joe was at Everton. He had played with Joe for the Combined Services during the war, and captained Scotland against Joe's England in the mid-1940s.

In 1966 the rivalry resumed, although both men stressed that the rivalry should always be friendly. Unfortunately, all City's old doubts and inadequacies returned. United were the more powerful side. At one point United's Denis Law was at the centre of a free-for-all. Players squared up to each other, fists flew, and the referee, Jack Taylor, surprised everyone by taking no action. Approximately six minutes later Denis Law upset the City players even further by scoring the only goal of the game.

After this, City slid down the table. Thoughts of success turned to thoughts of preservation. Joe Mercer: "We started well with three good results and seemed set for a fine life among the top-class teams. We were confident. Then Chelsea came north to Maine Road and ripped all our fancy notions to shreds. They took us apart on our own ground. They exposed flaws. They set us thinking. We wanted to survive in the First Division. This became our priority. Tony Book was installed as a sweeper behind the rest of the defence; a negative move that was mere insurance against further good hidings."

Chelsea had humiliated City 4-1 at home, and Joe and Malcolm agreed that something had to be done. In addition to the positional changes that took place on the field, the two of them worked on ways to improve the players' training. They agreed to bring in Derek Ibbotson, an England athlete, to help develop City as one of the fittest sides in Europe. Malcolm always believed that footballers should be top athletes, while Joe believed footballers should always be fit enough for any challenge. "Seventy or eighty per cent of football is fitness," Joe often said.

City's form continued to be poor. After the Maine Road derby with Manchester United - a 1-1 draw - City were in 19th place after 25 games. Joe needed to pick the club up before it was too late. In fact, City lost only four of the last 17, and supplemented it with good FA Cup form. For the second year running, they reached the sixth round of the competition. In later years Joe Mercer looked back on the sixth-round tie as a turning-point: "We were drawn away to Leeds United - ruthless robot-like Leeds they were then - in the FA Cup. The entire football world expected us to play it tight. But they reckoned wrong. They overlooked the moral courage, the gambling streak, the spirit of adventure that was always just below the surface of the Mercer-Allison partnership. We did precisely the opposite to what was expected. We attacked them! We threw everything in. We decided, in just as few words, 'What the hell have we got to lose?' City were brilliant that day. We gave Leeds a lesson and with the most outrageous luck lost by a solitary goal that should have been disallowed. We had been so much on top the result was unbelievable. Still, we had found ourselves. We were on our way, we started to stretch defences. Fear was scoffed at!"

It may be Joe doing all the shouting here, but the picture was taken the day before a subdued Malcolm Allison commenced a 28 day touchline ban in November 1966.

City took the game to Leeds. The team that had previously been rooted in a defensive style of play, broke forward and played exciting attacking football. Leeds were not used to teams going to Elland Road and attacking them. The only goal came in the 50th minute, following Leeds' first corner of the game. When Eddie Gray floated the ball towards the goal, Jack Charlton appeared to impede City 'keeper Harry Dowd. Charlton headed in, and City complained, unsuccessfully.

The discovery of an attacking style was perhaps more important than City's final position of fifteenth in the table. Also important was a new face, introduced towards the end of the 1966-7 season. Joe was always the first to admit that he had grave doubts about the player in question. Tony Coleman, signed from Doncaster on 16 March 1967, brought with him a reputation as being a bit of a hell-raiser. Most managers would not touch him. Joe was convinced, at first, that the player would be nothing but trouble. Coleman's past record seemed to back that up. Stoke City had allegedly thrown him out, Preston North End said he was 'unmanageable', Bangor City took advantage of no League team wanting him and then Doncaster Rovers took a real gamble by bringing him back to League football. At Doncaster it was reported that he had punched a referee in the face. No wonder Joe had doubts!

Malcolm Allison believed he could control the player. Others had tried and failed but Malcolm wanted Joe to take the gamble. Joe took some convincing. Malcolm Allison: "A famous Evertonian that Joe played with, TG Jones, was manager of Bangor. I went along to this match at Altrincham. Bangor were playing them in the FA Cup on a Wednesday afternoon or something. I'm watching the game and this kid was playing really well on the left wing - a lovely left foot. Now we needed another left-footed player. We had Neil Young and we'd converted Glyn Pardoe - he wasn't really a left-footed player - so I told Joe and he said, 'Yes, you're right, we really do.' So, anyway, I came back from the game and I said, 'Joe, I've seen one - we can buy him for £3,000 from Bangor.' So Joe said, 'Oh, great, I'll ring up TG. Who's the player?.' So I said, 'A boy called Tony Coleman.' Joe immediately went, '**Oh, no, not Tony Coleman, no, no** - I was at Lilleshall when he threw the bed out of the window! He did all sorts! **No, Malcolm. No!** He was in serious trouble with a referee!' So I said, 'But, Joe, he's a good player.' Anyway, after that he was transferred from Bangor to Doncaster Rovers, and so I'm watching this match in midweek, and this kid was playing again - he was outstanding. Well, we were still looking for a left-sided player. So I went to see their manager after the game and asked, 'How much do you want for him?' I think the price was about seventeen, so I said, 'No, that's too much,' and I managed to get him down to twelve thousand. So then I said I'll have a word with Joe and we'll ring you in the morning - I'd really agreed to pay twelve thousand, though, because we were doing quite well for money. I saw Joe and said, 'Joe, I've found a left-footed player for twelve thousand pounds.' He said, 'Oh, good, great - who?' I couldn't wait! So I said, 'Tony Coleman.' He went, 'Oh no, no - not him again. **No!**' Anyway I eventually managed to talk him into it. We went and signed the player, and he did a good job for us.'"

Joe was not the only person who knew Tony Coleman from Lilleshall. Mike Doyle did too: "He had a crew-cut, seemed to have tattoo marks all over his arms, wore jeans and a tee-shirt, and spoke with a Scouse accent you could almost cut with a knife. The men in charge of the course were Walter Winterbottom and Joe Mercer, and all the youngsters paid them due respect. Only one guy didn't address either of them as 'Mr'. Right from the start, it was 'Walter' and 'Joe' to Tony. We were at Lilleshall for eight days, and I remember that, when he had an hour or two to spare, Tony would borrow a bike and sneak off to Newport to enjoy himself there. When the course was drawing to an end some of the lads became a bit bored and decided to liven things up. There was some horseplay in one of the third-floor rooms, and the next thing you knew, a bed was flying out of the window. The story went the rounds that it was Tony who started the ball rolling, to inject some excitement into what he felt was becoming a repetitive sort of existence."

Despite everyone's concerns Coleman soon settled in at City, although it's true to say

Joe and Malcolm
caught in the middle
of a tactical discussion
at Maine Road.

there were a few 'adventures' along the way. The Coleman signing proved that Joe and Malcolm would back each other if one was convinced he was doing right for Manchester City. Even Joe would later look back on the signing with great affection: "Tony Coleman? I was the only manager he didn't hit. He had a great left foot. One day we gave him a rollicking about not scoring enough goals. 'I can score goals,' he said. 'It's just that I don't like being kissed.'"

Sometimes Malcolm would find a player, sometimes Joe, but they had to agree before completing a signing. Joe went for Summerbee, Malcolm convinced Joe about Bell, Book and Coleman. There was one player they agreed on from the start but were unable to sign. Both Joe and Malcolm believed they needed a world-class goalkeeper. Harry Dowd was City's main 'keeper at the time and, although he was good, he was not quite the class of 'keeper City fans had come to expect. Dowd had had the unenviable task of following Bert Trautmann, who many believed was the world's best goalkeeper. Before Trautmann there had been England's Frank Swift, who many City supporters regarded - and some still regard - as the greatest City and England 'keeper of all time.

Malcolm did not care what a top goalkeeper might cost - money was 'no object' to him - while Joe was aware that he had the directors to satisfy. In 1967, when one of the world's top 'keepers became available, and Malcolm and Joe were both keen to sign him, only the price stood in the way. Malcolm Allison: "The only time we didn't get the player we wanted was when we went for Gordon Banks. Leicester City let him go because Shilton was coming through. They were letting him go for £50,000, so that he could do well out of the deal himself. Now Joe was a bricklayer's son and money was always an important factor to him, whereas to me it meant nothing at all. So I said to him, 'Joe, ring up Leicester City and tell them we'll buy Gordon Banks for the £50,000.' So Joe said 'Okay Mal, I'm going to do that anyway'. So I went away training. When I came back, I said, 'Have you signed him then, Joe?' So he said,

Three men with strong Everton-City connections. Dixie Dean (left), Everton goalscoring legend who netted against City in the 1933 FA Cup Final; Joe Mercer and Tommy 'Tosh' Johnson (right), a star with City in the late 1920's whose move to Everton caused uproar in Manchester.

'I've bid £40,000.' He always wanted to do a deal! He couldn't do anything straightforward, he always wanted to haggle. In the end Banks went to Stoke for the £50,000! A few years later he cost us the Championship - he was outstanding in our game against Stoke. It was 1972, when Derby County won it."

Although Joe's keenness to strike a bargain prevented the legendary Banks from signing for the Blues, Joe believed that the City squad was not too far from becoming a very good side. He had been happy with the team's performance at Leeds, and was pleased that the last few weeks of the season had seen the Blues move well away from the relegation area. As City's strength improved during the two seasons under Joe, so did his own health. By the start of the 1967-8, Joe Mercer was more or less fully recovered. He was thoroughly enjoying himself.

Joe hard at work behind his manager's desk at Maine Road.

Chapter Eighteen

THE BLUE BALLET

I was looking at your match on Saturday and I think you have the best workmanlike team I've seen since the old days - nothing fancy, just a set of lads making it easy for themselves as it should be. Tell Mike [Summerbee] to keep getting them that way and he is a certainty for a white shirt.

Letter from **Billy 'Dixie' Dean** to Joe Mercer, December 1967

WHEN THE 1967-8 season started, on 19 August, Joe Mercer still believed the City side needed strengthening. Neither he nor Malcolm Allison were fully convinced they had all the players needed to mount a serious challenge for the League Championship. Tony Coleman was an exciting forceful player but the Blues still needed another quality attacker. Johnny Crossan had now moved on to Middlesbrough, and Pardoe and Doyle had been pulled back into defence and midfield respectively. In the first few games of the new season Joe and Malcolm tried different combinations without really finding the necessary blend.

Only one point - a no-score draw at home to Liverpool - was obtained during the first three games. After that Joe tried the youngster Paul Hince at number seven. Hince had played in only one League game the previous season, when he scored twice in a 2-2 home draw with West Bromwich Albion. Now he was given his chance again for a home game against Southampton. The Blues found their goalscoring touch and went on to win five League games in a row. One of them was against Nottingham Forest. Malcolm Allison: "We were playing Nottingham Forest and Paul Hince played quite well at outside-right. In this particular game he absolutely mesmerised the Forest full-back - he was running him inside and outside and totally slaughtering him. Anyway this full-back got involved in an incident and the referee sent him off. Paul Hince went, 'Oh, don't send him off ref - he's easy! I'm enjoying it!'"

Mercer's men scored 18 goals in those five wins. They played in the attacking style that had surprised Leeds the previous season. City moved up the table and by mid-September found themselves in the top five. During this run Joe gave a début to the young Stan Bowles, who scored an incredible four goals in his first one and a half games. (The half was when he came on as substitute in a League Cup tie against Leicester and scored twice.) City's fine run ended with a 1-0 defeat away to Joe's old team Arsenal.

The next game was another Manchester derby. Almost 63,000 poured into Maine Road to see City take on the reigning Champions. City included their new signing, goalkeeper Ken Mulhearn from Stockport County, but only because regular-choice Harry Dowd had dislocated a finger in training. On derby day, Mulhearn arrived at the ground about one and a half hours before the other players - he was so excited. Malcolm Allison spotted him and immediately realised that Mulhearn was very nervous. Allison locked Mulhearn in the medical room until the new goalkeeper had calmed down. When Mulhearn was let out, the other players thought he had only just arrived! Mulhearn admitted that he was nervous about playing in front of over 60,000 at Maine Road rather than a couple of thousand at Stockport. He says the only moments of the game he remembers are when Bobby Charlton scored his two first-half goals. City had started the game well, Colin Bell scoring after only five minutes, but with typical unpredictability went down 2-1. City were still Manchester's second team.

Mulhearn retained his place for the rest of the season, and City returned to form. After losing 2-0 at Wolves, on 14 October, they were unbeaten in the next ten games. This great run coincided with the signing of Francis Lee.

Both Malcolm Allison and Joe Mercer remembered Lee from his games for Bolton Wanderers against City in the Second Division, and from the a Bolton-City League Cup tie in 1966-7, when Lee had scored. Joe and Malcolm went to watch Bolton's League Cup game with Liverpool in September and the player was outstanding.

Lee was far from happy with Bolton at the time. He was unhappy with the terms of the contract offered, and disenchanted with the club. On Friday 29 September 1967, he told Bolton manager Bill Ridding that he was walking out. Bolton decided to transfer him to City without delay. The move suited the player because he had business interests in the Bolton area. It was something that Grocer Joe would have understood!

Joe Mercer and Malcolm Allison travelled to Bolton to meet Bill Ridding and the player. Even at this late stage the move did not go smoothly, much to Francis Lee's disbelief: "The next day was Friday, and I went back to Maine Road and signed. Already Bill Ridding had told the Manchester City officials that I would not get my ten per cent of the transfer fee because I had asked for a move. But even he did not bargain for the Football League reaction. I had my boots with me and was all set to move out with the team to play at Sunderland in a First Division game the following day. But the League refused to rush my registration through, and just as I thought my future had been settled Joe Mercer came out of his office to say, 'It's all off, the League won't accept the registration.' Finally, however, it was ironed out and the following Monday I signed. I remember Joe's words. 'I hope you will sign,' he said when we first met. 'We feel we've got the start of a good side. We are just one player short, and we think you are that player. The odd goal or two will turn us into a great team.'"

Joe was right. From the moment Lee signed, on 9 October, City were a more powerful side. A team was now in place: Mulhearn, Book, Pardoe, Doyle, Heslop, Oakes, Lee, Bell, Summerbee, Young, and Coleman.

On 9 December, the strength of that City side was there for all to see as the Blues defeated high-flying Tottenham Hotspur 4-1 in a game that has become known as the 'ballet on ice'. Almost 36,000 witnessed a game played on a snow-covered Maine Road, and that night around five million more had the pleasure of watching it on the BBC television's 'Match of the Day' programme. It was classed by many as television's match of the season.

At first, many doubted that the game could go ahead on such a snowy pitch. The City groundstaff worked hard to make the pitch playable, but when Jimmy Greaves scored for Spurs in the seventh minute at the Platt Lane end many wished the groundsmen had not bothered. By the end of the game the City fans were ecstatic however as City tore Spurs apart. Indeed, City were such an attacking force their defence was barely troubled again.

The equaliser came from Colin Bell, who, to many, remains the greatest ever to play for City. His skill, stamina, and tremendous power has never been matched. Joe Mercer, despite his earlier doubts, was convinced of greatness by this stage: "He's the best player since Peter Doherty, and he will get even better. He has got fantastic stamina, but also this unusual combination of speed and stamina, like Matthews or Finney. Players usually have speed and no stamina, or

Action from the famous 'ballet on ice' - City 4 Tottenham 1.
Above: Colin Bell (far left) strikes City's equaliser after Jimmy Greaves had given the visitors an early lead.
Below: Mike Summerbee, hampered by two defenders, heads City into a 2-1 lead.
See overleaf for goals three and four...

Above: Tony Coleman jumps for joy after scoring City's third goal against Tottenham.
Below: Neil Young (left) watches as his effort crosses the line to complete the scoring... 4-1 to City.

stamina and no speed, or speed and stamina but no balance. But Colin Bell has all these. He is best when he is given free rein and coming from the deep. He is a good tackler and covers every inch of the pitch."

During the game against Spurs, Bell's wide-ranging skills were much in evidence. The snow continued to fall but City's forwards mastered the conditions. Neil Young's shot brought an outstanding save from Pat Jennings. Another Young effort hit the right-hand post. Finally, in the second half, Young crossed from the left and Mike Summerbee scored from six yards with a brilliant header.

In the 64th minute, Tony Coleman, the rogue Joe had doubts about, scored the third when he followed up a Francis Lee shot that had hit the left post. Local-boy Neil Young made it four with one from close range. The Blues continued to push forward, and shot after shot went towards the Spurs goal. In one attack Tony Coleman latched on to a pass from Bell. Coleman's shot hit the left-hand post, and Young followed up by hitting the right-hand post.

Neil Young was an unsung hero of that City side. He ended 1967-8 as top scorer and Joe Mercer rated him as "the player with more talent than anybody else at the club". Joe believed the only thing he lacked was confidence, something that Malcolm Allison worked on. Young was to be one of City's most valuable players over the next three or four years.

After the game, City made all the headlines and received praise from all over the country. Among the letters Joe Mercer received was one from Billy 'Dixie' Dean, Joe's one-time idol at Everton.

Joe and Malcolm talk tactics.

A United fan called Bobby Greenroyd wrote: "I am a regular Manchester United fan but after Saturday's game your next home gate will be increased by one."

Mr G Firth from Barnsley wrote: "I have recently had the good fortune to watch Manchester City three times in the last four weeks, and I felt that I just had to write to you and compliment you and your training staff for producing the best team in Britain."

Others wrote in saying that if ever City were playing in their town then they would certainly go along to the game to support the Blues. Clearly, from the way neutral supporters wrote to Joe and the club in general, many people hoped that City would win the Championship. They still had a long way to go but the Spurs game proved that the Blues were capable of producing terrific results. A couple of setbacks in the Christmas League matches were soon followed by something even more embarrassing. Third Division Reading came to Maine Road for a third-round FA Cup tie, and City were lucky to escape with a goalless draw. Fortunately, for City, they went to Reading for the replay and won 7-0, Summerbee scoring a hat trick, and were back on course for a great season. As the players left the pitch the tannoy system carried an announcement around the ground: "Ladies and Gentlemen, you have just seen one of the greatest teams England has produced in a long time."

Peter Doherty, the great Irish inside-forward who starred for City in their 1936-7 Championship season, was at the match. He told Joe that the performance was "quite brilliant" and one of the best he had ever seen. Arthur Shaw, a former Arsenal colleague of Joe's, was also at the game. Shaw had had little recent contact with football, but City's display and Joe's enthusiasm revived his love of the game. He later went on record as saying that the Reading match had turned him into a Manchester City supporter and he predicted that five of the players who played that night would go on to win international caps.

Confidence soared throughout Maine Road as the Blues put in some great performances. There were still occasional setbacks, like the 4-3 defeat at Leicester in an exciting FA Cup fourth-round replay, but City were gaining ground on United in the League. On 16 March Mercer's men went top of the table on goal average after annihilating Fulham 5-1 at Maine Road. In an interview around this time, Joe was asked about the secret of City's success. He answered: "We do everything quick and simple and we're remarkably fit. We don't mind who comes and sees us training, or sees us playing, you know. We feel it's a simple game and we try to keep it simple."

City lost their next match, 2-0 at Leeds, and United took a two-point lead. No matter what the Blues did, the Reds still seemed one step ahead, and City's role as Manchester's second team was continually reinforced by the media. Mercer and Allison longed for the opportunity to break the United stranglehold, and their chance came on Wednesday 27 March. It was one of the most important dates of Joe Mercer's managerial career. A City victory in a Manchester derby was long overdue.

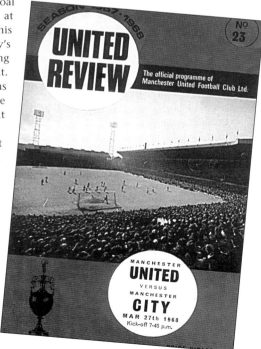

Chapter Nineteen

'MARS NEXT STOP'

The balance of power which has kept Manchester United perched so long beyond the reach of their poor relations from Maine Road took a violent swing in this drama-packed derby. For magnificent Manchester City, who came from behind after a shock start that would have shattered the nerves of many sides, outplayed, outfought and out-manoeuvred the team who carry England's hopes in the European Cup. With two points so richly deserved, if only for the relentless power of their non-stop running, they leap-frogged on goal average over United to second place in the table, and made it a three-club deadlock at the top. Leeds, Manchester City and United are all on 45 points ... a situation to set Manchester soccer fans tingling!

Ronald Crowther, Daily Mail, 28 March 1968

"*I* WAS NOT a United fan," Joe Mercer said later in life, "But I was a Busby fan." In the 1960s, the rival managers of City and United met regularly and played golf together. They even traded stories about their players. Matt told Joe about the first time he saw George Best play, his memory of the young Irish lad collecting a short corner, cutting in and bending the ball round the goalkeeper and in at the far post. Joe entertained people with occasional "stories about Bestie". Here's one of Joe's favourites, told in his own words, his eyes twinkling, a smile never far away: "One day at Old Trafford, United were playing Bolton, who had hard men like Hartle and Banks who would kick the tops off your stockings. Well, Bestie went through them all like a fox in a hen run, put the ball in the net. Some young reporter in the press box said, 'What time was that goal?' Arthur Walmesley replied, 'Never mind the time, what was the date?'"

When Joe and his side arrived at Old Trafford for the 78th City-United League derby, few rated their chances. After all, as United fans boasted, City had only won the Second Division Championship during the sixties while the Reds had won two League Championships and the FA Cup. Now, in 1967-8, United had a team full of stars - George Best, Bobby Charlton, Denis Law, Pat Crerand, etc - and had great hopes of becoming the first English team to win the League and the European Cup in the same season. To United supporters, the Manchester derby mattered only in so far as it would show City just how far behind they really were!

On the night of the derby, Joe took his place in the directors box, and exchanged a few friendly words with Matt Busby while they awaited the start. Sir Alf Ramsey was there, too.

Manchester United 1 City 3, 27th March 1968
Above: United's Alex Stepney is stranded as Colin Bell's shot gives City the equaliser.
Below: George Heslop scores his first League goal for City to make it 2-1.

Over 63,000 packed into the Old Trafford stadium for what was, in effect, the Championship of Manchester.

Joe sat down as the game started, and saw City go a goal down after only 38 seconds. Tony Book realised he was responsible: "An unforgivable error on my part let in George Best early on with a mistimed back-pass. I knew I should have stopped him and what's more I knew that had I been alert I could have stopped him. It didn't need the groans of our fans to make me aware of what a zero rating I was getting because this was one meeting where neither side could afford slip-ups. As captain, my team-mates looked to me for example, but on this occasion it was their attitude, their example, which promptly put behind me any thoughts of getting depressed about the incident."

At first, all the old concerns came back to haunt City fans. The first ten minutes of the game were desperate for their team. The Blues almost appeared to give up, then, just when it was needed most, Colin Bell began to control midfield, Mike Doyle won important tackles and City gradually got on top. After 15 minutes Bell started a right-wing move and then ran yards to reach the final pass and blast the equaliser past United goalkeeper Alex Stepney.

City were extraordinary that night. They pushed forward time after time, and were reward-ed with a second goal after 57 minutes. Tony Coleman curled across a free-kick and centre-half George Heslop scored his first goal for City with a firm downward header.

Joe was delighted, but there was still more to come. Colin Bell, who had spent most of the evening demonstrating to the Manchester public how special he was, raced clear and headed for goal. He was hauled down by Francis Burns, and Francis Lee scored the resulting penalty. City went on to win 3-1, and the only blemish was that Bell was carried off on a stretcher with a knee injury after the penalty incident. He would miss the next four games.

The important part about the victory though, was that it had finally restored pride to the City ranks. Now there was debate about which was the best team in Manchester. For almost all the post-war period, the answer had been obviously "United". No wonder City fans held their heads high. Indeed, there were even poems composed about the event. One of them, 'City's Night Of Glory', had eleven verses, and covered almost every incident in the game. Another, 'The Crushing Of The Reds', reproduced in *From Maine Men to Banana Citizens*, started as follows:

27th Day of March, A Wednesday night,
United they did die of fright,
Although Best scored in the first minute,
After that they were never in it.

It is difficult to stress what the victory meant to supporters of Manchester City. Joe and Malcolm understood. They had witnessed the disdain which United supporters held for City. They had assessed the discrepancy in the column inches applied to each team in the press. Now, City fans had their chance to pour scorn on the Reds. Joe would have none of it though. Although Malcolm frequently boasted about the power of the Blues, Joe controlled those boasts. He gave Manchester City the best image possible.

From that game on 27 March 1968, for the rest of Joe's reign at Maine Road, City dominat-ed the Manchester derby in a way that neither club had previously. United's next League derby victory was on the last day of the 1970-71 season, when Eamonn Andrews walked on to the pitch to announce, 'This is your life, Sir Matt Busby.' Joe was pleased for his great friend, on a day when the result was not vital.

Joe was City's 'elder statesman' who gave the club the respect it deserved. There was a spe-cial aura around Joe that gave the impression of a likeable, friendly, sincere, jovial character. Throughout his playing career he was admired for his fair-minded approach and respect for losers. At Manchester City his presence prevented the club from trying to gain revenge over

United for all the insults and the ridicule endured throughout the late 1950s and early 1960s. Joe's view was that the football should prove City's power, not scorn.

Following the 1968 derby match, Joe and Malcolm tried to keep the side's momentum going. It was not easy. Missing Colin Bell, they lost to Leicester and Chelsea in the next four games. Mike Doyle remembers Joe's attempt to push his players further: "We'd got one point out of two games. From there we went to Southport for four days, and got the biggest bollocking from Mercer we'd ever had. He said, 'The Championship is there to be won, either you want to win it or you don't. You'll train together tomorrow morning and then I don't want to see you again. It's up to you after that.' He knew we'd get together and talk it out. One night there was me, Neil Young, George Heslop, Belly, Mike [Summerbee], Oakesy and Glyn Pardoe discussing the situation. We reckoned we could do it, and I don't think we lost another game from then on."

Against Sheffield Wednesday, a lucky deflection gave City the only goal of the game. At home to Everton, Tony Book and Tony Coleman scored the goals in a 2-1 victory. City were then a mere two games away from glory, but faced two difficult away games - at Spurs and Newcastle. "It'll be like climbing Everest and K2 in one week," said Joe.

The first game, away to Tottenham, resulted in a terrific 3-1 victory. Much like Joe's old Arsenal side, City were an 'all attacking, all defending' side. One minute they packed their defence, the next they launched a six-man attack. Colin Bell scored twice and Mike Summerbee got the other.

Brian James, in the *Daily Mail*, stressed City's power and claimed that their success was down to "bloody hard and selfless running". He claimed that Spurs were "a team of much talent sparsely applied" while City were "a side of fair quality, brilliantly inspired". James went on to say that "City's output should be rewarded by not less than the title".

City and United were level on 56 points, and each had one game to play. City's was at Newcastle. United's was at home to lowly Sunderland. United had a better goal average than City, so the Blues had to ensure a better result at St James' Park than United's at Old Trafford. Also, if both City and United failed, Liverpool, with two to play, could leapfrog them and win the Championship by a point. Joe knew that his players were capable, but he realised that the pressure might get to them.

For the first time all season the media seemed to realise that the Blues might just pull off the unthinkable. For a decade City had played second fiddle to United and, quite simply, were not used to the media attention. Joe was worried. He told one reporter that City were the side with all the pressure now. They were the side who had to live up to the public's expectations. He went on to point out his great fear: "I am more afraid of my own team than I shall be of Newcastle United next Saturday. The danger is that the boys might think too much about the game during the next few days. But we just have to feel confident now that we have won at Spurs."

Tony Book, City's remarkable captain, who had come from oblivion to the verge of great success, admitted that "the next six days will seem like six years". Mike Summerbee attempted to lighten the mood. When he walked into Maine Road on the Monday after the Spurs game, he couldn't help but notice that the ground was full of photographers and reporters. For City, at that time, the attention

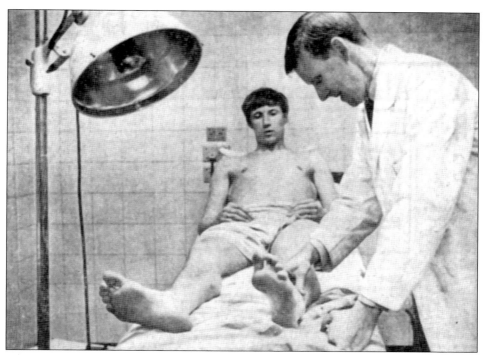

Colin Bell receives treatment from physio Peter Blakey in the build up to the title decider at Newcastle.

was new. Summerbee looked at the crowd and called across to Joe in a mock serious tone: "What's happened, Boss? Has there been an accident?"

Leading up to the final game, both City and United found themselves tipped for the title. Almost every footballing personality available gave his view. After the game at Spurs, Jimmy Greaves told Tony Book that City were the best side he had seen all season and the Blues deserved to win the title. Stan Anderson, the Middlesbrough manager, called the Blues the "team of the season ... exciting, tremendously composed." Bill Shankly, the great boss of Liverpool, more or less conceded the title when he declared: "I regard City as favourites now. Any team that can do what they did at Tottenham must have a great chance."

Incredibly, George Best, who was presented with the Footballer of the Year trophy the week before the season's end, predicted that City would win the title in style: "When they came to Old Trafford and beat us, I'd only seen them a couple of times before that and didn't think much of them. But that night we never saw the way they went. I've never seen a team run and achieve the workrate they did. I felt like demanding blood tests on them afterwards. They may lack United's individual ability, but if they can keep working and running they must be in with a great chance of beating Newcastle United on Saturday. It won't be easy, but I fancy them to do it. We at United have thrown it away by our inconsistency. We only needed a point at West Brom - and we were playing them only 48 hours after their Cup semi-final. They should have been exhausted, but they gave us a good hiding. Yet five days later we go and stick six past Newcastle. That's what I mean about our inconsistency."

Best went on to outline City's virtues, and then spoke about one of City's best players, Mike Summerbee. Said Best: "Even though he's my mate I never rated Mike as a great winger. But at centre-forward he's a different class. One of the best in the country. He does work for the other players that the fans don't see. I'd like to play a game in the City attack just to see what it's like."

This side is better, says Barkas

SAM BARKAS, captain of Manchester City in their one and only championship win to date, walked into Maine Road yesterday to wish Joe Mercer's side success on Saturday.

'In many ways this present side is a better one than we were and I don't mind admitting it,' said this old-time City stalwart, who captained his team from full-back as Tony Book does today.

'Modern coaching and training techniques have had a big impact on the game and there is something quite exceptional about the style of this modern City side,' he added.

'I can think of only two men from that 1936-37 team who could have slotted straight into this side of 1968 and they would have been the "big fella" (the late Frank Swift) and Peter Doherty.'

But Barkas, like many other people, sees grounds for comparison in the styles of Peter Doherty and City's present-day dynamo, Colin Bell.

Bell, he believes, is rushing towards football maturity at such a speed that it is difficult to believe he is only 21.

Regret

'There are no limits to what this young man can achieve with so many years ahead of him,' said Barkas, who also paid a compliment to Mike Summerbee.

'He must be the most unselfish centre forward I have seen in many years.

'He absorbs so much of the weight of every opposing team's defensive concentration and accepts so many hard knocks as a result. His unselfishness has probably cost him appearances in the England team.'

'It isn't easy to make comparisons between teams of different eras and some people might consider it unfair,' said the former England captain. 'But I don't live in the past, and I consider that this team does a lot more running and chasing than we did.'

Barkas's one regret is that the tension on the present-day side is greater than it was for his own team. 'A run of 21 games from Christmas without defeat put us in a strong position,' he added. 'We had to win the last match but one—against Sheffield Wednesday at Maine Road—to clinch it, and we did this by 4—1.

'But it will be great to see my old football home, Maine Road, on top of the world again. They've got fans there who deserve it, and I'm quite sure this side is going to do it.'

RONALD CROWTHER

As Best realised, City were a true team. Although they had some great individuals, no player was bigger than the team itself. Sam Barkas, who had captained City's 1936-7 Championship team, believed Joe's City side combined to make a very good attacking side. He told reporters: "This present side is a better one than we were, and I don't mind admitting it. There is something quite exceptional about the style of this modern City side. I can think of only two men from the 1936-7 team who could have slotted straight into this side of 1968, and they would have been the 'Big Fella' [Frank Swift] and Peter Doherty."

Bell and Summerbee were struggling to be fit for the Newcastle game. They had pulled out of England's midweek match against Spain, a game they were keen to take part in. Throughout the season Joe had been concerned about injuries to his players. Often players took part in games when they really should not have even been considered. Joe's squad was one of the smallest in the First Division, and was certainly the smallest of the top five or six clubs in the table. In the week leading up to the Newcastle game he was asked if it was true that many of his players had turned out when in fact they should have been rested. He responded: "This has been true at times of Alan Oakes, Glyn Pardoe, Tony Book, and Mike Doyle, as well as Colin Bell and Mike Summerbee. There have been games in which they have gone out with pain-killing injections, games before which we have left the final decision with the player himself. It has taken moral courage for them to put the good of the side before personal discomfort and, on many occasions, to insist on playing when decisions about their fitness to do so were not easy to arrive at."

Joe admitted that the squad was not really big enough for the long, hard race for the Championship. He admitted that the Blues had performed to a standard better than he had expected. He had always believed that it would take more than a couple of seasons to turn City from a side heading towards Second Division obscurity into major Championship contenders. The next step for Joe was to build strength in depth, although he made it quite clear to the footballing public that, at a time when professional footballers were beginning to be criticised for greed and lack of commitment, the City players gave their all: "People often talk very disparagingly about modern professionals, and try to make out that they don't give quite so much to the job as they did in the old days. They claim that everybody today wants things easier. But never in all my long association with football have I seen greater dedication than that of these Manchester City players. In the old days, fear of unemployment was undoubtedly a motivating factor. Today, with these players, pride is the driving force - pride in their performances, pride in what they are trying to accomplish."

Glyn Pardoe, Joe Mercer, Ken Mulhearn and Mike Doyle, with the ace up his sleeve, relax at a Newcastle hotel prior to the big game.

FORECASTING the result of the Football League championship that will be decided today is, I am assured by everyone, a simple formality.

Everyone seems happily certain that Joe Mercer's Manchester City will win at Newcastle today and make Manchester United's victory over Sunderland add up to a fraction less than enough . . . that Maine-road will take over the title from Old Trafford.

It has all been worked out with logic, statistics and facts—rather like algebra. The theorists make comforting sense when they point out that because the Manchester teams have proved to have not only better players but sounder tactics, more impressive records and greater incentives than Newcastle and Sunderland, they will win.

The slight snag is that football is not as logical as mathematics nor as leisurely as chess.

Joe went on to tell the press that there would be "no hiding place" at Maine Road for any of the club's players. Business would carry on as normal. Everybody had to be aware of how important the next few days were: "This week brings the crucial test. It requires a special quality of which Champions are made. We can't sweep the situation under the carpet and forget about it."

For all of Manchester the final week of the season was a tense affair. United had their pride at stake, while City had their chance to overtake their rivals. Joe was convinced the Blues could do it, and laughingly told the reporters that he had been practising the walk from Maine Road to Stretford ready for collecting the trophy from the reigning Champions: "I shall personally take great pleasure in walking down to Old Trafford on Sunday morning to pick up the trophy."

The game against Newcastle has been documented in almost every City publication since that famous day in 1968. City appeared nervous in the opening minutes. The 20,000 City supporters there that day must have realised that, more than ever before, the team needed their backing. The City supporters roared on their side in an attempt to give the jittery Blues the confidence and belief they needed.

Newcastle's Jim Scott hit the City crossbar in the third minute. Then City scored in the twelfth. Mike Doyle took a quick free-kick, and Colin Bell raced towards the Newcastle goal, swerving round full-back Frank Clark before pulling the ball back. Doyle shot towards goal and Mike Summerbee flicked the ball into the net.

As City fans celebrated, Newcastle came back. A defensive slip-up allowed Jackie Sinclair to gain possession. Sinclair fed a pass across the goal area where young Glyn Pardoe found himself facing three Newcastle players. Bryan 'Pop' Robson was the one who scored.

Newcastle had the control and composure that City needed. Tony Book played a true captain's role, in the leadership style of Arsenal's Joe Mercer, and tried to calm his players. After 30 minutes, Book saved the Blues when he cleared a header from Wyn Davies that looked a certain goal. Then, within two minutes, the Blues took the lead again.

A quickly taken throw-in by Summerbee was pushed goalwards by Colin Bell. Alan Oakes tried a shot, but the ball spun towards Neil Young who, with a typical goalscorer's instinct, volleyed a glorious goal with his left foot.

It didn't last. Three minutes later Newcastle were level again. City's George Heslop cleared the ball, but only as far as Newcastle's Jim Iley, the ex-Sheffield United player. Iley fed Sinclair, who scored with a fine 15-yard shot.

Although Neil Young had the ball in the net again - Francis Lee was adjudged offside - the score was still 2-2 at half-time. When the interval came, Joe and Malcolm wanted to give the players a bit of a roasting. Malcolm remembers what they saw when they entered the dressing room: "I was going to go in at half-time and give them a right going over in the dressing room.

Above: Mike Summerbee scores City's first goal at Newcastle.
Below: Francis Lee beats Iam McFaul for the fourth and decisive goal... City are champions!

When I got there, though, I could see that they were all tensed up. So I just told them that they had had 45 minutes to get used to it, and now they had to go out and play."

City were more composed in the second half. After only four minutes Colin Bell slipped the ball across the penalty area to Neil Young, who powered the ball in from 12 yards to give City a 3-2 lead. From then on City showed the class and style of football that had thrilled not only their supporters, but the whole of football. They were a joy to watch. Francis Lee had one effort ruled out, but he scored with a 12-yard shot in the 63rd minute, after Doyle and Bell had worked well to get the ball to him. Lee went straight to the crowd with his arms in the air. The City fans were ecstatic.

City played such exciting football that many Newcastle fans were now hoping that the Blues would win the Championship. Four minutes from time, John McNamee scored Newcastle's third. City were still ahead, 4-3, but the pressure was on. Although the last few minutes were tense, the City players were determined to keep their lead. As referee John Thacker blew his whistle, the celebrations began. The supporters chanted, "Champions, Champions", as many of them swarmed on to the pitch to celebrate with their blue-shirted heroes.

Joe was immensely proud with the way his side had played, not just on the day but throughout the season. With Manchester United losing to lowly Sunderland, City were Champions by two points. The Blues won praise from all the nation. The newspapers viewed City's success as being good for the game. City were stylish and a real joy to watch.

The day's only black spot came when the BBC announced that Manchester United's 2-1 defeat at home to Sunderland would be shown as the 'Match of the Day'. It seemed that no matter what City did, the media would always look to Old Trafford first. That season the Blues had been featured on 'Match of the Day' only three times, while the Reds had appeared eight times. Out of the top nine teams that season every team appeared on the programme more times than the Champions except one, West Bromwich Albion, and they won the FA Cup.

At least the newspapers were glowing in their praise. The *Sunday Mirror's* Vince Wilson highlighted the side's strengths: "City were magnificent. A blue-coloured lightning-fast outfit refusing to change a mood which spelled only victory. Twice City suffered the agonising, stomach-turning pain of losing a goal lead when fighting Newcastle stormed back to equalise through Pop Robson and Jackie Sinclair. But City came back as only one team can - a team of Champions. These blue streaks said it with goals - four thrilling, unforgettable goals from Mike Summerbee, Neil Young (2), and Francis Lee. And for those who think City had it easy, let me say this. It is many a long week since the Magpies played so well at home. The essence of City's win personified their whole exciting season - not a player stood out above the others. Not even Neil Young, possessor of that left foot extraordinary which struck cracking goals in each half. You can take your pick of the stars. Was it Young or George Heslop or Francis Lee or Mike Summerbee. The true answer lies with them all."

In the *Sunday Express* James Mossop gave his view of City's Championship victory: "There could be no more popular, sentimental success story. City are - were - the poor relations of the Manchester clubs. Three years ago discontented fans were throwing stones and abuse at the

Brilliant victory at Newcastle

MANCHESTER CITY
DIV 1 CHAMPIONS

Joe and Malcolm enjoy a joke at the post-championship decider press conference.

board-room windows. The crowds had dwindled to a starvation level of 8,000. But in an amazing spell of hard work and dedication Joe Mercer and Malcolm Allison have lifted ordinary players into the Champions of the Football League. They are just a grand set of lads, mostly young, and the best all-round team in England. It is desperately difficult not to get emotional about Manchester City, about such a major success born out of honesty, bravery and complete dedication. This victory was the pinnacle of the season. An afternoon coloured with skill, blessed with fair play and above all applauded in the end by every man, woman and child in the 50,000 crowd. These people will never forget it. Many thousands of them swarmed on to the pitch in a dancing, swirling sea of blue and white at the end. They were cheering for the new champions. For 90 minutes City, the team that has won more friends than any other in a season of imaginative attacking football, turned on the style."

On the day of City's victory over Newcastle the Championship trophy remained at Old Trafford, where if United had been victorious in winning the League it would have naturally been brought out. However, as United lost, the trophy seemed to disappear. *Daily Express* reporter Alan Thompson decided to find out where the trophy was. He started questioning the Old Trafford staff: "Secretary Les Olive was under the impression that a League official had taken it earlier in the week, Matt Busby was not at all sure what had happened to it, and for a minute or two it was lost until a member of the female staff admitted that it had been locked up 'in the vault'. You are at liberty to allow full rein to your imaginations in concluding exactly

Joe orchestrates the celebrations on the return journey from Newcastle.

where the 'vault' is at Old Trafford. But the centre of the board-room table, where the League Championship Cup has stood proudly for the last 12 months was occupied by five shillings worth of flowers. Sit down the City fan who says symbolic."

Joe Mercer arranged a friendly match against Bury for the following Tuesday night. He hoped they would be able to collect the trophy from Old Trafford, and make Tuesday a night of celebration.

The celebrations, of course started on Saturday night, both in Manchester and the north-east, where many Blues remained after the game. On the Sunday, City held a press conference at Maine Road. Mercer, Allison and Book talked to reporters about their success and, of course, their hopes for the following season when they would play in Europe for the first time. All three men were laughing and joking. All three knew what it was like to have been overlooked or rejected earlier in their careers. It was a great moment for all of them. Malcolm Allison had proved himself one of the best coaches in the world. Tony Book had proved a great role model for all people starting late in any career. And Joe Mercer had proved that he was able to bounce back and manage a truly great side. After leaving Villa Joe had said that he wanted to take control of a side that were capable of beating his old club. When Joe's City won the Championship, Aston Villa were in the lower half of the Second Division. Joe had lifted City away from the struggles that Villa now faced, while at the same time, he had emulated Ted Drake and Alf Ramsey, the only men to both play in and manage a Championship-winning side. He was immensely proud.

At the press conference, Joe stressed that City might have to change their style for European games: "It will be more difficult next season. We have played attacking football because it has suited us, because we have been playing to our strength. But I will make no excuse if we find ourselves having to play negatively, mean and tight. Every case has got to be taken on its merits. Every team should be defensive when their opponents have the ball."

Joe went on to talk about improvements he would like to make, and then made his prediction for how far he believed City would go in the European Cup: "The first priority is a good

IT'S MARS NEXT STOP

side. And we want a bigger staff. But I'm sure this side will survive the first two rounds of the European Cup."

Malcolm Allison chipped in with his own view: "I think we will be the first team to play on Mars." The next day the quote appeared in the *Daily Mail* under the headline 'Mars Next Stop'.

When the press conference was over, Joe went back to his house in St Werburgh's Road, Chorlton. The Mercers had moved there when Joe took the job at City. That afternoon Joe relaxed with Norah and David, David's wife Joan and Joe's two-year-old granddaughter, Susan. Joe played with Susan in the garden as well-wisher after well-wisher telephoned to congratulate him. Bill Shankly, whose Liverpool side just missed out on the championship, was the first. Then telegrams came from Matt and Jean Busby amongst others. Norah told reporters that the Sunday afternoon had been the first time he was able to rest for weeks.

On the Monday morning, it was work as normal for all the players and staff. Autograph-hunters waited for the players, the press waited for interviews, and Joe looked to the future. He told *Manchester Evening News* reporter Peter Gardner of his plans: "This is just the beginning of a bright, new era for

Manchester City. I honestly don't know how great they are going to be. It is impossible to sit back and logically say this side will improve. They will only improve if the attitude of mind is right. They must learn to wear this mantle of League Champions with dignity. But, most important of all, they must not consider that they have a divine right to go out and win every match just because they are the Champions. This is the start ... by no means the finish. It is the point from where we must build for the future. The more success, the bigger the demands come but there is only a certain amount that flesh and blood can take."

No longer could the club be described as "dear old City". From now on, opponents would say, "Oh dear, it's City." Joe, like everyone else connected with the club, wanted to end the unpredictability. He wanted to forge a side as powerful and respected as the old Arsenal side. He did not want a side that, as Francis Lee once put it, would "win a cup for cock-ups".

The Championship trophy was presented to Tony Book prior to the friendly with Bury. The players then went on a lap of honour with the crowd celebrating the end of a 30-year wait. When the players returned to the Main stand side of the stadium Joe ran on to the pitch to hug Malcolm. Tony Book then gave the trophy to Joe who lifted it above his head to the roar of the crowd.

Joe returned to the directors' box for the game. City won 4-2, with most of the excitement coming in the closing ten minutes. George Heslop was substituted and his replacement was none other than Malcolm Allison. Allison quickly threw himself into the game. He forced a

great save from Neil Ramsbottom, the Bury 'keeper, and had a goal disallowed. The City supporters chanted 'Allison for England', and then called for Joe to take the field. Joe sat smiling in the stand. He realised his playing days had long gone, although he probably wished he could take part on the pitch and celebrate with his players. At Aston Villa, Joe had played in friendlies, but at City he left the "guest appearance" role to his assistant. Maybe the only thing that stopped Joe was the realisation that there was not enough time for him to change into a City strip.

Celebrations continued after the game. A local reporter went in search of Joe for a quote, and found him on his own eating a bag of chips that he had sneaked out to buy. Now that's the way to celebrate winning the Championship.

'Allison for England' were the chants after Malcolm put on a City strip for an appearance in the celebratory friendly with Bury.

Joe relaxes at home with grandaughter Susan after winning the championship.

City, first in the
First Division
with a first-class
manager!

Chapter Twenty

THE GLORY CONTINUES

"This man must move a mountain." This was the *Manchester Evening News* headline on the day that Manchester City made Joe Mercer their sixth post-war manager. The last spadeful of apathy has just been removed, thank you very much. Manchester City are firmly back on the soccer map as English champions and roaring headlong into Europe for a first crack at the rich rewards that have all previously gone Old Trafford way. Joe Mercer has been on the bridge, Malcolm Allison down in the engine-room stoking up the Blues for one of the finest seasons the Maine Road club has ever enjoyed. Today the mountain has been moved.

Peter Gardner, *Manchester Evening News*, May 1968.

WITH the Championship trophy safe in the Manchester City board-room, Joe took the side on what was meant to be a relaxing tour of North America. In fact, the tour had problems, as the Blues suffered injury after injury. Tony Book suffered damage to his Achilles tendon, and at one point it looked as if his playing career may be over. Fortunately it was not, but he missed the early part of the 1968-9 season.

In one tour game City 'keeper Harry Dowd had to be brought on as an outfield substitute. Malcolm Allison was also forced into action. If the injuries had continued, even Joe may have got his chance. Despite the setbacks Joe came away with some good memories: "When we went on tour to America we landed in Montreal, went to Chicago - Mal went missing for a few days and I thought Al Capone had got him - up to Vancouver, back to Los Angeles. We had Bobby Kennedy with us, and when his name was announced he was either booed or cheered depending on the political allegiance. One night the lads were out on the town - well, it was the close-season after all - and little Albert Alexander [the City chairman] and I were in our rooms watching television. Albert Alexander was such a kind man. He knew nothing about football at all but he'd been a Manchester City fan all his life. His father had been on the board. He never swore. He was so kind and friendly. Then on came the news that Bobby Kennedy had been shot. I 'phoned the chairman and said, 'Have you heard the news, Bobby Kennedy's been shot?' 'What's he doing out at this time of night?' came the reply. It was a laugh a minute."

The Bobby Kennedy that had been shot was of course John F Kennedy's younger brother, and not the Manchester City player.

City's tour lasted a month. On Tuesday 11 June, they arrived in Mexico City to play the Mexican First Division side Atlante at the Aztec Stadium. A couple of hours before kick-off, the Mexicans cancelled the game, claiming that City had broken their agreement. Joe argued that there had been no breach of contract, but the Mexicans insisted that Joe had agreed to field

Two City matches cancelled

MEXICO CITY,
Wednesday.

Manchester City's match with Mexican First Division side Atlante was cancelled only hours before it was due to start at the Aztec Stadium here last night.

The promoters alleged that Manchester City had failed to comply with their contract, but they did not elaborate.

Joe Mercer, City's manager, said there had been no breach of contract.

The promoters had apparently expected City to field the side which won the Football League championship, but injuries and calls by the England team have reduced the strength of the City team.

City's game to-morrow with America, another Mexican First Division side, has also been cancelled and they will now fly to Atlanta, Georgia, for a return match with Atlanta Chiefs on Sunday.

City return to England on Monday.—Reuter.

exactly the same side that had won the Championship at Newcastle. The injuries had made this impossible, and City's next game, against another Mexican First Division side, America, was also cancelled. City hurriedly arranged a replacement game in the USA. Atlanta Chiefs agreed to play City for the second time. The Chiefs won again.

Of the nine tour games, City won only one, against Rochester. They drew four, and all four were against fellow tourists Dunfermline. Joe was disappointed with the results, and the injuries posed problems for the next season.

Back in England, City were the focus of much attention. Joe was interviewed for a number of pieces covering the highs and lows of his footballing career, but anything that was controversial also made its way into the newspapers. The worst 'sensation', as far as the *Daily Mirror* was concerned, came when many City players made an early departure from a civic reception given in their honour.

The reception had been delayed because of the trip to America, and when it took place the players were back in pre-season training. The team were under a strict no-drinking ban. For the first hour of the reception they sat, bored out of their minds, hatching a plan to escape. The players started sneaking out in small groups, hoping not to be noticed, while the band started playing 'Congratulations'. When Joe was told he was furious. He had been talking to the Lord Mayor, Alderman Harold Stockdale, at the time. Then the Town Hall doorman told him the players had gone to a night-club and, worse still, claimed that Malcolm Allison was leading them.

Joe sent out a 'posse' of club officials in search for the players, and one of them telephoned at nine-thirty,

Mirror
Tuesday, July 30, 1968
Manchester (STD code 061) 832-3444

SOCCER CHAMPS WALK OUT OF CIVIC RECEPTION

THE Football League champions Manchester City walked out of the Lord Mayor's show last night staged . . . for the Football League champions!

They quietly disappeared as 500 people danced in the Town Hall, following a reception, in celebration of the team's little win last season.

The players had sat it out for an hour.

Then, with the band playing "Congratulations" the teetotal team —under a strict no-drinking ban—walked out in small groups and into a nearby night

The event couldn't have been going the way they would have liked it.

But City's manager Joe Mercer, was an angry man as he said just before the dance ended: "If they are still

By MIRROR REPORTERS

were going straight to bed when they left the reception.

"They have a very heavy training programme tomorrow. I explained this to the Lord Mayor and he

champions and nothing less will do for me."

Earlier Mr. Mercer had said he was baffled as to where the players could be.

"I have been away myself for some time, talking to the Lord

tery: "They have gone to a night club."

It was then that Mr. Mercer asked David Ewing, one of the club's training staff, and Peter Blakey, physiotherapist, to make inquiries.

When Dave returned an hour after the team had vanished (at 9.30) he said: "I understand they are

an hour after the players vanished, to say that the players were now in bed. Imagine Joe's surprise at eleven o'clock, when a *Daily Mirror* reporter told Joe that the players were still in a Manchester club. Joe responded in anger: "If they are still clubbing it I'm going to be asking a lot of questions in the morning. And if they have been drinking I will be doing more than just asking questions. As far as I'm concerned all my players were going straight to bed when they left the reception. They have a very heavy training programme tomorrow. I explained to the Lord Mayor and he understood the position. When I heard they had called in at a night club I sent two of my training staff straight round there from the Town Hall to get them out - and home. If they have disobeyed these instructions there will be trouble. As League champions they have to act as League Champions, and nothing less will do for me."

The *Daily Mirror* splashed the story across its back page, causing much embarrassment for Joe and City. No details of any punishment were revealed. One thing was certain, though, the young stars of Manchester City would have to watch their actions as any event, no matter how trivial, would be under public scrutiny, especially in the swinging sixties, when the north-west was such a leader in fashion, sport and music.

Around this time the media wanted to find out more and more about the personalities connected with City and "life with Joe Mercer". Joe's wife, Norah, was often asked about her husband. She had always shared Joe's footballing life. She had experienced the trauma at Villa Park and, as was often quoted, she never really wanted Joe to take the manager's job at City. In a close season interview, she looked back to the space in Joe's life after leaving Villa: "I do not wish him to be anything else but connected with football because, during that year away, he was positively miserable without it. It was a trying time. Then I thought he had come back too quickly to Manchester City, but it has worked out for him. I feel so happy for him at times like this."

She went on to talk about how important it was for Joe to relax: "I think he likes best of all a round of golf or to be with the family, to get the car out in the summer and drive quietly through the Cheshire lanes. And you want to see him when we can manage a day with our son David and his family. He's thrilled to death with two-year-old Susan. It makes his week to have a few hours with her."

Joe's family had helped him through those difficult days after leaving Villa. There had been a number of black moments in Joe's career - his final days at Everton, his broken leg at Arsenal and those difficult early managerial days at Sheffield United - and Norah had always been there to help. She has always played her part in making the Mercer family the greatest team Joe was ever a part of.

The people of Ellesmere Port also supported Joe during his career. After City's success, Joe found that the pupils of his former school, John Street Infants, were compiling City scrapbooks. When Joe found out about their project, he wrote to the children and arranged for photographs and autographs to be sent to them. By doing that Joe ensured that the good name of Manchester City was being spread. He always believed in the value of public relations. Throughout his time at City he acted as an ambassador, and the club took on a lot of his warmth, friendliness and accessibility.

Malcolm Allison, of course, was always in the news, especially during 1968-9. He was often in debt, and there were rumours about gambling and "bad company". He was banned from the touchline by the FA after a series of arguments. He spent ten days in Italy assessing whether he wanted the Juventus job. And he was breathalysed after a motoring incident.

At times, Joe found Malcolm's exploits entertaining. Driving down Princess Parkway one day, going to the City training ground, Joe was pulled up by a police car for speeding, and he immediately thought, "Christ, now what's Malcolm done."

The 1968-9 season opened with the Charity Shield match against FA Cup winners West Bromwich Albion. In those days this curtain-raiser was played on the home ground of the Champions, and City outplayed West Brom to record a 6-1 victory. Joe hoped the season would follow in the same style. Unfortunately it did not.

City missed the injured Tony Book. Only one of the first nine League games was won, and the next match was the home leg of City's European Cup first-round tie. The Turkish champions and cup holders Fenerbahce came to Maine Road with the reputation of being about English Second Division standard. Even the Turkish press men told their English counterparts that City would dominate both the home and away legs of the tie. But it wasn't the case. City missed chance after chance, and the result was a shock 0-0 draw. Mike Summerbee, booed by a section of the crowd, was determined to do better in the away leg.

The Blues flew out to Turkey in a specially chartered Comet aeroplane. The players were in buoyant mood. Mike Summerbee had been married the day before, and the whole team were still celebrating. Joe and Norah had attended the wedding at St Michael and All Angel's Church, Mottram, near Hyde, and George Best had been Summerbee's best man.

CITY LEAGUE CHAMPIONS
VERSUS
WEDNESDAY SEPTEMBER 18th 1968
Kick-off 7-45 p.m.
FENERBAHCE S.K. Champions of Turkey
MANCHESTER CITY FOOTBALL CLUB LTD.
European Champion Clubs' Cup
OFFICIAL PROGRAMME ONE SHILLING

City players board the plane for Istanbul.
Above: The programme from the first leg at Maine Road.

When the players arrived at the stadium on the day of the game they noticed that the pitch was bumpy. They also discovered that the whole of Istanbul were keen to see the match. The stadium was packed with about 55,000 people. The official attendance was given as 45,000, but a member of the groundstaff proved to City officials it was much more than that.

When the game started, the noise produced by the partisan crowd was deafening. Even so, the Blues took the lead. Tony Coleman latched on to a cross from Francis Lee, controlled the ball, went round Fenerbahce's Yavuz and stroked the ball home. In the second half, however, the Blues needed to defend for all they were worth.

Less than a minute after half-time, the Turks equalised. Ogun crossed for second-half substitute Abdullah to score with his first kick. The Blues were still technically in the lead - the away goal would count double in the event of a draw - but Fenerbahce now had the initiative. Twelve minutes from time Ogun scored the winner.

The Turks invaded the pitch, fireworks zoomed into the sky, and then at full-time the celebrations began again. Over one hundred celebratory fires were lit on the terraces, and for the first time City experienced baton-wielding riot-police clearing a path for them to reach the dressing room.

The Turkish press described it as the most important result in the history of the country, and City were deeply ashamed. The English press regurgitated all the boasts made by Malcolm Allison at City's championship press conference. Even now around twenty five years later Allison is often reminded of his 'scare Europe to death' comment. Indeed, Allison enjoyed relating the tale on Radio Five in 1993 as he warned Manchester United about Cup ties in Istanbul.

Allison was not the only one to have his quotes ridiculed. Joe Mercer had stated that he expected City to reach the third round at least, and this now returned to haunt him. City were not allowed to forget their European experience, especially as Manchester United had won the trophy the previous May. United's European Cup victory had overshadowed City's League success.

The League season continued to disappoint Joe. There were some superb results - Sunderland (4-0), Tottenham (4-0), West Brom (5-1) and Burnley (7-0) - but they did no more than lift City to a safe mid-table position. As City had been knocked out of the League Cup in September, all that remained was the FA Cup. Prospects were helped by the return of Tony Book in January.

In the third round City beat Luton 1-0 with a Francis Lee penalty. In the fourth round, City gained a replay with an exciting goalless draw at Newcastle. Afterwards, Joe was full of praise for Tommy Booth, his young centre-half: "We were under a lot of pressure during the match, but did not give them many clear cut openings. Tommy Booth stuck right with Wyn Davies, so that he was not able to turn quickly or break effectively. Both sides must have done a lot of rethinking after Saturday, but there is a great spirit between us and there will be no recriminations after this game. Newcastle are enjoying a successful run, and there is lots of running in the team. It's not so hard when you are running for victory. But when you find yourself a goal down you get that 'here we go again' feeling. That's football."

Colin Bell puts the Luton 'keeper under pressure.

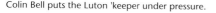

When Joe was asked if he was optimistic about beating Newcastle in the replay he simply responded: "An optimist is a happy man who is rarely right, A pessimist is an unhappy man who is rarely wrong."

Joe's style with the press was also shown in his response to questions about the injured Colin Bell: "He's an unusual character, Colin. He doesn't say very much. But I can tell you he was a lot happier today. Knowing Colin as I do, I have a feeling that we shall soon have him back. And, by heck, it can't be too soon for me. Or the lads for that matter! They have all had to share his running. But I have news for them, they will all have to carry on doing it when he comes back."

City won the Newcastle replay, 2-0, with goals by Neil Young and Bobby Owen, a close-season signing from Bury who had impressed in the celebratory friendly with City.

Tony Coleman's shot soars past Blacklaw for City's fourth goal in the fifth round game at Blackburn.

The fifth-round tie with Blackburn was postponed several times before City won the game 4-1 with goals by Tony Coleman (2) and Francis Lee (2). Within a week they were beating Tottenham Hotspur 1-0 in the quarter-final, Francis Lee's shot creeping in off a post.

City's semi-final opponents were Everton, the side Joe Mercer had played for and supported. The pre-match build-up was a chance for Joe to relive happy memories, not only of his days at Everton, but of his Cup career in general. There had been those Cup Finals with Arsenal in the early 1950s, an exciting Cup run with Sheffield United in the late 1950s, and two FA Cup semi-finals and two League Cup Finals while Aston Villa manager in the early 1960s. Joe certainly had plenty of Cup experience.

For the 1969 semi-final, City were without Tony Coleman, who was replaced by Dave Connor. Connor was told to mark Alan Ball out of the game. He managed to annoy Ball so much that the Evertonian lost his temper, fouled Connor and was subsequently booked. Joe Mercer later recalled how the tactic came about: "We put a lad named Connor on Alan Ball. I said, 'Look, Mal, I once played against Bolton and they had Westwood, and Jock Thomson said, "We'll play ten against ten." And I had the job of putting Westwood out of the game.'"

City won the semi-final with a last-minute goal from 19-year-old centre-half Tommy Booth. For the first time since 1956, City fans experienced the joy of knowing their team would play a Wembley Cup Final. Joe and Mal were heroes again. In the Villa Park dressing room, champagne was opened and cigars passed round. Joe stood proudly in the centre of the room with a glass in one hand and cigar in the other. He looked at all his players, at the press, and the well-wishers before he hushed the gathering and simply told everyone present: "The tension is over now. We shall go to Wembley to play football."

Years later, a discussion about backroom staff reminded Joe of another incident in the

Tommy Booth scores the only goal of City's Villa Park semi-final with Everton.

Villa Park dressing room: "The secretary takes a load of trouble off you, and the chairman is so important. We had little Albert Alexander. He knew nothing about football. A lovely man who loved Manchester City, masonry, Rotary and his wife, in that order. He was so naive. I'll never forget, we beat Everton in the semi-final at Villa Park, and just imagine the atmosphere. The press are in there, the champagne's flowing, everything is happening, and little Albert comes and says, 'Oh, great, we're in the Final, we'll make a lot of money and then we'll be able to buy some good players.' Well, the place exploded."

City played eight League games in between the semi-final and the Final. Results were mixed, but a 2-0 victory over their Cup Final opponents, Leicester City, gave the team a psychological advantage, especially as Leicester had a relegation battle to fight.

In the weeks leading up to the Final, Joe announced that City would not be wearing their traditional sky-blue shirts: "Since both teams have the same colours we decided to switch to our auxiliary strip. Our fans may think it important that we should play in our own colours, but this strip is very distinctive and after all it's the man inside the shirt that counts."

Rather than settle for City's traditional change strip - maroon or maroon-and-white stripes - Malcolm Allison had persuaded Joe and the others that AC Milan's red-and-black stripes would provide the same kind of invincibility the Italians enjoyed. City had tried the strip out a number of times during the season, including the Cup games against Blackburn and Everton, and Allison's idea seemed to work.

The 1969 Cup Final, played on 26 April, was Manchester City's seventh final. They equalled Arsenal's record of six Wembley Finals. They also broke with tradition by allowing young Paul Todd to be the first mascot at a Final. City smuggled him in on the players' coach and the boy sat next to Joe as the coach entered the stadium. Young Paul was also given a privileged position from which to watch the game when he took Malcolm Allison's place on the bench next to Joe. Allison was actually banned from sitting on the touchline because of his so-called 'excessive coaching' earlier in the season. Allison made his way to the stands: "I imagine that the FA enforced my touchline ban and ordered me to sit in the stands at the Cup Final

His Wembley worry

Allison can beat that F.A. ban

Says TONY CARTER

THE loose wording of the FA ruling that bans Manchester City coach Malcolm Allison from "sitting at or near the touchline" during matches surely offered the club an escape route for the Cup Final at Wembley on April 26.

Although the FA confirmed yesterday that they would still operate the ban at Wembley, where can they draw a line between a position "near" the touchline and a seat outside the limit?

SEPARATED

If Allison were to sit on the club bench during the final he would be separated from the pitch by two stretches of grass and a greyhound track — that's farther than he sat during the Villa Park semi-final last Saturday.

Then he was in the front row of the stand immediately behind the trainers bench and, as you can see from the picture on the left, h‑‑‑ ‑‑‑‑‑‑‑‑‑ ‑‑ ‑‑‑‑ ‑‑‑‑

because they thought I might lose my head in the emotional atmosphere of Wembley. They need not have worried. I reckon the 'hothead Allison' was one of the coolest men in the 100,000 people there. My seat was actually nearer to the playing pitch than the trainers' bench."

The game was not a classic, but it did produce some fine moments. Leicester's Allan Clarke, at that time the most expensive player in Britain at £150,000, had a superb shot which City 'keeper Harry Dowd finger-tipped to safety. Neil Young and Tony Coleman then both saw their attempts miss their target as the game seemed to swing from Leicester to Manchester. After 23 minutes, Mike Summerbee gathered a throw-in from Francis Lee, raced down the right, slipped past a Leicester player and then centred the ball to Neil Young. Young crashed the ball past the England under-23 goalkeeper Peter Shilton, into the top corner with his left foot to put City in front.

Joe jumped up from his seat to celebrate. He was immediately interviewed by the BBC and asked how he was feeling: "Much better after that. Mind you, it was against the run of play I thought. They had a couple of chances that could have gone in. But Summerbee's playing magnificently and I think he made the goal. Of course, Neil Young, when you put it on his left foot, well, it's just his chance."

Young's goal was enough to bring City the FA Cup.

At the end, the trophy was collected by City captain Tony Book, who had been voted joint Footballer of the Year (with Dave Mackay of Derby County) earlier in the week. Book had been

Neil Young scores the Wembley winner.

delighted with his award: "To receive an award that my boss, Joe Mercer, and Stanley Matthews, Tom Finney, Bert Trautmann, and men of their calibre were given is truly astonishing. It is an honour for which the greatest credit goes to Joe Mercer, Malcolm Allison, and the team. I've had some wonderful help on the way."

Above: A special moment - Joe shows off the Cup to City fans at Wembley.
Below: A special partnership - Joe and Malcolm Allison enjoy being winners.

Going home with the Cup - by train (above) and then through the streets in an open-topped bus (below).

When the FA Cup presentations were over, and the City players had stayed to cheer the losers, City took the trophy to their supporters. At one stage Joe proudly lifted the trophy to the fans. Earlier, together with Malcolm, he had conducted the fans' singing. The two men had shared a few moments together on the pitch laughing and joking. To have won England's two major trophies within a year was really special. It meant that City, under Joe and Mal, had won a trophy every season except 1966-7. While City were celebrating, Mal turned to Joe and said, "Boss, I'm worried." Joe was puzzled and asked him why he should be worried after City had just won a trophy. Mal replied: "Well, Boss, I can't help wondering what went wrong in 1967 when we didn't win anything!"

The celebrations continued in the dressing-room. The Cup was filled with champagne, well-wishers filled the room, and the press demanded quotes. The press asked about City's chances in next season's European Cup winners' Cup, and, wisely, both Joe and Mal refused to say how far they believed the Blues would go. They limited themselves to speaking about the Cup Final. Joe was truly proud of his side that day, and of the fact that he now entered the record books as the only person to win both the League and the Cup as a player and a manager: "It was great to get my hands on the FA Cup once again, but I believe our Wembley victory is only the start of a truly great future for Manchester City. We go back into Europe still reflecting on our bitter experiences of earlier this season and determined not

to make the same mistakes again. Europe is where the lolly is, so instead of being idealistic we have to be more financially minded. Our defeat by Fenerbahce in Istanbul in October taught us a firm lesson in that we should never underestimate the opposition - any opposition. We must get down to basics all the time and I sincerely believe that we have still to see the best of this City team. I don't really like talking about potential but we have here a great bunch of players, who are going to become a really great side. Things didn't go so well for us earlier this season and, quite naturally, I was disappointed at our results because I knew, Malcolm knew, that the entire team was capable of so much more.

"There is absolutely no substitute for experience, and this latest experience of a Wembley Cup Final victory will help to make these boys more mature for next season. And one player in particular who must be watched out for is Tommy Booth. What a fabulous young centre-half he is - he's the find of this or any other season. And he didn't cost us a penny. We found him on our own doorstep. I thought Tommy had a great game, but then who had a bad one? It was a magnificent performance. Sure I was worried. You've got to be worried with only one goal tucked under your belt. But the boys really did us proud. And how superbly they overcame the electric atmosphere that always charges Wembley on Cup Final day. We told them before the game that though there would be plenty of emotion, they should leave it to the fans to get worked up."

The celebrations went on well into the night - about four o'clock for most players - as City first had a celebration banquet at the Cafe Royal, then went on to a West End night club. Telegrams arrived from supporters and well-wishers.

The next morning, Joe woke up in his hotel room. On the bedside next to him was the FA Cup. He toasted the trophy with tea. Later, he told reporters: "I feel absolutely marvellous. Really on the ball."

City's homecoming saw the party travel by rail from London to Wilmslow, where more than 25,000 people turned out to see the players board an open-top bus for the trip to Manchester. John Humphreys, a City director and director of Wilmslow-based sports kit manufacturers Umbro, had suggested the Blues start their tour from the quiet Cheshire town. It had seemed a ridiculous idea at first but, as that part of Cheshire is strong in its support for City, it was agreed that it would be worth doing. Joe could not believe the welcome, especially as this was twelve miles from the city centre.

The journey was tremendous. It seemed that the whole of the Manchester area had come out to welcome their heroes. The bus was actually the same one United had used the previous year for their European Cup return. Even the bus driver, Bob Jackson, was the same, and he found City's welcome moving: "It was fantastic. I would say there were more people about than for United's homecoming, and I was very proud to be in the procession."

It was estimated that over 250,000 people welcomed Manchester City home. Joe and the others just could not believe it. The reception was far greater than Arsenal's in Islington in 1950.

The Albert Square crowd chanted the names of the players, and called for Joe Mercer and Malcolm Allison. At one point they simply chanted "Joe, Joe, Joe" over and over again, until Joe spoke to them. The vast crowd went silent as Joe spoke about the warmth of the welcoming, about the supporters, and of course the Cup. It was one of the proudest days of Joe's life and he had never looked better. At one point Joe simply summed up the feelings of the City staff: "We are thrilled to bring this Cup back to this wonderful City."

While all this was going on, the telephone rang in the Mercer household. Norah Mercer picked it up and recognised the voice of Ron Wylie, a former Aston Villa player. "Eee," said Wylie, laughing. "It's a good job you didn't let him go back into football!"

Norah Mercer laughed.

Joe relates highlights of another successful season to Maltese TV interviewer Lewis Portelli.

Chapter Twenty One

EUROPEAN SUCCESS

City are a young side and they have so much skill. They can reach a standard of skill which I doubt anyone in England can equal. They are capable of thrashing any side. While some teams are content to beat you, City want to go and thrash you. They can murder a team with their skill.

Bill Shankly, May 1969.

T THE START of 1969-70, City's first taste of competitive action was the Charity Shield match against Don Revie's Leeds United, the League Champions. Leeds won 2-1 at Elland Road.

Bill Shankly, the famous Liverpool manager, predicted that the two teams of the 1970s would be Manchester City and Leeds: "We now regard them as our two biggest rivals in the game. They are two teams to be feared. Everybody must respect them. If they don't they are either stupid or blind."

Shankly frequently told the press that Joe and Malcolm were a great combination who had wisely invested in young and experienced players: "Their buys have been good buys. Men like Book. Nobody else seemed to want him or even look at him. Bell is already a tremendous player and will be even better. Lee was floating around for a long time before City stepped in to buy him. They have won the League and Cup in successive seasons and now they are in a position to do what we did - win the League, the Cup, and then the League again."

In fact, City did not make a major impact on the League. Their final position of tenth was only three places higher than the previous year. There were a few high points - the double over Manchester United included a 4-0 win at Maine Road - but City's League form was mixed. The Cups were a different matter. The Blues chased glory on three fronts - the FA Cup, League Cup, and the European Cup-winners' Cup.

Tony Coleman had moved to Sheffield Wednesday, leaving an opportunity for Ian Bowyer, and Joe Corrigan was now the regular goalkeeper, but otherwise City's team was much the same as the previous season. Malcolm Allison worked hard to turn Joe Corrigan into a top-class goalkeeper and felt he could be "as great as Swift". Indeed, City supporters eventually rated him in the same bracket as the club's two greatest goalkeepers - Swift and Trautmann.

The departure of Harry Dowd, to Oldham, was the loss of a loyal servant. Mike Summerbee: "The best part of the team talk was when Harry Dowd was in goal, because Harry wasn't interested in football he'd rather be doing plumbing. I remember in London, Joe Mercer used to have to say, 'Look, Harry we're playing Arsenal today ... and they play in red and white!'"

The League Cup run started with a 3-0 win at Southport in the second round, and a 3-2

Joe with Athletic Bilbao's English manager Ronnie Allen.

home win over Liverpool in the third. In between those two League Cup games City also faced Athletic Bilbao in the away leg of the first round of the European Cup-winners' Cup. This time Malcolm and Joe were better prepared. Despite Joe's extensive playing experience, and his many games for England, he had hardly any experience of European competition. The previous season's game in Turkey had taken him into a new area.

There was a shock in store in Bilbao too. After 15 minutes City were 2-0 down to a team managed by Ronnie Allen, the former West Bromwich Albion and England star. Neil Young's goal reduced the deficit just before half-time. In the dressing room at the interval both Joe and Malcolm spoke calmly to the players. City already had a vital away goal. If the score stood the Blues simply needed to win 1-0 at Maine Road, so there was no need for hysterics. In the second half, however, the Spaniards scored their third. But before City could be written off, they fought back to 3-3 with a goal by Tommy Booth and an own goal from the Bilbao captain Luis Echeberria.

At Maine Road, Joe urged his players not to be too complacent about the second leg. In fact, City won 3-0, with goals from Colin Bell, Alan Oakes and Ian Bowyer. Bowyer, a youngster from Joe's home town, Ellesmere Port, was proving to be one of Joe's best finds. There was only

Colin Bell nips in ahead of goalkeeper Engelen to head City's fourth goal against SK Lierse at Maine Road...

one drawback, as Joe later explained: "The crowd never appreciated him. He played deep and did so much graft. He was a bit clumsy, a bit awkward, and the crowd didn't realise the graft that he did."

City's next European opponents were the Belgian part-timers SK Lierse. The two sides were a class apart. City won 3-0 away and 5-0 at home, and then had a long wait, until March, for their quarter-final tie.

Before then, though, there were plenty of other Cup fixtures. In the League Cup, City beat Everton 2-0 in the fourth round, and swept aside Queen's Park Rangers, 3-0, in the quarter-final. The two-legged semi-final saw City drawn against their great rivals - Manchester United.

Joe, as much as anyone, valued the competition: "Not only is the League Cup a means of getting into Europe, it is a competition from which clubs who go all the way can earn as much, if not more, than in the bigger competition run by the Football Association."

At Aston Villa, Joe had won the trophy in its inaugural season, when the competition was not taken as seriously. Many major clubs, like Manchester United, boycotted it. In fact, 1969-70 was the first season that all League clubs participated. United, like the others, realised that the competition offered them a way into Europe.

In the first leg, at Maine Road, City set the pace from the start. Colin Bell scored the first goal after 13 minutes, and, as the Blues continued to attack, United somehow withstood the pressure. At the start of the second half, United equalised through Bobby Charlton, but City scored the winner in the 88th minute. Francis Lee darted towards the goal, United centre-half Ian Ure stuck out a despairing leg and Lee crashed to the ground. Referee Jack Taylor gave the penalty, and Lee sent the ball low to Alex Stepney's right. City had a 2-1 lead from the first leg.

As the game ended, George Best exchanged words with Jack Taylor, and appeared to knock the ball out of the referee's hands. Best was later charged with bringing the game into disrepute, fined £100 and suspended for a month.

At Old Trafford, in the second leg, Ian Bowyer put the Blues further ahead after 17 minutes but a goal from United's Paul Edwards soon made it 1-1 on the night. In the second half, Denis

... and strokes home his second to complete the scoring, 5-0.

Above: Ian Bowyer pounces to put City one up in the League Cup semi-final second leg at Old Trafford.
Below: The City players show their delight.

Above: Mike Summerbee scores to send City to Wembley for the second successive year.

Law scored to put United ahead on the night and level on aggregate. United kept pushing forward but could not increase their lead. With just eight minutes left the game was settled in the most unlikely way. Willie Morgan fouled Bowyer about 20 yards from the United goal. The referee signalled an indirect free kick. Francis Lee either missed the signal, or simply ignored it, and fired the free-kick towards the United goal. Alex Stepney could have let the ball enter the net because the free-kick was indirect. Instead, he went to catch it, fumbled, and Mike Summerbee followed up to bury the ball in the net. City won 4-3 on aggregate. Joe described the semi-final as the "two of the most momentous games ever played in Manchester".

In the FA Cup, City defeated Hull 1-0 in the third round and then were drawn against Manchester United at Old Trafford. Manchester just could not believe it. It meant that the Blues would face the Reds a remarkable five times that season.

Tell me how to nail Georgie Best down and City are in with a great chance

In the build-up to the fourth-round tie, Joe organised a small get-together for the management teams of Maine Road and Old Trafford. It was a chance to show that Manchester was the top footballing city in Britain. Joe and Malcolm welcomed Sir Matt Busby and Wilf McGuinness to Maine Road for a champagne toast. The FA Cup was brought out and photographs were taken of the four men wearing big red or blue rosettes. Joe looked forward to the game: "This toast shows how we look on these encounters. For us it's a game ... a very important game, but not a war. We will do everything we can within the laws of the game to get our opponents down. But if we don't get to Wembley in this tournament, then I'll be hoping Manchester United will."

Joe went on to talk about the successes of the last couple of years, including the League Championship when United just missed out, and then he added with a smile: "United keep on getting their chances to get their own back." He compared the series of matches to a television saga: "Like the Forsyte one, only more exciting."

Before the game, United were the favourites even though George Best was suspended. Busby was convinced his side would win: "I like the air of confidence in our side. I think we can win this time, even without so many top-class players."

Busby was proved right as United defeated the Blues 3-0. At least the defeat spared City a further fixture chaos. As it was, they played 61 first-team games in 1969-70, excluding friendlies.

The first leg of their European Cup-winners' Cup quarter-final, against Académica Coimbra, in Portugal, took place only three days before the League Cup Final against West Brom. Said Joe Mercer: "We want to win the League Cup on Saturday, but we also want to win the Cup-Winners' Cup. So it won't be a case of holding anything back for Wembley."

Tactically, City now had a more controlling midfield rather than out-and-out attack. The new team pattern was still in its early stages. At the time, Joe Mercer said: "It still has to prove that it can be successful, but it could make us much more resilient and ward off shocks such as the one we suffered in our first game in the Cup-Winners' Cup against Athletic Bilbao. Our formation may look a little negative now, but for a long period we were boldly positive, perhaps a bit too bold at times."

City seeking final boost

Joe Mercer is given a farewell hug by his granddaughter Susan.

-Players denied-

From RONALD CROWTHER in Portugal

MANCHESTER CITY, with Neil Young back in their attack, intend to turn tonight's Cup-Winners' Cup-tie here into a morale-booster for Saturday's League Cup final at Wembley.

Manager Joe Mercer's last words to his men before they face Academic Coimbra will be: 'A powerful performance here can put us on the way to victory against West Brom. Defeat tonight could be demoralising.'

After a training session here last night, Mercer announced what he now regards as City's strongest team. And, barring mishaps or below-par performances, it is the side that Mercer has in mind for Wembley.

In a 4-3-3 formation Arthur Mann will carry on at left back, Glyn Pardoe will share midfield responsibilities with Alan Oakes and Colin Bell, and Francis Lee, Mike Summerbee and Young will be the front-runners.

Frank Carrodus, the 20-year-old engineering student who has had a first-team fling of three senior games, is the forward who gives way to back-in-favour Young.

He's

Significant

But the most significant feature of the side is City's greater concentration of players in midfield after

Coimbra were believed to be a fairly weak side. Even their coach Julio Pereira said they would be outclassed by City as some of their players were university students. Mindful of his experience against Fenerbahce, Joe would not listen to any talk of the game being a walkover for City: "We've heard all this talk before about teams having no chance and then we've seen them go out and play like world-beaters. Some of these fellows are no more students than Russian athletes are amateurs. My players will go into this tie with a realistic approach and without any nonsense about being on an easy thing."

The tie proved to be extremely difficult for the Blues. As Joe had suspected, the Portuguese were more capable than their coach and the media had suggested. The Blues were happy to get a goalless draw. They were not happy, however, with the events of the next twenty-four hours or so.

The City party stayed on in Portugal after the game. It was Joe's idea to "play the match, then stay on late to give us a chance to relax - and let Albion do the worrying." Unfortunately the plan backfired. While West Bromwich Albion, their League Cup Final opponents, lay in bed in their Surrey hotel, City were struggling to get home. An airport strike in London diverted the party to Birmingham after appalling weather had caused a delay to the flight. The Blues were weary when they eventually arrived back in England, thirty-six hours before the Wembley kick-off. The journey took over ten hours, but Joe was convinced it would not make his side suffer: "No team has ever approached Wembley by such a roundabout route. But these are the sort of things that professionals have to take in their stride. I refuse to get steamed up about

A nightmare for City

SNOW AND STRIKE RUIN FINAL PLANS

Home at last! Manchester City's injured captain Tony Book and George Heslop, who could be a surprise Final choice, relax at Birmingham Airport after the ordeal of their flight from Portugal.

such things and I think the players adopt the same approach. A good lie-in in the morning should see them all right."

The long journey delayed City's Wembley pitch inspection until Friday afternoon. When Joe saw the pitch, he was disgusted. He had described the Wembley pitch as looking like a "cabbage patch" before the previous season's FA Cup Final with Leicester, and now it was even worse. Joe saw workmen covering the worn turf with straw to protect it from the freezing conditions. He told the press his lads could handle it, but in reality feared that the conditions would prove too tiring for his players, especially after their experiences earlier in the week.

Neil Young, who had spent the day before the League Cup Final celebrating the birth of his daughter, was dropped from the team. Glyn Pardoe wore the number-eleven shirt with George Heslop returning to the side to play alongside Tommy Booth. It was certainly an unusual defensive formation, although both Joe and Malcolm told the press that the Blues were not going to make the game a defensive stalemate.

This was Joe's sixth Cup Final - two as a player and four as a manager. There had been the FA Cup Finals of 1950, 1952 and 1969 and the League Cup finals of 1961, 1963 and, now, 1970. Joe was asked by the Manchester press about his previous League Cup Finals: "It was not quite the same then. Those two-legged Finals did not quite have the same impact as the big one at Wembley these days. The competition was born to make more money for the clubs. The very fact that the Final as well as the semis was on a two-legged basis proved this point. But there was so much uncertainty over dates. And with many of the top clubs opting out there was not the same impact. However, it was still an honour to reach the Final and Villa did exceptionally well beating Rotherham 3-2 on aggregate in 1961. Two years later we were back in the final and this time there was the added spice of a derby, our opponents being Birmingham City. It was rather like City and United only on a slightly lesser plane. But this time we lost 3-1 on aggregate ... and deservedly, too, I might tell you."

Malcolm Allison sat in the stands at Wembley. Joe's request for a reprieve of the touchline ban was turned down by the FA. It did not really matter where Mal or Joe sat, as the players had all been prepared and simply had to go out there and perform. Once again, City wore red-and-black striped shirts.

After five minutes, Joe Corrigan missed a cross and Albion's Jeff Astle opened the scoring. City dictated most of the play after that, but it took nearly an hour to score an equaliser. Colin Bell headed the ball across to Mike Doyle, whose first-time effort entered the net. City lost Mike Summerbee, who limped off the cloying pitch to be substituted by Ian Bowyer, and Albion replaced Asa Hartford with Dick Kryzwicki. The Albion substitute almost gave his side victory as he seemed set for a goal before Tony Book somehow managed a timely tackle.

At full-time the score was 1-1. Although most people now expected Albion to have the fitness and pace to overcome City, it was City who looked the stronger. Malcolm Allison had always preached about fitness to the City players. The club's gruelling training sessions made City the fittest side in England, and the benefits were plain as they dominated extra-time.

Glyn Pardoe scored City's winner in the 102nd minute. The goal was set up by Francis Lee, who had one of his greatest-ever games for City. His performance was certainly noticed by Alf Ramsey as he finalised his plans for the 1970 World Cup. Lee was definitely on his way to Mexico after this.

City were now accustomed to celebrating. Not only had they won the League Cup, to add to the League Championship and FA Cup, but they had qualified for a place in the Inter-Cities Fairs Cup. City fans sang and danced in Trafalgar Square.

Joe was asked his view of another great day: "This was very probably the most professional performance we have ever given. Physically, it must have been the toughest test ever. Just to

The League Cup winning goal crosses the line, but scorer Glyn Pardoe (No. 11) has already turned to celebrate.

Skipper Tony Book is chaired around Wembley by his delighted team-mates.

play 120 minutes on a pitch that has begun to look like the biggest dump in the world was an epic performance after cup-fighting a thousand miles away in Portugal only three days earlier. But to win in such a manner as we did was magnificent, and I cannot speak too highly in praise of the bravery of my men. We're absolutely thrilled about this League Cup triumph. But I hope nobody will misunderstand me when I say that this isn't the big one for us this season. The big one for us still has to be won in Europe, and with the bravery, the character, and the teamwork that our players showed on Saturday, I think they can do it. If we can win the Cup-winners' Cup and so qualify to defend it next season, maybe the authorities will let us flog our Fairs Cup place to the highest bidders."

Life-long City supporter Eddie Large, one half of the comedy double act Little and Large, met Joe on many occasions during this period and says that his lasting memory of City's greatest manager occurred just after the League Cup Final: "When we won the League Cup back in 1970 I was waiting back at the hotel to greet my heroes, when in walked Joe holding the League Cup. He came straight up to me, handed

THE LEAGUE title and a proud Joe Mercer shows off the trophy

THE F.A. CUP and skipper Tony Book is on a lap of honour

THE LEAGUE Cup and it's Book again with another silver trophy

THE MERCER MAGNIFICOS

All-out effort earns a unique hat-trick

THE GOAL that won the Cup for City ... Glyn Pardoe (No. 11) has scored, and Bowyer is triumphant (right). Below, Mick Doyle cracks the City equaliser.

Manchester City 2, West Bromwich Albion 1

ON THE WORST Wembley surface I have seen— a "pig of a pitch" in Joe Mercer's words— Manchester City completed a unique hat-trick of football's major trophies.

Although it took them extra time, they beat West Bromwich 2—1 to win the League Cup ... adding it to the F. A. Cup won on the same Wembley pitch only 10 months ago and the League Championship won the year before that.

It is a truly great triumph which has demanded endless effort and will power ... and never more than yesterday.

Towards the end the players must have felt like men running up and down wet sand dunes with hidden hands pulling at their leg muscles.

Francis Lee was the star of stars—an unstoppable streak of red and black lightning

JEFF ASTLE gives West Bromwich the lead

JAMES MOSSOP says

OUT OF WEMBLEY'S football in a farmyard—for that is what the mud and water ... up ... there came a ...

ALAN HOBY'S Wembley report

The man

me the Cup, and said, 'Have this, Eddie, and I'll play you at golf for it next week!' Needless to say I was dead chuffed, and the next week Joe won it back. During his time at the Maine Road Academy I got to know Joe well, often playing golf with him, usually on a Friday afternoon before a home match. Joe was Joe. He was friendly, genial, very down to earth and a great guy. I played many games of golf with Joe, and you have to bear in mind that at that time I had never appeared on TV. I was just a 'normal' City punter, but Joe never ever talked down to me and was quite happy to discuss football all day. A great man who is idolised by everyone who knew him."

In addition to the welcome at the hotel, City enjoyed what Joe described as "a fantastic homecoming" on their return to Manchester, despite the abysmal weather. The temperature was just above freezing, a complete contrast to that in Portugal. Joe said at the time: "We have proved again that the British footballer must be the most adaptable of all. One day we are basking in the sunshine of Portugal. Less than twenty-four hours later we are back in the Siberian climate of England, sweeping down the M1 in a snowstorm. Then in the mud bath of Wembley we become League Cup winners."

Winning the League Cup was another major achievement, but, as Joe had pointed out, there was also Europe. City still had to overcome Coimbra at Maine Road to reach the semi-finals of the European Cup-winners' Cup. It was another hard game. Colin Bell and George Heslop were injured, and City were prevented from playing the kind of football they enjoyed. Chris Glennon and Tony Towers came on as replacements, and the break-through came with almost the last kick of extra-time. At about 9.50pm, Towers scored a magnificent goal to give the Blues a 1-0 victory.

The semi-final opponents were Schalke '04 of West Germany. Schalke had been so successful a club prior to World War Two that they were Adolf Hitler's favourite side. They were still a formidable team, and in the first leg, in Germany, they beat City 1-0. In the return, however, Joe's side tore into their German opponents with style. Goalkeeper Joe Corrigan, who was playing with a broken nose, was rarely troubled. The Blues won 5-1 with goals from Bell, Lee, Doyle and Young (2).

City were through to a major European Final for the first time in their history. Three days after beating Schalke '04, City played a League game at Leeds. United manager Don Revie, a former City player, and his wife, Elsie, were good friends of Joe and Norah. Before the game, Revie lined up his players to applaud City on to the field: "I am delighted City have got through and naturally I hope they win the trophy." City won the game 3-1.

City did not know their European Cup-winners' Cup Final opponents until seven days before the game itself. Gornik Zabrze of Poland eventually beat AS Roma of Italy in a replay in Strasbourg. As Joe had come to expect, he was unable to field his strongest possible side. Mike Summerbee was out with injury, and Alan Oakes played when not fully fit.

The 1970 Cup Winners' Cup final was played in torrential rain in the uncovered Prater Stadium in Vienna, and City won 2-1. They were two up at half-time through goals by Neil Young, following up a Francis Lee shot, and Francis Lee, from a penalty after Young had been fouled. In the 68th minute Oslizlo pulled one back but City remained in control.

At the final whistle the Blues fans, who numbered some four or five thousand, started the celebrations. Many of them raced on to the field. They were drenched but happy. Many of them had followed City through the lean years of the early sixties, and claimed to have been

Leeds plan salute to City success

LEEDS UNITED, who failed to reach a European final at the last hurdle, will offer a sincere salute to those who made it tomorrow.

An ironic twist has thrown Leeds against manager Don Revie's former club, Manchester City, for their last League game.

DERBY RIFT

And City, who reached the Cup Winners' final with a spectacular 5—1 victory over Schalke '04 on Wednesday, will get the full treatment at Elland Road.

Revie will line up the Leeds players to applaud City's finalists as they go on to the field.

'I am delighted City have got through and naturally I hope they win the trophy,' said Revie on his return from the bitter disappointment at Hampden Park.

Leeds were still counting the cost of defeat yesterday. Gary Sprake and Mick Jones will be

Carving it up! Joe at the opening of a restaurant in which Malcolm Allison (right) had shares.

Above: City skipper Tony Book exchanges gifts with his Gornik counterpart Oslizlo before the Cup-winners' Cup Final in Vienna.
Below: Neil Young knocks home City's first goal after goalkeeper Kostka had blocked a Francis Lee effort.
Right: Francis Lee's penalty beats Kostka for what proved to be the Cup-winning goal.

present when City suffered their lowest moment in the club's history in 1965. To those supporters the Mercer-Allison partnership was the greatest thing to have happened to the Blues.

For Joe Mercer, the success in Vienna gave him the satisfaction of knowing that he was one of the most successful men of football. He had won both the FA Cup and League Championship as a player and a manager - no one else had achieved that - and had been involved in seven major finals. Now he had seen his side become the first English side to win a domestic and European trophy in the same season. No one could ever take away those successes, and more importantly, no one could ever say that Joe was a failed manager. He was

Tony Book lifts the European Cup-winners' Cup.

Joe makes it through the waiting crowds to board the bus on City's triumphant return to Manchester Aiport.

Joe and Tony Book show off the Cup-winners' Cup to adoring fans in Manchester.

immensely proud of what had been achieved at City in just five years. Manchester City were now a major, successful club. The success of the sixties and early seventies resurrected the club's status as a giant in the game, while, thanks to Joe's careful planning and public-relations skills, it remained a friendly club.

Joe told the supporters that he was enjoying life at Maine Road. He also told them of his experience in Vienna: "A funny thing happened to me on the way to our greatest achievement ... the winning of the European Cup-winners' Cup in Vienna. For the first time in forty years in professional football I had to watch that final in the Prater Stadium as a spectator. The rain on the most wonderful evening ever in the history of Manchester City was more than an April shower. It was like a tropical storm sent to dampen the enthusiasm of even the most ardent follower of football. It failed because football fans are a hardy race, and those of Manchester City are perhaps a little hardier than most. In Vienna, though, when managers, directors, press and fans alike had to brave the elements together in the open air, I had to sit there with rain running down my neck, my coat was saturated and my shoes were filled with water. But neither Malcolm Allison nor myself would budge from that spot as we watched our players drive home their superiority to prove themselves a major force in Europe as well as one of the top teams in Great Britain. This has truly been a magnificent season for us all. I am pleased for the players - that is what this great game of ours is all about - I am pleased for Malcolm, a man who is so right in his outlook towards Europe where he believes their coaches are afraid to attack, I am pleased for our chairman, Albert Alexander, who, unfortunately missed the big one, and I am pleased for the fans."

Around this time, returning from a European trip, Joe was set up during the flight home.

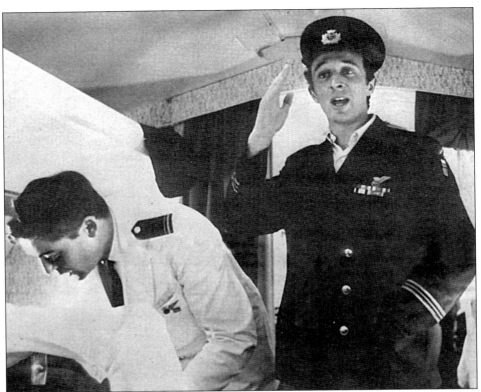

City's joker and prankster Mike Summerbee, dressed here as a pilot, tricked Joe into believing there was a hijacker on board one of the flights.

Mike Summerbee, one of the club's chief pranksters tells the story: "We were sat at the back of the aircraft on this trip, and Francis [Lee] noticed that the Boss was sat on the edge of the aisle and there was this vacant seat between him and a man who we didn't know. We were on a charter flight and there was a man we didn't know! You should know everybody on a charter flight. So Francis calls the stewardess over and writes down a little message, gives it to the stewardess and asks her to give it to Joe Mercer. The Boss looks at the message and it says, 'The man in the corner is a suspected hijacker, please keep him talking. Don't panic!' Joe kept him talking for about four and a half hours. The 'hijacker' turned out to be relief crew!"

Amid all the exultation and celebration, Joe Mercer remained level-headed, in more ways than in dealing with a potential hijacker: "We must never become greedy. We must not become complacent and believe that now we have a divine right to win trophies. Despite all our successes and achievements in the past we cannot now go out and demand glory. We have still got to work for it. We will plan and we will scheme for the future, but perhaps one day these players who have worked so magnificently for us will fail. And that is when we have got to be good losers as well as lively winners."

Chapter Twenty Two

RUINING THE DREAM

Bad feelings were beginning to replace the drive and thrust which had carried me - and City - into such a position of strength in the game. I felt terribly frustrated. I couldn't put my mind to the job. And Joe and I were no longer intimates. We had begun to drift apart and there were moments, for the first time, of real hostility between us.

Malcolm Allison, *Colours Of My Life*, 1975

IN 1970, Manchester City were a major force. Joe Mercer and Malcolm Allison, written off six years earlier, had won five trophies in five seasons. Surely, with so much success, the partnership could not possibly fail, could it?

Well, yes it could. As City entered the seventies, a period of board-room disharmony was about to affect the relationship between City's two great leaders.

According to Malcolm Allison, the seeds of the later problems may well have been sown on the team coach before the opening game of the 1965-6 season, when Joe had made his comment that "two years will do me". At that time, Joe was conscious of his health problems, and aware of the stress he had suffered at Aston Villa. He probably did not even consider that both his health and the position of Manchester City could improve so much.

Malcolm could see the change: "He improved so much in that first year that he was really good, really alive. Once we got going and won the First Division, the FA Cup, the League Cup and the European Cup-winners' Cup, with big crowds and a great atmosphere, Joe was really good, he was fine then. It was frustrating for me, though, for some time. Once he'd said to me about the two years it became three years ... four years ... five ... Because of the success we'd had he didn't want to lose it. You see, it's difficult to understand when you are young. When you get older you begin to realise that people don't like to relinquish success. They don't like to give up the power. They want to stay in that position. I didn't quite realise that at the time."

Joe found so much happiness at Maine Road. There was no way he wanted to part from the club. His love for football was too strong anyway. As can be seen by Joe's playing days, he was never a man to quit. He had always attempted to extend his playing career as far as possible, and now it was the same with his managerial career. There was nothing wrong with that. Equally, there was nothing wrong with Malcolm Allison's ambitions to achieve full control.

The Mercer-Allison partnership had started to become strained, but it was still alive. The two men were still working for the good of Manchester City. Then, following the club's successes, a number of people started to show interest in controlling the club. A board-room take-over is rarely an easy operation. At City, it was blown up into a major war with front-page newspaper articles informing the public of every stage in the battle. Even Mal and Joe were

I have power at City—Smith

By KEITH WARD and PETER GARDNER

BUSINESS TYCOON Mr Joe Smith today declared that he had power in Manchester City FC.

Mr Smith, boss of a £4M double glazing firm in Oldham, said that he and four colleagues had a legal agreement to guarantee that the 331 shares of City's vice-chairman Mr Frank Johnson would come to them.

Said Mr Smith : "This document was signed a few weeks ago... It is a legal document that I have made private request. I can now say that I now have power in the City club.

"He said he was keeping in touch with his four colleagues, Mr Chris Muir, Mr Simon Cussons, Mr Michael Horwich and Mr Ian Niven over the City bid.

Mr Smith also pledged his loyalty to the club's chairman 70-year-old Mr Albert Alexander and declared that he wanted him to stay as head of the Board.

Talking of Mr Alexander and his future role at Maine Road, Mr Smith said : "Our people are getting at Mr Alexander and saying that he will be out when we move.

"It is a certain clique that are intimidating him.

reasons putting him bid for Manchester City were finally settled yesterday when Malcolm Allison says with the players.

Settling the club a bid getting big enough stated game. Mr Smith said he knew Allison and the players

were upset about the gates, and that surely in the end Joe was going to demoralise the players.

Mr Smith denied controlling Mr Alexander over the shares deal. He said he had told Mr Alexander that two former members of a "group group" were involved with him, Mr Muir and Mr Horwich.

Talking about Malcolm Allison, Mr Smith said City's men are confident he was going to "co-operate" in his position at Maine Road.

Added Mr Smith : "Allison can work with the present chairman, and he gave him our full co-operation. He can talk to Albert. If anything, God forbid, was to happen to the chairman

and a new chairman was elected and Allison could not work in the new atmosphere, he might be tempted to move to some other club.

Mr Smith continued : I will do my utmost, everything of my power, to co-operate in any way to any project with Mr Allison to better the club. He is the greatest man in football."

The Manchester City board meets between then 344 where...

Said Mr Muir today : "I have been involved in business dealings with the club. Now all I want is to be in harmony with the officials of Manchester City for the continuation of success for four even greater days.

"... it is not the outcome of vindictiveness in any nature. The past is history. It is the future that counts now.

But late this afternoon Mr Alexander said he was twice when the club needed an explanation which was accepted, and so far as the board is concerned, as the matter is closed."

Earlier Mr Alexander said that Mr Smith had ended his bid.

Mr Alexander said he had seen an agreement 'connected Mr Johnson's shares.

"This latest explosive situation...

★ Turn to Back Page

stop press

NEWS DESK 061- 412 7200

Albert Alexander *Chairman* — Frank Johnson *Vice-chairman* — Eric Alexander *Director* — John Humphreys *Director* — Sydney Rose *Director* — Chris Muir *Ex-director*

Two suspended men get their jobs back

---

16   DAILY EXPRESS Tuesday November 24 1970

THE TAKE-OVER MEN

BIG FIVE WAIT ON MANCHESTER CITY GO-AHEAD

By JAMES LAWTON

THE take-over of top football club Manchester City seemed to be moving irresistibly forward last night.

Joe Smith, leader of the group ready to assume power at City, is now waiting for a phone call from the club chairman Albert Alexander.

That was the result of a day of phone calls, meetings and negotiations.

The call from Mr Alexander, it seems certain, will signal the success of the five-man move to wrest control from the present board of directors.

After his 9 a.m. meeting with chairman Alexander, the 81-year-old Mr Smith spent the afternoon at the offices of his double glazing firm in Oldham, then held an evening meeting of his take-over group.

make the next move now. We have stated our position and Mr Alexander knows the situation. I was delighted with the friendly nature of our meeting this morning and obviously this is going to be done reasonably.

"Unfortunately with the match against an Australian team coming up on Wednesday Mr Alexander is entertaining, etc. ... and so it could be that we may not hear from him until Thursday, or even Friday. But he has given me an assurance that he will now contact me the moment he has taken my number."

The take-over group arrived at the offices last night for their final discussions after phone calls the move to take control the most successful team to England over the last two years

Buoyant

They mood was buoyant, and one of the key figures, Michael Horwich has set the common between them and the City board. "We are all confident...

PHOTO SPORT ... features the men who seek to take control of Manchester City. From the left: Chris Muir, Simon Cussons, Joe Smith, Michael Horwich and Ian Niven.

Picture by Brian Dutt

KIGU OF LONDON Compacts

NO. 21,107

Daily Mail

WEDNESDAY, NOVEMBER 25, 1970   PRICE 6d.

MONEY MAIL TODAY

Watch it, Malcolm

MALCOLM ALLISON, assistant manager of Manchester City, was rapped by his club chairman, Mr Albert Alexander, yesterday.

He warned: 'Malcolm had better watch his step in future.'

This was Mr Alex-

ander's reaction to Allison's open support for Mr Joe Smith, who yesterday described Allison as the greatest man in football.

Parting shot from the City chairman: 'We aren't going around with our eyes closed. And I would like Malcolm to know that.'

CHAIRMAN ALEXANDER AND DEPUTY JOHNSON AFTER THEIR MEETING YESTERDAY

WHO'S THE BOSS?

Manchester City director calls off £50,000 deal

By HAROLD PENDLEBURY

AN about-turn by Manchester City's vice-chairman, Mr Frank Johnson, yesterday threatened to start a legal battle over a £110,000 bid for control of the club.

Mr Johnson, who has been paid £50,000 on account by Mr Joe Smith for his 510 shares, suddenly announced that he was not going ahead with the deal.

Comment

The rescue that wasn't

NOTHING fails like failure.

Post chief Lord Hall is sacked

By MONTY METH

LORD HALL, the £17,500-a-year head of the Post Office Corporation, was called to meet Minister of Posts Mr Christopher Chataway last night and sacked on the spot.

The shock dismissal is bound to lead to a storm in Parliament and protests by other nationalised industry chiefs now feeling the wind of change.

The Government will be charged with making a political 'sacking' because Lord Hall is a middle-of-the-road Socialist.

He was a leading financier until he was plucked from City obscurity by Mr Wilson to head the Post Office.

The Government must have decided to use the sudden axe on Lord Hall because he was due to oppose the Post Office

HOW WE FOUGHT LORD HALL

IN August this year Lord Hall temporarily capitulated to a Daily Mail campaign against a proposed computerised telephone directories scheme.

Under the scheme names are listed alphabetically only up to the initial letter of the subscribers' Christian names.

But street names of subscribers with the same surname and Christian name are listed alphabetically.

He agreed to suspend the

Union man in Heath's team

The first trade unionist to be appointed to the Conservative Government to a top Whitehall job as an industrial adviser was named last night.

He is Mr Ken Graham, 42, Cardiff area secretary of the electrical and plumbers' union, and South Wales leader of the Confederation of Shipbuilding and Engineering.

LATE NEWS

brought into the conflict, a conflict that would eventually end their relationship at Maine Road.

The main mover in the early days of the take-over, according to Malcolm Allison's autobiography, was Malcolm himself. Nowadays, Allison admits that the whole take-over business was so involved that he has long since forgotten who took what actions. In his autobiography, *Colours Of My Life*, Allison described it like this: "I realised, bitterly, that Joe was hanging on. I suppose it was then I decided to organise a take-over of Manchester City. Apart from my impatience over status, I was not satisfied with the way the club was being run. I felt the club had become big, but that the people in control in the board-room had not grown with it. I liked and admired Albert Alexander, the little, twinkling chairman, but some of the people around him staggered me with their lack of vision. I knew that the City vice-chairman Frank Johnson was ready to sell a huge chunk of shares for £100,000 and that the man who bought them had only to make one or two available alliances and he would win control of the club. So I said to Ian Niven, a fanatical City supporter who is now on the board, 'Find me a man with £100,000, and we will get control of the club.' Niven came up with the man within a fortnight, Joe Smith, a double-glazing 'tycoon' from Oldham. I had had enough of being patted on the head. I thought that if I was not going to be given what was my due, I would attempt to take it for myself."

Malcolm Allison met Smith, who immediately promised that once he gained control of the club, he would give Allison a 20-year contract to manage the Blues. That was just what Mal wanted. A man with the power to give Mal his full managerial rein.

By November 1970, news of the take-over overshadowed City's performances on the pitch. Joe Smith had called on 78-year-old chairman Albert Alexander to explain his plans. Alexander told the press: "I hadn't had my breakfast when he called on me. I told my wife to ask him to wait while I washed and shaved. I didn't recognise him. In effect he came to me as a total stranger. As far as I know, he has no shares in the club at the moment. If he had, I would know about them. But I understand he is in a position to acquire the necessary number to gain control."

Alexander saved the exact details of what was discussed for the next City board meeting, on the afternoon of the 24th. For Alexander the prospect of losing control of the club must have been deeply upsetting. He had been associated with the club for over fifty years, and had supported the team all his life. He had seen the club through the difficult pre-Mercer era and on to the successes of the sixties. He was not a glory seeker. His commitment to the Blues was total.

Throughout the early days of the proposed take-over, Smith and his supporters made much of the fact that they would make Malcolm Allison manager, and would provide him with an enormous contract to keep him at the club for years. There was little said about Joe Mercer's position, although there were rumours that Joe

Chairman Albert Alexander - "I hadn't had my breakfast when he called on me."

would be given the title of general manager. Joe himself was uncertain what the future held. He had been ill with influenza when the take-over news broke, but was determined to make it to the board meeting. He told reporters: "I have been doped up to the eyebrows. I want to get to this meeting to see exactly what is going on. It has blown up in my face since I went down with 'flu." As a final comment he turned to reporters and asked, disbelievingly: "How do you start to take over a successful club?"

The board meeting was a stormy affair, although the outcome was pleasing for Albert Alexander and his supporters. City vice-chairman Frank Johnson changed his mind about selling 510 of his 521 shares to Joe Smith and agreed to back the present board. Johnson claimed that he had been misled by Smith. He had not understood that Smith's consortium included Chris Muir, a former City director who had been asked to resign the year before for what the *Daily Sketch* described as an 'illegal action', and Michael Horwich, a Manchester solicitor and alleged close friend of Malcolm Allison. This was how Johnson explained it at the time: "Had I known these people were involved I would never have entertained the idea of transferring my shares. There have been personality clashes in the past. I am remaining loyal to the board. The money was very tempting - even though I'm not short of a bob or two. But money isn't everything. There's such a thing as loyalty. I thought Mr Smith would make a good director. After all, we have only five and the full complement is seven. Some of my directors had been urging me to look around for someone who would be a good acquisition. Mr Smith impressed me as that man. I had no intention of transferring my shares to him immediately. There was a verbal agreement that nothing should be said about it till next September. It was like a blow in the ribs when I saw it had got out. I hadn't told the chairman about it because I didn't want to upset him - his health has not been too good. You can judge my horror when I read the story. I had told no one - not even my wife."

The Mercer-Allison relationship was under pressure throughout this period. Malcolm was firmly in favour of the take-over, while Joe remained loyal to Albert Alexander and claimed the club was being hijacked. It was becoming more apparent that if the take-over succeeded Joe would find himself in a difficult position, and in all probability would have to leave the club. If the take-over failed, Malcolm would be on his way out. Neither of them could win, and the real loser would always be Manchester City.

BOO-BOY READY TO REPLACE LEE

Bowyer gets call-up for Cup

INTO EUROPE

By RONALD CROWTHER

IAN BOWYER, the teenage forward whose life Manchester City fans have made a misery, is ready for a dramatic recall to European Soccer warfare tomorrow night.

If an inflamed groin forces England leader Francis Lee to miss the Cup-Winners' Cup-tie against Linfield, Bowyer will play his first full senior game since the barrackers began last season.

r, who named Bowyer among o fly today to Northern Ireland, never kept Ian out of the side because of the barrackers.

'His absence this season has just been due to the way things have worked out, for Freddie Hill was the man to come in when Mike Summerbee was missing.'

Both Mercer and assistant manager Malcolm Allison have expressed their disgust at the fans' treatment of 19-year-old Bowyer.

While Bowyer was struggling to regain first team recognition, Allison told me: 'Their conduct towards this fine young player has been disgraceful.

'I don't regard such people as genuine supporters of City. They haven't got the interests of the club at heart.'

Suffer

MANCHESTER CITY

NEWS 1/- 5p

VERSUS

LINFIELD
OF BELFAST

EUROPEAN CUP WINNERS' CUP
16th FINALS—1st LEG

WEDNESDAY
16th SEPTEMBER 1970

Kick-off 7-45 p.m.

ALL ALONE: Colin Bell heads in the second goal against Bilbao on the way to last year's Cup Winners' Cup Final. Picture: Daily Express

When Johnson was first approached by Smith he was told that Smith would help the club overtake Manchester United as the area's most famous club. Johnson was excited by it all: "He said he was a good friend of Malcolm Allison and that he felt that Malcolm could lead the club to even greater success and he would like to be a part of that success. For my part I assumed he was talking about both Joe Mercer and Allison. There was no suggestion of ditching Joe."

In the board meeting the role of both Joe and Malcolm was considered. Now that Johnson had decided to keep hold of his shares, the likelihood of Malcolm being asked to leave increased. Albert Alexander was angry that Mal had chosen to support the Smith consortium openly. He told a *Daily Mail*

All-weather City

Mercer men plough through mud and rain

Manchester City 2 Honved 0: aggregate 3-0

MIGHTY Manchester City powered their way through pouring rain and a paddyfield of a pitch last night into the quarter-finals of Europe's Cup-winners' Cup.

Their hopelessly inferior and ill-equipped rivals from Budapest presented no problems to them compared with the appalling conditions.

But City proved themselves the true

LEE GETS A VIEW OF GLORY

Where there's action there's Francis Lee. He's on hand to salute Manchester City's first goal from Colin Bell (above) and then watches his own cross nudged home by a defender for City's second goal.

reporter: "Malcolm had better watch his step in future. We don't go around with our eyes closed. And I would like Malcolm to know that."

But Joe Smith was not going to give up. He would not accept Johnson's change of mind, and told the press that he had a signed agreement. Chris Muir told the *Daily Mail* that the consortium would continue its fight for control: "I've had difficulties in the past at Maine Road, but as far as I'm concerned they are over. It may take a day, it may take a week, it may take a few months, but eventually we will be in control."

While the directors continued to discuss the take-over, Joe and Malcolm tried to normalise the playing side. On Friday 27 November Mal took the players for a short training session and was amazed at their treatment of him: "The players were a little hostile towards me. Francis Lee, Mike Summerbee, and Colin Bell came to me and said, 'Why try to change the club, Malcolm? We have done well. You don't change something that works.' I was very much out on a limb. Joe Mercer came out on to the pitch and said that the directors wanted to see me. As we walked back towards the board-room, Joe said to me, 'You are on your own now, Malcolm.' When he said that to me I knew that the relationship had gone. I turned to him and said: 'That doesn't bother me, Joe.'"

Despite trying to work together, both men were now on opposing sides. Joe rightly believed Mal was trying to force the take-over in a bid to give him the power he wanted, while Mal understandably wanted full control of the club. Somehow there had to be a compromise.

When Allison met the board they asked him why he was backing the Smith consortium. He spoke honestly about his ambition of turning City into a truly great club. He told them that Joe Smith and his supporters could help Mal fulfil his ambition. What was perhaps not obvious at the time, though, was that City **were** a great club. At the time City were on a par with Liverpool and Leeds - two of the era's greatest clubs - and had nothing to be ashamed of. Tremendous success had come their way because of the strength of the Mercer-Allison partnership. The only remaining obstacle was the other great power in the city - Manchester United. United's popularity throughout the world angered many associated with the Light Blues. No matter what City did, how successful they were, United would always be considered the bigger club. The Smith consortium convinced Malcolm that their support would help City overtake the Reds. Mal had wanted that since he arrived in Manchester and met United followers: "Their feeling that they were the greatest things that ever walked had really got inside me. I loathed the bumptious, patronising tones of some of their players, their hangers-on, and many of their supporters. I wanted to punish these United people who believed that there could only be one team in the city."

Joe had the same feeling, although he was a little more diplomatic about it. He knew that United were in a transitional period and believed that the Blues could overtake them if the club remained together: "When I first came to City with Malcolm Allison we found everyone was obsessed with a jealousy about Manchester United. We decided that we must emulate them. We have not done too badly, winning everything we have gone in for. But support is a traditional thing. If we can keep winning things for the next five years I would expect our ground to be full every week."

After Mal's meeting with the board, he was convinced he was on his way out of Maine Road. He had not been sacked, but he believed it was inevitable. The following day City played Leeds at Elland Road. During the coach ride to Yorkshire Joe went and sat next to his lonely partner and told him: "Son, I have thought it over, and it is you and me together. We <u>are</u> this bloody club."

Joe believed there was still hope for the two men. Later that day Joe was given the chance to prove that he really was supporting Malcolm. It came at six o'clock in an Elland Road corridor after City's 1-0 defeat. Albert Alexander came up to Allison and told him that the board had decided to sack him. Malcolm had expected it but he did not expect what happened next. Joe arrived to hear the conversation. He turned to the chairman and said: "If he goes, I go."

The board cancelled their press release. Joe's threat caused a change of mind, and Malcolm Allison was reinstated. The Mercer-Allison partnership continued ... but not for too much longer.

City's 1970-71 season saw a lapse in form. After hovering around fifth in the table, about the time the take-over bid was announced, the Blues won only four of the next 25 League games. The team finished the season in eleventh place.

The Cup competitions were particularly disappointing. In the League Cup they lost to Second Division Carlisle at the first hurdle. The FA Cup saw them well beaten by Arsenal in the fifth round, what Arsenal captain Frank McLintock described as "a 2-1 massacre". That left the European Cup-winners' Cup as City's only chance of success. They reached the quarter-finals with relative ease, and faced old adversaries Gornik Zabrze. Both legs were 2-0 home wins, so City were forced to replay in Copenhagen. Controversy surrounded this replay as Gornik claimed that the City players had taken drugs during the second leg. The Gornik president, Ernest Wyra, demanded City's players be tested after the replay. Joe told his players not to get involved in the dispute as he believed it was Gornik's none too subtle way of gaining an advantage: "I don't want you wasting energy by getting worked up over this business. You must ignore this kind of thing, no matter how distasteful it may sound and concentrate everything on beating Gornik in the play-off."

Joe reluctantly agreed to the drug tests, but told his players to forget all about them until after the game, which City won 3-1 with goals by Tommy Booth, Francis Lee and Neil Young. Then came a dope-testing fiasco. Colin Bell, David Connor and Derek Jeffries, the three City players whose names were drawn out of a hat, were unable to provide urine samples. Orange squash was taken into the medical room for the players, but still no luck. Joe finally got very angry. He marched to the medical room, banged on the door and shouted: "What the hell's happening in there?"

When Joe came out, he was still fuming: "It's an absolute farce in there. I am disgusted. What Gornik have done to us is scandalous and disgraceful. Their conduct in this affair is an indignity not only to the players, but also to our club and to British football. I resent it very bitterly. Even after our fine performance this has put a damper on what should have been a happy sporting series of games."

As the wait continued, Malcolm Allison arrived with a bottle of champagne. He demanded entry to the medical room, but quickly returned laughing: "They won't allow them to have this!"

Eventually samples were produced and tests were negative.

Around this time, Malcolm Allison had been in trouble once again with the FA. He was banned from all football activity for a couple of months, leaving Joe in full control of the side. Joe did not warrant for the number of injuries City suffered prior to the first leg of the European Cup-winners' Cup semi-final against Chelsea. After four League games in six days over Easter, Mike Summerbee, Glyn Pardoe, Alan Oakes, George Heslop, Colin Bell and Mike Doyle were all on the injury-list. Joe was worried about the Chelsea game but was adamant his side would give it everything: "We are sick for the crippled players who had set their hearts on this tie against Chelsea. But we are not sick for ourselves. We are still in good heart and we don't seek sympathy from anybody. Obviously, we ask ourselves when all this injury toll is going to end. But our spirit isn't broken ... not by a long way. I've never been more proud of my players than I am at this moment. The ranks may have been thinned but the mood is right. So far as we are concerned, the game goes on. I won't even consider an appeal to the European Union for a postponement. We fought on against the Polish team, Gornik, despite our injury setbacks. And we fight on against Chelsea."

Brave words, but the situation was desperate. Prior to the first leg, at Chelsea, Joe revealed his inexperienced team, which included 17-year-old Jeffrey Johnson for his second game, and solemnly told the waiting press: "And may God bless this ship and all who sail in her."

Goalkeeper Joe Corrigan, who played the game with his left eye half-closed through injury, bravely kept Chelsea to one goal. City had been forced to play a defensive game and had succeeded in keeping themselves in with a chance of reaching their second European Final in two seasons. Joe was proud of his players: "We had to play it in a negative way to some extent and it was a very difficult match, but it went more or less as we planned it, and Joe Corrigan in particular was magnificent. We made one mistake and we lost, but we showed that we know a bit about defensive football and you don't learn it all on the Continent. But we must not delude ourselves into thinking that it will be easy at Maine Road. This is still a difficult tie to win and I am going to talk to Chelsea manager Dave Sexton about possible venues for any play-off that could become necessary. It could be as close as that."

We fight on says Mercer

NEW INJURIES WON'T STOP CUP BATTLE

By RONALD CROWTHER

MANCHESTER CITY manager Joe Mercer refused last night to plead for a postponement of a European tie after his team had suffered two more crushing injury blows.

Colin Bell and Mike Doyle are the latest victims of City's injury hoodoo.

They would have been key men in the Cup-winners' Cup semi-final at Chelsea tomorrow night.

Both were in hospital last night after the goalless draw at Newcastle. And City will now be without six senior players at Chelsea.

But defiant Mercer said: 'So far as we are concerned, the game goes on. I won't even consider an appeal to the European Union for a postponement.

'We fought on against the Polish team, Gornik, despite all our injury setbacks. And

JOE CORRIGAN
Home with a black eye

DAILY MAIL
Manchester: 061-834 8600
Telex: 668995

DAILY MAIL, T

A City in ruins!

Bell and Doyle now out of Europe in new injury crisis

By DOUG WEATHERALL

Newcastle United 0, Manchester City 0

COLIN BELL and Mike Doyle, two of Manchester City's outstanding Cup-fighters, lay in hospital last night after their club's savage injury hoodoo had struck again.

Both men, who were carried off during yesterday's goalless draw at Newcastle, will miss tomorrow night's European Cup-Winners' Cup semi-final against Chelsea at Stamford Bridge.

And, as a result of the serious injuries that will keep both of them out of football for the rest of the season, cruelly-hit City will have to face Chelsea without six senior players.

The others who have no chance of playing are Mike Summerbee, Glyn Pardoe, Alan Oakes, and George Heslop.

In addition, they will be without teenage goalkeeper Ron Healey, who had made such a brilliant entry into their Cup-fighting side in recent weeks, and there is still no certainty about the fitness of another brilliant young key man, Derek Jeffries.

Good heart

For City fans the news from Newcastle was grave. Bell, who had taken over the captaincy of City for their magnificent quarter-final conquest of Polish team Gornik, needs an immediate cartilage operation that also puts him out of England's squad for the European Nations' championship game against Greece. Doyle has badly damaged knee ligaments.

And giant goalkeeper Joe Corrigan, who had just made a heartening comeback, suffered a severe facial wound yesterday. But this will not keep him out of the Stamford Bridge game.

Despite the blows which have made his job a nightmare, manager Joe Mercer was in defiant mood as he journeyed back to Manchester with the remnants of his brave side last night.

Five Leeds stars in doubt

By BILL MALLINSON

Huddersfield 7, 0, Leeds U. 0

LEEDS paid a heavy price for the point Don Revie said would satisfy him before this bitterly contested local derby last night.

They may be without five of their stars against Liverpool in the Fairs Cup semi-final first leg at Anfield tomorrow night.

Bremner and

Anxious Manchester City boss Joe Mercer (left) and physiotherapist Peter Blakey supervise the carrying off of Mike Doyle and Colin Bell

---

DAILY MAIL, Thursday, April 15, 1971

THE DOUBLE CHALLENGE FOR A FINAL PLACE IN EUROPE

Incredible City!

By RONALD CROWTHER

Chelsea 1, Manchester City 0

INCREDIBLE Manchester City bravely shrugged off their injury burden and achieved a result at Chelsea last night which few teams in their unhappy plight would even have dared to hope.

They lost the first leg of the Cup-Winners' Cup semi-final at Stamford Bridge by a single goal, but they won the profound admiration of countless London Soccer supporters by their courageous struggle.

Admittedly, there was a desperate struggle in a nerve-racking battle in which the talent of their make-shift team was stretched to fearsome pressure.

Chelsea started with the bold and aggressive manner of men who believed they might win by a cricket score.

But, for all their breathless effort, they found themselves pitted...

It's another super show from those Mercer minors

...nothing in spirit or determination even though they went into the lead without six of their injured senior stars.

The goal for which Chelsea had to settle was scored by Derek Smethurst a minute after the interval. It resulted from the one unfortunate mistake that City made.

...

the game as substitute for Charlie Cooke, and he's swift use of the ball stepped up the tempo for the home side and gave their onslaughts greater power.

When he crossed the ball from the right, young Tony Towers failed to get it under control and David Webb swept it through to Smethurst on the left. Although Tommy Booth, he...

BEATEN HERO City 'keeper Joe Corrigan ... this one as Smethurst scores at the second attempt

---

City had more players missing from the second leg, which was played 48 hours after a League game with Liverpool. Joe Corrigan and Tommy Booth were both out. Ron Healey took Corrigan's place and was unfortunate when, two minutes before half-time, he turned an in-swinging free kick from Chelsea's Keith Weller into his own net. It was the only goal. Chelsea won 2-0 on aggregate and at least went on to beat Real Madrid in the final to keep the trophy in England.

Joe was disappointed with the defeat but proud of his inexperienced side. Malcolm Allison, though, was unimpressed. He believed Joe had made a number of mistakes during his enforced absence. Those alleged mistakes more or less ended the relationship between the two men. Malcolm relates his side of the story: "The worst moment was when I was suspended and we were playing Chelsea in the Cup-winners' Cup semi's. I said to Joe when we play Newcastle

Before the Manchester 'derby' at Maine Road in May 1971, which United won by the odd goal in seven, Eamon Andrews surprised Matt Busby with the famous 'This is Your Life' red book. Joe, a subject himself the previous year, was one of the guests.

don't play Doyley, and don't play Colin Bell. In fact I told him to leave out three players for this league match, which wasn't a very important game. Remember I was suspended and Joe was in complete control of the team. In the end Joe played them all because he wanted to win the match. Two of them got injured and they couldn't play in the semi-final, and I was really, really annoyed at him, really angry. He wanted to win it without my advice because, well, we've all got egos and he perhaps wanted to prove he could do it without me. I told him that he was foolish, but now thinking about it I probably would have done the same thing. Even so, at the time I was really annoyed because those players wouldn't be playing in the semi-final ... and it probably cost us the game. It was the blackest moment for me."

The partnership was soon to end.

Chapter Twenty Three

END OF THE ROAD

There'll only be one manager of Manchester City ... and that's Mercer. He was a man respected like Sir Matt Busby and Bill Shankly. Loved by the people, a character in his own right, a fatherly figure. There will never be another like him.

Mike Summerbee, interviewed by *Blueprint*, 1990

*T*HE SAGA of City's board-room take-over continued through the summer of 1971. There seemed confusion over who had agreed to what. In April 1971, Peter Swales was brought on to the board to play the role of peace-maker. On 5 October 1973 he became City's chairman. By that time, both Joe Mercer and Malcolm Allison had left Maine Road.

When the 1971-2 season commenced, Joe was still team manager. Two months later, the new board-room set-up, which included Joe Smith, appointed Malcolm Allison team manager. Joe Mercer was the new general manager. He was far from happy with the situation, and still wanted to be involved in the playing side, but Malcolm wanted no interference at all. Malcolm had his opinions and stuck to them. But even Mal was unhappy with the new brooms: "The new board, which contained Joe Smith and his allies Ian Niven and Simon Cussons, failed to please either of us. Joe Smith asked me what I wanted. I said I wanted a good contract and that I wanted to be boss. Mercer said that I should be made team manager, but that he should continue to have the final say. I was terribly disillusioned with Joe Smith when I saw my new contract. It was full of loopholes. My solicitor spent several months working on it and still it wasn't right. I remember saying to the directors: 'My contract isn't worth a light.'"

Malcolm Allison took over the team for the home clash with Everton on 9 October. After City's 1-0 victory, the press asked him how good a manager he would become. In typically cocksure Allison style he replied: "Probably the best that ever was. And I'll tell you something else, it will be nice to walk out at Wembley ahead of the Cup Final team."

Joe Mercer now felt that he had no real position at the club. Then, in March 1972, Allison bought Rodney Marsh for £200,000 from Queen's Park Rangers. Joe was unhappy that the maverick Marsh went straight into the first team. Marsh was certainly a great entertainer and a tremendous flair player but at the time City were heading for the League Championship and had really gelled as a team. Marsh disrupted that team. Mike Doyle, a player renowned for being City blue through and through, remembers Marsh's first game: "He made his début against Chelsea. They left Tony Towers out, who'd been playing really well. We should have hammered Chelsea that day. Tommy Booth scored and we managed a 1-0 win. He did mix

Mike Doyle with £200,000 City signing Rodney Marsh (right).

with the lads to a certain extent, but really it was clear Marsh just wanted to do his own thing. You don't win anything with players like that in your side. But the writing was already on the wall. All we had to do was to win three games to get the Championship. But they persisted in playing Marsh and we just lost all our rhythm and everything. We blew it."

City ended that season in fourth place on fifty-seven points, only one point behind champions Derby County. They had also been knocked out of both Cup competitions in the early rounds. Maine Road's succession of trophy-winning seasons was over. Joe ridiculed Malcolm's decision to play Marsh. "£200,000 is a lot of money to spend to throw away the Championship," he told the press.

The partnership ended that summer. In June 1972 Joe left for Coventry City. He had become increasingly disappointed with his role at Maine Road. It was obvious to him that Malcolm no longer wanted him at the club and the bulk of the directors appeared unconcerned whether he stayed. Joe's title of general manager was dissolved and witnesses at the club claim his car-parking space was taken away and his name removed from his office door without him being consulted. The story goes that Joe arrived at the ground one morning in June to find he had to park his car elsewhere, and then, when he walked down the corridor of City's Main Stand, he found his office was no longer his. Joe was devastated and, understandably, angry at the club. His pride was wounded.

When the Coventry offer came along, Joe realised he could leave all the disharmony of Maine Road for a fresh challenge at a club where he knew he would be appreciated. Once away from Maine Road he told reporters of the role he had been offered at Manchester City: "The humiliating part of this sad affair is that at one time the board were saying there was a job for life. But the new regime of directors had no real confidence in me and I finished up by being offered a three-year engagement plus a thirty-three and a third per cent cut in salary. However, the thing that hurt most of all was that they just didn't know what to call me. All my life I have been known as Joe Mercer the footballer, or Joe Mercer the manager. Then suddenly they can't find a title for me. That was when my pride was hit most of all."

He went on to tell the press that he believed City could have found him a position at

Maine Road similar to that of his old friend Matt Busby at Old Trafford. Instead, all that was offered was a public-relations position. If the board had wanted him to stay on then surely they could have found a way of letting him continue. After all, in the late eighties they gave Jimmy Frizzell a position at the club when his managerial involvement ended. Without being disrespectful to Frizzell, it is clear to anyone connected with Manchester City that Joe Mercer achieved rather more at the club.

Joe saw Malcolm Allison's new role as an inevitable progression. The quibble was about his own. He told the press: "I always wanted him to have the job, but at the same time I wanted to retain some control, although that can only be done on a mutual understanding. I did not want to be shorn of all authority, but unfortunately it was not to be. I am the sort of person who has got to be involved in the footballing side of football, helping to create and build teams, making and taking decisions and formulating policy."

When Malcolm Allison heard the news of Joe's departure he was in Cape Town, South Africa. He seemed shocked at first but then quickly defended his own role in the affair. A reporter explained Joe's criticisms of Malcolm, that he no longer listened to advice, that he had always wanted to overthrow Joe. Malcolm responded by saying that he no longer needed Joe: "Before I left Manchester to come to South Africa I told Mercer all there was to be told. He knew exactly where he stood. Why must the questions be brought up again. Mercer knows how I feel. In effect he was relegated to opening the mail."

Throughout the events of June, Joe received tremendous backing from City supporters. They condemned all the men who appeared to force Joe out, and Malcolm Allison was given a rough time. To this day many still blame present City chairman Peter Swales for not giving Joe a position of respect at the club, not just in 1972, but in the years that followed.

Joe Mercer had rebuilt Manchester City, although Joe was always the first to share the credit: "There was Mal, Dave Ewing, Johnny Hart and a great scout, Harry Godwin, who could get where castor oil couldn't reach. And Ken Barnes came in to look after the youth team."

In 1972 the supporters wanted Joe to know that they, at least, appreciated all he had done for the club. The City supporters' club invited Joe to their annual dinner, and Les Saul, the supporters' club chairman, presented Joe and Norah with a silver tea service. Frank Horrocks, the vice-chairman, explained: "It's a token of our appreciation for what Joe has done for us in his seven years with the club. We were determined that he wouldn't leave us without knowing the gratitude and goodwill we have for him."

Mike Summerbee was also at the dinner, and he made sure that Joe knew what the players felt. When Joe accepted the tea service, Summerbee and the supporters gave him a tremendous ovation. Joe was clearly moved. He told them: "Forget what's happened over the last couple of weeks - just go out next season and give the lads the same support you gave them when I was

Joe Mercer and his wife Norah with farewell gifts last night

Joe during his last couple of years at Maine Road... the North Stand is being built in the background and many fans felt it should have borne his name.

here. Tonight's occasion is sentimental enough without me adding to it. This game is not about sentiment - it's a man's game. It's a tough game, and these things happen. The first six - the good years - are the ones I'll always treasure, I'll just forget what happened last year."

After Joe's speech the supporters queued for autographs and to wish Joe well. They told him what he meant to them and Joe was quite touched when one supporter turned to him and said, "I hope your new team does better than us next season."

After the presentation Joe spoke about the future for himself and for Malcolm. He told the press that he was proud of the success that he and Malcolm had enjoyed: "Never ever let anyone forget the contribution Malcolm Allison has made to City. Never let anyone undervalue what he has done, but I would warn him that there are more things to managership than coaching. If I could offer him a piece of advice it would be to listen. Please yourself what you do afterwards, but do listen to others first. For when you stop listening you stop learning."

With Joe away from Maine Road, Malcolm had his chance to prove what he could do alone at City. It never really worked out though, and within a year he too left the club. Two reasons were stated; firstly he felt he could no longer motivate the players, the second reason was that he was unhappy when the board forced him to sell Ian Mellor. The Mellor transfer to Norwich City gave the club a lot of bad press and it appeared to many supporters that City no longer knew how to portray the right sort of image. When Malcolm Allison left, he was drained and in need of a break.

In an interview several years later, Joe gave his view of what caused the split: "They [the directors] broke up the combination. Mal was tremendous as part of a set-up. He and I were right. We had all the success, but then kicked the basics out of the door. Mal had a way of getting the best out of some players - yet he upset some by having favourites. At the time Johnson and Alexander owned the shares, controlled the club, although the others had a vote obviously. Johnson wanted to be chairman, Albert didn't want to stand down: 'He knows nothing

Happier days... Joe with Albert Alexander and Malcolm Allison.

about it.' Johnson sold his shares to Joe Smith and all of a sudden there was no benevolent dictatorship. The most important thing in a club is continuity. It's controlled, a benevolent dictatorship. Even if they're talking tripe, as long as it's consistent tripe. A manager must be confident. There mustn't be intrigues. Arsenal, Everton, Liverpool ... all these teams have continuity. Directors must direct, the manager must be allowed to manage, players must be encouraged to play. In the last years, intrigues came into it. There's no way I'll ever knock Malcolm. He wanted to manage the club, which is understandable. I thought Mal stopped listening. He was adventurous, creative, but you can't neglect the basics. Mal loved the Marshes. I didn't want the back-heelers. I didn't want players who played at other people's expense."

Although the partnership broke down with the two men appearing to be at war with each other, neither Joe nor Malcolm regretted their partnership. Once they parted Joe made sure he didn't criticise Malcolm for wanting control of the side; after all, he would probably have wanted the same if he had been in Malcolm's position. Malcolm Allison preferred to remember the good times at City. He spoke about the strength of his friendship with Joe, and, of course, about the fun they had: "Overall, the first five years were phenomenal, they were absolutely marvellous. It was a great friendship. All the club was really close-knit - the players, the young players, the groundstaff and the coaches. That was really a good feeling. It was a wonderful atmosphere. Joe and I would go out to dinner sometimes and I'd take him to restaurants that I'd been to. He used to look at the menu then say, 'Phew, dear me, this is a bit expensive, Malcolm.' Even so he used to love it."

Malcolm Allison felt a deep bond with Joe: "An important thing in life is that when you feel things you should say them. A lot of people feel things and then when it's too late they've never managed to say the things they wanted to say. It mostly happens with children and parents. They don't say things they should say like 'I love you, Dad' or 'Thanks for this' or whatever. But Joe and me did say things to each other. We told each other the truth, and we never really fell out. Once, we were in a restaurant and he turned to me and said, 'Mal, these have been the best five years of my life. I wouldn't have traded them for anything.' He meant it. He must have looked back over his life and thought, 'I've been lucky, life's been good to me.' We had a great relationship really. I enjoyed it all and I think, like Joe, those first five years were the best-ever for me. I think that fortune favours the brave, and I think that sometimes you have to be fortunate where you work and who you work with. I was very lucky when Joe got the City job, and took me there. And we started right from the grass roots, right from the bottom and took them to the top. That is real achievement."

Joe Mercer formed good relationships, and was well-loved wherever he went. On scouting trips, he radiated warmth in the board-rooms and tea-rooms of other clubs. He was always good for a story or a laugh. He was always good company. For instance, there was a time he went with Malcolm Allison to watch a young player near Ellesmere Port. "I think I played with his Dad," Joe said. "You mean his granddad," Malcolm teased him. After the game, Joe's former colleague came rushing up: "Hello, Joe, how are you?" "I'm fine, how are you?" Joe replied. "I've just come to see a lad with your name." "Ah, yes, it's me grandson." Malcolm Allison loved it, and Joe Mercer laughed too.

David Mercer drove his father around for a time. He remembers one scouting trip: "We went to Port Vale's ground once, and we stood on the slag-heap. Joe had this big hat on, because he didn't want to be seen. It lasted about five minutes, and somebody sent a message down that said, 'Tell Joe that if he wants to sit in the stand he can do.'"

On another of Joe's scouting trips, the directors' box at Crewe was full of managers and scouts. They were all watching a big, raw-boned left-half, but the young lad had a poor game and made a few basic mistakes. Just before the end of the match, the player set off in a one-on-one chase for the ball but was left for dead. Joe's quiet voice could be heard by those around: "Christ, he can't run either." Everybody laughed.

Right: Joe and Bill Shankly... two of the game's greatest characters.

The players Joe left behind at Maine Road had nothing but admiration for him. Obviously they were unhappy that the partnership came to an end but, like Malcolm Allison, they had some great times to look back over. Glyn Pardoe, one of the young players when Joe first arrived at Maine Road, remembers Joe's strengths: "I think he was a real gentleman, a very nice man, very honest. I think he always told the truth. You could not go wrong with him and I think he controlled the other side of the game tremendously. Malcolm dealt with the coaching and Joe was the other side. He always looked after the lads and was a real gentleman. He was so relaxed and people could talk to him about anything you wanted and there were no problems. If he could sort it out for you he would do. He was that kind of person. All the lads respected him and everyone got on well with him."

Pardoe, who gave tremendously loyal service to City as a player and a coach, says that Joe really looked after everyone as if the club was his own: "We had a lot of success. We went to Wembley a few times and we had banquets afterwards and Joe and Norah were a different class - they always came round, looked after the wives, spoke to them and so on. It sounds biased when you say it now, but Joe and Norah really were something special. They would always look after everybody. Joe used to check on everyone on the coach trips, or in the hotel, he used to make sure we were all okay. He was tremendous. Success spoils people sometimes, but it never spoilt Joe. He remained exactly the same."

Tony Book, City's great captain during that period, remembers that Joe was prepared to listen to any problem: "He was always there to lend an ear to whoever. He would come and put his arm around your shoulder, without you having to say anything, and he would take you for a walk with him around the track. He loved to talk to you about the game. Outside of the football itself, he must have been the best public-relations man there's ever been at a football club. And it means a lot at a football club to have someone like that. They say nice people can't win things in the game, but I think Joe proved that theory wrong."

Colin Bell, a man regarded by many City supporters as the greatest player ever to appear for the club, remembers that Joe knew exactly when to dispense advice: "If you needed advice he

Glyn Pardoe

Tony Book

would give you advice. There are different times when you need advice or you don't need it, and he knew the moments to come in and talk, and the times to leave you alone. His judgement was near enough always spot on, every time. The period when he was at Maine Road, those seven or eight years with Malcolm, were terrific. It was a real family atmosphere, and Joe was like a father figure over everybody. And, like in a good family, he gave everyone advice when they needed it, and a clip around the ear when they needed it. If you did wrong you expected it, you expected a belt around the ear. You didn't bear any grudge, you accepted it. It was for your own good. Joe was a one-off. He rubbed nobody up the wrong way. He was just so friendly with everybody. He was probably the easiest, most likeable manager there has ever been. I've only really had a couple of other managers, but I doubt there was someone better than Joe Mercer, more likeable, more friendly, more like a father to us. City

Colin Bell

could not have had a better figurehead for the club during those years. He had time for everyone ... supporters, whoever. If you wanted a chat, he would talk to you."

The players have different views on why the Mercer-Allison partnership blended so well. Bell's view is that they knew how to relate to each other: "They were good for each other. They had a lot of mutual respect and one could say something to the other, and he would take it in good spirit - the way it was meant. They gave each other guidance and were a good balance for each other. A nice partnership. Joe was on the quiet side, and although Malcolm was the other way, they compensated for each other. They didn't need each other, but it worked out to be a very good combination. Looking back in hindsight, it's easy to say, 'Well, that's the way it should be', because it worked, but it could have gone the other way. The reason it worked so well was because they looked after each other and respected each other."

The players agree that Joe Mercer contributed to a tremendous atmosphere at Maine Road. Francis Lee, like the others, believed the Allison-Mercer partnership was extremely good for football: "I think it was the perfect combination. Malcolm was probably the best coach I've worked with in football and he motivated the players and got them going and thinking, while Joe was the father figure, pouring oil on troubled waters every time Malcolm stirred up problems ... or caused them ... but I think they were a great combination. Matt Busby was the manager at Manchester United and Joe gave Manchester City the same sort of dignity that Busby gave United. It was a great combination."

Tom Finney, the famous Preston and England winger, has no doubts at all about what Mercer and Allison created at Maine Road: "Joe had great success at City - there's no question about that. He should be remembered for that tremendous side he put together, with a lot of very talented players. They were one of the best footballing sides of all time. A good side to watch. People like Franny Lee, Mike Summerbee, Neil Young, Alan Oakes - they were one of the most exciting teams ever. Remember also, they had Manchester United to contend with. I think City had gone through some real traumas before Joe - although going back over the years, I remember pre-war it was City who were the great side and United were a nonentity in those days."

Tom Finney went on to stress that the City side of the late sixties and early seventies was one of England's greatest, and that no one should ever forget the success achieved: "There's no question about it Joe did a tremendous job there. People should remember these things. I don't think anyone who has watched City for any length of time will ever forget that era. They will always talk about it and remember it with tremendous affection. There's no doubt that Joe had a great influence on City at that time, and together with Malcolm Allison, who had a tremendous rapport with the players, they put together a great side."

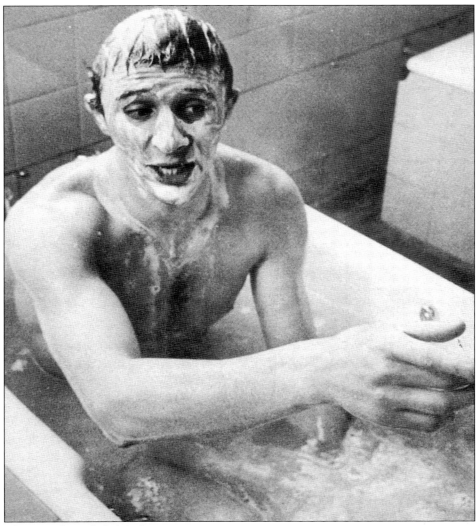

Mike Summerbee... all of a lather!

Chapter Twenty Four

THE FUN RETURNS

Joe Mercer suddenly approaches his sixtieth birthday not just as Uncle Joe, one of the best loved characters in football, but as one of the game's big successes. Asked to take over as caretaker manager of England when Sir Alf Ramsey was sacked by the Football Association for having failed to take the national side to the 1974 World Cup Finals in Germany, Mercer brought a new freedom back to English soccer.

Frank Butler, *News of the World*

*A*FTER Malcolm Allison, Joe Mercer's next partner was Gordon Milne at Coventry City. Milne had been a cultured midfield player with Preston, Liverpool and Blackpool, winning 14 England caps while with Liverpool in the 1960s. As player-manager of Northern Premier League team Wigan Athletic he had helped prepare the club for the day when they would achieve Football League status. When he took the Wigan job he was aware that he could have joined a number of First Division clubs as coach, but he felt it important to learn football management from the basement: "I wanted to learn all about the job, and there's only one way to do that - by starting at the bottom."

When Joe and Gordon teamed up at Coventry City, the combination, though different to the Mercer-Allison one, seemed promising. Joe, fifty-eight when the 1972-3 season began, was no longer out with the players - that had not been possible since the early days at Manchester City - but had great experience and knowledge of the game. Also, because he was so well-loved he was able to bring publicity and interest to Highfield Road.

Gordon Milne, on the other hand, was still young enough to get on to the practice-pitch and show the players what he wanted and how it had to be achieved. Milne was only thirty-five when the two men came together. He was also manager of the England Youth team.

The two men took over a team that had struggled to avoid relegation the previous season, a situation that had contributed to the sacking of manager Noel Cantwell in March. The Mercer-Milne partnership quickly agreed to avoid the more negative style that had accompanied the fight against relegation. The supporters wanted to see football played with style. Joe, realising this, simply announced his plan: "We shall attempt to play the attractive way." Gordon Milne added: "Players need to be expressive."

When the season started the side tried to play attractive football, and went six games without a victory. Having assessed the players at the club, Joe and Gordon decided that new faces were needed. In October they set about improving the club's position. They sold Jeff Blockley to Arsenal for £200,000, and signed Colin Stein, a Scottish international striker from Glasgow Rangers, as part of an exchange-deal with Quinton Young. Tommy Hutchison, a great

Gordon Milne and Joe toast their new partnership on the way to Highfield Road.

entertainer, came from Blackpool and soon became a firm favourite at Highfield Road.

When the new line-up came together for the first time, the visitors to Highfield Road were Joe's former club - Manchester City. The result was perfect for Joe. The new-look Coventry side matched City throughout the game, playing thrilling football, and ended 3-2 victors. Joe was a very happy man.

Further excitement followed when Coventry faced Arsenal at Highbury. Tommy Hutchison was proving to be a great buy and a terrific crowd pleaser, and at Arsenal he scored a fantastic goal. He started his run in his own half, went past virtually half the Arsenal side, side-stepped goalkeeper Geoff Barnett, and sent the ball into the empty net. The Coventry supporters loved it.

The first half of the season saw Coventry play some exciting football, and clearly the supporters were pleased with the effort being put in by the new management team. Both men were helping Coventry rediscover the excitement that the club had enjoyed in the mid-sixties, when Jimmy Hill had taken them from the Third Division to the First in five seasons.

Early in 1973, Coventry won FA Cup ties against Leyton Orient, Grimsby and Hull. When they were drawn to play at Wolverhampton Wanderers in the quarter-final, Cup fever spread throughout the Midlands. Before that game, though, the side went to Maine Road for the return match against Manchester City. Joe told the press that he was keen to return to the scene of so many of his managerial successes: "This is the first time I've been back to Maine Road since I joined Coventry and it's something I've been looking forward to for some time. Because, make no mistake about it, it's full of happy memories, plenty of laughs, and the only thing we didn't win was the Grand National. This is an important game for us, the last and best

14th October 1972, Coventry City 3 Manchester City 2. Joe (top left corner) and Malcolm Allison (bottom right) watch the game. Allison, alongside City directors Eric Alexander, Joe Smith, Peter Swales, John Humphreys, Ian Niven and Simon Cussons, doesn't look too happy with City's performance.

preparation for our Cup game next week with Wolves. Apart from that it would be that much nicer to come here and get a result. I'm well aware though that the City players will be keen to show how good they really are. Looking back over the years I was at Maine Road I suppose winning the European Cup-winners' Cup was the highlight. I'd done everything else. A soaking wet night, a stadium almost deserted. It's funny how your own big moments sometimes don't touch others quite the same way. The relationship Malcolm and I had in that period was unique. He's got a good side here now, there's no doubt about that. It's fabulous to see how well players like Derek Jeffries and Tony Towers have done, and Willie Donachie too. It will be good to see Maine Road again. I've a lot of friends here and I'm hoping to bump into them. I'm enjoying myself at Coventry. There's a nice bit of atmosphere about now that the city has been stimulated by our Cup run. But I'd really enjoy winning today."

Joe was a little unsure about how he would be greeted at Maine Road. He realised that the true supporters still loved him - his welcome at the supporters' club dinner proved that - but he was unsure what sort of a welcome he would get from the staff. He need not have worried. Joe was made welcome throughout the club, and his proudest moment came just prior to the game when the crowd of over thirty thousand gave him a magnificent ovation. Joe was deeply moved.

Coventry won 2-1, with goals from Colin Stein and Willie Carr. Joe was not only pleased with his side's performance, he was also happy that one of his old favourites, Tommy Booth, provided City's only goal. Incredibly, Francis Lee, who was now known as 'Lee Won Pen' because of his record number of penalties in 1971-2, missed a penalty. Perhaps even he felt the day belonged to Joe.

After the FA Cup quarter-final, which Coventry lost 2-0 at Wolves, Gordon Milne and Joe Mercer faced a slump in their team's form. Gordon Milne later looked back on his first season with Joe: "We finished fourth from bottom and it wasn't a false position. We had a terrible start to the season, a great middle and a disastrous finish. The League position at the end of a season is a fair guide to a team's achievements. We bought players, and our policy has always been to play positive attractive football. If we had been more sensible and a little more cautious we would have picked up another half a dozen points and finished level with Manchester City."

Joe's former side, Manchester City, had managed to reach eleventh position, but were only six points ahead of his new side. He was not too unhappy with Coventry's eventual position, and pleased with some of the attacking football they had played. Joe's attitude still favoured a relaxed team. "If you can't laugh, you can't win," was the sort of thing he would say. David Mercer tells one story which illustrates it well: "After he'd left City, we met a couple of the players one night. They were saying, 'We're going to win the League. We're a better team now than we've ever been. It's not funny any more. There's nobody having a laugh. It's serious. We're all down to it and we're all working properly, and we're all getting down to it.' We walked away and the old fellow says, 'Well, that buggers that, being serious. They ain't good enough to be serious. None of them are good enough to be serious. If they're not laughing and doing it because they're enjoying it, they're never going to do it by thinking about it.'"

In his later years Joe would remark on how tense players often looked when they were coming down the tunnel at the beginning of the game. He would argue that in his playing days they had smiles on their faces, looking as though they were going to enjoy it.

The following season, 1973-4, was again one of mixed fortunes. The Coventry Sky Blues finished the season in an improved sixteenth place - still not good enough for Milne or Mercer, but nevertheless respectable - and reached the League Cup quarter-finals and FA Cup fifth round. The side was strengthened by the signing of Norwich goalscorer David Cross for £150,000.

Joe, still with a great deal to offer, receives the Bells' Manager of the Month award for November 1972.

The relaxed and happy atmosphere Joe encouraged at Coventry can clearly be seen here.
Below: Joe with Jimmy Hill.

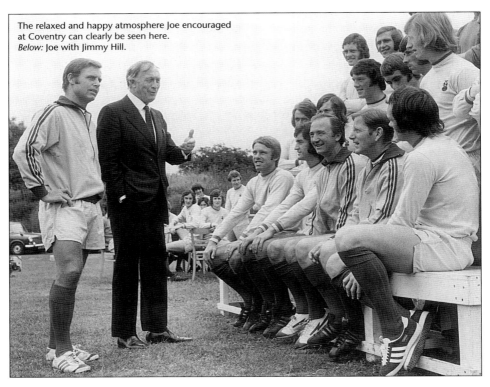

By the summer of 1974, the Mercer family was settled in the Midlands. Joe and, in particular, Norah loved the area and the people. They had found a great deal of peace and happiness after the problems of the last year in Manchester, and had made many friends. Few people expected Joe to move on, and even less expected him to hit the headlines again as "the saviour of English football". But that is exactly what happened.

On Valentine's Day 1974, the Football Association set up a new committee, called the 'Future of Football', to consider the future of the England international team. In reality, the committee was more concerned with the future of Sir Alf Ramsey, the man who had guided England to World Cup glory in 1966. England had failed to qualify for the 1974 World Cup Finals and most of the English press had firmly laid the blame at Ramsey's door, saying that the time had come for him to be sacked. Once the 'Future of Football' committee met, they decided that Ramsey's contract should not be renewed.

Ramsey heard the news early in April, and an agreement was made that the announcement would be delayed until 1 May. This gave Sir Alf the opportunity to inform his family while the FA searched for a replacement. By the time the next committee meeting took place, on 30 April, the FA had decided they wanted a bit of breathing space before a full-time appointment. One of the committee members, Dick Wragg of Sheffield United, was given the task of seeking permission from Derrick Robins, chairman of Coventry City, to approach Joe Mercer. When this was given, Joe was duly appointed caretaker manager for seven matches - three home internationals, a friendly with Argentina and a tour of East Germany, Bulgaria, and Yugoslavia. Joe was delighted. It seemed the perfect climax to his managerial career.

When Joe arrived at Lancaster Gate, headquarters of the Football Association, to discuss the terms, the Belgian-born receptionist did not recognise him. She asked, "Do you have an appointment?" Quick as a flash Joe replied: "Yes, for seven matches!"

Joe was determined to put the fun back into international football. The England team had become too serious. The players no longer appeared to enjoy playing, and Joe wanted the sort of relaxed pre-match atmosphere that he had enjoyed as an England player. Whenever possible Joe had a quip at hand to lighten the mood.

Joe talks tactics with Harold Shepherdson and Les Cocker at his first England training session in May 1974.

CALLED TO HIGHER THINGS!
Joe was given the England job at the same time as Ramsey, the Archbishop of Canterbury was succeeded by Archbishop Coggan.

MERCER SUCCEEDS RAMSEY

Manchester Evening News

NOLAN

Joe with his England squad. The array of talent included Mike Pejic, Martin Dobson, Dave Watson, Alec Lindsay, Malcolm Macdonald, Tommy Booth, Colin Todd, Trevor Brooking, Keith Weller, Ray Clemence, Peter Shilton, Mike Channon, Emlyn Hughes, Kevin Keegan, Frank Worthington and Duncan McKenzie.

His first game in charge was against Wales at Ninian Park. He immediately got the result he needed as England won 2-0 with goals from Kevin Keegan and Stan Bowles, one of Joe's former Manchester City players. The next match was at Wembley. Joe brought in Leicester City's Frank Worthington, one of football's greatest characters, and ensured that training and every other activity connected with the England squad was enjoyable. It was another good result. England beat Northern Ireland 1-0 with a goal from Leicester's Keith Weller.

Joe was already being hailed as the saviour of English football, but, as always, he played down his achievements. He told reporters that football is a simple game, and that international football is really just a game for eleven good footballers: "I call 'em all footballers. If they're good enough, I pick 'em. If not I leave 'em out."

Joe's third game was the Scotland-England fixture at Hampden Park. The Scots won 2-0 - two own-goals - and shared the home-international championship with England.

By now everyone was talking about how Joe had restored some pride and fun to the England set-up. His long-standing friends and colleagues were delighted for him. Many were hoping that Joe could take the job on permanently. Malcolm Allison hoped that Joe would ask him to help. Had the Mercer-Allison partnership survived at Maine Road until Ramsey's reign came to an end, then almost certainly the two men would have been given an opportunity to guide England to the 1978 World Cup. Once the partnership at Manchester City had ended, the two men did not work together again, not at another club, nor with England. They did, however, enjoy each other's company. At the 1974 Football Writers' dinner the two men talked for well over an hour about football, and Malcolm wished Joe well in his new role as England caretaker manager.

After the home internationals, England's next game was a friendly with Argentina at Wembley. An exciting, entertaining match ended in a 2-2 draw, and once again Joe was credited with attracting a new following. Seven days after that game, Joe and his England party were on tour in Leipzig, East Germany.

Throughout the tour Joe encouraged everyone to have a good time and, more than anything else, enjoy the games. When problems arose, Joe did his best to help everyone forget the difficulties and look at the positives. At one point he learned that the England party's hotel was condemned as being unsafe, that some of the players would have to sleep three to a room, and that the press had been thrown out of the hotel to make room for the players. After a major

dispute, more rooms were found in another hotel and several bottles of Polish beer were given to the English on the house, while Joe helped to calm the atmosphere. Peter Corrigan of *The Observer* commented: "With Joe Mercer around it would be difficult for the atmosphere to be anything but chummy, and he, more than anyone, deserved to see England beat East Germany. I would not recommend that his relaxed approach to training and off-field discipline should become a permanent feature of the English abroad but he has rightly judged this to be correct for this particular period."

England managed a 1-1 draw in East Germany. Joe's side attacked, upset Germany's composure and put tremendous pressure on the German goal. England hit the post five times, and were unfortunate

Bare-chested Joe watches his team train in Sofia prior to a 1-0 win against Bulgaria.

that a goal from Southampton's Mike Channon was their only reward. Joe could not believe how close his side had come to victory. After the game someone brought him a bottle of champagne. The England manager took the bottle and tried to open it. When the 'tight' cork eventually came out, it popped with so much force that it hit the ceiling and rebounded back towards Joe. "Christ, we've hit the post again," Joe exclaimed before coming out with tale after tale of how close England were to winning the game.

Joe told the press what he thought of the game, and singled out one particular player: "When I was at Manchester City I would ask Colin Bell, 'Why can't you play for England like you play for me?' But these last four games have been wonderful for him - I thought he was our best player in Leipzig."

The players enjoyed playing for Joe, and, in turn, he put his faith in a number of players who had never really been given a chance before. David Miller, in *The Argentina Story*, comments on some of them: "The new players whom Ramsey had earlier spurned, such as Brooking, Todd, Keegan and Watson, gave England a lift which suggested that, had they been in the finals about to begin in West Germany, they would have been among the more entertaining sides. Mercer smiled his way through his brief appointment, consistently getting the names of players wrong, even in team talks - one was actually missing when addressed at some length - but he succeeded in reminding everyone that football is, after all, a game."

Joe Mercer later looked back on his approach: "We had a good time. We had one or two fellows who could play a bit. Frank Worthington could play. The object of tactics is to allow

FA Secretary Ted Croker was a great admirer of Joe's.

the people to play naturally. You pick a player to blend in. You've got to be complimentary. What's the use of not allowing them to play their natural game? You've got to encourage them to play their own natural game. We didn't have many tactical talks. I'd just say, 'You're picked because we feel you'll fit in that position, so I dare you, go out and play, play your natural way.' Frank Worthington was my biggest success. How they never kept Frank in the side after I handed over, I'll never know.'"

FA secretary Ted Croker was another who took to Joe's happy nature. Before his death, late in 1992, Croker recalled Joe's England period: "Joe didn't want the job full-time but he wanted to make sure that his brief spell in charge was enjoyable, not merely for himself but for everyone. He was laughing and joking all the time and I admired his fortitude on the tour of East Germany, Bulgaria and Yugoslavia, because he kept smiling despite a painful back condition which partially immobilised him."

After the game with East Germany, England defeated Bulgaria 1-0, thanks to a Frank Worthington goal. Before that game the press had asked Joe, in one of his typically relaxed press conferences, what he knew about the Bulgarians. He replied, "Not much. Have you heard anything?"

Four days after the victory in Bulgaria, England faced Yugoslavia. A reporter told Joe, "These Yugoslavians are a bit special." Joe replied: "Good! It should be a great game to watch then." And it was. England drew 2-2 with Yugoslavia in Belgrade. Mike Channon and Kevin Keegan scored the goals.

Before that game, however, the England players were involved in an incident, and the game was almost called off. It started when Kevin Keegan was taken to a room by local police to be questioned about a disturbance at the Belgrade Airport. They believed he had been causing trouble and, at one point, looked as if they would be charging him. The other England players wanted to fly back to England immediately. Joe tried to calm the situation. "We can all go home, no problems," he told the players, "But Kevin won't be able to come with us. He'll probably have to stay behind and answer charges. The only way we'll get him out is by sticking together and answering them on the field. It's their country off the field but they can't stop us on it."

Joe's speech convinced the players to stay, while Ted Croker and other FA officials managed to secure Keegan's release. The FA lodged an official complaint, and the Yugoslavians tried to make peace by claiming it was all a big misunderstanding. It was quite fitting when Keegan headed home the equaliser.

The Yugoslavian game was Joe's last as England manager. Many people wanted Joe to remain in charge, and some journalists predicted that he would be offered the job. Peter Corrigan of *The Observer* wrote: "In the general guessing that still drags on about who will be the next manager Mercer cannot be overlooked. Indeed, I understand Mercer has already been asked if he would consider extending his caretaker period. Mercer will not give exact details before discussing the position with Coventry but he seems keen at the success so far achieved. If things go right during the rest of the tour he could be with us for a while yet."

Brian Madley of the *Sunday People* wrote that Joe had told him: "I'd love to keep this team together and take them to the next World Cup."

Years later, Joe explained why he didn't take the job permanently: "I had the most terrible sciatica to start off with. I was almost a cripple with sciatica. That was one of the reasons. I was offered the job but I wasn't fit enough. It was as simple as that. I had sciatica which goes right down the middle of the right leg, and I was in agony most of the time."

The FA appointed Don Revie of Leeds United to the post, and Joe backed Revie's bid for the job, believing him to be the right choice. Years later, when Revie left the job for an appointment in the United Arab Emirates, Joe felt let down. To Joe, the England job was not one any fit man should walk away from. He felt that Revie was wrong.

Under Revie, England failed to qualify for the 1978 World Cup Finals. Some reporters felt that Joe might have done better, and when Revie left, in 1977, Joe's name was again linked

Joe with England players Colin Bell, Keith Weller, Roy McFarland and Emlyn Hughes.

with the post. The *Sunday People's* Brian Madley, when reviewing the England managers of the seventies, claimed that Joe was the best for inspiring his players: "The best England team I've seen in the past five years didn't have a manager, didn't have any dossiers and had the shortest tactical talk ever - 'Go out and show them what you can do.' And for three matches that's what they did, with a flair that we hadn't seen for many years before, and a style that we certainly haven't seen since. The man who inspired that short-lived burst of English pride was Joe Mercer - a darling of a man who would still pay to watch England play if he had to. He simply told the players that English football was still the best in the world and they believed it, and played accordingly. Anyone can pick the best team. Making that team perform at its best is the secret. Mercer had that secret, and we need someone like him now. A lively young man in a track suit gets quickly bored with the pace of international football. Let them get on with their theories in the rush of League football. Leave the big job to a man who is big enough to handle it, smart enough to live with it and proud to have it."

A lot of football people still recall how Joe gave England a new spirit. Tom Finney remembers the time: "England had a spell where Joe was made caretaker manager and it turned out to be, probably, one of their most successful spells of playing good football. They had a new attitude to the game. They were enjoying themselves and Joe was picking players who were really skilful. It was probably Joe's experience more than anything else. He often used to say, 'If you get really good players, they don't need to be told how to play ... or at least they shouldn't have to.' He was a great believer in that. He did not believe in using a lot of technical theories. Some managers or coaches spend too much time talking about the game, and the players go out all befuddled and spend most of the game looking towards the bench saying, 'What am I supposed to do now?' Joe believed the player should be able to sort it out himself, on the pitch."

By this time Joe Mercer was known and respected as a successful man of experience and wisdom, a true lover of the game with a gift for telling stories with a smile. In short, a very unusual man.

Joe receives a silver plate from the Duke of Kent to commemorate his time as England manager.

Chapter Twenty Five

RETIREMENT

A lifetime's contribution to British football by one of Ellesmere Port's most famous sons, Joe Mercer, has been rewarded in the Queen's New Year Honours List. He has been awarded the OBE. Despite his immense success, Mr Mercer has never forgotten his home town and Ellesmere Port has never forgotten him. Among the many functions he has performed for the town have been the official openings of the Youth Centre, the Stadium, and the Municipal Golf Club. He was also present at the opening of the Wing Half, Stanney Grange, which was named in his honour.

Ellesmere Port Pioneer, 8 January 1976

ONCE JOE'S reign as England manager came to an end he returned to Coventry City. By this time it was not really possible for Joe to return to managerial duties - he would have been intruding - but the club recognised that his knowledge and love of the game could be put to good use. Coventry City, unlike Manchester City, realised that Joe Mercer's presence at Highfield Road gave the club prestige.

To ensure Joe remained in the Midlands, Coventry asked Joe to be a director. Both the club and Joe had something to gain from the appointment. For Joe it meant that his future was assured and that his long association with the game he loved would continue. The uncertainties and doubts over the future that Joe had at Manchester were now banished. At Coventry Joe was wanted and appreciated. "Coventry have been marvellous," he said some time later, "yet I've done less for them than anybody else."

As a Coventry director, Joe helped in whatever way he could and, as he had throughout his footballing life, he made sure he met supporters. He attended social evenings, opening ceremonies and visited schools, and he was a regular after-dinner speaker. He was a natural in his role as football's elder statesman.

Throughout the seventies Joe was often quoted, interviewed, and mentioned in the media. He continued to tell anyone who cared to listen about the beautiful side of his sport. He entertained many with his stories and anecdotes.

At Arsenal and Everton, Joe was made welcome. They recognised him as one of their all-time greats. His contributions to Everton, Arsenal, Manchester City and England were enormous. It was no coincidence either that he was around Aldershot, Coventry City and Tranmere Rovers at great times of their histories. At Sheffield United and Aston Villa, he achieved some success and left many fond memories.

OBE FOR JOE MERCER

A LIFETIME'S contribution to British football by one of Ellesmere Port's most famous sons, Joe Mercer, general manager of Coventry FC, has been rewarded in the Queen's New Year Honours List. He has been awarded the OBE.

Mr. Mercer has been better known in recent years for his contribution to the managerial side of the sport, but he had a distinguished career as a footballer.

He played for Everton, captained Arsenal to an FA Cup win, and played for England on a number of ocasions. He started his football career, however, here in his home town.

an early age and he was one of the star players in the Ellesmere Port Schoolboys' team of his day. Then followed spells with Town FC and Elton, before starting with Everton who paid him £5 for his first game.

Mr. Mercer's contribution to management began at Sheffield United. After a spell at Aston Villa he went to Manchester City before moving on to his present

In January 1976, his services to football received the recognition they deserved when he was awarded the OBE in the New Year's honours list. Joe and Norah were delighted that his life's devotion to, and promotion of, football was recognised both inside and outside of the game. At sixty-one, he had achieved so much that the OBE may have seemed like just another trophy but, for Joe, it was something very special. Winning the League and the FA Cup was tremendous, but those successes were down to Joe and his colleagues. With the OBE, and the Footballer of the Year award, it meant that he was other people's choice.

In 1981 the unbelievable happened - Joe Mercer retired from professional football. He was sixty-six. His involvement with football did not end there though. Having moved to Hoylake,

Joe could not end his involvement with the game. Here, at the age of 70, he is part of the selection panel for the Robinson's Barley Water Young Player of Year. Mark Wright is the choice on this occasion.

Opposite: Joe on his way to receive his OBE from the Queen in 1976.

Joe, Ted Drake (centre) and Stan Mortensen (right) with 'Dixie' Dean after Dean had had a leg amputated.

back on the Wirral, Joe continued to be involved with various footballing panels and committees. He was one of the judges for the 'Spotting The Ball' pools competition, and joined up with personalities such as Ron Greenwood, Jackie Milburn and Bill Nicholson as a member of the panel that selected the 'Young Player of the Month' awards. In November 1986 he returned to Maine Road to present Manchester City's Paul Simpson with the award for October. It was a weekday presentation; had it occurred prior to a City game, Joe would have been guaranteed a tremendous welcome by the City faithful.

He supported his local sides, Everton and Tranmere Rovers. Those disagreements with Theo Kelly in 1946 were insignificant now. Joe still loved Everton, and he had always been an Evertonian. In the 1980s, he enjoyed the club's success during Howard Kendall's first managerial period. In 1978 he had written a foreword to the club's centenary history, stressing the pride he felt as an Everton player. He used to remind people how he had been treated in the early days at the club: "When I was only twenty-two they had given me a benefit amounting to £650 and you would go through fire and water for a club as generous as that."

How much Everton meant to Joe Mercer can be gauged by an incident in 1951, when he attended a stormy annual general meeting after the club had been relegated to the Second Division. Joe was an Arsenal player at the time, but he addressed the meeting as an Everton shareholder: "The greatest thing in football is loyalty. The best thing is to rally round the club once more. We are all part of a big family and success in football is brought about by everyone pulling together."

Joe kept in touch with the many friends he had made during his long career. They included Billy 'Dixie' Dean, his former Everton colleague. In 1976, when Dean had his right leg amputated, Joe made it his business to help his former idol. On one occasion he took Dean to see a specialist. Dean was keen to do any physical exercise necessary that would help him gain the mobility and fitness he needed before he could have an artificial leg fitted. The two Everton greats entered the waiting room, and Joe remembered the scene: "The room was filled with

Joe in 1980.

Joe pictured at home in the late 1980s surrounded by pictures of Arsenal's glory days from the 1950s, and holding the 1950 Cup Final ball.

chaps who had limbs missing, and Bill took a good look at them all and cracked, 'Aye-aye, I see Tommy Smith's been in 'ere!.'" Joe and Billy were together on a number of occasions at Goodison Park. They were there for a derby match with Liverpool in March 1980 when Bill Dean collapsed and died. On television, that evening, Joe gave a moving tribute, and was close to tears.

The F.A. honoured Joe by appointing him a Vice-President and he attended international matches, Cup Finals, any game he could. He was at Wembley for most of the major games. Prior to the 1981 FA Cup Final - Manchester City against Tottenham Hotspur - he was introduced to the crowd, and was given a tremendous reception. Naturally, he was disappointed that City lost in the replay.

In 1986 Arsenal celebrated their centenary by introducing players of all eras to the Highbury crowd. Keith Fisher described the scene in *Arsenal Greats:* "A massive crowd gathered on that cold, winter afternoon but the ground was soon warm with nostalgia and bursting with pride as the fans recalled exploits over 100 glorious years. Arsenal had invited players past and not so past to attend the centenary celebrations - from Ted Drake to Alf Kirchen; Laurie Scott to Reg Lewis; Joe Baker to John Radford; and Pat Rice to Malcolm Macdonald. Great players who illuminated almost every era of the club's history. At half-time Arsenal's golden oldies were introduced one by one and cheered onto the pitch by delighted fans eagerly taking a journey back into time. Then came the moment that brought the house down. First came the famous 'grin'. Then the famous 'cowboy legs'. Joe Mercer had arrived! Younger fans, enriched by stories of his greatness from their fathers stretched to catch a glimpse of a Gunner who is still held in awe in the marbled halls of Highbury. Older fans just felt very warm inside at seeing once again the man who, for eight glorious years, led Arsenal into the second great era of their history. 'Uncle Joe', 'Genial Joe', 'Dear Old Joe' - the memories came flooding back. A wonderful example of a man and a footballer."

During the eighties, Joe regularly watched Tranmere Rovers, his father's old team. Tranmere made Joe very welcome, and gave him what was called "the freedom of the club". Peter

The Mercers Arms in Coventry (seen in background) must have benefited from Joe's time at Highfield Road!

Bishop, Tranmere's programme editor and club historian, remembers the time: "If Joe Mercer enjoyed a love affair with Arsenal but a marriage to Everton it is somewhat ironic that his local club Tranmere Rovers, where his father once played, offered the greatest warmth and companionship in his twilight years. Genial Joe was a regular visitor at Prenton Park, where he had his own seat in the directors' box. I would often meet Joe, and sometimes Norah, at the top of the stairs leading to the directors' lounge and was always met by that engaging grin, a firm handshake followed by a warm embrace. He met me with the warmth and concern you would offer to a long lost son. 'Everything alright? Wife and kids okay?' he would enquire sincerely, adding with a wink, 'We'll win tonight don't you worry about that?' The reference to Tranmere as 'we' was significant. After his retirement, Joe became a regular 'fan', even following us to Wembley before his death in 1990. He hardly ever missed a home game. Though Joe's memory began to fail him in later years, I always felt honoured that he should remember my name, even my address - he occasionally called at my house for a chat - when I'd hardly played a significant role in his past. Joe's great strength was his humility. He never lost his common touch. Having known him personally for around eleven years, I can well appreciate how he must have inspired his teams. Players would, I'm sure, run through brick walls for Joe."

Joe thrilled audiences with his footballing tales when he became a successful after dinner speaker.

None of the players who played for Joe ever forgot what he did for them. In the late eighties, Francis Lee organised a special birthday treat in Joe's honour. Glyn Pardoe remembers the occasion: "Franny did a great thing for Joe. It was Joe's birthday, a couple of years before he died, and Franny took Joe and about six or seven of the lads to his box at Haydock Park for Joe's birthday. Joe didn't know, it was a surprise, so Norah fetched him from their home to the racecourse. We were all waiting inside in Franny's box. Joe was brought in and he was as delighted as anything. It was a great surprise for him. That's how much he was respected - you just wouldn't find that today. How many players would do that for one of today's managers? Franny gave him a great day out. Joe watched all the races, had a nice meal and drink with us. It was tremendous."

Although Joe continued to make public appearances throughout the late eighties, his health had deteriorated. He was still physically fit, but he was not mentally alert. Throughout his managerial days he had forgotten players' names, but that was just Joe's way. As he got older he started to become more muddled, and it became apparent that he was suffering from a form of Alzheimer's Disease.

Alzheimer's causes a progressive decline in the ability to remember, to learn, to think and to reason. The causes are not fully understood, and a cure seems to be a long way away. For anyone with the disease it is obviously terrible, but for those close to sufferers it is probably worse. The Alzheimer's Disease Society offers help. They issue information sheets and provide examples of what to expect: "The symptoms of Alzheimer's disease vary from person to person and, at first, they are not always distinguishable from the forgetfulness that occurs with being depressed, bereaved, under stress, anxious or with gradual ageing. The loss of short-term memory is an early and most striking sign. Disorientation, confusion with time and place, sometimes leading to the inversion of day and night, and wandering are often symptoms. As Alzheimer's disease progresses the loss of the ability to think becomes more and more marked. Simple tasks (like tying shoe-laces or telling the time) can become impossible. As the disease takes hold, people become increasingly less aware of their condition - though they can still experience anxiety and distress. The course of the disease varies from one person to another. The decline can be rapid in some people, gradual or uneven in others. In all cases the family and friends of people with dementia are put under enormous strain."

Investigations into the causes of Alzheimer's still continue, though there is a theory that head injuries can sometimes create the condition. Some scientists believe that the brain responds to a head injury by producing a protein, amyloid, as protection for nerve functions. This process may continue with excess amyloid being produced. This excess forms clumps of protein, disrupting the functioning of the brain and leading to the loss of nerve cells.

If head injuries do affect the disease, then the long-term effects of a footballer's career need to be looked at. Studies of boxers have proved that ongoing blows to the head have an affect. Who knows what footballers have suffered from years of heading the ball, especially with the heavier balls of the thirties, forties and fifties? Other footballers from the era Joe played in are known to suffer from Alzheimer's, but so far there is no actual proof that regular headers of the ball are more susceptible than other sportsmen. Perhaps, if there was proof, there would be a case for Alzheimer's to be treated as an industrial injury with the necessary funds being allocated to make the sufferers comfortable and ease the burden on the carers.

Joe's family, especially Norah and David, did everything they could to ensure Joe was happy. It was a very difficult time for them. Alan Percival, one of Joe's lifelong friends, remembers that the disease caused Joe to forget the simplest of things yet he could remember events and people from years before: "In the latter stages, to give Norah a rest I used to go to their house and get the old photograph albums out and sit with Joe. We used to look through the albums of City, or whoever, and Joe would remember people or stories. Going right back he was alright. After a couple of hours it would tire him out and he would go to sleep. The next day we'd go through another set of photographs. It was incredible how he could go back and remember things that no one else could. A photograph appeared in a local paper just before his death and it was under the headline 'Do you remember this team?' Joe remembered it. He could name all the players and he pointed at the photo and said, 'And that's me down there.' There was a little boy with a great big cap on his head, and I'm sure it was Joe. The newspaper said the ground was Ellesmere Port's new ground, but we knew it wasn't. It was the old ground at Grace Road because Joe and I recognised the old tongue and groove boards - we used to pull these boards apart at the bottom to make a 'V' so that we could go through and watch the game. But Joe could remember this. I couldn't even remember the photograph being taken."

To all who met or knew Joe during this period it was sad to see the deterioration from a man who had dedicated his life to being superbly fit to someone who could barely remember the day's events. Tom Finney recalls seeing Joe at this time: "It was sad. When you get to this age you like to see a person who has been a great sportsman, extremely fit, you like to see them keep their fitness. You don't like to see them when they deteriorate. It was only towards the end, I think, when I noticed it particularly, but it was sad to see him like that. My former colleague Stanley Mortensen went exactly the same way, where he couldn't remember what he was saying. It's very sad to see, especially when you've known them in their peak."

Tom Finney believes that, under the circumstances, Norah gave Joe tremendous support: "She has always been a real stalwart for Joe, and Joe was the first to acknowledge that. He often said that he didn't know what he would have done without her. She really is a very charming person, and remember she had an awful lot to do for Joe. I remember every time there was an event and Joe was there, so was Norah - she'd do the driving. Then at night when the do was over she'd be there waiting to drive him home. Norah is a very nice person, so friendly, and makes you feel so at home."

Alan Percival believes that Norah played a tremendous role in keeping Joe up and about: "Joe could discuss details from years back, but if we went out for a meal to somewhere like Eastham Golf Club - he was president there - within a couple of minutes he would forget where he was and would ask what he was doing there. That's how he deteriorated. He was not the Joe Mercer we knew, but I think Norah was absolutely right keeping him in circulation, because he was quite happy in the past - it was just the present he had difficulty with. This Alzheimer's Disease is so cruel, it really is."

I also recognised a change in Joe. When I first visited him and Norah, in 1987, as part of the research for my first book, Joe was a little forgetful - he seemed no worse than anybody else in their seventies - but basically he appeared well. I saw him a few times after that and he did deteriorate, but by the time I last saw him on 31 May 1990, he was much worse. Even though we had met a number of times before, he kept asking where I was from. On that occasion I took along Steve Cawley, my co-writer on *The Pride Of Manchester*. Time after time Joe repeated the same question: "You're from Manchester. Who do you support?" When I answered "City", Joe just said, "Great days!" It was all quite sad. I realised that day that Norah must have been under tremendous pressure, yet somehow she got on with looking after Joe. It must have been extremely difficult for her but, as she had proved throughout her life with Joe, his happiness was vitally important to her.

On Thursday 9 August 1990 the suffering ended. Joe was celebrating his seventy-sixth birthday with his family. He relaxed in his armchair after an enjoyable day and then passed away peacefully.

The following day, as news of Joe's death spread, Norah told the local newspaper, *The Pioneer*, of Joe's final moments: "Joe had not been well for a while. He had just had a nice meal on his birthday last night and sat down in an armchair and went to sleep and never woke. It was very peaceful."

The funeral service took place the following Tuesday. Over four hundred people packed Hoylake Parish Church with a further hundred or so lining the street outside. The Mercer family could not believe it. They had no idea so many people would attend. Among the congregation were footballing friends and colleagues from every period of his life - Sir Matt Busby, Dave Hickson, Bobby Charlton, Ian Bowyer, Alan Oakes, Francis Lee, Mike Summerbee, Joe Corrigan, Tony Hateley, Billy Liddell, Ian Callaghan, and Bob Paisley.

Tom Finney, fighting back the tears, gave a short address during the service. Remembering that day and the way Joe was admired he told me: "I think the indication of how well Joe was looked upon and admired was the fact that I've never heard anybody say anything bad about Joe, which is most unusual. You usually get some critic somewhere along the line, but Joe was the sort of person that everybody liked. Of course it was a very sad occasion when Joe died, and I was asked to say a few words at his funeral. I was delighted to be able to do that because he had done so much for me during my playing career. It was a packed house. I remember saying something along the lines of 'if Joe had have been here he would have been very pleased with the gate'. But, you know, he really was a tremendous person and I think the great thing about Joe is that he enjoyed every moment he lived. He had so many happy memories to take him through the ordeal that he had. He had a tremendous passion for the game. Every time I saw him he never got tired of talking about it and was so interesting to listen to. He followed the game right up to the end. I've never met a nicer chap in the game, and I've met an awful lot of people. He was a superb person."

At the funeral Tom Finney spoke these words: "I am a proud man to be asked to say a few words of appreciation to a great friend and colleague. He was a true gentleman - a lovely man. He was a legend in his

MERCER: Popular

JOE'S DEATH STUNS SOCCER

By RALPH ELLIS

JOE MERCER was the man who proved that nice guys do win.

His death on Thursday night — his 76th birthday — left the world of soccer mourning the loss of one of the game's great characters.

As a brilliant player then successful manager, he stood aloof from the seedy side of the game he loved and created teams that matched his own beliefs in attack and entertainment.

The history books will record genial Joe as one of only six men to have both played in and managed championship-winning sides. He was also caretaker manager to the England team for seven games in 1974.

Flair

But the quality and flair of those sides deserve to live longer in the memory.

Mercer began his playing career as an amateur with Everton in 1931 and ended with Arsenal just before his 40th birthday.

He learned the ropes as a manager at Sheffield United and Aston Villa — but it was with Manchester City in a flamboyant partnership with Malcolm Allison that he made his name.

England boss Graham Taylor said: "Joe was a wonderful man who achieved the almost impossible by being popular with all sections of the game."

own lifetime. We have lost a great man and a friend. He will be sadly missed but not forgotten. He will be remembered for all the good things he gave to the game - sportsmanship, honesty and integrity. We will always remember him for his infectious smile and cheerful approach, whether in victory or in defeat. We may never see his like again."

After the service a private cremation took place locally at Landican. It was clear from the many messages of sympathy, and the number of people at the funeral, that Joe was much loved. Joe Mercer always had time for people. He was never malicious. He made friends wherever he went, and he even had time for the people who had harmed him. Years after leaving Everton he made it clear that he held no grudge against Theo Kelly. After Manchester City, he refused to blame Malcolm Allison. He had no enduring quarrel with Aston Villa. Such was the measure of the man that he always looked for the positives, and if they could not be found he simply smiled and cracked a joke.

Prior to Manchester City's first home fixture of the 1990-91 season, there was a minute's silence out of respect for Joe Mercer. Fittingly the opponents were Everton. A few days earlier, at White Hart Lane, City supporters had commenced their singing with several verses of "To See Joe Mercer's Aces". World Cup heroes like Niall Quinn, Gary Lineker and Paul Gascoigne were on show, and football had entered the nineties with multi-million pound players, but Joe Mercer had left a legacy of the game's real enjoyment.

The lasting memory of Joe Mercer is of a happy, interesting, hugely successful man who made the difficult seem easy and would never look down on anyone. Joe Mercer was not only one of the most successful football players and managers ever, he was one of football's greatest people. He achieved so much and yet remained approachable, open, and honest. He stayed in the game because he loved it, and he lived his life in football with a smile.

Tears and pride at the sad farewell to Joe Mercer

by Rachel Halliwell

THE world of soccer and the people of Merseyside said a moving farewell to the legendary Joe Mercer yesterday.

Former England star Tom Finney led the final tribute to the ex-Everton and England captain, who died at his Hoylake home last week on his 76th birthday.

Infectious smile

Mr Finney, a close friend of the family, gave a short address during the service.

He said: "I'm a proud man today to be able to say a few words about my great friend and colleague.

"We will always remember him for his infectious smile and cheerful approach, whether in victory or in defeat.

"We have lost a great man and friend. He will be sadly missed - but not forgotten.

"We may never see the likes of him again. He was a legend in his own lifetime."

More than 400 people packed Hoylake Parish Church, and around a hundred more lined the nearby street to pay their respects.

Overcome

Among the mourners were a gallery of stars from the world of football. They included Sir Matt Busby, Dave Hickson, Ian Bowyer, Ian Callaghan, Tom Finney, Bob Paisley, Tony Hateley, Bobby Charlton and Tommy Docherty.

There were also players from his title winning Manchester City and an official party from Everton.

One youngster dressed in full Everton kit was overcome by the day's events and wept with his father as the coffin passed. He was among dozens of children and teenagers dressed in various football colours.

After the service Bobby Charlton said: Joe was a great, great person and we don't say that about many people.

"You can tell how great he was by the number of people who also have turned up today.

"He was also a genuinely great player and manager and I will miss him very much."

Tranmere Rovers manager Johnny King offered his condolences and said: Joe was a wonderful man and a real gentleman. I considered him a very good friend and he will be sadly missed."

Tom Finney

Joe Mercer

Francis Lee and Dave Hickson

Sir Matt Busby

Among the stars paying tribute yesterday were Bobby Charlton, Ian Rooney, Ian Callaghan, Alan Oakes, Dave Hickson, and Tony Hateley

Pictures: RICHARD WILLIAMS

Smile on the face of a football great

Mercer . . . humour, fun and fine football

Joe Mercer with the England boys of 1974, including, front row, from left to right: Weller, trainer Harold Shepherdson, Hughes, McKenzie, Worthington, Shilton, Bell and Clemence

❝ He illuminated the game for 50 years ❞

STEVE CURRY
. . . Express chief soccer writer, pays tribute to an endearing hero

A SMILE has gone from the face of football with the death of Joe Mercer on his 76th birthday.

For 50 years he illuminated the game, first as a defender who clearly enjoyed playing, and subsequently as a manager whose sides, including England, exemplified entertainment.

Joe came from Ellesmere Port, close enough to Merseyside to have inherited the Scouse wit. And it was as an Everton player in the pre-war years that he first made his name.

Slender of build but belligerent in the tackle, he made a nonsense of his frail physique. His famous spindly legs persuaded Dixie Dean to tell him: "Those legs wouldn't last a postman his morning round." In fact, they lasted him over 20 years as a player in two distinct phases of a fine career. He made his Everton debut in 1933 and won the Championship with them in the 1938-39 season.

His wing-half performances won him five England caps, a total that would have been much higher but for the War. Joe was turned 30 when the hostilities ended and with knees that seemed unable to stand the ravages of the game.

But Tom Whittaker thought otherwise and backed his judgment with a £7,000 transfer fee to take Joe to Highbury, where he was re-vitalised. Arsenal were second from bottom when he signed in December 1946, but the following season he captained them to the League title, a feat he repeated in 1952-53.

He later forged a famous managerial partnership with Malcolm Allison at Maine Road.

Manchester City enjoyed their finest hours with Joe picking up the pieces of Allison's occasional recklessness. But their team, which included Lee, Bell, Summerbee and Doyle, played poetic football.

For one wonderful Indian summer in 1974 he was England's caretaker-manager on a tour of Eastern Europe still remembered for its humour, fun and fine football.

Ron Greenwood, who took over as England manager, said yesterday: "He was one of the game's characters, not only a great player but a successful manager and a fine person."

Soccer mourns Uncle Joe

Death of true-Blue legend

JOE MERCER, one of soccer's best-loved sons and described by Goodison boss Colin Harvey as "a magnificent Evertonian", died peacefully at his Hoylake home on his 76th birthday.

The great Dixie Dean once told him: "You've a pair of legs that wouldn't last the postman his morning round," yet Mercer's famous bowed, spindly legs were to carry him on a playing career that did not end until his 40th year.

Illustrious

In an illustrious career, he not only skippered Everton, Arsenal and England but also managed Sheffield United, Aston Villa and Manchester City as well as becoming England caretaker-manager in 1974 after Alf Ramsey was dismissed.

He was one of only six men who have played in and managed League title-winning sides.

Mercer won his first championship medal with Everton in 1939 when war clouds were looming and then, after a £7,000 transfer to Arsenal in December, 1946, helped the London club win the first division title twice in 1948 and 1953.

In between, he also led them to an FA Cup final success against Liverpool in 1950.

Arsenal were at Wembley again two years later but lost to Newcastle.

In 1954 came the accident which was to finish him as a player

● **JOHN KING:** ❛ People talk about Bill Shankly being an all-time great, but Joe Mercer belongs alongside him in the football hall of fame.
● ❛ The biggest compliment I can pay him is that

Chapter Twenty Six

TRIBUTES TO JOE

Joe's life was totally devoted to football. From the moment he could kick a ball to the day he died, Joe was totally committed to the people's game. In his later years, he was able to look back with pride at all he had achieved during his long and distinguished life. It must be said though, that Joe only ever wanted to play football. The success was great, but Joe was at his happiest simply playing the game. Playing football was everything to Joe.

All the people I have spoken with agree that football really was Joe's life. In addition to reinforcing that view, the following comments give an insight into how Joe was viewed by his colleagues and by the supporters of his clubs. Whilst writing this book I have been contacted by people from all walks of life who, quite simply, wanted to stress what Joe actually meant to them.

Gary James

STAN CULLIS

There was a unique similarity about the life of Joe and myself, which almost seemed the work of a script writer. We both played in the same team for Ellesmere Port schoolboys and the war period saw us both playing for England - the half-back-line of Britton, Cullis and Mercer was a regular part of the England team.

After I was posted to Italy in the Army Joe took up the captaincy of England, and later we both took on managerial roles, myself for Wolves and Joe for Aston Villa. The difference between Joe and myself in our managerial outlook was that Joe had a truly remarkable sense of humour whereas I was living in a complete state of tension. Joe had a quite remarkable rapport with other people and it is no exaggeration to say that he was one of the most popular characters in the game.

Joe was a formidable opponent, either on the playing field or as a manager, but he was also a person of impeccable honesty who, at least as far as I was concerned, was someone whose friendship you treasured. In the summer break when I went home to my parents at Ellesmere Port, I sometimes played golf with Joe at the Hooton Golf Club. He played golf in the same fashion he played soccer, and I very rarely finished on the winning side.

Summing up, I would say that knowing Joe was a privilege, and being a friend was an added bonus.

JIMMY HILL

I first met Joe as an opponent. Old Joe versus Young Jim, Fulham v Arsenal, Craven Cottage, March 1952. The score was 0-0, a kind of victory for the relegation-threatened Fulham and I was so much in awe of the great man that anything I managed to achieve in midfield took on magnificent proportions. To be allowed to kick the same ball was a privilege. As a football crazy teenager in the war, Britton, Cullis, Mercer, Aldershot's half-back-line, was worshipped; godlike and invincible. Thus the seeds of my admiration were planted.

In later years, our paths crossed as opposing managers, fellow directors and warm friends. I hardly ever remember him without a smile on his face, and particularly on the last occasion we met, when Fulham played Tranmere during the 1989-90 season. Joe brought joy to everyone on or off the field, and his memory still does.

MIKE SUMMERBEE

I knew Joe Mercer since I was sixteen, and I only signed for Manchester City because of him.

He wanted you to express yourself on the field, to play as though you were enjoying yourself. People warmed to him because of it. He was a charismatic figure, a leader. Like Bill Shankly, Matt Busby and Bill Nicholson, he will never be replaced. There will never be another like Joe Mercer. He was like a father to me and all I ever achieved in the game is down to him.

FRANCIS LEE

He got my career off the ground. Everybody liked Joe, and all the players respected him because he had been a great player himself. He was a great character as a manager, always ready with a funny one-liner. But he was tough when he had to be and although he seldom lost his temper, you knew when he had, usually at half-time!

TONY BOOK

The man was a legend. He had done it all. To all the players who knew him, he was a father-figure.

JOHN MOTSON

Dear old Joe. That twinkling smile which we all loved used to be permanently etched on his face, especially in later years when he was able to enjoy the game he loved, but which caused him a lot of stress in his early years as a manager.

I first met Joe in my BBC radio days, when I was sent to Vienna to cover Manchester City's European Cup-winners' Cup

Final against Gornik in 1970. As a rookie reporter desperate for an interview, I interrupted Joe's pre-match nap. He was kindness itself.

Later, in his Coventry days with Gordon Milne, and in his brief tenure as caretaker manager of England, he remained a firm friend. When England played at Ninian Park in his first international, Joe asked me to sit next to him and tell him the names of the Welsh players!

In his retirement years, he helped me with a video about the history of Everton. Then I realised, for all his success at Arsenal, that his heart as a player still lay at Goodison Park. He could recite Everton's 1933 FA Cup winning team without blinking an eyelid.

Joe received inestimable support from Norah, but right up until his death on his seventy-sixth birthday in 1990, he remained the charming personality loved by everybody in the game. Joe belonged to the 'old school', and what a legacy they left. He once told me Peter Doherty was the best player he ever saw, and talking football with Joe was both pleasure and privilege.

TOMMY LAWTON

I've known Joe ever since I joined the Goodison staff, and he's always been the same; even tempered, good-humoured, a great, hard-working footballer and one of the shrewdest judges. To hear Joe describe a match was something worthwhile.

BOBBY CHARLTON

Joe was a great, great person and we don't say that about many people. They don't produce people like him very often. He was a true great, along with the likes of Bill Shankly.

BRIAN LABONE

He didn't have an enemy. Everyone loved him.

JOHNNY KING

Joe was a wonderful man and a real gentleman. I considered him a very good friend. I can't speak highly enough of Joe. People talk about Bill Shankly as being an all-time great, but Joe belongs alongside him in the football hall of fame. He was a superb player who performed at the highest level and then moved into management. He was called upon by England and there's no greater honour than that. But most of all he was a gentleman who had a great feeling for the game and along with Shankly was one of the true cavaliers.

The greatest compliment I can pay him is that players wanted to play for him and as a manager that's what you're aiming for.

Joe was proud of his England connections, hence the FA badge on his jacket.

Joe shakes hands with Newcastle captain Joe Harvey before the 1952 Cup Final.

RON GREENWOOD

Dear old Joe was one of the game's characters, not only a great player but a very successful manager and a fine person. He was always a good companion and a fine after-dinner speaker.

I still cherish the memory of playing against him when I was a lad and with Chelsea and he was playing for Aldershot during his wartime service. There were lots of characters when Joe was a player and a manager, but he was one everyone remembered - as a player, a manager, and a person.

He took over as England manager from Alf Ramsey, then handed over to Don Revie, but he deserved to manage England in his own right. His partnership with Malcolm Allison was good for both men and good for football.

MALCOLM ALLISON

The first time I met him I knew he was a star, a man who had been given so much more than the natural ability which it takes to become a merely famous footballer. There was a puckish humour which cut through the pompous like a knife stroke. There were biting, colourful phrases which rolled off his tongue on their way from a great fund of shrewdness and knowledge of life. He bailed me out of trouble so many times. He was a father figure and a partner.

Between us we had it all. I charged into situations like a bull, full of aggressive ambition and a contempt for anyone who might be standing in my way. And Joe came behind me, picking up pieces, soothing the wounded and the offended with that vast charm which touched and affected all those who came in contact. He was the boss, he had the controlling voice.

GRAHAM TAYLOR

Joe was a wonderful man and achieved the almost impossible by being popular with all sectors of the game. It was always a pleasure to be in his company. Joe enjoyed telling, and I enjoyed listening, to his fascinating football stories.

He was a highly-respected figure and an honourable man, I always found him very approachable. He was an inspirational player who excelled at First Division and international level.

LAWRIE McMENEMY

When I first started in management he was a senior figure alongside Bill Shankly, Harry Catterick, Don Revie and Jock Stein. They were always there if you wanted to ask for advice. Joe always reminded us that the job could be done with a sense of humour. He was loved by managers, players and the public alike.

JIM GREENWOOD, *Everton Chief Executive*

Joe was a truly great Evertonian. Wherever he went after leaving the club, he always regarded Everton as his home. We saw him regularly here, and he never missed many of our matches. Joe was a truly great football man and it was always fun when he was around.

GEORGE WILLIAMSON,
Secretary of the Ellesmere Port Sunday League

Joe was just one of the great guys of football. He could talk about the game to anyone and always had a fair word to say. I never heard him speak ill of anyone and if he did level criticism it was always justified.

PETER SWALES

When I joined Manchester City in 1972, Joe was coming to the end of his career at the club. However, he did visit us on many occasions over the next 16 to 17 years. I had a very good working relationship with Joe and he had a great knowledge of the game and is probably the most popular managerial figure ever to be connected with the club. I had the pleasure of seeing him many times at Wembley with our involvement on the International Committee and I also sat with him at dinners. I can honestly say that I never heard anyone have a bad word to say against him and was one of the very few people in the football world you would find very difficult to criticise.

NORMAN WISDOM *(Comedian)*

Joe Mercer was vital to the Arsenal team. Joe had the ad lib touch. I doubt if he ever read a script or planned anything on the field. He just went out and played football as his instinct told him and the creative sparks flew off him.

PHIL FLETCHER, *Manchester United supporter*

I support the most charismatic, legendary (and hyped) club in Britain - Manchester United. However, I am not the sort who bluntly hates every other club, and I enjoy watching *any* good football. My Dad is a City fan. When we were slum-cleared out of Hulme to Wythenshawe I found an allegiance with MUFC - to my dad's disgust. He used to take me to all City home games, but to no avail.

Late Sixties. City v Fenerbahce. European Cup. Me and my Dad are about to enter the Platt Lane Stand when Dad spots Joe walking from the car-park to the players' entrance. I didn't know him, being only ten years old, but Dad tells me to go and get his autograph. Joe signs the back of my ticket and Dad says to him, "Sorry Joe, but he's a United fan. I keep trying but I can't change him." Joe, realising I'm in awe of him, said, "Now a good lad should always do what his Dad says. Enjoy the game and obey your father!"

My second memory of Joe took place fifteen years later. The team I play for hold a Sportsmans' Evening each year at the Cresta Court Hotel (Altrincham). It was either 1982 or 1983 that Joe was booked as guest speaker. He entered the room to a standing ovation from Reds and

Blues, and then kept a 300-plus audience totally silent and entertained by his stories and the older members of the audience marvelled at his powers of recall. People at our club still talk of the great night Joe gave us.

When Joe died, the local and national press did not do him justice. My Dad always says he was "a gentleman, a great player, and City's greatest-ever manager". That's how he should be remembered.

TOM SMITH, *Aston Villa supporter*

I've been a keen football follower all my life. I've been a Villa man for more than seventy years. Although I saw many internationals in which Joe played I never had the pleasure of meeting him until the end of World War Two at the Army Physical Training Corps, where instruction was given on the "finer points of physical training". Several internationals were there teaching skills - rugby, hockey etc. And of course Joe was there with football. A great player and a perfect gentleman.

I was demobbed and lost touch with him until he took over the Villa. I made contact with him and sent him a photo as proof that we had met at the APTC. He kindly asked me to make myself known at the next home match. I met him and had a chat and a cup of tea. He was highly delighted as I was with our chat about old times in the Army. I went home a very happy supporter. He was truly a great man.

MIKE CAIRNS, *a Portite*

As a boy brought up in Ellesmere Port, I was very conscious of Joe being an old 'Port' boy. The town was always boasting of its childhood links with him and Stan Cullis. In fact after the war, for nearly ten years, Joe used to organise a friendly match with Ellesmere Port Town FC at York Road. This always took place near the end of the season. In fact, one year he brought the *full* Arsenal team after they had played a game at Blackpool.

Joe takes England training with Martin Peters Trevor Brooking and Mike Pejic.

I have a vivid memory of watching Joe training at York Road, wearing a red track suit with 'The Gunners' emblazoned across its back. Joe never forgot his roots and always showed interest in Ellesmere Port Town FC and always remembered his ex-associates. There are still many people who know him well and were very proud of him. There is little doubt Ellesmere Port never forgot Joe Mercer, and I know Joe never forgot Ellesmere Port.

MAX KESTER, *Arsenal supporter*

I have one vivid memory of Joe and that was the occasion when Arsenal were playing Sheffield United at Highbury. Alex Forbes was playing for United at the time, and he was bursting through the defence towards the Clock End. He was in top flight when, one could say impetuously, Joe stretched out a foot and caught the trailing foot of Alex Forbes who, because of the speed at which he was travelling, resulted in him doing almost a complete somersault. He landed heavily and he lay inert.

A lot of players these days would have spread their hands gesturing their innocence or walked away but Joe wasn't concerned about a booking, he was more concerned about Alex Forbes, and I was close enough to see the look of horror on Joe's face when he caught Alex's trailing foot. He immediately ran over to the fallen player to see if he was badly hurt, then urgently beckoned the United trainer on to the field. He fussed around like a mothering hen until he was assured that Alex wasn't badly hurt. With so many cynical fouls around it was quite refreshing to see a player being so concerned about a fellow professional.

BILL PEEL, *Manchester City supporter*

I worked for the late Louis Edwards, who was United's Chairman, as a director running the transport as a separate company. I introduced safe-driving awards for the drivers who had an accident free year. I used to arrange dinners for the lads. At this particular time Joe was managing City. I was and still am a supporter of City, in spite of Louis' threats.

I arranged a dinner at the Town Hall and invited Joe to present the awards, but kept his name secret for most of the lads were United supporters. In fact, on the night, 95 per cent were Reds. When Joe came in sight the lads went very quiet. I heard one say, "If he's presenting the awards I'm not having mine!" I thought, "Hell, this is going to be a flop."

After dinner Joe stood up to a mild clap, and for the first time he told that much repeated joke about the boy climbing out of 'Old Trafford and a policeman ordering him back. This brought a little laughter. After five minutes the lads began to warm to him, and after ten minutes they were all on their feet cheering.

He was fabulous. His stories and genuine feelings of a good sportsman really took over.

DENIS COMPTON

He was a lovely, lovely man. It's extraordinary when you think he became a celebrity that I've never heard anyone say one word against him. The players loved him.

MIKE SLOAN, *president of the Ellesmere Port Junior Sunday League*

Even when he was ill he attended our various functions, he was an absolutely marvellous man, one of life's natural gentlemen without having to try hard. He was what football is all about. He played the game hard and fair, and rose to be top man at his job; that is where he deserves to stay. We do not get many heroes in this life, but Joe was one of them.

Above: Joe, Sergeant Instructor in the Army, takes a PT class in Cheshire, November 1939.
Below: In action for Arsenal at Portsmouth during the 1948 Golden Jubilee Match.

Joe Mercer - soccer legend

By GILL ISTED

SOCCER legend Joe Mercer died on his 76th birthday last Thursday.

4The former England, Everton and Arsenal wing-half who managed Sheffield United, Aston Villa, Manchester City and was caretaker-manager of England in 1974 collapsed in an armchair at his Hoylake home, shortly after birthday celebrations with family and friends.

Mercer, born in Ellesmere Port on August 9, 1914, was raised in the town and owed much to his father who played football for Notts Forest.

He showed exceptional ability as a schoolboy footballer when he was coached by Mr. Bill Roberts, former head teacher of Cambridge Road School, later of the former Sutton Secondary School and manager of England Schoolboys.

Joe himself played for Cheshire schoolboys along with such well known names as Stan Cullis and Frank Soo, later to become international colleagues.

There followed a period with the Town F.C., Shell, and Elton. When he left school at 16 he was recommended to Everton by Mr. Tom Corley.

Progress was swift and spectacular and it did not take him long to establish himself as the best all-round left-half in the country as Everton won the championship in 1938-39.

His skills were recognised by the England selectors and he played in all five internationals that season.

The outbreak of war brought his full-time career to a temporary halt, though he did play regularly in the England team durig those dark years.

At the end of the war he returned to Everton, but in 1946, following a cartilege operation, he was transferred to Arsenal for £7,000.

He stayed with them for seven seasons, captaining the club in two cup finals and leading them to be Cup Finalists in 1950 and League Champions in 1947/48 and 1952/53.

He was selected 'Footballer Of the Year' in 1950 and in recognition of this and his FA Cup success was accorded a civic reception and presented with a silver tea service at Ellesmere Port's Masonic Hall.

Shortly before his 40th birthday he broke his leg in a collision with team mate Joe Wade during a match against Liverpool at Highbury, and this marked the beginning of the end of a brilliant career.

But though his playing days may have been over, managerial ones were just beginning. First Sheffield United then Aston Villa.

A period of illness followed before he joined Manchester City as manager in 1965, with Malcolm Allison as coach.

Over the next five years the team rose to unprecedented heights to win the second division title, the 1968 League Championship, the 1969 FA Cup and, the following year, the European Cup Winners' Cup and the League Cup.

Allinson's appointment as manager in 1972 resulted in Mercer moving to Coventry as general manager, but he was not out of the front line for long.

When Sir Alf Ramsey was sacked as England Manager, Joe Mercer took his place in a caretaker capacity, during which time he led the team on an unbeaten tour of Eastern Europe.

With the appointment of Don Revie, Joe Mercer returned to Coventry and in 1976 was awarded the OBE for services to soccer.

Sometime during his busy career he found time to meet and marry Miss Norah Dyson, daughter of an Ellesmere Port grocer, and towards the end of his career the couple started a similar business in Hoylake where they also made their home.

Mrs. Mercer said on Friday: 'Joe had not been well for a while. He had just had a

● FLASHBACK to September 11, 1968, when Joe Mercer opened the Ellesmere Port Stadium.

nice meal on his birthday last night and sat down in an armchair and went to sleep and never woke. It was very peaceful.'

Many former colleagues from the football world had already been in touch with the family to express their sympathy.

Many of them mixed with local people at Joe's funeral at St. Hildeburgh's Church, Hoylake, on Tuesday, which was followed by cremation at Landican.

● SEE ALSO PAGE 4.

Every day was sunny for Joe

by James Mossop

A slight tremble and pause entered Tom Finney's delivery as he quietly spoke: "Wear no false air of solemnity or sorrow. Laugh as we always laughed . . ."

Behind him stood the coffin of Joe Mercer, a man whose lifetime's currency had been laughter, and Tom was providing all our farewells.

Up there somewhere with old footballing soldiers who departed earlier, Joe will be looking down with a twinkle in his eye because all his days were sunny.

His captaincy of Arsenal after the war was as vital to Highbury as Alex James's wizardry had been before.

He played for his favourite team, Everton, and managed Aston Villa, Sheffield United and Manchester City where, with Malcolm Allison, he created unprecedented success.

Malcolm was his young and outrageously controversial assistant and when a police car with a blue flashing light stopped Joe on a

fast stretch of road he greeted the patrol man with the words: "What's Malcolm done now?"

When Joe took over as England's caretaker manager in 1974 he gathered the squad around him. They waited for a stern lecture on discipline only to hear him say: "I didn't want this bloody job in the first place. We are going on tour and we are going to have a laugh and a joke." They were unbeaten.

He consulted Emlyn Hughes about a player in the squad and received the thumbs up. "No," said Joe, "definitely not. I've never seen him smile. We'll send for Alec Lindsay. He's a happy soul."

Joe was of that distant school of football cavaliers. He could be hard, and injuries left him with legs as knobbly as blackthorn sticks.

He was a born leader; his own man. And as he fell asleep for the last time on his 76th birthday he may have been dreaming Tom Finney's very last words: "Just around the corner all is well."

JOE MERCER playing for his favourite club, Everton

BIBLIOGRAPHY

Allison, Malcolm and James Lawton, *Colours Of My Life*, Everest Books, 1975
Barnes, Walley, *Captain of Wales*, Stanley Paul, 1953
Brassington, David, Rod Dean and Don Chalk, *Singers to Sky Blues*,
    Sporting and Leisure Press, 1986
Cawley, Steve and Gary James, *The Pride Of Manchester*, ACL & Polar, 1991
Clareborough, Denis, *Sheffield United FC - The First 100 Years*,
    Sheffield United Football Club, 1989
Cullis, Stan, *All For the Wolves*, Rupert Hart-Davis, 1960
Doyle, Mike, *Manchester City - My Team*, Souvenir Press, 1977
Edelston, Maurice and Terence Delaney, *Masters Of Soccer*, The Naldrett Press, 1960
Ellis, Arthur, *Refereeing Around The World*, Hutchinson & Co., 1954
Gardner, Peter, *The Manchester City Football Books*, Stanley Paul
Hapgood, Eddie, *Football Ambassador*, Sporting Handbooks, 1948
Hodgson, Derek, *The Everton Story*, Arthur Barker, 1979
James, Brian, *England v Scotland*, Pelham Books, 1969
James, Gary and Keith Mellor, *From Maine Men to Banana Citizens*, Temple Press, 1989
Johnson, Ian, *The Aston Villa Story*, Arthur Barker, 1981
Joy, Bernard, *Forward Arsenal*, Phoenix House, 1952
Kelly, Stephen F, *Forever Everton*, Queen Anne Press, 1987
Lawton, Tommy, *Football Is My Business*, Sporting Handbooks, 1946
Lee, Francis, *Soccer Round The World*, Arthur Barker, 1970
McParland, Peter, *Going for Goals*, Souvenir Press, 1960
Matthews, Stanley, *Feet First*, Ewen and Dale, 1948
Mercer, Joe, *The Great Ones*, Oldbourne, 1964
Miller, David, Stanley Matthews - *The Authorised Biography*, Pavillion, 1989
Morris, Peter, *Aston Villa,* The Naldrett Press, 1960
Mortensen, Stanley, *Football Is My Game*, Sampson Low, 1949
Prole, David, *Football in London*, Robert Hale, 1964
Roberts, John, *Everton - The Official Centenary History*, Granada Publishing, 1978
Soar, Phil and Martin Tyler, *Arsenal 1886-1986*, Hamlyn, 1986
Swift, Frank, *Football from the Goalmouth*, Sporting Handbooks, 1948
Thornton, Eric, *Manchester City*, Robert Hale, 1969
Wall, Bob, *Arsenal From The Heart*, Souvenir Press, 1969
Ward, Andrew, *The Manchester City Story*, Breedon Books, 1984
Whittaker, Tom, *Tom Whittaker's Arsenal Story*, Sporting Handbooks, 1957
Wright, Billy, *Football Is My Passport*, Stanley Paul, 1958
Young, Percy, *Football In Sheffield*, Stanley Paul, 1964

In addition, a number of books in the Breedon Books Complete Record series

Football is a great game. It is all about goals, goalmouth incidents and end-to-end attacking football. There is nothing wrong with the game; plenty wrong with managers, players, directors, legislators and the media. Football has been very kind to me and I really mustn't complain so can I leave you with this thought - The object of playing any game is for enjoyment. If you have enjoyed it and done your best you have won no matter what the result!

JOE MERCER, circa 1980